KU-579-638

KU-579-638

GOD'S ARCHITECT
A Life of Raymond McGrath

GOD'S ARCHITECT

A Life of
Raymond McGrath

by

Donal O'Donovan

Foreword: Nicholas Robinson
Architectural Analysis: Alan Powers
Catalogue Raisonné: Catherine Lawless
Design: Ted and Ursula O'Brien

KILBRIDE BOOKS

First Published in 1995 by Kilbride Books,
14 Rosslyn, Bray, Co. Wicklow, Ireland.

Copyright © Donal O'Donovan, 1995
All rights reserved.

ISBN 0 948018 30 5

Special Edition: ISBN 0 948018 31 3

Apart from any fair dealing for the purposes of research or private study,
or criticism or review, as permitted under the Copyright, Designs and
Patents Act, 1988, this publication may not be reproduced or utilised in any
form or by any means, electronic or mechanical, including photocopying
and recording, or by any information storage and retrieval system without
permission in writing from the publishers.

Design and Production by Ted and Ursula O'Brien, Oben Design
Typeset by Oben in 11pt Times, with title hand-lettered by Ted O'Brien
after a style designed by Eric Gill in 1907

Printing and Reproduction of Photographs by W. & G. Baird Ltd

TRIBUTE

The author is deeply grateful to the Commissioners of Public Works in Ireland for their warm encouragement and generous support, without which this production would not have been possible.

At the travel and research stage, invaluable assistance was rendered by (the then) Córas Tráchtála and by Aer Lingus.

The author also owes a great debt to three private patrons.

Acknowledgments

To all the people who in their many supportive and encouraging ways have brought this book to birth, I offer my heartfelt thanks. Kingsley Aikins, then our man in Sydney, was endlessly helpful, and Paul Bennett brought his technical genius to the production. Geoffrey Cains, unseen but not unsung, made an act of faith, while Séamas Daly was an early agent of practical help with research. Brian Fallon employed his blue pencil to effect on the first draft, and Louise and Shay Fortune continue to use their skills in my cause. Allan Gamble was an informed guide to Sydney University, John Graby put constructive ideas on behalf of the Royal Institute of the Architects of Ireland, and the Director of the Irish Architectural Archive, David Griffin, always smilingly offered his knowledgeable support. Catherine Lawless was unendingly patient in researching the catalogue.

Norman McGrath used his high professional skill to photograph Finella, St. Ann's Hill and his own collection of his father's pictures. His wife Molly was supportive in more ways than one. Eddie MacParland made many valuable suggestions and Louis McRedmond prepared a most useful and understanding reader's report. Seán and Rosemarie Mulcahy followed the publication saga with sympathy and practical proposals.

Words are not enough to describe my gratitude to Ted and Ursula O'Brien, who have surrounded my text with an aura of their own design magic. But for Michael O'Doherty and Freddie O'Dwyer, the Office of Public Works would not have made an important, sagacious and encouraging contribution to the book. Alan Powers has provided an admirable and witty overview of McGrath's architectural and design oeuvres, filling a gap in my comprehension. Nick Robinson's foreword is an empathetic model of concision and nostalgia. Andrew Sayers, Janet Sheehy and Stuart Smyth have played their parts in the construction, Andrew as my mentor in the Australian National Gallery, Janet in the hidden world of computers and Stuart in the demanding role of photographer of other people's pictures. Bob Warnock's generosity in giving me the work done by his late son John on a life of McGrath will not be forgotten.

Donal O'Donovan
Bray,
May 1995

Foreword

If you become involved with a body such as the Irish Architectural Archive, a vehicle occasionally draws up to your door, and from it are carried into the Archive parcels wrapped in brown paper, pipes of drawings, and tea chests filled with books, and photographs, and manuscripts of a newly acquired collection. For the first time in many years, perhaps, the albums and sketch books are opened, and the drawings are unrolled. It is a great moment when you realise that you are looking at treasure trove. This happened when, for the first time, we looked at the Burgage Collection, and at the Ashlin and Coleman drawings. It happened most memorably when we looked at the collection of papers and drawings of Raymond McGrath, transferred to the Archive on permanent loan in 1978 by his daughter Jenny and her husband Donal O'Donovan.

I had long been an admirer of McGrath's work. One of his pictures had by this time become a favourite: a drawing of the Parthenon in which he had managed to express in his spare line just what his admired Corbusier wrote of in the same building: "The fraction of the inch comes into play. The mouldings contain a number of elements, but everything is ordered with a view to strength… Brutality, intensity, the utmost sweetness, delicacy and great strength." It was a pity that McGrath never published his book on Corbusier.

But the documents carried into the Archive that day told us more. There were, of course, drawings for his major *projets*, executed and unexecuted, and superb examples of his work as a war artist. There were designs for chairs, and carpets, and textiles, and Christmas cards (the Four Courts in 1942, Trim in 1945). And there were nostalgic evocations of a vanished Dublin: menu cards which he designed for the Royal Hibernian Hotel (offering you lobster mayonnaise at 11/6, and Galtee cheese at 1/-), and a bird's-eye view of a city with landmarks such as the Dolphin Hotel, the Red Bank and Jammet's, and the Queen's Theatre. This is the city which was lucky enough to attract Raymond and Mary McGrath in 1940.

Seán Rothery in his book *Ireland and the New Architecture* has described the Ireland that McGrath found: the last paragraph of Rothery's last chapter records McGrath's arrival, as if thus to point to the opening of a new episode in the history of modern architecture in Ireland. McGrath was a distinguished modernist. Behind him was the design of Finella ("In 1928 the place to meet if you were possessed of an interest in the arts and were within visiting distance of Cambridge", according to *The Architectural Review* in 1977), and of an advanced house for A.L. Schlesinger at St. Ann's Hill, Chertsey ("like a big cheese, with a slice cut for the sunlight to enter the whole house", as McGrath himself described it). He had been the Decoration

Consultant to the BBC for their new headquarters in Portland Place, and the collaborator there of Serge Chermayeff and Wells Coates. He had written *Twentieth Century Houses* and – with his brother-in-law Albert Frost – *Glass in Architecture and Decoration*, two important texts in the development of ideas about modern design. His British and Australian careers had been brilliant preludes to what promised to be a triumphant maturity.

Dublin, as we know from Rothery, was not unprepared for, or unacquainted with, those ideas of a new architecture which, germinating in Continental Europe, had inspired McGrath's radicalism. The Irish pavilion at the World's Fair in New York in 1939, with its flat roof and undulating walls of glass, advertised a country which seemed to be presenting itself to the world as ready to embrace the avant garde. As we know, McGrath did not assume the leadership of the new architecture in Ireland. Many of his major commissions here proved unsatisfactory for him: a Gallagher Gallery which he did not get the chance to finish, an unbuilt concert hall, and unbuilt transformations of Dublin Castle. And here his path crosses my own once again. His alterations at Áras an Uachtaráin are individually elegant and, in that historic context, evidence of McGrath's principled commitment to the twentieth century.

As we know from the parentalia of the younger Wren and the younger Gandon, it is the great advantage of the relative as biographer to have access to family material unknown to others. And Raymond McGrath's papers are rich and detailed. Indiscreet comments confided to a private letter or diary can become glaring when exposed in print. If this happens now and again, we can all rejoice elsewhere at McGrath's satire: the account of dispatching Corbusier – intent on exploring the seamy side of London – into a cab bound for Dirty Dick's must count as one of the more exuberant episodes of recent architectural biography.

The drawing of the Parthenon I mentioned earlier, in aiming for objectivity, achieves an impersonal quality familiar from some of his other drawings in which human figures are indicators of scale rather than individuals. Yet his great drawings speak of a fastidious, witty and passionate draughtsman. He was so gifted that it is a pleasure to pay, and to appreciate, a tribute to him. I suspect that over the years McGrath, who was more committed to the practice of his art than to its politics, will attract a growing number of tributes. Briefed for the defence, Donal O'Donovan's lively and affectionate life will be a good foundation for these, with its portrait of the objective draughtsman – drawing "like an angel" – as husband, father, friend, and partygoer.

Nick Robinson

*To my wife and helpmeet Jenny, who was
unstinting in her giving of sometimes painful recollections,
I dedicate this book on her father.*

CHAPTER I

Raymond McGrath first saw the light of Australian day in an insignificant township upriver from Sydney. Gladesville lies on the Parramatta, its most imposing building the mental hospital where Raymond's father was a clerk. Herbert and his wife Edith lived in a small timbered house called Thornhill on Wharf Road where Raymond was born on 7 March, 1903. A month later, the child was baptised at the Anglican Christ Church.

Herbert Edgar McGrath had married Edith May Sorrell in 1899. Their first-born, Ivor, died in infancy. The cause of death was bad hygiene and Herbert as a result conceived a lifelong dislike of dirt in any form. He was twenty-seven when Raymond was born. The happy event encouraged him to work even harder to climb the ladder of the New South Wales mental hospital system.

The Commonwealth of Australia was only two years old. Parliament sat in Melbourne and the rivalry between Victoria and New South Wales was rising to its peak. Brash, thrusting, confident though the young continent was, its people still numbered fewer than 4.5 million. Two-thirds of them were Protestant like the McGraths and 22 per cent of them Roman Catholic underdogs striving for social respectability and ultimately political power. Religious denomination was a significant label up to much more recent times, and it may not have been thought sensible for Herbert to boast of his Irish Catholic descent.

Nor was much made of Edith's Irish links, which were Scots-Irish. We know that James Bell, a native of Coagh, Co. Tyrone, was born in 1820, and in that village, in the lovely Presbyterian barn church that has stood there since 1708, he married Mary Edmiston. Straight after their wedding in 1841, the couple emigrated under the Bounty System to Bourke in New South Wales. The ninth of their ten children was Margaret Jane, who married William Thomas Sorrell of Liverpool, New South Wales.

That union first produced Raymond McGrath's mother Edith. His father Herbert was the son of a couple who dispensed with the Bounty System and took their time reaching the antipodes.

John McGrath was one of a large family of poor Irish farmers from Bagenalstown, Co. Carlow, and became the only child who "backslided" (Herbert's word) from the Roman Catholic religion. He made the change in London in order to marry Elizabeth Hannah of Holland Park, Kensington, and their first home was in Gibraltar.

There John worked for Thomas Cook, the founder of organised travel, and there their first child, Blanche, was born in 1868. John picked up the

Herbert and Edith McGrath, married in 1899

John McGrath,
Raymond's grandfather

Elizabeth McGrath, wife of John
and grandmother of Raymond

rudiments of nursing as an orderly in the medical corps. Soon he emerged as a ship's doctor.

Their second child, Florence, was born in Cairo, and in Ceylon either Edward or Ernest joined the crew. Herbert, although he was born in Auckland, New Zealand, in 1876, moved at the age of six when the McGraths sailed for Brewarrina in northern New South Wales. There Alice, the youngest, was born.

John established a pharmacy in Brewarrina and was doing very well until alcohol took over his life and he had to sell out. Elizabeth worked as a hospital matron in these harsh times during which Edward and Ernest died, one of disease and the other by drowning.

When Herbert was eleven, his teacher announced that he had no more to teach him and Herbert was sent by coach and train to Fort Street School in Sydney.

When Herbert left Fort Street, he had passed the Junior University and Public Service Entrance examinations. He went up to Bourke where he became a postman provided with his own horse. But he had acquired a taste for the greater Sydney area and he soon got an office boy's job in the mental hospital at Parramatta, the first settled town in Australia. New South Wales at the end of the nineteenth century had a well-developed mental hospital system with handsome buildings set in spacious grounds and an enlightened management structure. In a relatively small area west of Sydney, Herbert worked at the hospitals at Parramatta, Gladesville, Callan Park and Rydalmere.

By the time Raymond was born, Herbert McGrath had secured a clerkship at Gladesville. About 1906, Herbert was transferred back to Parramatta Hospital and the family moved to Rostella, at the corner of Grose Street and Sorrell Street, Parramatta. There, on 25 September, 1907, Eileen was born and from there Raymond first went to school. He spent three years at Parramatta North Public School until, about 1911, his father was appointed assistant manager of Callan Park Hospital, now known as Rozelle.

Raymond was sent to Gladesville Public School from which, the local paper recorded with pride, "at a very early age he won a high school bursary". Eileen later joined him at the Gladesville School.

Herbert, who had a talent for handiwork as great as his wife's gift for gardening, had built a week-end cottage at Queenscliff, North Manly, then a very beautiful and quite untamed strip of shoreline on the Pacific Ocean. He sentimentally named this house Rayeileen, combining his children's names, and the family moved in there for two years after his promotion to Callan Park. Herbert soon was able to buy a new house on Wharf Road. He named it Rostella. It had a large garden and a stable in which Raymond, says his sister, "liked to raise the dust in cowboy-style play".

This was to be Raymond McGrath's last home in Australia, the house in which he grew up. Across the road was bush country, then a stream flowing into Glades Bay; more bush and then the wall of the mental hospital with its boathouse. There the McGraths kept their 16-foot sailboat, used by Herbert and his son to explore the vast Parramatta River, its headlands, inlets and islands.

Up the road at the junction was Gus Bowes' cinema where Raymond's lifelong infatuation with the moving picture was conceived in black and white and jerky silence. Down Wharf Road was the pier from which in their teenage years the McGrath children took the Ryde ferry down-river under Drummoyne Bridge and past Cockatoo Island to school and later university and college in the city.

Life at home was full of warmth, love and encouragement. Edith grew her flowers, designed the flower-beds and read gardening books, of which she built a serious collection; while Herbert constructed a tennis court, fernery, summer house and hen run. Everywhere there were books. Edith loved poetry, especially about flowers and gardens, and both parents and children took photographs and made up elaborate albums. They had no motor-car until 1927, after Raymond left for England, but when they did buy a Chevrolet they made great expeditions throughout New South Wales.

Eileen McGrath, sister of Raymond

Eileen remembers her father as a man of patience, vision and imagination, very well liked by all who knew him and much in demand in the hospital as a counsellor. Although his job was strictly administrative, he had the ability to soothe and comfort the troubled. He was a pioneer in the use of cheerful pastel colours in the wards and ensured that the walls were well washed. He introduced occupational therapy, a novelty then, and encouraged the patients to make toys in bright colours and arts and crafts for pleasure. In later years as his authority grew he set up and ran a model pig farm using the left-over food from the hospital. Edith he induced to try pottery making and, after weekly classes at Miss Holden's studio at Warrawee, she became quite skilled. Some of her pieces still adorn at least one house in Ireland. When she was dead, Herbert himself at the age of 75 became a potter and gave classes in County Dublin.

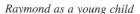

Raymond as a young child

Raymond's early interest in drawing and painting was fostered by a neighbour who gave him lessons in oil painting when he was about twelve. Later his father allowed him to paint a ship in full sail on the wall over the livingroom mantelpiece. His room was a mess, covered in books and drawing materials. "He was always", says his sister, "pottering and tinkering with something." He made the McGrath family's first radio set inside a cigar box, the cat's whisker finding the sensitive spot in a piece of mica. The excitement in the household as they listened to the voices of people far away was palpable.

Tennis, sailing and long family walks in the bush; learning about birds, animals, and plants; and constant sketching and photography all added up to a busy life. Yet there was also school and homework, the making of manuscript books and the writing of articles and poems. A pattern of diligence was forming in the young man that was never to leave him.

While Raymond was always doing or making something, he did not lack for friends. Of these Roy Booth was the staunchest. He in turn valued Raymond's friendship so highly that throughout his life he collected every letter and Christmas card that he received from Europe. To his Sorrell and Smith cousins Raymond was a kind of *Wunderkind*, a little remote though entirely admirable. But to his sister Eileen, he was always close and more than that — easy to be close to. She too, although more than four years

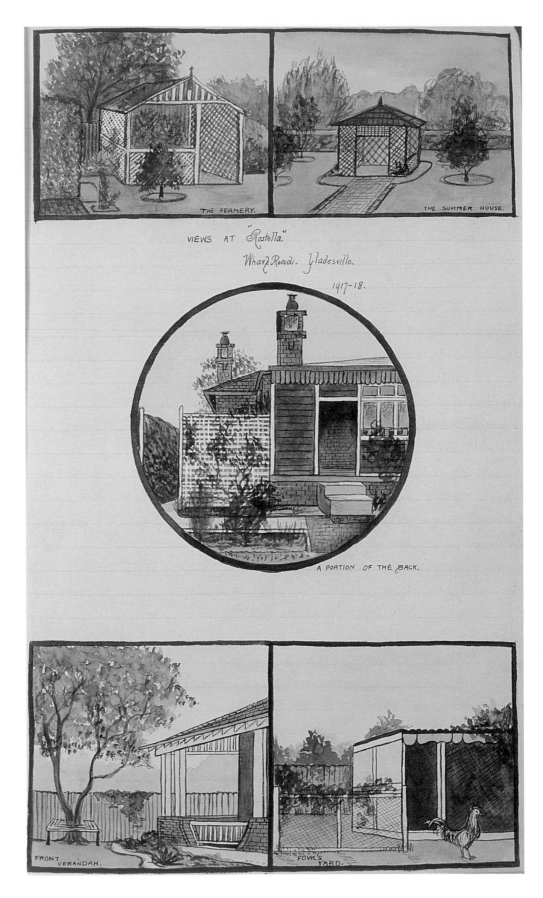

THE FERNERY.

THE SUMMER HOUSE.

VIEWS AT "Rostella"

Wharf Road. Gladesville.

1917-18.

A PORTION OF THE BACK.

FRONT VERANDAH.

FOWL'S YARD.

Raymond's view of Rostella, painted in December 1917. From 'Fragments of Prose and Verse'.

younger, was designing the matrix of her life as an artist. Whenever she asked Raymond for help with a drawing, he always refused, saying: "No — you do it. You must do it yourself." At the same time he took an intense interest in whatever she was doing.

Across the Parramatta lay another ferry wharf at Abbotsford. If no ferry-boat was due, one could call "cooee" from the rocks in Glades Bay and a rowing boat would fetch the callers across the water. From Abbotsford, the tram would take them along the Great North Road to Burwood, where Granma Sorrell lived.

Herbert McGrath did not like dogs, but there was always at least one cat at Rostella, as well as canaries and hens. Annual holidays were a generous three weeks and they were always taken at Ettalong Beach, near Woy Woy about 50 miles north of Sydney on Broken Bay. The journey by train and launch took the best part of a day. Tanks of rainwater operated the washing system in the rented cottage and kerosene provided fuel for lighting and heating. Edith complained that it was fine for the others but it was not a holiday for her. The staple diet was fish, which was easy to catch from their boat.

Ettalong to Raymond was a very special place. One of his earliest manuscript books, 'Rain Prince and Fire Demon', is sub-titled 'A Book of the Bush' and dedicated to "my dear mother".

The book, written in 1918 when Raymond was fifteen, is lavishly illustrated with landscape, animal and fairy pictures that foreshadow one of his later difficulties as a draughtsman. He drew and painted landscapes, urban scenes and buildings with an accuracy and feeling that made him the envy of other artists throughout his life. But he never did master the human figure. The lumpish and ill-featured forms that one would expect from a young adolescent did not mature and he quite sensibly ceased almost entirely to portray men and women when he reached London.

A full-page picture of six species of birds on branches is brilliantly coloured and showered with a loving detail that makes one wish he could transfer his gift from the animal to the human world. Raymond's delight in nature is undeniable. In 'A Day Among the Birds' he writes: "…We will watch the waves breaking in foam on Ettalong, and a tiny schooner with white sails spread in the wind will go slowly by, and somehow we will feel that there is no place on earth like it, this beach."

Rowing up the calm river or taking the quiet road on his bicycle or on foot, Raymond escaped from the noisy tramcar rattling in from the city and felt close to the beautiful bush, "filled with the song of the birds and the perfume of the gums and the wattles".

His advice is to start early, for dawn is "the rose-bud of the day". Night has bedewed the road so that it is never dusty and the sun will not tire you before your journey's end.

On a bird-watching expedition with some mates he asks: "Who does not know the Kookaburra, the laughing kingfisher, Australia's own bird?" His ornithology and indeed his botany were both academic and sympathetic, and his sense of national pride, stirred by the Australian contribution to the Great War just ending, was reflected in his feeling for birds:

The Bungalow, Pretty Beach.
From 'Dreams of the Orient'

"By the lonely bank of the grey lagoon, shrouded beneath the mists of morn..."
Watercolour from 'Fragments of Prose and Verse', painted when McGrath was 14 years old

We had just skirted the pond and entered a clump of She-Oaks when there burst upon our ears the strains of perhaps the most beautiful song our bush holds, sweet, full and yet plaintive, a whole tuneful little lyric in itself. And where was its gifted minstrel? Instinctively we scanned the boughs for some big princely songster, but we saw none. Then came the beautiful song again and why, there he was at our very shoulder, the tiniest little sombre creature of olive and yellow, with a pure white throat. It was the Native Canary, the prince of all our small warblers.

At Rostella, Herbert planted fruit trees; two plums, two oranges, two apples and an apricot. Eileen recalls with joy: "sitting in the apricot tree, eating the fruit and reading a book — I thought that was just heaven. It was a simple life."

6

CHAPTER II

Raymond McGrath did so well at Gladesville Public School that he was awarded a high school bursary to Fort Street,[1] his father's alma mater. Founded as the model school of the national system of public education for the colony of New South Wales, Fort Street was on Flagstaff Hill, Sydney, near Australia's first suburb, The Rocks, and was accessible by tram from George Street and Essex Street, or by the Erskine Street ferry. It was adjacent to Fort Phillip, the site of the present Observatory, and up to 1916 the school was housed in the old Military Hospital.

At the beginning of 1916, Raymond took the ferry from Gladesville, climbed up the hill and presented himself to Alexander James Kilgour, the autocratic Scotsman who was headmaster. Kilgour was a devotee of Latin, one of those old-time people to be found especially in England. Unless a person had Latin he could be neither a gentleman nor a scholar.

Harold Mathews was a contemporary of Raymond's. Mathews' father, a doctor, had decreed that Latin was a waste of time and that the boy should take the business course — "commercials", Kilgour called the boys in this stream dismissively. Raymond took the Latin stream while the commercials studied shorthand, book-keeping, geography and business principles. The two boys did not even meet until after the Intermediate examination. The number of business students had dwindled to the point where they had to join the majority for the last two years leading to the Leaving Certificate.

Fort Street School in 1916.
Raymond is second from the left
in the back row

Raymond wasn't a personal mate, but we all admired him for his artistic ability and in class, where he was an outstanding member liked by everybody. He was not shy or retiring, but he was not strong on sport either. He was a very observant and sympathetic person, a quiet genius.

The boys abandoned short pants in the first year and graduated to knickerbockers, known as "shit-catchers". There was no uniform. The pursuit of excellence was the primary purpose and indeed when Raymond graduated from Sydney University in 1926, so did 48 other Fortians.

The greatest event in the life of Fort Street was the move to Petersham. A chronic shortage of space had plagued the school, and a £20,000 purpose-built structure was erected in 1915. The site was at Petersham in the western suburbs. Continuity was maintained by requesting Petersham's Municipal Council to change the name of Norwood Street to Fort Street. The boys ended their last class on Flagstaff Hill on Saturday 10 June, 1916, and through the superhuman efforts of Kilgour and his staff, the doors of the finest school building in New South Wales opened two days later. Fort Street Boys' High School was in business. Desks, exercise books and fountain pens were all the boys had on Taverner's Hill on their first day. The girls stayed behind in Sydney.

Fort Street High School, 1984.
Drawn by Ian Marr

Of greater significance to the Commonwealth, if not to the school, was the Great War, which for the whole of the British Empire began on 4 August, 1914. Fort Street boys responded to the call to arms by offering their services in large numbers. The officer commanding the Fort Street Cadets was besieged with volunteers. Soon the best of Australia's blood was spattered on the sands and cliffs of Gallipoli. More than 1,300 Fort Street boys enlisted for active service overseas: 142 did not come home. Some 21 were awarded the Military Cross, and one even a Croix de Guerre. The word Anzac (the Australian New Zealand Army Corps) entered the dictionary.

THE SPINEBILLED HONEY-EATER.

LUNULATED HONEY-EATER.

*Above: The Spine-billed Honey-Eater
and the Lunulated Honey-Eater, and
Left: The Regent Honey-Eater.
From 'Fragments of Prose and Verse'*

HONEY-EATER

ve probably one of the most delightful group of birds

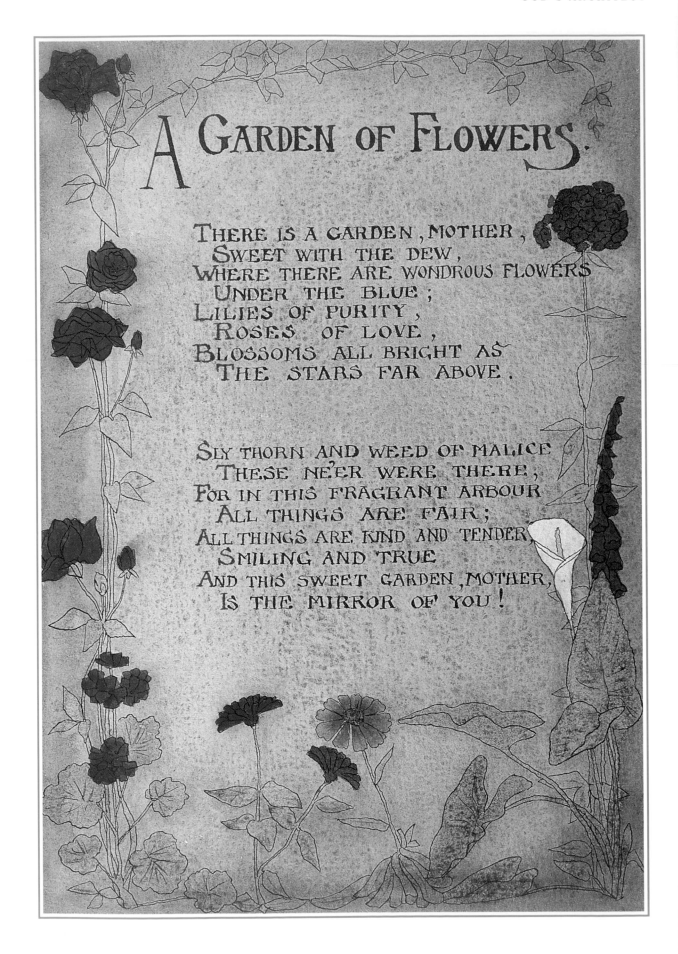

A Garden of Flowers.

There is a garden, mother,
  Sweet with the dew,
Where there are wondrous flowers
  Under the blue;
Lilies of purity,
  Roses of love,
Blossoms all bright as
  The stars far above.

Sly thorn and weed of malice
  These ne'er were there,
For in this fragrant arbour
  All things are fair;
All things are kind and tender,
  Smiling and true
And this sweet garden, mother,
  Is the mirror of you!

Obviously moved by the war news, Raymond demonstrated his innate pacifism which stirred him even at the age of twelve to write the first of his war stories. 'Fairyland' was written in 1915 and published as a prize-winning entry in the *Town and Country Journal* in 1916. The tale begins with a tall, graceful fairy standing at the great gate of Fairyland changing children into fairies while the fish, the flowers and the birds proclaimed: "peace, happiness and goodwill to all who dwell within the fairy gates."

The source of the children was revealed to the narrator:

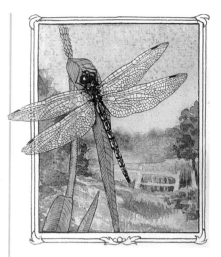

A dragonfly. Book illustration from 'The Paddock' in McGrath's 'Dreams of the Orient'

> Then I gazed down upon the world of strife and turmoil below, I could see the smoke of battle rising over the treetops, I could hear the noise and din of battle rising over the treetops, I could hear the noise and din of battle and the cries and shouts of the soldiers. Then I heard the roar of a great monster gun and saw the awful havoc it wrought in the nearby city.
>
> Now let us hover over the blackened walls of the town and peer into the gloom of a wretched cottage. I can see the prostrate form of a child upon the bed, I can see the poor mother leaning over her child, the cruel shells of the invader have done their awful work. The little child's spirit had departed, it had gone to a land of sunshine, to Fairyland. And as that mother leans over the still form a voice seems to whisper: 'Fear not, he is happy, in a land that knows no sorrow.'

In countries all over Europe — Germany, Austria and Turkey, the enemy, are not excluded — the same terrible tale is told. The story goes on to describe the adventures of two tin soldiers found by a Turkish commander near his camp. There is no trace of jingoism, no evidence even of national bias in Raymond's writing. The *Town and Country Journal* should have been awarded a special prize for tolerance, for this was the year of Gallipoli.

Nearly three years later, Raymond wrote 'On the Western Front', a poem in ten verses of which these two will serve to show his horror of war:

Facing page: 'A Garden of Flowers' and (below) 'The Cicada', both from 'Dreams of the Orient'

"No man's land" is full of flowers, round the craters song birds sing,
And above us in the heavens, sweet and soft, the soaring lark
Pours his song upon the battle, pours his song upon this waste
Of human life and careful labour, till the day is blent in dark.

* * * *

There the shell-holes, overflowing, bloom with blue forget-me-nots,
There the field is red with poppies, yea! the field that once hath been
Red with blood of dead and dying, red with human waste of war,
Ah! I hunger for green meadows and a quiet and peaceful scene.

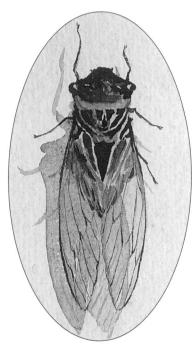

Although he wrote a more conventional war poem on 'The Ghost of Gallipoli' in 1917, he redeemed himself by getting second prize for 'Daisies on the slope' in the same year. Raymond's pacifism was to endure. In 1923, he was at home in Gladesville when he heard of a new poison gas to be used in chemical warfare. He asked himself: "What are the barbarian tortures of the middle ages to this?"

Yet he was a patriot. In 'Dreams of the Orient and Other Poems' (1921) he writes of 'My Australia':

Nations rise and Nations fall,
Kneel in blood and weep in thrall,
Peace she loves above them all,
My Australia!

This is the first of four bland verses, and they are echoed in 'An Australian's Heritage' in which the last verse goes:

Fair land! beloved of God and sage,
What more could mortal find?
Beauty and love, and peace of mind,
A smiling country, silver lined,
A proud Australian's heritage!

'Dreams of the Orient' is the loveliest of four illustrated manuscript books that Raymond made. It is bound and covered by him in blue suède with a light gold frame and lettering. Each line of the poems is decorated with a red initial capital and there is a brilliant use of colour in the illustrations. He uses handmade deckle-edged art paper throughout.

The greatest single influence on a highly impressionable boy was Dr. George Mackaness, deputy head and English master at Fort Street until 1924 and then lecturer in charge of the English department of Sydney Teachers' College. His literary output was prodigious and included a life of William Bligh in two volumes; books on the Australian connections of Sir Joseph Banks and Robert Louis Stevenson, and 'Inspirational Teaching'.

Mackaness it was who cultivated the writing of verse and prose in the *Fortian*, the school magazine that he edited. This gave Raymond a large platform for his writing. His mentor also made a point of monitoring developments in the teaching of English in America and the United Kingdom, though a survey of Raymond's English notebook would not discover much study of writers outside the mainstream.

All in all, George Mackaness was a teacher of unusual breadth of vision and depth of knowledge; and he had the gift of imbuing his students with a love of the language and especially of the classics. He was not, however, universally loved. Harold Mathews[2] admired his advanced teaching methods but now feels that as a man he was not fully respected — "a bit of a bluff, not quite as good as he pretended to be". He also lacked the strength to stand up to Kilgour, and on the sports union committee would never say a word to support any ideas that Harold Mathews as the student representative would propound. As a result the ideas were dismissed with a lordly wave of the headmasterly hand. "It was a one-man school run by a despot, and other teachers later told me what a bad time

The National Art Gallery of New South Wales, from 'Dreams of the Orient and Other Poems'

From the Fortian *of September 1920*

they had under Kilgour", says Mathews, who himself went on to head Australia's first experimental school on the principle of trust and confidence in the children.

When Raymond McGrath was in his last year at Fort Street, he became a prefect, as did his life-long friend Roy Booth. Harold Mathews was captain of the school. He is pictured under Kilgour in a drawing of masters and pupils done by Roy Booth and Raymond under the heading "A glimpse of the old familiar faces". This drawing appeared in the *Fortian* of September, 1920, and shows Raymond as the artist with flowing cravat, easel and pallet; and Booth at the piano wearing tails and mop of unruly hair. Mathews is throwing the discus.

The next four pages reveal Raymond's developing taste for whimsy. In an essay entitled 'Taverner's Hill Five and Thirty Years Ago' which the editor informs us first appeared in 1955, Raymond writes as Charles McLamb. He tells us of his move from the humble day school at Gladesville to Taverner's, "that classic pile with its venerable, collegiate aspect and sweet garden scenes... Come back into memory, like as thou wert, comrades of these happy schooldays." Kilgour is "that Roman", a kind friend and a firm master. Than H. Roy Booth no finer friend ever lived. "Be he what he may, he is first and foremost the musician... with the strains of his own-created melody." Booth in fact became one of Sydney's best-known lawyers, but not chief justice as Raymond prematurely wrote.

"Nor shalt thou, good Harold [Mathews] of the cordial smile, be quickly forgotten", he ends this article by "Charles McLamb, 1955, autrement Raymond McGrath." Done first as a class essay, the piece was so highly regarded by Dr. Mackaness that he decided to publish it.

He later went further. In his own book 'The Study of the English Essay', he comments on 'Taverner's Hill':

> Super-excellent in its kind, probably the most brilliant essay that it has ever been my good fortune to procure as a class essay, is the imitation of Charles Lamb published below. It is by Raymond McGrath, then aged 16.

When Mackaness edited Raymond's work, he corrected the spelling. But he did not eradicate some of the mistakes that Raymond continued to make up to his death. He could not, to take the worst case, ever place the apostrophe in can't, isn't, wouldn't or any kindred word.

Such were Raymond's results in the Leaving Certificate that he had no difficulty in obtaining a scholarship to Sydney University. So obvious was it that his talents lay in English language and literature that the arts faculty was an automatic choice. Dr. Mackaness suggested journalism as a career.

CHAPTER III

Sydney University in 1921 was just 70 years old and still maturing. Maturing in the sense that in the year Raymond McGrath enrolled in the Arts faculty, the university first opened its architecture school under Professor Leslie Wilkinson. With the notion of becoming a journalist, Raymond studied English literature, history, mathematics, geology, philosophy and psychology, a basket of disciplines that left him with the option of specialising.

At university as at school, the greatest single influence was wielded by his professor of English. John Le Gay Brereton was an exceptional man and, as it turned out, an exceptional friend to the young McGrath and his family. Like Dr. Mackaness at Fort Street, Brereton encouraged Raymond to write and soon he was producing poetry and prose for *Hermes*, the undergraduate magazine. He became art editor of the magazine and as well as redesigning it, gave its cover and title page a distinctive style of decoration. With 'The Boy from Berrima' he won the Knyvett Memorial Prize and with 'The Journey of a Joeadjan', the Adrian Consett Stephen Memorial Prize. It was the first time a student had gained both prizes at the same time (1925).

Berrima, like Richmond, Camden, Goulburn and Ballina, held a real place in Raymond's heart. He took some tranquil photographs of it and he used his story to inform us of his views on aborigines. Biddie was a "titled lady of royal blood" and a regular and honoured visitor to the house. Very old and very dirty, she never tired of begging money and getting very drunk. To the question of where she would go when she died, Biddie replied: "Me plurry good as you boss. Me black, you white. No more care. God die you, you go Heaven. God die me, me go Heaven too."

"Biddie", says the narrator in Raymond's story after she drowned, "is of more account than Caesar."

There were several tribes of blacks in the district and the boy from Berrima was drawn by curiosity to see a corroboree by the riverside. A great many blacks gathered in the moonlight and suddenly began to beat upon pieces of wood with a melancholy clattering, and to dance together.

Their black bodies, curiously streaked and painted with white mud, glistened in the moonlight against the mysterious shadows of the trees, and they stamped and jumped about in a strange frenzy of happiness. But no sooner, weirdly and lustily, had they begun to sing together:

moondang-um-um- waam-ma mogin

than of one accord Billy and I turned on our heels and ran…

John of Paris, which appeared in Hermes, *1924*

Though the black men frightened me sometimes still I always loved them, and it fills me with sadness now to think that their kingdom is past and they themselves are vanished like the leaves of the autumn. Rum and trousers and the white man's civilisation have been their downfall.

There was Aboo, the best black tracker in the district. A little white girl was missing so they sent for him. But first he must have tea, then sleep for three hours. Awake, he shook himself like a dog and set out. "Sometimes he would sniff the air and set off at a run and sometimes he would stand stock still. Once when I asked Aboo if I might see the track, he bent down and showed me a broken blade of grass, no more." And sure enough Aboo found the child, sleeping beside a log.

There is in Raymond's writing on the aborigines a sense of equality, of respect, of acceptance if not of understanding of their otherness, that was unusual 75 years ago. In the pages of his book 'Loaranneleah' is a brief version of this tale. The aborigines have now departed.

Another award that he plucked each year from 1922 to 1925 was that for the University Prize for English Verse. 'What the Wind Brings' (1925) is a romantic verse in 12 stanzas. It is of its time and would not merit more than a critical glance in this era of realism and the laying bare of deep feelings. Strict metre and tortured rhyme were the rule in a society that had not yet met even Hopkins or Thompson across twelve thousand miles.

In one of the large manuscript books that Raymond made appeared some of the poems that later were published in *Hermes*. His intimate knowledge of the waterway that lapped the Gladesville wharf led to the 25 stanzas of 'The Parramatta River'. It ends thus:

> I ask this only: when my spirit flies
> From earth's rude corse to haunt the honeyed flow'rs.
> To hear this river breathe the music sung
> When daylight and the faeries touched my eyes!

Lennox Bridge from McGrath's poem 'The Parramatta River', which won the University Prize in 1922. From 'Dreams of the Orient'

The handmade book was 'Dreams of the Orient and Other Poems'. It was all his own work. The last of these books, 'Loaranneleah', had decorations by his sister Eileen. It was subtitled 'Some Pieces in Verse and Prose 1920-1926' and it was bound in July 1926, just a month before

Raymond set sail for England. Here the hand-scripting aspires to the heights he achieved in his thesis on Chinese architecture, and it was these two books that he brought to England and showed to interested guests after dinner.

Here too, in 'Loaranneleah', appeared 'Matthewtown', which described in detail the architecture of an imaginary town 50 miles from Sydney up the Hawkesbury River. It was this story, published in *Hermes* in 1924, which convinced John Le Gay Brereton that Raymond should transfer from arts to the school of architecture.

Matthewtown stood "as far from the feet of the hills as Georgian Windsor". Founded in Raymond's fancy by his great-grandfather John Herbert McGrath on a Government grant he received in 1839, it was a commune, "an idealistically conceived community… the haunting Mecca of my adolescent and maturer pilgrimages". The finest house, Inigo, was John McGrath's, the fruit of his travels in Europe and the Near East. The inn served as art school, town hall and post office as well, and the steepled church of St. Matthew-of-the-Firs had a bell cast by a tailor whose hobby was the making of bells near the old toll-gate in Parramatta.

John McGrath was not an architect, "but he was a true builder. The love of creation that flowed in the veins of Lachlan Macquarie flowed in his too. He had no Greenway at his side, but he had brought many beautiful books with him from England and in them lay the germs of his desires."

So Raymond expressed in his fancy his tribute to the two Australians who as creators of the built environment of New South Wales meant most to him. Lachlan Macquarie was Governor from 1810 to 1821. He was a tolerably liberal Scot who knew what good buildings were but lacked an architect. Fortunately for Sydney, he found Francis Howard Greenway among the convict ranks. Greenway (1777–1837) had been in practice in Bristol when he went bankrupt, forged a contract and was sentenced to death. In those enlightened years, a death sentence usually was commuted to 14 years' transportation. From about 1816, Macquarie placed Greenway in charge of all Government works. The best of the buildings designed by Greenway transformed the architecture of the colony, and on the end of Macquarie Street in Sydney can still be seen today his Hyde Park Barracks facing his St. James' Church. He also designed St. Matthew's in Windsor, which gives us a clue to the provenance of Matthewtown.

One of the events that most moved Raymond was the sad death of Ernest Shackleton, the Irish-born Antarctic explorer:

> O fierce white world! Long-Haunted, step and stair,
> There is one pride-wed hamlet in Kildare
> That breathes thy solemn spell; whose oaken beams
> And crumpled thatch will harbour frosty dreams
> Till they are wormwood; and whose quiet stones,
> Rain-rotted in the grass, like fleshless bones,
> Will stand, a troop of snow on Irish hills,
> Beside rank thyme and drooping daffodils
> When living lips are dust.
>   O glory fled!
> The white, unselfish pioneer is dead.

Another view of the Parramatta River, from 'Dreams of the Orient'

Illustration from Hermes, *Lent 1925*

And so on for 18 stanzas. But his poetry was maturing and the fairies were being eclipsed. 'The Death of Shackleton' brought him the University Prize for English Verse in 1923.

Another death and even more untimely brought Raymond to lament the memory of John Hunter. A Fort Street boy two years older than Raymond, Hunter was already Professor of Anatomy at Sydney University when he died at 26. A.J. Kilgour contributed an appreciation to *Hermes* where Raymond's 'In Memoriam' also appeared, with a delicate decoration showing the young widow weeping.

Nor had his pacifism been eroded. The Great War was well concluded when he wrote 'If the Bugles Blow':

O sleeps he still and sound,   What echoes bid him wake?
The dreams he loved so done,   Dear Peace, he stirs and saith:
His pictured pageantry   'O if the bugles blow
Deep-set beyond the sun?   Or if the hell-horse neigh,
To Time's last trumpetings   God, wilt thou lift thy hand
Beneath the blooming briar,   And brush these sounds away?
Where long lean olives sweep   The champ of martial steeds,
A dirge with winds of Tyre?   The tread of marching men,
Nay, clouds have hid the stars   I had not thought to wake
In night more keen than death;   And hear such sounds again!'

In 'Dreams of the Orient and Other Poems', Raymond was searching for the poet he felt lay in him. Two of his pieces, 'The Rubbish Bin' and 'The Haberdasher' were published in *Hermes* in 1922 and 1923. A fellow student and later the family lawyer was Elmo Pye,[3] who became a warm family friend and lifelong admirer of Raymond's and Eileen's work. He says that "quite an amount of Raymond's verse had decoration and drawings nearby. I always found his hand printing unusual and attractive. He was influenced in some degree in the combination of verse and drawing by the work of William Blake. 'The Rubbish Bin' was included in the anthology done by Mackaness, 'The Wide Brown Land', and in a later book, 'An Anthology of Australian Verse'."

Pye makes a telling comment: "One rarely finds expressions of strong feeling in Raymond's writing. But [in 'If the Bugles Blow'] I think the horror of conflict and war are well and originally given. It and the accompanying drawing appeared in *Hermes* in June, 1924, when Raymond was 21."

In all twelve poems, five short stories and two miscellaneous contributions appeared in *Hermes*. Countless decorations, illustrations and end-pieces either accompanied them or stood alone. The cover, title-pieces and sports section heading were constantly used during his art editorship. They are models of simplicity and elegance. He won the annual medal for English Verse four times; the Adrian Consett Stephen Prize for a short story twice, and the Knyvett Memorial Prize for a prose sketch three times, one of the sketches being 'Matthewtown', which changed the course of his life.

CHAPTER IV

lmo Pye entertained Raymond at his house in Emu Plains in 1921. He was with Raymond when he painted two scenes, one of Glenbrook Creek and the other the viaducts on Lapstone Hill. In Raymond's house in Ireland 33 years later, Pye made slide photographs of the two pictures.

The years 1921 to 1924 were for Raymond the time of the etching. 'The Old Church, Hunter's Hill' (1921) is a prime example of Raymond's early mastery of the etching process. Two years later, 'Windsor-Across-the-River', a quiet pastoral scene, was reproduced in *Art in Australia* for October, 1924. All his published etchings were listed in that magazine for September 1925, an indication of the high esteem in which the artist was held even at 22 years of age. Two years after his death a major exhibition of his etchings and wood engravings was held in the Deutscher Galleries in Armadale, Victoria. It contained 85 works and, with the aid of a lavish catalogue and biographical notes by Roger Butler, aroused a great deal of interest in an artist by then (1979) largely forgotten in his native land.

Emu Plains and the Viaducts on Lapstone Hill, from 'Dreams of the Orient'

Although the only McGrath etching in the Sydney University exhibition catalogue of its collection (1988) is his 'Great Hall' of 1923,

The Women's College,
Sydney University, 1924

prints of 'The Deserted Farmhouse, Ermington', 'Lennox Bridge, Parramatta', 'Hayshed, Windsor', 'The Charm of Ettalong' and 'Windsor-Across-the-River' can be found in various rooms in the university. Sydney does not possess prints of 'The Medical School', an edition of 20 done in 1922; 'The Tower', a linocut edition of 25 (1923), or 'The Women's College' (1924), a wood engraving done in an edition of ten.

During his years in the arts faculty, Raymond worked hard at the set subjects. But at the same time he studied painting at Julian Ashton's Sydney Art School and the Dattilo Rubbo School also in Sydney. In his art he was encouraged by Lionel Lindsay and Hardy Wilson, the eminent architect and historian. Adrian Feint, painter, printmaker and collector (1894–1971), was an acquaintance to whom he bade farewell before sailing to England.

A seminal event in Raymond's artistic development was an exhibition of woodcuts, wood engravings and linocuts held in Tyrrell's Gallery, Sydney, in September 1923. The artists included Margaret Preston (1875–1963), who as Rose Macpherson of Adelaide had been a pupil at Fort Street. There and everywhere she is now saluted as "the forerunner of modernism in Australian art".

At the Tyrrell's Gallery show too were Lionel Lindsay and Napier Waller. Lionel Lindsay (1874–1961) is one of the most popular artists in Australia and perhaps the country's best-known and most respected printmaker. He is well known too as a writer and critic and in 1923 was the first to write in *Art in Australia* about the woodcut and the English artists Thomas Bewick and William Blake. His pioneering 'A Book of Woodcuts' appeared in 1922 and was the first album of its kind in Australia.

Facing Page:
The Tower, Sydney University, 1923

Mervyn Napier Waller (1894–1971) was wounded in the Great War and learned to use his left arm for drawing. The first in Australia to make linocuts, he later did fine watercolours, murals and mosaics.

Above and below:
Wood engravings by Norman Lindsay
from Kenneth Slessor's 'Earth
Visitors', 1926

Preston, Lindsay and Waller especially gave Raymond McGrath a *tour d'horizon* of the woodcut, and later that year he made his first linocut, the linocut being the poor man's woodcut. Already he had discarded etching. He soon abandoned the linocut for the wood engraving.

An early letter to Professor Le Gay Brereton dates Raymond's conversion to early December 1923, when he wrote:

> The other day I was initiated into the mysteries of the real graver, and the making of one, by an old Austrian die-sinker whose present hobby is feeding birds and writing Hebrew proverbs. The real graver, as he showed me to use it, is fluent as a pen. Previously I had used a foolish 'carving' contraption of my own, the result [of] which was the little hacked cut I sent you. I can understand now the delicacy of such work as Howard Pyle's 'Sacking of Panama'.

Displaying a quite astonishing aptitude for his new-found craft, Raymond in the following year not only mastered the technique of wood engraving but published a book containing six full illustrations, three vignettes and a cover of patterned paper. This latter process even in England was confined to the work produced by the Curwen Press, which used paper designed and cut on wood by such people as Enid Marx and Eric Ravilious. Raymond used a linocut.

'The Seven Songs of Meadow Lane: A Book of Poetry and Woodcuts', was published in Sydney in 1924. Only 30 copies were printed, on Japanese vellum, on the handpress of J.T. Kirtley. Raymond's friends, Jack Lindsay, John Kirtley and Wal Taylor, helped him in this enterprise; and his father Herbert played a key role.

A letter which must have been written by John Kirtley (it is undated, addressed "Dear Harry" and only one page is extant) reveals a great deal about the publication of 'Seven Songs'. Raymond had the habit of calling to see Kirtley in Martyn Brownhill's office at 113 Pitt Street. He found Raymond "a slim fellow, quiet mannered, with precise formal type of spectacles, had a pleasant humorous outlook made [missing] decent by his assumption of humility".

The acquaintanceship became "a quiet sort of friendship without any special intimacy". Both liked nice books. The Lindsays [Norman (1879–1969) was a sculptor, painter, etcher, illustrator, author and maker of model ships, was the younger brother of Lionel whom we have met; and the father of Jack] regarded Raymond "as small beer and were supercilious, but he was much superior to J.L. [Jack Lindsay]". Kirtley was writing sometime after the Second World War while the Lindsays were alive.

He had bought some fonts of Cloister type — 18 point, 14 point — for a job and he decided to make first use of them by doing a book of Raymond's poems. Kirtley regarded Raymond as a "very good engraver... His print 'Is there anybody there?, said the traveller', is a superb effort, one of the best of the modern engravings, if not of all time."

The printing was a protracted job and Kirtley could not complete it before leaving for England. "My mother sold [Raymond] the bench hand platen, formes, trays and type for a token £10 so that he could do the job." He does not think any copies were sold and at the time of writing the books are "probably one of the rarest of Australiana". Raymond called to Kirtley at 5 Bloomsbury Square in London and gave him a copy.

Herbert McGrath's part in the making of 'Seven Songs' is described in an account he has left us:

Piece affixed to the cover, 1924

> This book was certainly printed on the hand-press of J.T. Kirtley but not wholly by that gentleman. He and Jack Lindsay were working together and undertook to print Raymond's book. Before the job was finished, however, they decided to go to England and in cleaning up their printery accidentally upset the cases of type, of which there were several founts. Not having time to sort it, the whole lot was swept up, litter and all, and emptied into kerosene tins.
>
> The press and type were purchased by Raymond at an agreed price and he and I set about sorting the type so that the printing of the book could be completed in the same fount. This took weeks of our spare time and when we had picked out what we thought was sufficient type to print one page at a time, I had learnt to set it up, for neither of us were printers.
>
> The three poems remaining to be printed were 'The Rubbish Bin', 'The Sunflower' and 'The Haberdasher' and all the woodcuts.
>
> I had not gone far with my typesetting when I found myself running out of small dees and hours of search through the remaining type did not produce the required number. To help overcome the shortage, Raymond altered a number of words with dees in them and had to almost rewrite some of the verses. We were further aided by using the abbreviation for 'and' but still there were insufficient dees. I then hit upon the idea of picking out another fount of type to help us out and this accounts for those verses printed in italics.
>
> The cover is a linocut by Raymond and was printed by me on the press. The bookbinding, I think, was done by Wal Taylor.

'The Haberdasher', 1924.
Decoration for the First Song of
Meadow Lane

The pictorial book-plate made its belated appearance in Australia at the end of the nineteenth century. The English writer, poet and public servant, Austin Dobson, had and has close relatives in Australia, one of them being Rosemary Dobson the eminent poet, who is his grand-daughter, and another her sister, the late Ruth Dobson, whose last diplomatic posting was as Australian ambassador to Ireland. In that capacity she formally opened a memorial exhibition of Raymond McGrath's art in Dublin in 1979. Austin Dobson had his book-plate engraved by J.D. Cooper after an 1883 portrait by Edwin A. Abbey, R.A.

A number of book-plates by the young Norman Lindsay became collectors' items, and his brother Lionel soon was seized of the same

Above and below:
Vignettes for 'The Seven Songs of
Meadow Lane'

enthusiasm. D.H. Souter executed a plate for Raymond McGrath's mentor, John Le Gay Brereton, and another for Percy Neville Barnett, the author of 'Pictorial Book-Plates: Their Origin; and Use in Australia', privately printed in Sydney in 1931 in an edition of 300. Raymond's copy is numbered 69.

Barnett's book illustrates two of Raymond's book-plates, one his own (dated 1926) and the other for Heather McDonald Sutherland (1925). An explosion of interest was the result of an exhibition of book-platers in Sydney in 1923. It led to the foundation of the Australian Ex Libris Society.

"Raymond McGrath", says Barnett, "of great talent in a variety of ways, produced several wood-cut plates, charming and skilfully cut."

When Raymond was in London he entered in his diary for 11 April, 1927, an amusing reference to Barnett:

"Well if it isn't Mr. O'Garth. How are you? That's the stuff", exclaimed Walter Bradley as I came down the iron stair into his basement printery in Percy Street. Bradley always calls me O'Garth and he pronounces it with such care that I never have the heart to tell him he is mistaken. Anyhow it doesn't matter much and I enjoy having two separate names. As a matter of fact I always feel more like Mr. O'Garth when I call on Walter Bradley for I am then in a different London. We set about the task of ruling up P. Neville Barnett's book of 'Woodcut Book-plates' and I was reminded that "Barney" in his last letter to me had said, concerning the [Frank] Brangwyn plates Bradley had printed for his work: "He hinted at me paying the printing expenses and postage." Now the trouble with Walter Bradley is not that he is mean but merely that he is poor, like a lot of other people in this rich city.

Another of Raymond's handmade books was the consequence of his skill as a woodcut artist. Gathering together the illustrations and vignettes he had done for 'The Seven Songs of Meadow Lane', he made them into a leather-bound book entitled '24 Woodcuts: 1924 to 1926'. He made two copies, one for himself and one for his parents. The additional woodcuts include a full-page illustration for 'St. Simeon Stylites' by Tennyson; the Royal Mint in Sydney; a book-plate for James A. Gardiner, and the Women's College, Sydney University. Jim Gardiner was a friend whom he later met again in London.

The artistic output from Raymond's hands between 1922 and 1926 was impressive. The Australian National Gallery has a list of 14 etchings done between 1922 and 1924 in editions no larger than 30 and as small as five. He featured in four exhibitions in Sydney. In the Society of Artists' annual exhibition for 1924 he showed four woodcuts illustrating verses from Walter de la Mare's poems. They sold for one guinea each. In the Farmers' Exhibition Hall in November he displayed the same four at an exhibition of etchings and drawings. In 1925, he had two woodcuts at the Artists' annual show; one was 'St. Simeon Stylites' and the other

'Tamburlaine' (proceeds to go to the Marlowe Memorial fund). His last "appearance" — he already had set sail for England — was at the 1926 annual show of the Society of Artists held as usual at the Education Department's Art Gallery in Loftus Street. His sole offering was 'When Shall We Three Meet Again?', a very fine wood engraving for which he asked 1½ guineas.

While he was a student under Wilkinson, Raymond also contributed to the Institute of Architects of New South Wales annual exhibition, which had a section devoted to the work of students of the Sydney University School of Architecture and the Sydney Technical College School of Architecture. "The work of Raymond McGrath stands out among the drawings", said the *Sydney Morning Herald*, which also commented favourably on a decoration based on a Chinese design, "one of the rarest things in the exhibition".

As Raymond made the transition to architecture in 1923, it is revealing to record the impressions of a famous Fortian who studied with him in the Philosophy Room of the university. Hermann Black had been Chancellor of Sydney University for some years when he died in 1990, and had been knighted. As students he and Raymond sat together listening to the slow, deliberate diction of Professor Bernard Muscio and later Professor Francis Anderson, whose level of eloquence was much higher.

"Raymond was a most attentive listener, his striking blue eyes always level save when, instead of taking notes, he would sketch various items in the setting", which was mural paintings of the famous philosophers.

Black's overriding impression was that Raymond's interest in philosophy derived from "his deeper aesthetic interests, forerunning his devotion to architecture". He seemed, although he engaged in no philosophical discussions, to be adding early Greek thinking to his general equipment. "I should think", says Sir Hermann Black,[4] "that an architect could do worse."

Black found Raymond a very private person, not distant in manner but not the easygoing effusive type. "In the '20s he was distinctive in giving an impression that he was an 'aesthete', a type which in those less sensitive days might attract a derisive comment." The two had an easy rapport but though Raymond "confessed" that he wrote poetry, he never showed his writings to Black. Anything he wrote, whether poetry or prose, always seemed to Black to indicate that "the rich resonances of Old Europe's cultures were the meat and drink he would value and seek".

Macbeth and the Witches, 1926.
'When shall we three meet again...?'

Raymond's Christmas card, 1926.
St. Paul's Cathedral, a kangaroo
shaking hands with a bushman and
buses full of onlookers

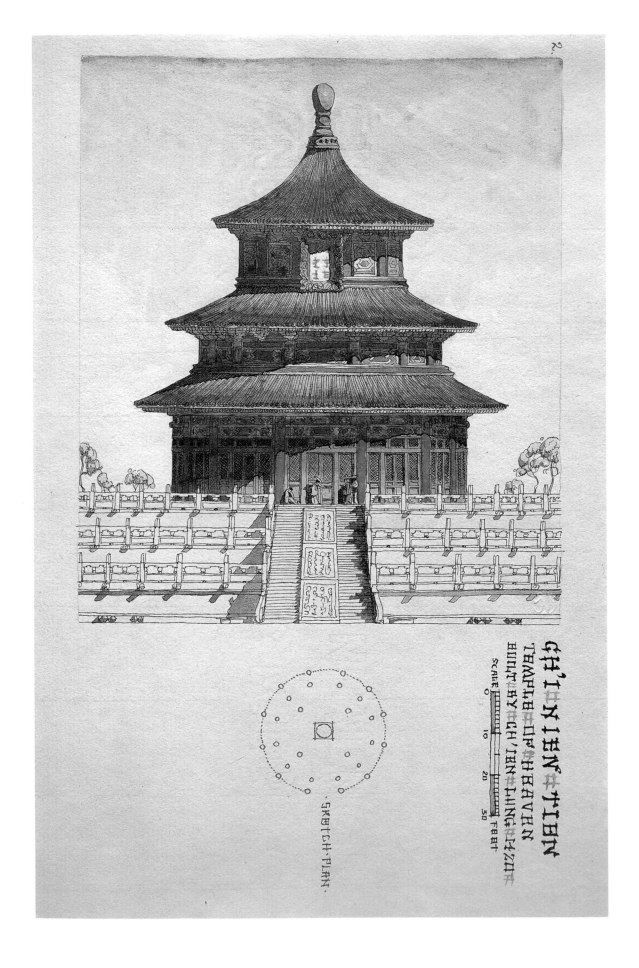

CHAPTER V

In 1977, Raymond McGrath reflected to Brian Hanson[5]: "In a way, I came to architecture through history." Professor James Fawthrop Bruce taught history extremely well and by good fortune the history faculty was specialising in the Italian Renaissance while Raymond was studying arts at Sydney from 1920 to 1923.

R.M. Crawford tells us that "many a student was to remember Bruce's lectures on 'The Renaissance in Italy', not for their verbal frills, but for their sheer driving enthusiasm for creative achievement in all fields of art from sculpture to statecraft. When Bruce forgot his notes to talk about these things, the conscious wordplay fell away, to be replaced by that easier felicity of phrase that comes to a master of words when he talks of something which really interests him more than the words themselves."

Bruce's influence and the work of Francis Greenway gave Raymond a real foundation in classical and renaissance architecture. The Victorian Gothic of Edmund Blacket's Sydney University itself left him unmoved.

The new school of architecture under the Englishman, Professor Leslie Wilkinson, was a year old when Raymond joined it. His passport consisted mainly of 'Matthewtown', which had won him universal praise on the campus.

In the school, the emphasis was on measured work, study of the styles of architecture and learning architectural history. There was no particular school such as Beaux Arts to be rammed down the students' throats. And there was Alfred S. Hook, associate professor of architectural construction, who had no notions about fashions. He was interested only in materials and structure and in Raymond's words he was "damned good". Hook once returned the compliment by saying of Raymond: "You give him a hint and it blossoms out into something quite original."

In the Sydney of the day, Spain seemed more European than France or Germany because a number of Australian artists had worked and studied there. So Spain, and Italy and Greece, became the foci of Raymond's European interest. Because of Hardy Wilson's book on colonial architecture[6], in which he developed the theory that there was an oriental influence in colonial buildings, Raymond was attracted for romantic reasons to the notion that some Australian houses had curved forms. In his last year at university he became interested in oriental architecture and tried to design a number of buildings in an oriental manner. He succeeded in at least one.

It is perhaps moving on too quickly to refer to Raymond's degree thesis. No matter. Its subject was 'Architecture of China and its adaptation

Facing page:
Selected page from McGrath's 'Architecture of China and its adaptation to Japan', 1926
(Courtesy of the Australian National Gallery)

ARCHITECTURE OF CHINA
AND ITS ADAPTATION TO JAPAN
AN ACCOUNT OF THE CLASSICAL ARCHITECTURE
OF THE PRINCIPAL PROVINCES OF CHINA

WITH SOME SUGGESTIONS
AS TO ITS VALUE IN THE
DEVELOPEMENT OF MODERN
ARCHITECTURE PARTICULARLY ON
THE AUSTRALIAN CONTINENT

RAYMOND McGRATH ⊗ ARCHITECTURE II
SYDNEY UNIVERSITY
JANUARY 1926

YUNG TING MEN OUTER GATE TOWER OF PEKING
FROM A CHINESE MEASURED DRAWING SHOWING ACTUAL COLOURS
THE PANTILES AND BRICKS ARE A SILVERY GREY

SCALE 0   10   20 FEET

to Japan: An account of the classical architecture of the principal provinces of China with some suggestions as to its value in the development of modern architecture particularly on the Australian continent'. It is dated January 1926, and is the apogee of his superb skill in illustrated manuscripts. Technically, it is "watercolour, pen and ink on paper bound into a volume", but to say that is to say nothing of the penmanship that went into writing a whole thesis in imitation Chinese characters, or of the startling combination of atmosphere and accuracy that marks the illustrations. And this from a man who had never left New South Wales, never mind drawn the Temple of Heaven from life. The thesis, each page of which is embossed "S.U." for Sydney University, was borrowed by Raymond when he was leaving for London. H.M. Green, librarian of the Fisher Library at Sydney, recommended the loan to Walter Selle. Ignorant of this information, McGrath's daughter Jenny gave 'Chinese Architecture' to the Australian National Gallery in Canberra in 1987.

His schooling in architecture turned Raymond, he thought, into a good classicist with "a fair training in construction". He was dismayed by the realisation that what the students saw being turned out by the profession at large was "just a commercial version of the classics".

Young Raymond McGrath in particular and the Sydney school of architecture in general were not among those who knew what the Germans and French were doing. "Europe was a closed book to us; the word 'modern' had not crossed our paths, and it's hard to realise how isolated we then were on the other side of the world."[7] Hardy Wilson remained the diehard traditionalist.

In the meanwhile there are examinations to be passed and holidays to enjoy. In a letter to Professor Brereton in December, 1923, Raymond informs him that "the next few days will see two or three studio mates and myself upon a land-loping, sketching vagabondage of the Hawkesbury River".

He encounters temperatures up to 113°F and finds that from 9 o'clock in the evening to 1 o'clock in the morning is the best time for rowing.

In a burst of gratitude to Brereton he says he is set to enjoy architecture. "Thanks to your intervention of two years ago I often think what I should have lost had I gone wandering on into the wilderness of journalism."

February 1924 finds him working "night and day for a month in a crescendo of energy" on a model of a bulk handling road materials depot for Norman Weekes, the Sydney city engineer. Built to a scale of 1/8" to a foot, the large and elaborate model had a branch railway line, truck elevators and local quarry and cement stores. Years before Meccano of Liverpool made the first Dinky Toys, Raymond and a fellow student built convincing model lorries with hinged sides. The whole thing had to be delivered within a few days of his writing to Brereton. He had had some practice with modelling when he made a scale replica of St. John's Church, Parramatta, for which the drawings took up 20 pages of his sketchbook. His partner was not too pleased with the £30 they got for the Sydney job, but he himself went on to measure up the Observatory and Old King's

Facing page:
The title page (above) of McGrath's thesis and (below) the Outer Gate Tower of Peking. 1926
(Courtesy of the Australian National Gallery)

McGrath's model of St. John's Church, Parramatta

School (formerly Government House) at Parramatta.

On his bicycle again, he rode over De Burgh's Bridge into Gordon, where he went to see "the most beautiful house I know of". The owner of Eryldoun was E.G. Waterhouse, but more important to Raymond was the fact that the architect was Hardy Wilson, "one of the truest artists in Australia". He stood an hour in front of the house, drinking in the beauty of its shady verandah and its flagged path, bordered with rows of riotous red China roses.

Nor had he outgrown his poetry. To the *Mail* he submitted 'Martin Place' (a plaza in the centre of Sydney). It begins:

> If there were fields in Martin Place
> It's green they would be now.
> It's brown would gleam the town-clerk's face
> As faces by the plow.
> Your typists country-sweet would walk
> Between the shimmering wheat,
> Such birds would sing, from stalk to stalk
> All down the tramless street!

Few of Raymond's activities as a student could be called normal or usual, but perhaps one of his more extraordinary undertakings was his work for the University Carillon Fund. Sydney University had lost nearly 200 of its members in the Great War and in 1924 decided that its memorial to them should take the form of a set of bells to be hung in the Great Tower. Raymond designed a striking three-colour poster with the theme: "Will you help to set the bells ringing?" and the newspapers of the day carried reports of the design and reproductions of the poster. They give full credit to "Mr. R.H. M'Grath" for a fine idea and artistic design. (The original drawing was later presented to the university.)

Simultaneously, Raymond and Eileen cast six-inch plaster painted figurines of a male and female chorister for sale in aid of the fund. At least one family in Sydney still displays these moulded models.

Professor Ernest Rudolph ("Sonny") Holme, who held the chair of English Language, went to England to raise money for the bells and was in London when Raymond arrived there. Raymond, who had considerable respect and affection for Holme, wrote to Professor Brereton: "What a wonderful piece of good fortune it is that Alfred Gilbert should be doing the bust of Professor Holme... Mr. Gilbert executed a very vigorous sketch model and is now working from life." The bust is still on display at Sydney University, where they tell the tale of Professor Wilkinson's first sight of it. Wilkinson put his hand inside, withdrew it and said: "Ah, just as I thought. Hollow."

Another war memorial in which Raymond was engaged was in fact his only building in Australia. It came about in this manner. His father was assistant manager of Callan Park Hospital where the manager was Robert Kirkpatrick. Kirkpatrick's son, who rejoices in the name of Michael Alexander Addison, had been at Fort Street with Raymond and was an arts

A fanciful watercolour of McGrath's war memorial at Callan Park Hospital, 1925
(Courtesy of Aidan Powell)

student at Sydney and a member of the literary staff of *Hermes* while Raymond was its Art Editor. Michael Kirkpatrick often went on rowing or sailing trips with Herbert and Raymond, sometimes to Rodd Island, sometimes under Drummoyne Bridge.

Callan Park had 128 acres of grounds, and the McGraths decided to ask the manager if Raymond could design and build a small war memorial to the staff members who fell in the war. A brick, concrete and timber structure of unusual design was erected. Eileen made her contribution by designing a drinking fountain with water spouting from a kangaroo's mouth. In each of the two end pillars of the memorial she inserted circular glazed plaques, one bearing the names of the dead officer and a private soldier; the other carrying a quotation from Rupert Brooke. Remarkably, though the drinking bowl is shattered and no water flows, the memorial stands yet, just inside the old gate of Rozelle Hospital. It is semi-circular, whitewashed red-tile-capped with distinctly oriental timber pergola extensions; no more than 40 feet in length, with a dimpled cement finish on its walls — an enduring

The war memorial as McGrath photographed it

31

monument to Professor Hook's instruction on building well. Raymond's rich and fanciful watercolour of this building is now in Dublin.

Leslie Wilkinson looked upon Raymond McGrath as one of his brightest students. So it is not surprising that when he graduated in 1926 it was with first-class honours and the University Medal for the most distinguished candidate. He was also awarded the William Charles Wentworth Travelling Fellowship for post-graduate study in England or the continent of Europe. It was announced that in addition he had completed nine courses in the Faculty of Arts. His was a *succès fou*.

Herbert McGrath was moved to write to Professor Brereton on May 6th: "The honours that the University has recently conferred upon [Raymond] are more than his mother and I ever expected and we feel that his success is in no small measure due to your advice and guidance upon the many occasions he sought it."

The Wentworth Travelling Fellowship was the rock upon which Raymond McGrath's future was built. It was named after William Wentworth (1790–1872), bastard son of an Armagh publican. Wentworth lived at Vaucluse House, designed by Francis Greenway. He was the founder of *The Australian*, an Emancipist newspaper which he used to lever himself up the social ladder. He went to Cambridge University, not to get a degree but to compete for the chancellor's gold medal for poetry when the subject was Australasia. He came second and sailed home instead with a printing press. When transportation to New South Wales was abolished in 1840, Wentworth's role as the Emancipists' champion disappeared and he spent his energy building up a reputation that would erase what he saw as the ignominy of his origins. In 1862 he gave £445 to accumulate until it was enough for a fellowship in the faculty of arts. The first was awarded in 1923, the second to Raymond McGrath in 1926. When he got the news, he told Elmo Pye: "I shall not easily forget the kind of daze I was in all day."

The travelling fellowship was worth a generous £250 a year for three years at most, and Raymond made the most of it. He booked his passage for late August on the R.M.S. Osterley bound for Tilbury. But first he had a task to perform.

Hyde Park in Sydney was named in 1810 after its famous London counterpart. Governor Macquarie designated it for "the recreation and amusement" of the inhabitants. In 1926, the then municipal council established a remodelling competition. The winner was Norman Weekes, the former city engineer. Probably because of his work on the road materials depot, Raymond obtained a job in Weekes's office. There he prepared drawings and caught the eye of Gwen Woodward in Sir Charles Rosenthal's office next door. She "fancied him as a good catch".

The adjudicators appreciated "the vision and masterly handling" of Norman Weekes's park of formal avenues and vistas, but modified it to some degree, with his concurrence.

This is the place to lay a small ghost. Professor David Saunders of Adelaide University wrote the obituary of Raymond McGrath for *Architecture Australia* (April–May 1978). It was a fine piece of writing but in regard to the Hyde Park remodelling Saunders was misled by Roy Booth. Saunders wrote:

> His friend Roy Booth remembers how the new graduate in the short period before he took up the travelling scholarship… which took him away from Sydney forever, was engaged by an officer of Sydney City Council to revamp the park. The layout and planting we know today are his.

The late John Warnock, who was working on a life of Raymond McGrath when he died at 45 in 1990; and Ms. M.E. Burn, helpful Mitchell Librarian in the State Library of New South Wales, have since set the record straight. We now know that the work on Hyde Park was Norman Weekes's and the role of the young graduate was confined to the preparation of some of the drawings.

'Skeleton of a City' by Raymond McGrath, 1925

Vaucluse House, Sydney, designed by Francis Greenway, from 'Dreams of the Orient'

CHAPTER VI

Raymond McGrath is simply incomplete without his sister Eileen. They grew up together, they worked together, their interests were inseparable, their mutual encouragement constant. (Three years before his death, Eileen wrote: "You do have a beautiful style with a pen."). But more than that, Eileen was so outstanding a sculptor that before she was 24 a book had been written about her work. Norman Lindsay and Leslie Wilkinson were among the contributors to this remarkable tribute, which was edited by her teacher, the sculptor Rayner Hoff.

After Gladesville school, Eileen went to Drummoyne Public School from which, in 1923, she was awarded a scholarship to East Sydney Technical College in Darlinghurst. There her exciting life as a sculptor began. It lasted ten years in Australia, culminating in the flawed triumph of the Anzac Memorial in Hyde Park.

Eileen McGrath was the favourite student of Rayner Hoff, the Manxman trained in England. At 32, Hoff met Hardy Wilson in Naples and took his advice to accept the post of public instructor in drawing and sculpture at East Sydney.

It is a measure of the cultural microcosm which Sydney was that Hoff's and Raymond McGrath's worlds touched, not just through Eileen, but through busts that Hoff did of John Hunter, Professor Muscio, Norman Lindsay and Professor Hook. Contrary to some opinion, however, Raymond did not study under Hoff.

Barbara Tribe, a fellow student of Eileen's and an acquaintance of Raymond's, paid tribute to Hoff's "great creative force and energy". But viewing Hoff in hindsight (1966), she saw him as coming at the very end of an era in art, isolated in an Australia that knew nothing yet of Brancusi or Picasso. The same criticism, if it is a criticism, could by extension be levelled at Eileen McGrath.

At the end of her first year, Eileen had to her credit a modelled, anatomised, half-sized study of Michelangelo's *Giorno*, and about then she decided to specialise, to become a sculptor. In 1926 and in 1928 she came second in the scholarship offered by the Artists' Ball Trust Fund. In 1929 she was placed second in the Society of Artists' travelling scholarship competition. She told Professor Brereton[8]: "I am sorry I was unable to pull off the scholarship, for I was looking forward to meeting my brother on the other side."

Eileen gained an honours diploma in sculpture, and B.J. Waterhouse, President of the Institute of Architects, deeply regretted that a travelling scholarship was not associated with the diploma "to enable so brilliant a

'Joan' by Eileen McGrath, 1929

Eileen McGrath

student to further pursue her studies abroad".

"It is given to few artists so young to be 'produced' in a de luxe edition, but to Eileen McGrath has fallen that honour", said *Woman's Budget* in July, 1931. 'The Work of Eileen McGrath' was a special number of *Art and Printing*, quite unusual in being a full book printed in capital letters by the letterpress students of the college under E.H. Shea. Eileen drew the decorations as well as having all her major sculptures shown in photographs. Norman Lindsay in 'A Footnote to the future' ranged widely on cultural values. "We can claim for the Australian mind", wrote Lindsay, "a cultural impulse towards plastic art and the investigation of physiological phenomena. There we stop. The response to music and poetry and prose is apparently nil."

"Miss McGrath", wrote Leslie Wilkinson, "is a sister of Raymond McGrath, a young Sydney architect who is making a name for himself in Cambridge and London, and to me having followed the career of the brother, the success of the sister comes as no surprise. There is a family of talent…"

It was left to Rayner Hoff to strike the only personal note: "Miss McGrath", he wrote, "remains a quiet, unassuming, almost diffident girl; rather apt, perhaps, to underrate her ability."

Fresh from the triumph of his remodelling of Finella, Eileen's brother sent her "the critical letter I promised you". He let her have it between the two eyes, attacking her carelessness about details in her figure pieces and finding in 'Tamburlaine' little distinction between the texture of the draperies and that of the hair.

"Why", he asked, "is your figure of 'Kitty' sitting on a lump of dough?" She should not approach her model in a spirit of reproduction. "Hence the uselessness of choosing a model for her personal beauty. You should have an idea to express…"

Raymond cites Chana Orloff, Antonio Maraini, Ivan Meštrović, Pablo Gargallo and John Skeaping as exponents of modern figure work whom

Eileen and Rayner Hoff working on the reliefs for the Hyde Park war memorial, 1930

she should study. In fact, when Eileen went to London in 1933 (the letter was written in 1930) she *did* study under Skeaping for a while.

Having dealt equally harshly with Eileen's relief work, he ends: "Pardon the presumption of a daring brother." Presumption it was too, coming from one who had long given up the search for mastery of the human form.

Eileen was 23 and Hoff's assistant when they became the prime movers in the sculptural works that formed the core of the Anzac Memorial Building in Hyde Park. It was only four years since her brother had helped with the new design of the park; but the siblings' connection was even closer, for Raymond as architect and Maurice Lambert as sculptor submitted their own design for the memorial from London.

There were 117 competitors for this most important commission, the assessors being Leslie Wilkinson, Alfred Hook and the Public Trustee, E.J. Payne.

The winning architect was C. Bruce Dellit, whose design incorporated a large quantity of sculpture by Rayner Hoff in bronze and synthetic stone, in the round and relief. Hoff did not set out to glorify or in any way present a romantic picture of war, and although two groups of statuary were not included in the final memorial, it amply fulfilled its function as, in the words of Lionel Wigmore, "a memorial worthy of the State and the Nation, in keeping with the magnitude of the event and the sacredness of the memory of those whose courage, endurance and sacrifice it is intended to symbolise".

A photograph of the model of the McGrath/Lambert entry appeared in *The Home*.[9] The design was rather "futuristic" for three conservative assessors. Raymond wrote to George Mackaness about his scheme "with its conventionalised column of flame springing from the rising sun". Only one person wrote to him about his design, which "seems to have had a cold reception".

The sole Australian member of the McGrath fan club was his friend John Moore, the artist and architect, who was most enthusiastic. "I saw your study", he told Raymond. "I must sit down straight away tonight and tell you how much I admire it. I think it is a magnificent piece of pure design so far above everything else in the show, so clear cut, so definitive, so very beautiful; far too fine a design to build here today. We would not understand it, but how wonderfully fitting for this country."

Maurice Lambert was two years older than Raymond, a brother of Constant Lambert, the composer, and a son of George Washington Lambert, the painter and sculptor. Maurice Lambert was born in Paris and worked in London. Mansfield Forbes, the Cambridge don who was Raymond's mentor and patron, was very excited about Raymond's prospect of winning the competition and told him: "The Lambert liaison seems devilish promising…"

Eileen's major contribution was the design under Hoff of the two bronze reliefs over the lower entrance doorways. Each is 32 feet long by 4 feet 6 inches high. One shows units of the Australian fighting forces on the Western Front; the theme of the other is the Eastern Campaigns. Most of the work was done in a spacious studio purpose-built in the Sydney Technical College for the memorial workers. The bronze was cast in Loughborough, England.

In July 1932, when all seemed to be going smoothly on the Anzac Memorial, the storm burst. The Roman Catholic Co-adjutor Bishop of Sydney refused to attend the ceremony of laying the foundation stone.

The Most Rev. Dr. Michael Sheehan made a two-pronged attack. He excoriated the nude female figure on a cross which was part of the symbolism of 'The Crucifixion of Civilisation'. And he complained that the ceremony itself was "obviously intended for Protestants".

Invitations to the ceremony, which included some hymns and a prayer of dedication, specifically were addressed to heads of all churches as well as other dignitaries; but it is true that the prayer was to be said by the Anglican Dean of Sydney, the Very Rev. A.E. Talbot. Dean Talbot also was Senior Chaplain of the Australian Military Forces. *Smith's Weekly*'s report lamented. "Such an unhappy difference of religious opinion is an entirely new experience in the post-war history of the A.I.F., since those days of battle in which Catholic, Protestant, Jew and Pagan fought as comrades side by side under the shadow of Death."

Although the subsequent furore centred on the indecency of the woman who hung from the cross, it would be naive to ignore the depth of sectarian feeling between the majority and the "Rockchoppers" (the Catholic Irish) in the Commonwealth then and for 30 or more years to come. One factor in this antagonism was Irish Catholic resentment against Australia's participation in a "British" war.[10]

The nude woman, "a perfectly nude woman", was in the words of the Archbishop's secretary, Father Edmund O'Donnell, "immoral and revolting in a memorial like that", "a travesty of the Redemption" and "gravely offensive to ordinary Christian decency".

The press, under headlines such as "Nude woman on Cross: R.C. Church attack", "Catholic Bombshell to Anzacs" and "Objection to Protestant Service and Crucifixion Statuary", embraced an ideal opportunity to blazon the naked figure on their front pages in both drawing and photographic form.

By September the attack had broadened out to the whole memorial. *The Daily Telegraph* used the official magazine of the Master Builders' Association to trumpet: "Builders' Journal Hits Memorial: Hideous Realism Is Charged: Naked Woman as Figure of Civilisation Resented. Artistry In It But War Horrors Too Raw and Figures Awry?"

The Society of Artists' Exhibition had by now opened in Loftus Street and *Construction* urged everybody worthy of the name of citizen to make it his or her business to see the figures. If not, the magazine thundered, "another offence against fine feeling will be perpetrated upon the people of Sydney, if these are allowed to go up...".

Archbishop Michael Kelly, the Roman Catholic primate whose assistant had first entered the lists, returned from the Eucharistic Congress in Ireland to tell the *Sun*: "Christianity today has to fight against animal passion. There are signs that the devil is in the streets working on the minds and hearts of the people."

For Rayner Hoff, Dr. Kelly's onslaught was the last straw and he replied in the next day's newspaper:

> It is a matter for extreme regret that the Anzac Memorial, designed in a spirit of reverence for those who made the sacrifices demanded by war, yet to avoid glorifying war lest we forget its folly, should have been made a subject of controversy by a section of the Church. Such terms as 'diabolic', 'outrage', 'blasphemous', 'indecent', and 'insulting to God', used by Dr. Kelly in his utterance yesterday, surely do not express the feelings of Roman Catholics generally, among whom are included many of the world's great artists…

By early 1933 it was clear that the trustees of the Anzac Memorial did not have enough money to cast in bronze the two controversial groups, 'The Crucifixion of Civilisation' and 'Victory After Sacrifice'. The 'Victory' group showed a young woman, mostly undraped, standing with upraised arms in front of Britannia bearing a sheathed sword while below are the dead who by dying made victory possible. Both Dellit and Hoff deplored the fact that the memorial would be opened in an unfinished state. It would be a countenance without eyes, a blind building. All of Eileen's patrons lent their names to a plea that the money be found. The models were never cast and Eileen says that although interested groups have tried to locate them, "mystery surrounds them and they have never been found".

A. Wallace, in the Melbourne magazine *Today*, wrote at length on Hoff's motives and was probably the first to state openly that "Mr. Hoff was a soldier in the Great War for three and a half years. For months he watched the agonised deaths and tortured lives of his fellows, and of himself, knowing that it was all a futility."

Eileen McGrath was the most talented of Hoff's students. During the Anzac Memorial period her parents sometimes took him and Eileen on long drives in the Chevrolet. But in 1933, Eileen's father got six months' leave from his work and the McGrath family set sail for England. Eileen had saved every penny she made on the memorial work and while her parents soon went back to Sydney, it was nearly 50 years before Eileen saw her homeland again.

Chapter VII

is leather-bound diary shows bewilderment in its first entry. On 22 August, 1926, Raymond McGrath begins his new life with: "What a strange unrealisable thing it is to leave home on a long journey." He was on board the Orient Line's R.M.S. Osterley sailing from No. 7 Wharf, Woolloomooloo Bay. He had begun the long migration and it was raining.

There had been faculty farewells, family gatherings and endless visits to patrons, former teachers and well-known artists, as well as his own circle of friends.

Raymond's cabin was a delight — half his mother's worries dissipated in a flash. Streamers innumerable — "these strips of coloured paper will bind us all together". The wharf fades — a last glimpse of his mother's face. Tears he cannot restrain put a mist over his eyes.

Only two weeks after he left Norman Weekes's office he is writing in a cabin bright with gum leaves, jonquils, violets, and reading the letter Roy Booth has thrust into his hand: "Probably at times you have found me a lighthearted and frivolous companion but I have always put a high valuation on your friendship… If I had my Varsity days over again I am afraid I should do architecture for the sake of keeping our paths close together."

Stewards are attentive, bathrooms have plenty of towels, the meals are haute cuisine and Raymond is forming firm friendships. Two of the passengers were at Sydney with him. Walter G.K. Duncan, B.A., a political scientist, had won the James King of Irrawang Travelling Scholarship. Ian A. Henning was appointed to the French Government Travelling Scholarship, having been awarded first-class honours in French and German and the university medal for the same subjects. He went on to hold the chair of French at Sydney.

John C. Beaglehole, M.A., of Wellington, New Zealand, came from a house full of books and music and had been teaching history at Victoria University College, Wellington, for three years. He joyfully joined the Sydney lads whom he found "right willing controversialists". All four were travelling first class free and enjoying the luxury of it.

Raymond's diary is an observant traveller's vade-mecum but at Colombo the writing ends and he does not take up his pen (filled even then with the architect's brown ink that served him to the end) until the middle of February when he has got to know London.

But as well as the diary he was writing letters home, letters that traced every leg of the voyage, letters that were written on the Osterley's

---

ORIENT LINE

List of Passengers by

R.M.S. "OSTERLEY,"
12,129 Tons.

Captain I. J. HAYES, R.D., R.N.R,
Commander.

From Brisbane, 11th August ;   Sydney, 21st August ;
Melbourne, 24th August ; Adelaide, 26th August ;
Fremantle, 30th August, 1926.

Mrs. T. E. Barnes
Mr J. C. Beaglehole
Mrs. L. Berry
Miss W. L. Berry
Miss Margot Best
Miss Calder
Mr. S. J. Dixon
Mr. A. L. Duggan
Mr. W. D. K. Duncan
Mr. and Mrs. H. R. Dunlop
  and child
Miss S. Edwards
Mr. A. R. Gerrard
Mr. & Mrs. C. P. Hainsworth
Mr. I. A. Henning
Miss M. Herbert
Miss Holden
Mr. L. Iser

The passenger manifest

Facing page:
Left: Raymond, bound for England
Right: Third Officer Whinfield
Below: The R.M.S. Osterley

inexhaustible supply of stationery, letters above all that his mother kept and had bound into a leather book. He has a nice turn of phrase now and then — "A strong wind is making white holes in the sea" — but these are letters to be passed around family and friends, and few hints of his inner feelings are allowed to show. And he is conscientious — "When I have told you all the news I will write to Aunty Alice, to Aunty Gladys and Grandma and Aunty Mat, to Mrs. Gillard, Professor Brereton, Jim, Roy, Mr. Weekes, the Dramatic Society and a few others. There's a list for you." Indeed.

Brereton[11] got his share of letters from the Osterley and is told things that Raymond's family misses. His cabin is one of the most comfortable on the ship and contrasts sharply with those below the deck which are very stuffy. In bad weather the portholes cannot be opened:

> It is very disturbing to compare conditions in the third class with our luxury and comfort, still more disturbing to compare with the conditions under which the seamen work… For the most part the third class seems to be full of foreigners. There the passengers are crowded together in the worst part of the ship… Their diningroom is rough and comfortless. Ours is a centre of expensive elegance. One poor Italian in the third committed suicide and was buried at sea; another foreigner attempted to throw himself overboard. He speaks no English and no one can understand him.

His fellow passengers are some of them genuine people but for the most part they are a shallow lot, "cradled and crawled to by the stewards".

During his two-day stop at Melbourne he took a cable tram to Flinders Street Railway Station. The tram seems to have operated on the same principle as the cable cars of San Francisco. Another novelty was a white line painted down the middle of the street to divide the traffic. Sydney had nothing like that.

His interest in architecture, domestic and public, was intense and he took Duncan and Henning to see Newman College, "the most important piece of work Walter Burley Griffin has done in Australia. I went to scoff… but I was really impressed". Griffin is the man who went on to build Canberra, to which the Federal Parliament moved in 1927. Raymond also saw Griffin's Capitol Theatre and found the originality of its lofty interior "a sheer delight… an ingenious piece of work".

In the National Gallery he found a collection of 40 of Blake's original illustrations to Dante's *Inferno* but while many other pictures drew him and "there is no doubt that the Pre-Raphaelites still hold their own", a painting by "the famous Claude Monet… I thought a daub".

The Hon. Mr. Conybeer, Speaker of the House of Parliament in Adelaide, was a friend of Duncan's, and Raymond on meeting told him he had a very painful tooth. Mr. Speaker at once telephoned his dentist friend Mr. Lipman, and the tooth was removed. His whole trip would have been spoiled by an abscess if the pain had not arrived just when it did. The gods were still smiling on the young traveller.

The three Sydneysiders got a great deal from John Beaglehole, who was going to London to further the study of history. He was an art lover, an excellent poet and an enthusiastic musician who played Beethoven, Chopin, Debussy, Elgar and Grieg on the ship's grand piano every evening. He was a great admirer of Walter de la Mare, knew all the illustrations and liked Raymond's woodcuts of de la Mare poems better than any he had yet seen. Beaglehole wrote home to his parents: "I should say that if [he] keeps on doing better work he will be a good deal heard of as a woodcut artist some day if not as an architect."[12]

A letter from Norman Weekes was full of praise for the way in which Raymond's mother bore the ordeal of parting, and Raymond allows himself to tell her: "I was very proud of you too, and of Dad and Eileen." And he says of Roy Booth: "I will miss Roy very much while I am away, but his friendship is something to look forward to when I return."

As the Osterley left Fremantle, Raymond saw the last of Australia, "the cluster of twinkling lights". Into the tropics, beef-tea at eleven was replaced by ice-cream; a tank swimming pool was built on the boat-deck and the fans began to work. In the quoit tennis tournament, he got as far as the semi-finals, and a fancy-dress cricket match was played between the officers and the ladies.

As one would expect, Raymond kept his accounts methodically. "I left Sydney with £29.6.7½, to be accurate and my expenses up to the time I left Fremantle were £2.12.6 which leaves me with a balance of £26.14.1½, which I think is very satisfactory."

"If I describe Colombo I cannot make it more than a dream, for I passed through its medley of beautiful things like a person transported and when we had left its shores behind I was as dazed as if I had attempted to frame an image of ten thousand pictures in my mind in a few hours."

The camera was to the four voyagers as good as a second pair of eyes. They bought, used, processed and sent home film all the time. Many of Raymond's photographs are extant and in good condition, testimony to his lifelong enthusiasm for taking pictures.

The passage up the Gulf of Suez gave a view of the coast on either side. On the right, the mountains around Sinai and on the left the ranges of Egypt. It was too much for the frenzied Beaglehole. He pointed towards Africa and exclaimed: "Do you realise that Cleopatra ruled over that land; that these waters are liquid history!"

Raymond is full of gratitude. "Every time I arrive at a new port I tell myself how lucky I am to have this glorious opportunity of seeing the beauty of the world… what a great deal I owe to my mother and father." Not every letter contains such an expression of real sentiment.

Port Said brought out Raymond's philanthropic instincts. "I shall not easily forget the coaling of the ship there. Two large coal-lighters, moving masses of humanity, came against each side of the ship. The natives ran planks up to the coal-traps on the side of the ship and carried the coal up these in baskets and tipped it in. A great cloud of coal-dust rose over them. People tell you glibly that the days of slavery are over. What then do they call this? It is a lasting blot on the humanity of Europe that these

Roy Booth

43

conditions have been brought about, are tolerated and encouraged. If you had seen those poor devils sweating and toiling you would understand. With their eyes choked with coal-dust they cried like children. That black legion will haunt me for many a long day."

A month out from Sydney, the Osterley entered the Straits of Messina. He was in Europe. They passed Stromboli, "lighthouse of the Mediterranean", and then, after four hours in Naples, Raymond is fully resolved to learn Italian and see all he could of Italy. He saw Italy many times but did not learn Italian or much of any other language. And he left it to Beaglehole to recall 20 years later "the insistence of that low fellow in trying to show us 'naked women' and the high souled way in which we repelled him".

Ruins crowned the hill on Elba and Beaglehole came up again with the *mot juste*: "A bloke would feel a bit peeved to be put there after mopping up Europe." Another reminder of French military power greeted them at Toulon where, because it was a naval depot, they were forbidden to take their cameras ashore.

There was no doubt about Raymond's stance on the Spanish dispute over Gibraltar — "this great pile of geological architecture". He and his friends remembered that "the place had been filched from the Spaniards long ago and retained by England contrary to her word of honour. Perfidious Albion!".

They decided to go to Algeciras instead, 4/- each for the return trip in a launch. "If this is only a very minor town of Spain, what must the real Spain be? I will not miss her for worlds." He could imagine himself in Matthewtown except for the buildings, and he felt quite at home. The same kinds of watercourse as in New South Wales; the same stubbled paddocks of cropped grass and stranger still, many gum trees with long pendulous leaves and silver-white stems.

They saw delightful little staircases and archways, sunny courtyards and "those lovely little señorita balconies you know from Lionel Lindsay's etchings". On the way back to the Osterley an English woman on the launch surveyed the Rock and said: "It fills me with pride every time I look at that little bit of England. It is the envy of all the world." The colonial worm turned and Raymond felt that the English people they had met so far had lived up to Beaglehole's epigram: 'The Conquering Race'. He had seen enough at Colombo and Port Said to believe that — until a few days later, when he first saw English hills. Looking at "this beloved island" in the early light "I thought instinctively of Flecker's lines:

> Day breaks on England down the Kentish hills,
> Singing in the silence of the meadow-footing rills,
> Day of my dreams, O day!"

Docked at Tilbury by the tugs, they saw a maze of ships, chimneys and smoke, "much rarer owing to the coal strike". Duncan shouted "Nigger" to a chap on the wharf. It was his brother, come from Manchester.

44

The train to St. Pancras station passed a short space of flat fields filled with haystacks and sheep, then "the interminable monotony of long straight streets and rows of sordid uniform houses… What sort of people can be bred here I wondered. Everywhere ugliness, interminable terraces, little straggling gardens in tiny backyards. Where was the great dome of St. Paul's towering over the wonderful city?"

It was a bad beginning to a lifelong love affair with London. On the underground to the Hotel Madrid on Cromwell Road, Raymond was fed up with what he had already seen. The Madrid, clean and comfortable and 7/6 for bed and breakfast, had been suggested by the Osterley's third officer, Mr. Whinfield, who had chosen well for them.

Next morning he took buses, saw wonders, recognised few of the landmarks he knew from books, and went home hungry for tea. He had forgotten to have lunch. You have, he was learning, to discover London for yourself. She is not a dramatic tableau ready for the traveller. She is a maze of locked doors and you have to seek for the keys patiently.

Cambridge Terrace, London, where at No. 7 Raymond took his first lodgings

CHAPTER VIII

Armed with introductions, Raymond began to make the rounds. He had no fixed idea of what he should do and he was open to the advice proffered freely by Australians and English people. His reputation as a talented artist and promising architect preceded him, but he was a colonial taking on the might of an Empire. If he had been less naïve or trusting, if his charm did not work on those he was relying on to advance his cause, he could have retired early from the fray and gone home disillusioned.

His first call was to Professor E.R. Holme, who had asked him to come to his flat at Granville Place. Holme, whose heart and soul were in the future of the carillon, and his niece Miss Munce, whom Raymond had also met in Sydney, wanted him to get the best out of his fellowship, to have the best advice and not to rush things. They sent him to Professor and Mrs. J.W. Mackail. Tillyard[13] describes Mackail lecturing on Pope in Cambridge: "Exquisitely turned out in black jacket and striped trousers, terribly distinguished with his fine features, glossy grey hair and soft yet somehow treacly eyes… a kind of high priest of aestheticism." Mrs. Mackail was a daughter of Edward Burne-Jones. He had dinner with them at 6 Pembroke Gardens amid glorious Pre-Raphaelite pictures, Morris wallpaper and Kelmscott Press books. The Mackails were the parents of Angela Thirkill the novelist.

It took him four or five weeks to get settled. Where should he work? Where would he be best able to further the studies he had begun? Most important, what was he going to be?

"I realise now," he wrote to Brereton, "that dearly as I love painting and drawing for themselves, I shall have to devote myself, as closely as it is reasonable, to one end. I have decided definitely for architecture."

That decision made, there was the question of whether he should study in London, Paris, Oxford or Cambridge. Mackail said he should lay sound foundations for drawing in London but should investigate the possibilities of the École des Beaux-Arts. Major Hubert C. Corlette, an Australian architect working in London and advising all Australian travelling architectural students, approved of this suggestion. He said Raymond should join the Architectural Association and propose himself for associateship in the Royal Institute of British Architects. He recommended the London County Council's School of Building at Brixton and thought highly of the value of a year at Oxford.

With Sir Frank Fox and Professor Holme Raymond went on his first enchanting walk in the English countryside. Fox was an Australian, deaf

Studio photograph of Raymond by Dorothy Wilding

47

Ian Henning

because of war injuries and full of lively talk, but he could not help on the question of the Beaux-Arts.

So Raymond went to Paris to see for himself. He got a hotel room through his shipboard friend Ian Henning, who had acquired a splendid big room in the rue du Cherche Midi. He met Raymond at the Gare du Nord and took him to the Hotel Montana.

So contracted has the world become that it is difficult to understand why Raymond had to tell his family that a croissant was "a kind of delightful short-bready roll shaped like a horseshoe". The secretary of the Beaux-Arts gave him most of the information he needed while Henning interpreted. The architecture course, Raymond learned, took five years. He would have to do a history essay and a French oral as part of the entrance examination, and once in would have to work in French. No allowance was made for any "foreign" degree, though by working extremely hard he could take the examinations in less than five years. All tuition was free.

"Perhaps I may eventually know sufficient French to work in an office in Paris", he told Brereton. In the meanwhile, he gave up all thought of a Beaux-Arts training and returned to London.

It was just as well for, like Rayner Hoff in Sydney, the Paris School of Fine Arts was nearing the end of its remarkable reign. Established in 1819, it enjoyed a tradition going back to Colbert's Académie Royale d'Architecture of 1671. David Watkin[14] says of it: "The prestige, continuity and high seriousness of a system of architectural education which was unique in Europe made France the natural centre for intellectual debate about architecture during the 18th and 19th centuries."

Duncan and Beaglehole took rooms in Brunswick Square and Duncan attended frenzied lectures at the L.S.E. for eight hours a day. Raymond went to see Oxford ("the most beautiful sight of my life, the domes and towers and spires of Oxford") and Cambridge, both "ancient places of sweet unworldliness". But they were not for him, he thought, and he became a student of the British Museum Print Room and the Westminster Art School under Walter Bayes. There Frank Medworth was a wood engraver of great distinction. "Wood engraving", Raymond said in this context, "is a very live art here and on the Continent", and of the practitioners Eric Ravilious "holds pride of place". Ravilious in those years was one of the artists contributing to the Golden Cockerel Press publications under the direction of Robert and Moira Gibbings.

Sir William Furse of the Imperial Institute had, like Sir Frank Fox, proved a good friend, and Raymond did not lack for expatriate dining rooms to visit, but an air of aimlessness crept into his life. Two visits to see Blake at the Tate confirmed in him the opinion that Blake is "the very greatest of English artists". But he seemed to be wasting his substance.

Eileen wrote from Sydney that she had seen Professor Brereton: "No one could help liking him. He is so young at heart and has the sense of humour which I admire so very much. We had ice-cream at the Union." Presumably they discussed Eileen's doing a bust of Brereton. He had told Raymond of his intention "to lay at your sister's feet my disreputable head, if she still wants it."

Raymond strongly encouraged her to take this chance to do "a most interesting portrait head". Ice-cream notwithstanding, the idea seems to have fallen through.

Raymond's enthusiasm for Walter de la Mare's poetry already had led him to illustrate six of the poems in his '24 Woodcuts'. It was logical then for him to tell de la Mare of his interest. The result was an invitation to Taplow Hill House in Buckinghamshire. He walked down a country lane between thick trees to meet his host, "a short, broad-shouldered man, sturdily built, with greyish hair and very roguish eyes". One son was Raymond's age, the other younger and an artist. Mrs. de la Mare was white-haired. They had supper by candlelight.

Raymond in gratitude for his meeting with the great man ventured to leave him his last copy of 'Seven Songs of Meadow Lane'. In reply he got a pleasant note from de la Mare:

> It was a great surprise and it is a rare delight to have it for its own sake, for the poems, the woodcuts and the inscription. Think of it, Henry Brocken set off on his journey in 1904. I like best the *first* song, the fourth, the *fifth* and the sixth: and of the woodcuts, the first, the Ice-cream man, and two little ones, tail pieces. Beautiful things.

Raymond had inscribed the book: "From a remote friend of Henry Brocken". ("Henry Brocken" was one of de la Mare's better-known books). De la Mare was then 43.

Of the profusion of ideas tossed about on the high seas between Sydney and London, one got a second airing when John Beaglehole expressed again his hope of publishing a little book of poems with "a woodchopping accompaniment of mine". He proposed to call it "Mouth-Organ Mumblings". The notion was still-born, though Raymond did a wood engraving for Beagle's 1927 Christmas card.

Raymond had a trial run on a new hobby-horse. "I am not", he wrote to Brereton, "a mere worshipper of the past, but some buildings are a balm to the soul, others fill you with anger. Some people laugh when I tell them I have made a solemn vow never to live in a London house built between 1870 and 1900. But I mean it. One must have some self-respect." This was Raymond at his most priggish.

He began to catalogue the destruction of London. Brunswick Square, in which his friends lived, and Wren's Foundling Hospital were threatened with demolition by "Beecham's Estates and Pills", which wanted to move Covent Garden Market to Bloomsbury. "May their scheme, and lots of others now moving in this unfortunate city, be confounded", said the young conservationist.

Campbell Dodgson took him to an exhibition at the Burlington Arts Club of paintings by Canaletto and his English followers. "They were a revelation and all the proof I desire of my contention" that London reached the zenith of its beauty at the end of the 18th century and had been withering ever since.

The Ice-cream Vendor from 'The Seven Songs of Meadow Lane', 1924

After a fall of snow and then a fog, Raymond was walking through St. Mary's Roman Catholic cemetery in Kensal Green when along an untrodden path he came upon Francis Thompson's grave. "It was like meeting him face to face, for I had lately been reading and growing more than enthusiastic about his poems. It was a simple sarcophagus with the ivy beginning to grow over it and apparently quite uncared for…"

FRANCIS THOMPSON
1859–1907
Look for me in the
nurseries of Heaven

If Raymond knew, he did not record that the tomb had been carved by Eric Gill, whom the commission had nudged nearer to Roman Catholicism because it brought him into touch with the Meynells, Thompson's patrons. Everard Meynell had given Gill the commission. The quotation is from Thompson's 'To My Godchild'.

Quite suddenly, as 1926 turned into 1927, Raymond's life acquired a direction. He went to Cambridge again, ostensibly to explore the possibility of applying for a studentship that would bring his income up to the "necessary" £350 per annum, and in the knowledge that Ph.D. work would be of value and acceptable there. But what really excited him was his meeting with Mansfield Duval Forbes, a fellow of Clare College who lectured in English.

Forbes was a Scotsman born in Ceylon in 1889, the second son of a tea and rubber estate manager. He was small, shortsighted and so incredibly youthful-looking that a photograph of 1924 makes him appear much the same as one taken in 1911. He was still only 22 when he was elected the youngest ever fellow of Clare and exchanged history for English as a discipline. He had a light voice and moved quickly. His small round steel-rimmed spectacles did not conceal the intense blue of his eyes, and he retained most of his boyish traits until his early death in 1936.

Among Forbes' many interests was the Russian ballet. Hugh Carey[15] tells the story of how a group of fellows was discussing disapprovingly the thorny question of whether their wives should call on Maynard Keynes' new wife, Lydia Lopokova, the ballerina. Manny, as we shall have to call him from now on, broke in and said: "I should think that talking to *your* wives is the last thing she would want to do." Keynes, later Lord Keynes, never became a friend of Raymond's but did cross his path several times. His interest in the arts was intense. Lance Sieveking first met him at Cambridge and recalls him as "rather tall, but… graceful and debonair. He had a gentle, attractive and very intelligent way of talking".

For the best part of nine years, Manny and Raymond maintained their curious friendship. Curious because Manny was 38 and Raymond 23 when they met; and curious because Manny was outgoing, gregarious and gay, whereas Raymond was shy, introspective and heterosexual. Perhaps the feminine side of Raymond appealed to Manny. Raymond's daughter Jenny describes his gift for flower arrangement and the family's tacit

Mansfield Duval Forbes

acceptance that all Christmas decoration was his province. It was, at any rate, a relationship that proved fruitful as well as complementary.

When E.J. Dingwall, a Clare College contemporary of Manny's, was 91, he offered this memoir[16] of Manny:

> …We met in King's Parade one day and he came beaming up and said: 'Oh Ding, what will you say, I had an orange this morning. Wonderful. They say, "Women for generation, boys for pleasure and melons for delight; so I thought I would try an orange".'

Manny and his Auntie Barty

Unhappy, an insomniac, a memorable lecturer, Manny was in ways a charming user of people. His troubles were always Raymond's and later his wife Mary's. Money, for example. It was widely thought that Manny Forbes had private means. He had only some shares, his fellow's stipend and a talent for winning overdrafts from bank managers and loans from friends, including Raymond. He wrote only one great book, but he could talk with insight, passionate zeal and a sense of fun. He had a nose for scandal. And he knew Gaelic. He was a great authority on his beloved Scotland, its history, archaeology and architecture. His sister's name — we shall meet her later — was Mhari, a version of the Irish name Máire, anglice Mary.

At the time Raymond met Manny, he told Brereton: "He is a rare soul, an artist to his fingertips. His knowledge of architecture is profound and he numbers the choicest architects among his friends. His enthusiasm and desire to help were very pleasing. He gave me books and letters and I felt immediately that if to go to Cambridge means association with men like himself then it was something to be hoped for indeed."

That night he slept in Sir Giles Gilbert Scott's new Clare College building. It was a sleep full of hopes and doubts. The sky was clear and serene after the busy streets and endless traffic of London. He could not take his eyes from the shadowy Backs stretching outside the window. One of his less successful poems ensued. The second of three verses will serve:

> My restless thoughts would rush
> Out through the frosty air,
> In the brightness of the hush
> Of the midnight over Clare

A few days into January, Raymond quite by accident met Mansfield Forbes (as he still of course called him) in a little café near the British Museum. Manny took him along to the Travellers' Club ("a delightful place by Sir Charles Barry in Piccadilly") and introduced him to J. Murray Easton the architect. He already had met Easton's partner Howard Robertson. Manny told him he must go to Cambridge. He seemed to think studentships were very scarce commodities there and asked Raymond "if a part-time job with the School of Architecture there would help!" That is not how it worked out.

St. Paul's Cathedral, this time without the kangaroo

CHAPTER IX

From his new rooms at 7 Cambridge Terrace, Hyde Park, Raymond sent his parents and friends a Christmas card. It was a wood engraving of St. Paul's Cathedral with omnibuses crowding the street in front of it. In the centre is an Australian bushman shaking hands with a kangaroo. The greeting is typeset and tells us that he has seen "St. Paul's, a pigeon or two, Christopher Robin and Christopher Wren, Peter Pan and Rima[17], and some top-hats and other sights of London…" He used the same design later, excising the kangaroo.

He could not, because there was no vacancy, get into the fifth and final year of the Architectural Association School that term, but he had no regrets about it although the subject for 1926–27 was town planning. "Unfortunately one cannot do everything", he wrote to Brereton.

He felt justified in doing life drawing at the Westminster School of Art because he was in much need of the evening classes. He planned to spend the next six months between the R.I.B.A. library, which he was now eligible to use, the British Museum, the Victoria and Albert Museum, the Westminster School and the Brixton Building School, with the emphasis on Brixton.

Brixton was a "thoroughly practical place and incidentally inartistic, but that will not matter. I will be able to refute those people who are accustomed to say 'Yes, it looks very nice, but can you build it?'."

At the school, the students were constructing an actual building, two storeys high and 60 feet square. All the trades took part and Raymond believed he would learn more there in six months than in the ordinary routine of an office in two years.

The Exhibition Division of the Foreign Office and the Board of Trade was directed by Major Longden, whom Raymond met at Christmas dinner with the Mackails. Longden had a French wife and was Norwegian himself. Add M. de 'Smet de Naeyer, who was president of the Art Society of Ghent, and you get quite an international gathering which yielded Raymond a cordial invitation to Belgium.

A visit to Alfred Gilbert the sculptor was interrupted by another visitor. "O come in", said Gilbert, "it is all right. I am only talking to one of my students." Raymond was "rather proud of that remark".

Gilbert's ideas inspired him. Gilbert told him that every face has a convex and a concave side and explained the bearing of that on his model. He talked of the endeavour "to combine all the fleeting expressions in one expression that will suggest many of them".

Sculpture was in Raymond's mind. He took to heart Brereton's remark about "the eager promise of the future imaginative success of Eileen's work", and felt that she must travel and see the wonderful collections in London. "London is like a great ant-bed into which is dragged the meat of the world." He could, one feels, have put the thing more delicately, especially when the flesh was his sister's.

At the Tate Gallery, he and Manny saw Carl Milles' work. Raymond "developed an almost insatiable appetite for sculpture, so much so that if I had sufficient courage, I might very easily try how my wings are in that quarter even now...". Milles' 'The Dancers' he thought a 20th-century masterpiece. It entranced Manny, who raged about the intolerable dullness of England.

From Cambridge came an encouraging letter from Mr. Priestley the assistant registrar, who had talked about Raymond to Professor Wilson of the Anatomy School and hoped soon to have him down to meet "some of the people that matter". Wilson then arranged for him to meet the Master of Gonville and Caius College and for two days before the meeting his heart sang. He bought violets from an old man and went back to buy more. The train to Cambridge passed through "an army of grass waving ecstatic plumes" and Wilson and he passed through "The Gate of Honour" into Caius. The Master, Sir Hugh Anderson, was a homely fatherly old man of natural politeness. When Wilson left them he drew up a chair in his study for Raymond and listened to his plan. He could see that Raymond would need £350 to carry it out and he "gave me to understand" that he could arrange it.

Raymond went to see Manny in his cheerful study with glasses of egg-flip all around him and papers, books and pictures all over the carpet. "By God, McGrath, how are you?" he asked, "I was wondering when you'd come in". He said Raymond must see Tommy (Harold Tomlinson, assistant to Theodore Fyfe at the Architectural school). He was "the man". Raymond found Fyfe a rather fussy little man, though very amiable in his way; and he was introduced to George Checkley, a New Zealander and Jarvis Scholar who was an assistant in the school. Raymond went to

The Memorial Buildings at Clare College

dinner with Fyfe at Pembroke, where Raymond gave a dissertation on white ants, "a subject about which I know very little".

Dining in hall with the fellows of Clare College, staying at John's College, visiting Professor Wilson's family and listening to a talk about the architecture of Frederick of Palermo — Raymond was acquiring quite a taste for the academic life. And Manny was working hard to get him out of the meshes of Caius ("a barbarous college") and into the care of Clare. Working on the bursar, W.T. Harrison, and Priestley, and all his other malleable friends, Manny contrived to pull it off.

On Wednesday, March 16th, 1927, Raymond's morning mail brought a letter from Manny Forbes:

My dear McGrath,

I hope you will be glad to hear that at a College meeting this afternoon, *Clare* College council (of master and fellows) agreed to guarantee you not less than £50 grant (studentship) per annum either for next term (ca. April 20) or from the beginning of the normal academic year (i.e. in October) — and for two years. Thirkill [Master of Clare] has seen the Caius authority and 'squared' the affair with them. To my joy finally I am glad to be able to add that the bulk of the opinion in our body is that it will be admirable to have an architectural exponent amongst us. I am overjoyed and amazed at the reception given to what one propounded, at the end of the College meeting, as a forlorn hope… Ever rejoicingly,

M.D. Forbes.

Harold Tomlinson and his wife

As a postscript Manny added the hope that within two years Raymond might get a creative job at the Architectural School in Cambridge helping Tomlinson to make "a really aesthetic school".

Raymond's delight knew no bounds. It took the form of buying a jar of ginger and a box of figs for Jessie the housemaid.

Now he is able to look ahead with "a degree of certainty I had hardly hoped would bless me". He is not only going to Cambridge as the first research student in architecture, but he is entering Clare College. He plans to be in London until mid-June and then to go to France for three months — "little enough in all conscience". In October (1927), with Professor Mackail's hearty concurrence, he will go up to Cambridge. Sir E. Guy Dawber, the president of the R.I.B.A., also thinks Cambridge a splendid notion. So Raymond is "feeling the sort of experience one has in shooting a wave in the surf".

His only anxiety was that the Wentworth fellowship might not be extended to a third year — "on that, all depends". His gratitude to Manny led to a long letter to Professor Brereton. "Mansfield Forbes", he wrote to Brereton, "is a great friend of I.A. Richards who wrote 'The Principles of Literary Criticism'." (Ivor Richards who "expounds the meaning of meaning", had been recruited in 1919 into Manny's band of brothers, those who gave Cambridge its English School and gave literary studies in English a new stimulus. Another supporter of the school, though he was an orthodox member of the English section of Modern and Medieval Languages, was F.L. Attenborough, father of Richard and David and later befriender of Raymond McGrath when Attenborough was principal of University College, Leicester.)

Raymond's paean to Manny has been sounded already but his view in the early months of 1927 will bear recital:

> He is such a lover of art and literature, and of all things beautiful, that his enthusiasm for them leaves one gasping at one's own torpidity. He has a rosy cheerful face, an infectious smile and a head of sandy hair which tumbles about without the attention of brushes and combs. He is a Highlander and known throughout Cambridge and liked by everybody. His faculty for getting things done amuses all his friends and they all refer with great respect and delight to his 'technique' in these matters. I am told that he wangled Sir Gilbert Scott into doing the New Clare college and George Kennedy into doing the new Library of King's etc., etc. His architectural knowledge and skill is astonishing. There is hardly a person of mark in the literary, artistic or architectural world whom he does not know. He has formed musical societies and every other sort of society. He will sail off in a car to all the rich collectors of art in the district and come back to Cambridge with enough material for an exhibition. Nobody minds his remarkable nerve.
>
> While I was at Cambridge he took me to a lecture he delivered to the Shirley Society on Scottish Architecture It was a revelation for I had no idea of the refinement of Scottish Renaissance buildings. He interpreted these lovely harled buildings, Castle Fraser, Craigievar etc., in the phrase of Blake, as organic designs which seem to be seen "not with but through the eye", and it was most interesting when he spoke of the sympathy these builders felt to exist between architecture and the human body. He is a splendid lecturer and his sense of humour is acute. He is a poet himself, was at college with Rupert Brooke and knew Flecker. He used to do a fair amount of landscape painting in Scotland but has since had no time to follow it up, though several of his pictures I have seen show how remarkably sensitive he is and make me understand why he appreciates pictures so intensely. His rooms at Clare are full of artistic treasures, a cartoon by Blake, designs by Boris Anrep, a lovely Alice-in-Wonderland picture of a little girl by Jean Marchand (for which he paid £80 to the great disgust of some of his friends), and drawings, woodcuts and books innumerable.

Professor Brereton[18] was fortunate to receive such a vivid pen-picture of this quirky little don whose dynamic quality of restless energy did so much for bonum, verum and pulchrum. In April, 1927, Manny went to America on a lecture tour which paid his expenses ("he has some Scotch instincts", said Raymond). Manny talked to the Carnegie Trust about cementing the artistic relations between the universities of England and America, a scheme for which he had "unlimited hopes".

On a spring day when the grass in Regent's Park was studded with yellow, purple and white crocuses and Nash's beautiful buildings were laughing in the sunshine, Manny arrived from Cambridge in the early morning to show Raymond "all the things I should not be missing". All the art galleries knew him and he acted like a lambkin among the pictures, taking them off the walls to study them in all lights and charging the proprietors with bad hanging.

In two days they saw everything, including Stanley Spencer's much-discussed 'Resurrection' at the Goupil Gallery. Manny delighted in Raymond's appetite for art. He was "quite mad" about Raymond's 'Chinese Architecture' book and insisted on showing it to everyone, even threatening to take it to his publisher friends, "which God forbid, for as I told him, a thing like that needs real care and originality if anything is to come of it". Manny told him he was absurd to think so.

They went to see Manny's attractive sister Mhari, Mrs. A.H. Parry. Arthur Parry, a stockbroker with Keen, Cobb and Lee and a musician, had been at Clare College. Their house at 5 Westbourne Street, Lancaster Gate, had just been remodelled by George Kennedy, who showed Raymond some delightful granite farmhouses he had done in Cornwall. Kennedy, who lived at 31 Oakley Street, Chelsea, also introduced Raymond to Hope Bagenal, the librarian of the A.A. and author of many books on recent architecture, and to Victor Hodgson ("Uncle Victor" to Manny), the Scottish architect who looked after the West Highland Museum. He also arranged that Raymond should have tea with him at A. Trystan Edwards' studio in the Strand.

The prospect of meeting Trystan Edwards really excited him. At Sydney he had read articles by Edwards in the *Architects' Journal* and knew that "his taste and mine had a very great deal in common". Edwards stimulated his interest in oriental design and he shared the common view that 'Architectural Style' was an epoch-making addition to the study of all forms of design. Edwards went to Oxford, where his father was a don.

We found him in his little Regency stronghold in the Strand (no. 430), a young boyish-looking man, slightly bald with an impediment in his speech when he is excited. He has the drollest humour imaginable… as keen as mustard and a modern crusader… He has refused to meet certain architects [one of them was Sir Edwin Lutyens] because he is bringing out a book on 'Some Enemies of Architecture' and he desires perfect freedom to say what he thinks about them, as he did about the people who were responsible for the destruction of the Old Regent Street. How they must have quaked in their shoes to read his powerful indictment of the ignorance and conceit which led to what he calls

'The Fall of Regent Street'. We are already good friends and I have permission to call him Arthur.

Edwards described his efforts to get satisfactory boys (i.e. without smelly hair oil) to type for him and he attacked the feminisation of Oxford and Cambridge. His dislike of Lutyens was based particularly on Lutyens' "unprincipled and concerted action" over Waterloo Bridge.

When Raymond told Edwards of his desire to measure up the Nash blocks on the east side of Regent's Park, Edwards nearly fell into his arms. "Must you go back to Australia?", he asked, "because England has need of you."

Through Edwards, Raymond added two more scalps to his belt: Captain Kidley, the secretary of the Institute of Structural Engineers, and Christian Barman, editor of the *Architects' Journal*. Barman, whom Raymond took to at once, fell for 'Chinese Architecture' and led Raymond to muse: "What a queer open sesame that exotic interest of mine seems to have been. But it has been a sincere and fruitful interest." Barman was the first of many editors, including the present writer, with whom he enjoyed cordial journalistic relations.

He was now very happy with his lot. He was accepted in circles that were not always so quick to permit the colonial to join, and learning what was fashionable as well as what was good, even if he did not always know the difference. "The future in my own belief is opening like a flower and I am well content with all my prospects."

He stuck to his programme, the Brixton School, the Westminster, the R.I.B.A. Library. He got to know the work of Sir John Soane, "now so deplorably neglected", and changed his mind about the brothers Adam. "Adam, Dance, Soane, Nash, these are the men who made an architecture of humanism the glory of England, and may God grant me the power and the opportunities to enrich my native land as they did."

A letter to his lonely friend Henning in Paris elicited a reply to "Dear Mac". Henning went on: "And listen to me my good fellow: let me tell you that the man who upholds Esperanto in this enlightened age is like the man who would advise the wearing of crinolines in the Paris Métropolitain."

A month before the great news from Cambridge, Raymond had written in his diary: "What is the good of architecture and woodcuts? Is it not only for the selfish and aesthetic pleasure they provide that I pursue these fascinating paths? If I had any courage at all I would set myself bitterly to work for the emancipation of the poor, for God knows this smug age needs the healing touch of socialism as much as anything. But what a hypocrite I am with my expensive books and prints and my precious tastes."

We shall hear little enough of egalitarianism from our architectonic fledgling as he settles comfortably into the Establishment nest.

CHAPTER X

The endless arguments about who was a good architect and who bad had less to do with real debate than with personal antagonism and envy. If Raymond listened to George Kennedy, he would be told that B.G. Goodhue was a great quack and a bad architect, whereas Robert Atkinson was the best architect in England. Philip Ker, the secretary of the Rhodes Trust, considered Lutyens the genius of modern English architecture. Ker was also friendly with Sir Herbert Baker, with whom Lutyens was designing New Delhi. They could not hit it off at all and each went his own way, said Ker. Baker, a protégé of Cecil Rhodes, did his best work in South Africa.

Raymond was asked to the R.I.B.A.'s annual dinner, "an informal and boisterous affair". "Tommy" Tomlinson and Major Longden were there, and he saw Professor Charles H. Reilly of Liverpool. Howard Robertson gave an after-dinner lecture on modern French architecture and the subsequent discussion, Raymond noted, "revealed all the English architectural diehards".

H.S. Goodhart-Rendel spoke in a very charming and accomplished way but Professor Reilly was one of the people who could not digest modern French experiments and was prepared to wait until the French had made themselves sick.

Raymond met Victor Hodgson again at lunch at the Architectural Association with Manny Forbes, Murray Easton and Hope Bagenal. Hodgson asked Raymond to help him with a booklet on Scottish domestic schemes designed to prevent the possibility of a fatality with the British Aluminium Company's housing scheme at Inverlocky. Raymond quickly learned his subject and a week later delivered a paper to Hodgson on "What shall we do with the Highlands?" He smiled at his own audacity.

At tea another day he met Clough Williams-Ellis the architect, "resplendent in his checked trousers... almost as baroque in his dress and conversation as he is in his design... Other architects are rather envious of his success, which is due in good measure to his social activities". Lance Sieveking[19] found Clough and Annabel Williams-Ellis "a striking couple: both very tall, graceful and handsome... that rare thing, a husband and wife who were both equally witty."

Clough Williams-Ellis was best known for "the assembly of little houses of every shape and colour he built at his famous resort at Portmeirion in North Wales" (Sieveking's words). Raymond later visited Portmeirion more than once, but at his first meeting with Williams-Ellis he was taken on a tour of the English-Speaking Union, a London clubhouse

The Hemming family: John; Louise (standing); Alice, who died in 1994; and Harold. Alice Hemming o.b.e. was for 40 years President of the Commonwealth Countries' League

which Williams-Ellis "concocted out of a very exuberant town mansion".

H. Harold Hemming was a Canadian who had served with the Royal Artillery during the war and won the Military Cross. When Raymond met him he was very keen on "balloon jumping" and was considered, with his writer sister, "the brightest Canadians I have met". Hemming took his sister, Manny and Raymond motoring through Edgeware to Ashridge, "an amazing neo-Gothic mansion with a glorious garden and estate". In exquisite March weather, Raymond felt an "irresistible" desire to roll on the grass or climb trees. He resisted the irresistible.

Hemming had been to Cambridge and knew Manny Forbes well. He was an influential mining financier and publisher, had married Alice Weaver, an English graduate of the University of British Columbia, and was a cousin of Ian Parsons of Chatto and Windus the publishers. Parsons, who was wealthy, was best man at the Hemming wedding and it was he who wound up Manny's estate later on. The McGraths and the Hemmings — Alice, who was an O.B.E., was godmother to Raymond's daughter Jenny — kept in touch, but with the decreasing regularity that accompanies the onset of old age and distance.

The president of the R.I.B.A., Sir E. Guy Dawber, invited Raymond to dinner at 25 Hamilton Terrace. Dawber was a round-faced and exceedingly jovial and companionable man "fond of his little joke". He was quite scandalised when Raymond butted in on the conversation his host and two Canadian guests were having about Stanley Spencer's flaunting of perspective and draughtsmanship in his 'Resurrection'. "Spencer", said Raymond, "is one of the few men now painting in England who has genuine artistic inspiration". Collapse of jovial party.

Dawber recovered to discourse amusingly on the habits of Continental boys on his sketching tours. He liked the French and Italian boys who did not worry the painter but he thought that Dutch boys were "dirty little beasts" who went so far as to spit on his paper.

Walter Gilbert a few nights later shared Dawber's view of Stanley Spencer. Indeed all the "modern tendencies" were shams and insincerities. Carl Milles was pagan and insincere, a statement rebutted by Gilbert's son Donald who said Milles was rich with Swedish tradition. Hot and heavy went the argument until "O damn you", said his father, walking out of the room. "Swedish tradition be damned."

Raymond asked Manny what sort of person Spencer was. "A lovely little fellow", said Manny, "like a crabapple. An acorn!"

When Christian Barman, whom Manny fondly called Jesus, saw Raymond's 'Chinese Architecture' he not only went into raptures on the spot, but tried to get Raymond to have the drawings unbound and exhibited. They were, he said, the loveliest architectural drawings he had seen. Raymond was mighty pleased with himself and noted smugly in his diary: "Like a thunderclap, I have met almost all the people I am interested in."

At the crowded Queen's Hall, a little man with a woolly mass of white hair, glasses and a deliberation and certainty of manner spoke for nearly three hours on Peter Breughel. This was Roger Fry, "the most original and stimulating of art critics", who held his audience as he discoursed on 'The Fall of Icarus', to Fry's mind as to Raymond's the most delightful and the most fantastic of Breughel's works.

At the end of March, 1927, Raymond took the Riviera Express from Paddington to Penzance. He was treating himself to a holiday. He took the motor bus to Sennen and enquired of a burly fisherman whether he knew a Mrs. Elsie Nicholas of Shelbourne. "Seeing as I'm married to her, I do", he replied. "I thought I'd come up and give you a hand with your bag."

The Nicholas's house overlooked Whitesand Bay. "I realised I had drawn an ace, so clean and cosy and comfortable it was." Mrs. Nicholas was a laughing little lady and she fed him well. A few days later a storm blew up and Raymond noted: "God have pity on all ships tonight, for this is the cruel coast indeed." He walked everywhere, up and down the Cornish shoreline; but he seems to have forgotten his camera. He did produce his first English watercolour, 'Escalls', done in the style of Andrew Wyeth.

'Escalls', McGrath's first painting in England, 1927

Molly Rohr

Bookplate for Heather Sutherland

After a week, he was back in London and found a typical letter from Manny: "Mon cher McGrath, First very many thanks indeed for the Witches woodcut — it has much *Stimmung* by my halidom — I envy you such creative sense…" The same post brought letters from Molly Rohr, the art student and friend of Eileen's, and from Heather Sutherland, by now a young architect. Molly in 1925 had done a life study using the same model and pose as Eileen. She now sent Raymond a photograph of her piece and Raymond's mother had scribbled on the back: "Don't insult Eileen by thinking this hers. It is Molly Rohr's to Ray". To the untutored eye, Molly's figure was quite as graceful as Eileen's. Raymond was clearly smitten.

"I like Molly for her simplicity and her enthusiasm, for her beauty and her natural good taste. Her actions were always gracious and the way she dressed always charmed me. There was a curious sort of wonder in the way she said: 'Do you think so?' and her laugh was a delight. Her admiration, which I could never account for, has made me her devoted friend." The three-quarter life figure she had just sent him was "a very beautiful piece of modelling". He had not seen her work before. Eileen thought that Molly was getting more serious than ever. "I don't think she believes firmly enough in Peter Pan." Raymond failed to understand that remark.

Heather was a very different sort of girl. "She has most of the tantalising characteristics of her sex. She can be very witheringly sarcastic… She had very large dark eyes and I found it dangerous to look into them." He had given her one of the precious copies of 'Seven Songs' and was happy with her reply: "I shall value it very much as a memento of student days and as much again for its quaint songs and woodcuts."

The eponymous department store was selling the Selfridge Bicycle at £5, such good value that it attracted Duncan, Beaglehole and McGrath. On their maiden outing to Elstree it rained most of the day but "riding in the rain is pleasant enough and quite usual in England". Cycling took Raymond's mind off Molly and Heather, who were quite forgotten by the time he took the inevitable tea with Trystan Edwards. Edwards had a scheme for making money — his 'Architectural Style' had sold only 200 copies. He would do some coloured drawings and create a market for them by putting n.f.s. on all but one, for which he would charge 150 guineas. Talking to Edwards Raymond found "a precious experience, his wit is so keen, his sympathy so human".

Christian Barman wrote: "A rather fine work on the royal palaces of Peking has just turned up for review." It turned out to be Osvald Sirén's wonderful work in three volumes, 'Palaces of Peking'. Raymond was delighted to review it for the *Architects' Journal*. Barman gave him back his "fascinating thesis which I have been reading both backwards and forwards ever since you left it with me". He then amazed Raymond by asking him to review the Institute Exhibition of Modern British Architecture. "You could have knocked me down fairly easily with a feather", he noted.

Barman and McGrath and his New Zealand architect friend Amyas Connell went at Connell's invitation to meet the London directors of

Dorman Long's the large construction company. They were shown all the working drawings for the Sydney Harbour Bridge and a collection of photographs of work in progress. In the yard on the Thames they saw riveting and planing machines. Boys were tossing red hot rivets from the forges to the riveters at work on the stanchions. Their host told them that during the war he had seen them toss red hot shells and catch them with a pair of pincers.

After dinner in the Piccadilly Hotel grill — music provided by de Groot the violinist — they inspected some of Dorman Long's London jobs: Lyons' new Oxford Street restaurant; the building half-completed in Bloomsbury Square, the Royal Hotel (for which the architect got the £100 design award and no more), and finally the Bank of England.

"Alas for this masterpiece", wrote Raymond. The remodelling by Sir Herbert Baker consisted of the total demolition of everything inside the stone screen wall on the street. "This greatest gem of London civic architecture is now gone forever", he lamented.

"When Sir John Soane [1753–1837] fancifully depicted his bank in ruins, overgrown with foliage like the remnants of Rome, he could hardly have imagined that bankers themselves would ruin it all in 100 years, though not quite as picturesquely as in Soane's engravings. It is a calamity of the first magnitude."

At Rupert Thompson's house at 13 Sussex Place, Raymond encountered the poet Siegfried Sassoon at dinner. It was Good Friday. Walter de la Mare's wife was there too because de la Mare had been in a nearby nursing home for five weeks. De la Mare had a reputation for asking questions. "Now I understand why I was interrogated about everything connected with Australia when I first met him." His new book, 'Stuff and Nonsense', was due out in two weeks with illustrations by Bold. Nobody knew whether he or she, but the pictures showed a great sense of humour.

Sassoon was a very tall man, well built, dark and with alert features which "indicate his keen intellect and sensitive taste". He came into the room in "a sort of curious swinging, gliding, impulsive way and shook hands with us all".

He is never still and hardly ever silent. He looks everywhere and at everybody and speaks with a great deal of expression, stopping sometimes in a half-amused way to collect his thoughts and then rippling them out so quickly that you are surprised to find he has told you what was on his mind.

His eyes and his expressive mouth forecast some touch of humour long before it has escaped his lips, and he has a way of rounding off a story most incisively with a few summary staccato remarks. He is blest with a sense of intellectual humour and describes a tragic event with a levity that renders it incalculably more poignant.

The talk led to typography. Rupert Thompson brought out the Nonesuch Press Bible with the beautiful engravings by Stephen Gooden.

63

Sassoon said he had begun to collect beautiful and limited books at Clare College when he could least afford them. "Now he has given it up and hates to have more stuff than he can pack up in a couple of hours." He had developed a tidiness mania, perhaps as a result of his war service in France and Palestine. T.E. Lawrence had sent Sassoon a copy of 'The Seven Pillars of Wisdom'. King George V wanted one but Lawrence tore up the King's letter and refused to let him have a copy because of the way the Government had treated the Arabs. The King, far from being annoyed, was pleased that someone should relieve the monotony of his existence by disagreeing with him. That at least was Sassoon's version of the story.

Mrs. de la Mare complimented Raymond on 'Seven Songs' and mentioned the rewriting of 'The Haberdasher' to suit the type available. Sassoon pricked up his ears and demanded to know all about it. He was most amused by the story, and then told them that Manny Forbes had asked him if he would publish one of his poems in 'The Book of Clare'. There were, said Sassoon, "signs of insanity" in Manny's delightful letter. Forbes, they all agreed, was a mixture of carefulness and dissipation. He had an amazing craze for patent medicines, on which he claimed he kept himself alive. He was perfectly careless about his diet and at one time, in France with Rupert Thompson, as often as not ended up the day on an absurdly indigestible meal of shellfish.

"One would never think", said Rupert, "that he was the product of a respectable and conservative tea-planter in Ceylon."

Let us interrupt the Thompsons' dinner party to describe the book to which Siegfried Sassoon had been asked to contribute. The sexcentenary of Clare College, Cambridge, occurred in 1926 and while it was marked with the building of the Memorial Court designed by Sir Giles Gilbert Scott, the fellows felt that the history of the college should be commemorated by the publication of a decent-sized book. Mansfield Duval Forbes, fellow and librarian of the college, lecturer in English, holder of a fine degree in history and with an interest in architecture and book design, was chosen for the task. It was to take up the best part of four years of his abbreviated life and to waste time, money and scholarship.

The two volumes, properly named 'Clare College 1326–1926' but called by most the Book of Clare, were heavy in every sense. Beautifully produced by Cambridge University Press, they appeared in 1928 and 1930, two and four years late. In a sense, since they were his only publication, they are Manny's memorial, edited with distinction and dash. Sir John Betjeman, later a friend of Raymond's in Dublin, tells the story of a college meeting at which Manny's failure to verify his references was discussed. His response was: "Of course I couldn't do that, you stupid old men; it would be too much trouble." Dates and facts were not his kind of history; they were mere "cover-the-groundism".[20]

The volumes cost the college £6,000; 2,000 copies were printed; few were read. They have not even achieved the status of rare books. Apart from the two untitled 1905 poems by Sassoon, the only interest for us lies in the frontispiece to volume II: 'A Prospect from the Air; Clare old and new' from a painting in tempera by Raymond McGrath, 1929. The Book

Facing page:
'A Prospect from the Air: Clare
old and new' by Raymond
McGrath, 1929

of Clare was, in two senses, monumental waste.

After dinner, Sassoon took Raymond as far as Marble Arch in his two seater. He told Raymond that he lived with Harold Speed the artist, in Hampden Square, Kensington. As they parted he asked if he might see a copy of the 'Seven Songs'.

He had been guessing all evening what Raymond was and Raymond's conversation had foxed him. Raymond told him, and said Sassoon's poem 'Alone' was his favourite. Sassoon agreed and said he felt that he had achieved in that piece rather more than in any of the others. 'Alone' was new, written in 1924 when he was 38, and published in 'The Augustan Books of Modern Poetry' series:

ALONE

"When I'm alone" — the words tripped off his tongue
As though to be alone were nothing strange.
"When I was young", he said; "When I was young."…

I thought of age, and loneliness, and change.
I thought how strange we grow when we're alone,
And how unlike the selves that meet, and talk,
And blow the candles out, and say good-night.
Alone… The word is life endured and known.
It is the stillness where our spirits walk
And all but inmost faith is overthrown.

Clare Bridge, c. 1929.
This engraving was to illustrate
Albert Frost's poem 'On Clare
Bridge' in Lady Clare Magazine
(Vol. xxiii, No. 2, 1929).
The woman on the right is almost
certainly Mary Crozier, whom
McGrath married in 1930

CHAPTER XI

Roland Stickles was a pseudonym that Raymond McGrath used several times in Australian and English newspapers. When a controversy raged about the siting of Alfred Gilbert's bust of John Hunter on the wall of St. George's Hospital, Stickles joined the fray. He had tried to view the work and somebody knocked him off the pavement. "I have now to content myself with embryonic glimpses from the top of an omnibus…"

At the same time, Christian Barman, not knowing the identity of Roland Stickles and using the pen-name Astragal himself, wrote of Raymond: "…a gentleman correspondent… evolves the equivoque that high art should not soar too high for comfortable enjoyment." It was the kind of cosy correspondence that amused the few, passed by the rest, and would not be possible in today's less elitist world in which *The Times* and the *Sydney Morning Herald* have better uses for their space. Raymond used the incident to remind Professor Brereton of previous letters in Sydney papers from the pen of Roland Stickles. "He comes from that city, as I happen to know."

Forbes said at this time that Raymond was not one of those people who can work in public rooms and libraries. When Barman felt like writing, he shaved himself and then bubbled with ideas. Keats, when he sought inspiration, put on his best suit. Raymond thought it was no good trying to write anywhere until he had ordered the thoughts in his mind and "prepared them for the order to advance".

He went to the R.I.B.A. exhibition that Barman had commissioned him to review. He and Major Corlette went to Conduit Street, where the institute's galleries were, and found themselves impressed by Easton and Robertson's Prestatyn Pavilion and R.S. Balgarmie Wyld's Mill Hill School Cricket Pavilion.

Raymond's latent feeling for modern architecture was stirred into life by Sir Reginald Blomfield's introduction to the catalogue — "very blum", as he said, "a diehard, a loadstone round the neck of English architecture".

He reacted strongly to Blomfield's statement that he was "quite unconvinced by the latest experiments now being made in France to evolve new forms out of reinforced concrete. Most of them are of an appalling and gratuitous hideousness"; and he cites Wyndham Lewis with approval: "I should have no compunction in having every London architect's head severed from his body at ten o'clock tomorrow morning unless he made some effort to apply a finer standard of art in his own art-practice."

A letter from John Beaglehole's fiancée in New Zealand revealed her amused despair at the loss of her garters. She had comforted herself with the thought that Beagle wore her garters every day. Now she has heard that he "gave them to a McGrath for one of his rotten little woodcuts... The only meet compensation is for you to forward us the aforesaid woodcut." Raymond does not enlighten us on the use to which he put the garters.

Raymond applied for the Brenforce Travelling Scholarship organised by the Institution of Structural Engineers. On May 7th he sat the esquisse for twelve hours. Where he had expected an architectural subject such as theatres, town halls or churches, what he got was "a combined water tower and tank on an eminence in moorland country". All the conditions were in engineering terms, and with little expectation of success he based his design on the Chinese pagoda and tried to use the concrete as one would use wood, "for in such a treatment I believe its future lies". Without knowing even how the designs were to be adjudicated, although he must have realised that Trystan Edwards was a member of the jury, he set off for a ride in the country with Duncan and Beaglehole.

At Greenwich they were about to take a photograph of the hospital when an attendant rushed up and said pictures were forbidden, the hospital being the property of the War Office. "If I'd known you wanted to take a photograph of course I'd a been inside. I wouldn't a known anything about it. But you see I was watching you and I'd a been pimped on, sure thing, for if the Secretary 'imself ain't looking out of 'is window, 'is wife is. Them women — O my God."

At dinner with the Parrys, Mhari said she was convinced that Raymond's ancestors were all Irish monks who did nothing else but illuminate manuscripts. (He had been asked to bring along 'Loaranneleah' and 'Chinese Architecture'.) Perhaps she was half-right: the Mc Graths, Mac Graths or Magraths (the personal name is *Craith*, not *Raith*) were a sept in Thomond (basically the county of Clare in Ireland). There they supplied ollamhs or men learned in poetry to the royal O'Brien sept who derived their name and historical importance from the family of King Brian Boru (d. 1014). By a coincidence, Forbes (which was of course Mhari's maiden name) is a synonym of MacFirbis and in Clare is pronounced Forbis.[21] So you have McGrath, Clare and Forbes. Perhaps there were other arcane links that drew Raymond and Manny Forbes together: certainly they had Celtic blood in common.

Raymond's design for the water tower was finished and delivered. It was vermilion surmounted by a yellow and green tank with a blue roof. He believed firmly that concrete, especially for isolated structures, was an ideal medium for colour decoration. "Architects are scared stiff of colour and it is hard lines that colour should have become the monopoly of post office authorities and firemen."

He did not win the Brenforce scholarship. All the more delicate and sensitive treatments were ousted in favour of the heavy style of "concrete couchant", as Trystan Edwards would have called it.

Manny's next visit to Raymond was the occasion for, "in accordance with our custom", a grand tour of the picture exhibitions. They saw

"Teddy" Wolfe's show at the delightful little Warren Gallery. Wolfe, Raymond thought, was a very effeminate painter and he judged that Manny's admiration for him stemmed from the fact that Wolfe was a friend of Mhari's. Pastiche Picasso or Matisse for the most part, but he "has captured the colour of Tangiers" and his drawings of Arabs were often very fine. Most of them were drawn on silver or gold paper "of the kind you sometimes see round firecrackers from China". Raymond must have changed his mind about Wolfe, for his family was left a very fine nude in the manner of Modigliani. Neither he nor Forbes bought at the Warren, but Manny paid £21 for an Ethelbert White at the R.W.S. Gallery. Manny always bought when he went up to London. It was no wonder that he was house-hunting in Cambridge.

At the Academy next day, Manny climbed out of the restaurant window in full gaze of the diners to see what the view up the light area was like. He was thrilled by it and insisted that Raymond should see it too. This was the kind of public exposure that Raymond always dreaded, but he did it. Later he gave Forbes the last copy of his 'Seven Songs of Meadow Lane' for the sake of Clare, in other words to mark his appreciation of Manny's interest in him. If the reader could have sworn that Walter de la Mare had already been given "the last copy", he is not alone. Forbes was "immensely touched and grateful — you could not give me anything more intimately personal".

After all those galleries they needed tea at Mhari's, and there Raymond met Ivon Hitchens, who had five pieces in the *Daily Express* Exhibition. The Contemporary Art Society was buying one of them for £50.

When Raymond later that week called on Hitchens for tea at Hampstead, he found the studio fascinating. The window looked out on an unpruned pear tree and some large fig trees. ("In England", he informed the reader of his journal, "figs never ripen".) Hitchens, a truly modern painter, had nothing fantastic about his person, which was mild and gracious. But his pictures were thrilling and romantic and "full of a wild poetry".

The rent of the studio at £60 was the devil to find sometimes, said Hitchens. And Sir Reginald Blomfield's opinions about modern art were a problem too. "You see", he said, "when Blomfield makes a speech and they publish it in the papers, all my aunts and cousins sent me cuttings about it with postscripts that say: 'There you are. I told you so. That's what an R.A. thinks of your modern art. If you had any brains you'd give it up and go in for some respectable occupation'."

Raymond had entered for an architectural competition in Perth, Australia. It was for Winthrop Hall and other buildings for the University of Western Australia. He worked steadily on his designs — "it would be just my luck to win a Gothic competition and be tied to the one branch of architecture for which I have the least facility" — and Major Corlette came in at 4 o'clock daily to look at the plans and mark them with crosses in unsatisfactory places.

But it was not all work and no play. Iris Wennström from Sweden and Frankie Rosen from Russia via Australia entered the quiet lives of Duncan, Beaglehole and McGrath for a few weeks and Raymond grew very fond of

Iris, who spoke Norwegian, German, Danish, Dutch and French as well as Swedish and tolerable English. Her conversation was a delight. She was witty and sarcastic. The bewitching curl of her lips reminded Raymond of Heather Sutherland — "another of those enigmatic, tantalising people". It was a great pleasure to know two such natural and unpampered girls, "so un-Londonish that I am glad London is not to be their home".

Little wonder then that Raymond's interest in Iris's homeland grew. "Sweden is the most remarkable country in Europe architecturally." He applied for membership of the Anglo-Swedish Society. He thought he would learn Swedish while he was at Cambridge and spend a year or so in Stockholm afterwards. He went so far as to do a drawing of the Månstenteater in Malmö, and signed it Rämun Makra.

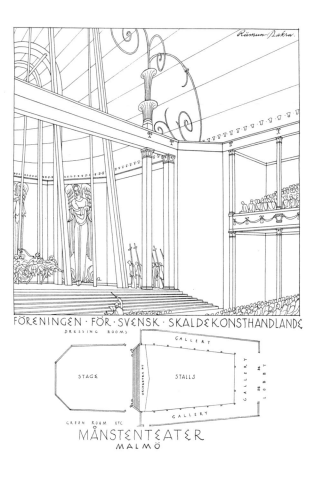

The Månstenteater in Malmö, Sweden, from Raymond's Clare College scrapbook, 1928

Raymond worked hard for Iris, who wanted to emigrate to Australia. He wrote to Sir Frank Fox and got a vaguely encouraging letter from him, which Raymond brought to her place with Sir Frank's card. They went to a little Greek café. She was in confiding mood and he could not help but admire her fine eyes and head of golden hair. He wrote of her:

> You speak, so slowly, that I hear the rain,
> Pattering and whispering, in between your words,
> And the sight crosses my fancy, again and again,
> Of showery haloes of lamps and of shadows like birds,

Of Åre far up in the mountains and under the pines
In a world that shines, suddenly deep, in your intimate eyes,
Where the drip of the leaves and the sound of the wind as it sighs
Are notes of some magical music my being divines
I have dreamed of you lost in the forests where day is no more,
Where day cannot come, and I called you in vain
Till I heard the last echo die in the leaf-laden floor
Of the cloisters of pines and heard only the drip of the rain
O Flower of Åre, why is it I dream and despair
When the leaves and the groves are so bright with the gold of your hair?

(Some years later, when he was married and settled into his architectural practice, this poem resurfaced as 'Home-driven Ships'. It had been subtly stripped of its Scandinavian associations.)

'Princess Charming' at the Palace Theatre in Charing Cross Road was a dazzling and clever performance, made the more memorable by Iris's company. But Raymond's time was divided up between Iris and pleasure, and Perth and his forthcoming visit to Paris. His competition entry now included the interior of the great hall and a bird's-eye view of the whole group of buildings. And all the time he was planning to go to Paris, the starting point of a journey to Spain. Already Duncan and Hubert Woodhouse were in France awaiting his completion of the Perth drawings.

He went to Cambridge to see about rooms for the coming year. The Dean of Clare, Dr. Telfer, gave him the addresses of four sets of rooms, each uglier than the one before until he settled on 43 Grantchester Street and Mrs. Withers. It and she did not meet his high standards, but she was nice enough and he would learn to live with her Edwardian chairs. "I suppose I am fussy", he admitted.

The Italian marionette show attracted Raymond and he went along with Jim Gardiner, his Sydney friend, Jim's sister and of course Iris. She surprised him by appearing in a yellow dress and stockings and silver-spangled shoes. She was in an "I-beg-your-pardon" mood and "by no means her usual self, for which I was sorry". If he had been a little direct with himself, he might have applied to Iris the phrase that he had used of London the day before: "One can stand a little honest wickedness but plain vulgarity is the stuff that kills."

On Saturday, 23 July, 1927, the Continent of Europe beckoned. Raymond sent round a bouquet of flowers to Iris as a parting token of his good wishes for her future success. There was, he confided to his diary, more to those good wishes than she might have imagined. "I have dreamed dreams and pursued strange hopes since first we met just a week or two ago. Now she is gone and when I shall set eyes on her again, see that proud golden head and look into those dear deep eyes I cannot say. She has been an inspiration and a despair... I have been consumed by the fear of finding others unhappy, and I daresay it is her unhappiness for which I fear most... I dreamed that she wandered bitterly over the world and vanished, like a little dust, into the utter darkness."

He would not return to England for two months.

The Moorish Tower & Church of S.Nicolás. Córdoba

Chapter XII

At the Hotel Azur in the Rue de l'Abbé Grégoire, the lovelorn lad sighed: "I breathe again, a little pensively… All the treasures of Paris are not as wonderful as a woman's hand." His company was Walter Duncan. Hubert Woodhouse, Jim Gardiner and Ian Henning, the resident Parisian. Duncan sported a black French felt, a red cravat and a moustache and side-levers. He had his hat pulled down over his eyes and was the picture of infantile innocence. Woodhouse was trés Woodhouse. No wonder a jeune fille approached Henning with an invitation: "Viens, bébé, fais l'amour avec moi." To which Henning replied with a drunken bar from Mistinguette's famous song:

Et quand j'ai pris mon anisette
Je m'en fou

The jollification carried them up to Henning's Louis XIV room, where they had a musical entertainment. They had bought a ukelele, which Jim Gardiner played, and two mouth organs. "It is surprising what joy one gets out of singing songs even badly", Raymond noted, all thought of Iris banished.

From Paris to San Sebastian, Raymond, Duncan, Woodhouse and Jim Gardiner went by train, stopping at Tours, Angoulême and Irun. Raymond was in his artistic element and determined to make the most of this opportunity to investigate what he had sensed at Algeciras the year before. He wrote and he sketched bountifully and beautifully, and a year later was able to publish in the *Architectural Review* a reworked account of his journey. It was a remarkable achievement for, in four successive issues of the *A.R.*, he was given generous space in which to display his own carefully scripted story. To our eyes, the manuscript makes difficult reading, but visually it is a world of wonder to behold, with vignettes and sketches neatly fitted into the text. Under the general title 'Spanish Moonshine: Some fragments from a travel diary', the *Review* carried the story from August to November 1928.

In November, Eyre and Spottiswoode did a reprint which faithfully reproduced the four full pages of text and drawings and carried a full page colour plate entitled 'Spanish Mediterranean'. It was a triumph, and we shall return to its reception in due course. Now we must go back to San Sebastian, where Raymond sketched the ships in the harbour.

In Valladolid, Woodhouse quoted as his philosophy of life and women a Spanish proverb that says: "God gives us walnuts when we have no

Facing page:
One of McGrath's illustrations for the Architectural Review *series 'Spanish Moonshine'*

teeth." At the Prado in Madrid, Raymond was highly critical of Titian except for his *Offering to the God of Love*; and of Rubens with his fat coarse women and oleographic colours. But "an amusing picture was the childish *La Via Lactea* with its humble fat woman squirting milk from her breast at a squabbling [*sic*] child".

As he moved from city to city, it became clear that Raymond's Spanish diary was being written with an eye to publication. When the train stopped at Bobadella, they found an Irishman called Dyer working as a waiter. A child of nine threw kisses at them on the platform and asked for "una peseta". The precisian in Raymond was moved to write:

> Nothing is more pathetic than to see children begging in Spain and it is a sin for anyone to encourage them. She was a most beautiful child with most expressive eyes and she was dressed in one thin and dirty garment which had once been white. She wore a woman's ragged stockings which were gathered and tied up over her knees and on her feet she had a pair of dusty sandals. Nothing would have given me more pleasure than to have given her a bath and a clean dress. While we were waiting in our carriage for the train to go she climbed up to our window and threw more kisses to us. Her brother, a child of about six, was with her. He did not look at all Spanish and it occurred to us to ask their names. After a little hesitation she told us it was Sophie Dyer. So they were our Irishman's children by a Spanish mother. We gave them some biscuits which they ate greedily…

In Granada, they reached the heights of the Alhambra by "the most amazing of all tramways". It wound up through the tortuous and narrow streets of the old town, leaving room for nothing else. As it turned it scraped the corners of the buildings; knocked against balconies, and ran over melons on the square. The shops and houses seemed to open into the tramcar. "You could", said Raymond, "put your hand out and take the razor from the barber's hand as you go past".

In Barcelona, he saw Gaudí's unfinished Sagrada Familia church, "probably the strangest church in the world… the elements of this building are most amazingly ugly and vulgar. Here all the principles of beauty which have governed design since the world began are flaunted and the art of a good sculptor has been ruined by a setting of the most brazen deceit, for it is almost impossible to believe that the architect of this work ever seriously believed that the building would be beautiful. Icicles of mud take the place of Gothic traceries, columns are toppled together in defiance of gravity, and all the forms that artists have laboured through centuries to perfect are thrown to the winds. The wonder is that Antoni Gaudí is taken seriously in Barcelona. It does not speak well for genuine taste… One hopes that it will never be fitted with lightning conductors." (He did not know that Gaudí had been killed in a tramcar accident outside the church only a year before. Nor that he himself would come to admire Gaudí's work).

Facing page:
San Francisco, Palma, 1927

74

At 24, Raymond McGrath had a strong preference for "the noble mass of Palma Cathedral" where one could find serenity and peacefulness. The people too were happy, happier and brighter than on the mainland. In Majorca, there were no beggars, no poverty. "Here man, nature and man's works seem to be in perfect harmony."

A glutton for punishment, Raymond wanted to see one bullfight before he left Spain in order to form his own impressions of it "in its actuality". He was not prepared to watch the spectacle before giving his opinion that "there is not a grain of sportsmanship in it, I am convinced. It is sheer butchery and one can only feel that a country which enjoys such a spectacle has not yet emerged from the barbarities of the medieval age".

The great arena was packed with people, including many women and even some boys and girls. The faces around him were mostly coarse and brutal, some of the women being positively repulsive. The band played; the attendants offered cushions for the hard concrete seats, and paper-sellers walked up and down. A hush was followed by an exhibition of lassoing by some cowboys. Two horses were driven into the arena, tantalised and thrown.

When the bullfighters entered, the torilero opened the door and the bull thundered into the ring. He was "stupefied and dazed" by the bright daylight. He was lassoed and rolled over on the sand, then he was teased by the capeadores waving their cloaks.

"The poor animal, thoroughly confused, made one sudden dash and to my surprise cleared the ring fence and raced around inside the alley. But he was soon in the arena again and once more began the torture," Raymond wrote.

After the bandilleros had done their work, the bull was bleeding from his bruised nostrils. "If there had been a Spaniard in that great crowd with any human or animal sympathies he would have intervened then. But there was none. A great shout went up from those who were eager for the killing… The famous Belmonte was there, in a suit of tawdry gold braid, a short fat lump of a man who stood at the fence calling off the capeadores when they took any risks."

And so on to the slow death in the afternoon. When the espada thrust his sword into the bull's heart, the animal went down wearily on his forelegs and rolled over on the ground, the blood gushing freely in a long stream from its mouth over the sand. Raymond got up, his head throbbing with anger, and left. It was his first and last bullfight.

By 1 October, Raymond was busy packing up and leaving Cambridge Terrace for the real Cambridge. Two days later, he dined in hall for the first time. The Master of Clare, Mr. Henry Thirkill; the assistant registrar, Mr. Priestley; the dean, Dr. Telfer, and Mr. Theodore Fyfe of the School of Architecture told him he was to have as much freedom as he desired, and Mrs. Withers the landlady turned into a charming woman.

"When you wrote from Spain about the rooms", said Mr. Withers, "I said to the wife: 'This sounds like the young gentleman you told me about, but are we sure it is him?' 'Yes', she said, 'I'm sure it is. He wasn't the ordinary undergraduate type at all. He was quite different. I would like to have him.' 'All right', I said, 'if he's anything like the sound of that letter, all right. But I want no more of the last kind. They go out, bag and baggage.' "

Iris Wennström came briefly back into Raymond's life. She wrote from Sweden pleading for a letter to prove to her father that she had a job waiting in Sydney. "Dear Mr. McGrath will you please answer me at once?" But there was no need. She broke with her parents and was left penniless. Raymond dreamed:

> All heavenly stars may cross my sleep,
> All rains my dreams explore,
> Yet star or tempest cannot keep
> This wanderer from my door.

That, and two more verses, was the end of Iris.

At Christmas, the antipodean expatriates formed a society of colonials in London called the Ahahlians. The first annual corroboree was held at 21 Brunswick Square, the home of Duncan and Beaglehole. Raymond passed his R.I.B.A. final.

Professor Brereton told Raymond at this time that he was "an indefatigable worker". Raymond responded: "I sometimes have grave doubts. I should write to you once a week simply out of gratitude for having helped to drop me into the middle of this glorious bubbling cauldron.

"I have been interested to observe changes in my own outlook — a broadening of vision, I hope. You will remember how busily I used to occupy myself with the poetic conceit of the barrenness of towns. But I have seen enough beauty in them now (and I believe it began with 'The Rubbish Bin') to forget all that."

In case Brereton was in doubt about whether Raymond still went on "scribbling verses", he assured the professor that "I do and I suppose I always will". But he has been reluctant to publish poetry — "(not because I am not conceited, as witness my delight in architectural articles) but because the few things I have written have been for the interest of one or two people..." He sent Brereton the first of his poems about Iris Wennström for his comments.

H.M. Green in 'A History of Australian Literature'[22] describes three young poets who, after publishing a book each, left Australia, not to return — Jack Lindsay, Raymond McGrath and Winifred Shaw. Raymond in 'Seven Songs of Meadow Lane' published "some light verses full of grace and fancy".

In this vein of grace and fancy, he did continue to write some verses. He gave to *Lady Clare Magazine* for Michaelmas 1927 the second of his poems to Iris, which he entitled simply 'Song'. But he published also his 'Macbeth' wood engraving from 'Twenty-four Woodcuts'; a full page illustration for Albert Frost's poem 'An Old Man's Song', and a delightful pictorial product of his Spanish tour called 'Montserrat'.

Already he was deeply involved in the magazine's life. The editor was

Montserrat, 1927

Christopher Millett as president of the Dilettante Society, sitting on Srabbit, the society's mascot. The drawing is by Ramón Majraz (Raymond McGrath)

Christopher Millett, "a good modern imitation of Benvenuto Cellini", as Raymond described him to Brereton. Millett, whose family lived in Switzerland, was clever and handsome, and therefore attractive to women. His prose was racy and funny, and when Raymond taught him wood engraving he proved an apt pupil with a prolific output. Kris or Chris was his nickname and he and Raymond rapidly became friends, if not boon companions. With J.F. Scott, Raymond was a sub-editor for the Michaelmas issue of 1927.

The secretary was A.C. Frost. Albert Frost was on a scholarship to Cambridge, where he was under Manny Forbes' supervision "in respect of his studies for the English Honours (Tripos) examination(s)", as Manny painstakingly wrote in a report on Albert's work to date. He went on:

> Frost is the best student I have ever had or can ever hope to have… His personality is equally attractive and his influence upon his fellow students quite invaluable… His intelligence is as fine creatively as critically.

A native of Carlisle, Albert Frost became Raymond McGrath's confidant, collaborator and eventually brother-in-law, so his career is inextricably interwoven with Raymond's. His poetry adorned the *Lady Clare* throughout his Clare years and he sometimes wrote jointly with Chris Millett or Manny Forbes himself. In Volume XXIII No. 1 appeared 'The Truth at Dunsinane':

> To marry, or to marry and to marry,
> Crops up this potty point from boy to boy
> To the last Jezebel of reported crime;
> And all our Registrars have plighted fools
> The way to frowsty flats. Out, out, brief cuddle!
> A wife's but a waiting widow, a sure stayer
> That sulks and frets herself into a rage
> And then is heard all day; she is a sale
> Sold to an idiot, full of bounce, and fussy,
> Dignifying nothing.

This anti-feminist bagatelle was signed:

$$\begin{matrix} \text{MD} \\ \text{AC} \end{matrix} \text{F}$$

and as a pastiche of 'Tomorrow, and tomorrow', in 'Macbeth', would have passed muster in a school annual. Manny Forbes was 39 and still an undergraduate in his heart. A great deal of the frenetic activity that he generated in his coterie was schoolboy stuff, as far removed from the revolutionary student spirit of the 1960s as it was from the conservative primness of today's campus.

The stories told about Manny Forbes were legion and often embellished in the retelling. But his endearing qualities quite outweighed his occasional silliness, and he had a loathing of class privilege which showed in his fostering of students such as F.R. Leavis, Elsie Phare, Denys Harding and Albert Frost, whose education depended largely on county scholarships.

Albert was among the most skilful players of 'Resumption', a game invented by Chris Millett. It had no fixed teams. Both sexes played barefoot and kicked a tennis ball towards no fixed goal. It was a free-for-all with no fixed time limit, the end coming with exhaustion or an injury serious enough to cause a halt to be called. It could then be resumed, hence 'Resumption'. Albert's childhood had necessarily, and unusually for Cambridge in the 1920s, involved him in street games, and he had captained his school rugby team. Thus his prowess at Resumption.

In 1928, Anthony Blunt founded an avant-garde magazine called the *Venture*. Blunt, who later became Surveyor of the Queen's Pictures and later still was exposed as a spy, was in his third year at Trinity College, Cambridge, and founded the magazine with two Magdalene students, Michael Redgrave, the actor, and Robin Fedden, later a Middle East expert and architectural historian.

To the *Venture* Raymond contributed some of his finest wood engravings while his friend John Beaglehole offered poems such as 'Molecular Theory', which begins:

> Noiseless, unnursed, the country rose
> Is born, and quietly it goes;
> The unheard bright anemone
> Blooms for the eye alone to see.

and ends:

> And yet, I think, could I but hear
> Once, suddenly, with quickened ear,
> Might I not start, as saw my eye
> A petal fall, to catch a cry?

In this poem of Beagle's, reprinted in the Michaelmas 1928 *Lady Clare*, one may hear the authentic voice of the poet. Another contributor to the *Venture*, though he was then a student of Merton College, Oxford, was Louis MacNeice. He and John Betjeman had been to Marlborough with Blunt. Julian Trevelyan[23] says that Julian Bell contributed, as did Mansfield Forbes.

This issue of *Lady Clare* (volume XXIII No. 1), in which Chris Millett's name appears under many illustrations, is remarkable for many reasons. Raymond was the editor, Albert a sub-editor, and the whole magazine was refurbished. The cover and title page were printed in Eric Gill's sans-serif type. Gill designed what commonly came to be called Gill Sans for the Monotype company in 1927. It represented the full flowering of what he called "absolutely-legible-to-the-last-degree letters". It is still fresh, undated, and in constant use. Raymond McGrath was one of the first to see its beauty and utility.

The end-papers

The end-papers are Raymond's. They show the programme and menu for the annual devilment of Forbes's Dilettante Society, of which Chris Millett was then president. The Dilettante, which might have been subtitled 'The Lark in the Clare Air', was more Mannymania. The programme for Thursday, December 6th, 1927, included "pyrotechnics; consequences; the druids' egg or serpent's secret well out; Clarewitch and luminous tortoises" and so on. It is a peculiarly English form of humour not truly appreciated by others.

The menu contained "S'mushrooms", a reference to the secret language of the members, who prefixed certain nouns with s' or s, from the 18th century form of words such as strewth (God's truth). Thus "Srabbit" was the society's mascot. 'The Story of Srabbit' by Chris Millett had decorated — if decorated is the word — one of the 1927 *Lady Clares*. And Raymond earned the ridiculous nickname Smoon McGrath because of an unfortunate verse of his which began "Say Moon, how have you left Valencia?" He himself was responsible for Roland Stickles the letter writer, and for Ramón Majraz, the name he used for fragments of his travel diary. The briefest appearance was made by Rämun Makra.

His attempt to improve *Lady Clare* involved a larger format, better paper and wider margins. Its quality was enhanced too by his drawings and woodcuts and by some lovely work by Chris Millett. From Forbes's Clare Book came some woodcuts entitled Dialogus Creaturarum I – III (by permission of the editor), one of which illustrated a limerick that goes:

> Said the Mare, "I deplore recent traffic
> In literature candidly Sapphic;
> Aristotalization
> Is much better for the nation
> Than novels that approach on the graphic"

A piece of self-indulgence by Manny spans two pages of Volume XXIII No. 1. A "wookcut" by Raymond McGrath is captioned: "The fallowing poem, noow frashly illustred in wook, is thocht to beling to the early yahs… and has been resigned by Offessor A.D. Hoc…" and so on ad nearly nauseam. The "poem" is coyly called "Wookman! Spahir θot Treeh!". It is remarkable only for its tedium and the pity is that Raymond's woodcut, showing a Little Lord Fauntleroy character crying halt to the burly woodman as he lays his axe to the tree, is one of his finest. It should be added that Christopher Millett in 1983 wished that he still had "an incomparable poem by Manny illustrated with an exquisite woodcut by Raymond". *De gustibus…*

The *Cambridge Review* of 27 April, 1928, congratulated the *Lady Clare* on its new size and scope. The text, it commented, "displays less spontaneity and a more conscious effort at parody… but in doing so reflects the more faithfully that naïf spirit of *diablerie* which characterises so many of the activities of this college, and in particular those with which the omni-active Mr. Forbes has anything to do".

With the omni-active Mr. Forbes, Raymond went motoring in Dorset

'Wookman! Spahir θot Treeh!', 1928

and Surrey. Their chauffeuse was Manny's cousin "Pud" Batten, a great Hardy enthusiast with an Eton crop which gave her a boyish look. With them was Pud Batten's employer A.R. Powys, who was secretary of the Society for the Protection of Ancient Buildings. Pud owned the car. Raymond recalled for Brereton:

> I shall never forget Manny's star turn when we went to Cerne Abbas and climbed up on the hill to look at the famous Cerne giant outlined in the chalk. Manny sprinted down its great penis and skipped gleefully from ball to ball…

The Cerne Giant was similarly described by Lance Sieveking[24] as "that outstandingly virile prehistoric man 180 feet high", but unlike Manny, Sieveking, who was travelling through Dorset with Paul and Margaret Nash in 1943, sat only at the foot of the hillside.

Above and right:
San Gimignano, 1929.
Two versions by McGrath

CHAPTER XIII

In April 1929, Raymond fulfilled the promise he had made to himself at Naples. He visited Italy. Indeed it could be said that his self-determined itinerary of Europe was being fulfilled at a rate that indicated no immediate shortage of funds. Christopher Millett, excellent musician and imaginative draughtsman, went with Raymond from London as far as Brigue in Switzerland. They were driven by Christopher's father, who also carried Christopher's girlfriend Derry as far as Clarens, where Chris went to see his old nanny at the clinic. On the way to Brigue, they ate a lunch of hard-boiled eggs and potatoes in their skins in the middle of a pine wood. Then the two Cambridge men went south by train.

For a week or so, they were joined by Bob Hurd, a Scottish architect, and in Florence they saw among the wonders the Loggia di S. Paolo, which seemed to Raymond the "most grateful arcade" done by Brunelleschi, whom Gloag[25] has called "the most gifted of all the pioneers of the Renaissance".

From Florence to Poggibonsi, the two took third-class railway tickets. Then they chartered an old man's sulky and drove through Certaldo, hilly birth-place of Boccaccio, to San Gimignano. "The smell of the open country, the barley fields and the bean-rows made me feel strangely homesick", Raymond confided to his diary.

Terraced on the hilltop, San Gimignano is a city-in-miniature, containing four piazzas, ten churches, town hall, theatre and museum as well as the many family palaces remarkable for their thirteen towers which crown the hill in a compact group. From the distance, these towers he later thought might be the skyscrapers of Corbusier's 'Ville Contemporaire'. This quality of monumental miniature is "the great charm of the place…".

At the time, Raymond was able to pull his eyes down from the towers to the very beautiful blonde girl on the pensione stairs. She had an "irresistible attraction" for him and at the risk of being thoroughly vulgar, he could not take his eyes off her face at dinner. Chris thought he was excited: he admitted that he was. Next night he again caught her eyes — she was of course Scandinavian. "For two pins I would have sent Christopher back to Florence without me. But what use?"

They walked from San Gimignano, one of the most perfect places in the world, to Certaldo. "A strange subtle feeling of loss seemed to have possessed me", he noted as he headed back to Florence and Cambridge.

Christopher Millett was good company. He spoke German and French

'Ray', wrote Christopher Millett (above) 'never took a good picture: he always came out like a dying duck with digestive troubles, but I rather like the one I took of him framed in the window with the towers of San Gimignano in the background.'

as well as he spoke English, and he was used to climbing up among the pines of Switzerland or tramping in the Black Forest. It pleased Raymond that Chris had been such an apt pupil of the woodcut, and that his mother was an Australian. Chris's charming Irish girl friend talked about her adopted country, Arizona, "as if it were some marvellous province of Samarkand". Chris was counted among "my immediate friends who include Frost, George Yeats [a Californian] and of course 'Manny' Forbes". Frost too had a passion for climbing mountains, and Yeats went on walking trips in Spain. It was the era of the *Wandervogel* all over Europe.

Manny was not the least of the hikers, especially in Scotland. Early in 1928, among his 101 enthusiasms was the establishment of architecture as a subject in the schools. He was also working on the Book of Clare, and lecturing on English Romanticism and talking to "a brilliant constellation" of artists, architects and poets at breakfast in his rooms. There he sat in the middle of a long narrow medieval table — like Christ at the Last Supper, thought his protégé. A low bookcase ran round the big cream-coloured room with its chintz curtains. On it stood dozens of valuable pictures, vases, Indian bronzes, negro sculptures, and broadsides. The carpet was "littered with magazines, bristling with newspaper cuttings".

The Cambridge architectural group, Raymond smugly informed Brereton, "with whom I am of course very intimate", comprised Harold "Tommy" Tomlinson and his wife, George Checkley and his wife, H.C. Hughes and Ian Parsons. Mrs. Tomlinson was a Cambridge architectural student who married her lecturer. When they were in England, Mr and Mrs Sweeney, "the two most likeable of Americans", were of the group. This couple, later to live in Ireland and become closer to Raymond and Mary McGrath, were James Johnson Sweeney and his wife Laura, also an architectural student. "She is the only married woman I covet", Raymond told Brereton, the sole receptacle of this kind of confidence.

Other members of the group not residing in Cambridge were Trystan Edwards, Christian Barman, George Kennedy, Edward Maufe, Hope Bagenal and Boris Anrep.

Settled in his mind on 'Entertainment Architecture' as the subject of his thesis, Raymond saw cinemas, theatres, opera houses, concert halls and restaurants as a very important group of buildings that "need not be as vulgar as they usually are". He had begun to gather examples and had had a very polite response from some prominent Continental architects. He expected to be travelling and already had Germany "mapped out like a war campaign". He was studying lighting, ventilation, acoustics (which he felt should be on the Sydney University course) and decoration. He already had been in touch with "every London firm that does anything interesting in the way of decoration". He knew all the possibilities of modern flooring materials, wallpapers, modern paints, glass and mirrors. He even found a place in modern architecture for chocolate papers as a wall covering.

"The virtue of being in touch with all these firms is this", he told Brereton: "You see what can be done with copper for example, and you are given introductions to owners of houses or buildings in which use has been made of the material. Manny Forbes… has been my constant accomplice in all this and his great influence has enabled us to see many rather guarded interiors."

The founding of an import agency in Sydney occurred to him. All the beautiful things he had been discovering — Swedish glass and wallpapers, German textiles, Italian Murano glass, French metalwork — needed an Australian outlet. And why, he wondered by extension, could not Australians see modern German films?

This letter to Professor John Le Gay Brereton, dated 3rd August, 1928, is quite remarkable for two things. First, it is written on the backs of postcards from Italy, a trick copied from Manny. But vastly more important is the fact that only on page seven does he mention Finella, the project that set him on the road to success as a modern architect and designer in London.

Casually he wrote: "Various things are keeping me busy this vacation. I am modernising and decorating a house on the Backs for Mansfield Forbes. About £2,000 is being spent on it and I hope later to tell you all about it."

Such insouciance in the face of his first commission is not easy to comprehend unless the frenetic activity and consequent public interest in the house built up rather slowly. Another and more likely explanation is that Raymond was trying to construct a sequential story for Brereton, to whom he had not written since February. Seen in this way, the role of Manny as "constant accomplice" can better be understood. The visits to firms and private houses were conducted, not to flesh out Raymond's thesis, but to work out ideas for the remodelling of Finella. Certainly by 10 September, Raymond reported to Manny: "Things begin to take shape."

Finella, Fenella, Finola are anglicisations of the Gaelic *Fionnghuala*, white shoulder. She was a legendary Queen of Scotland, said to have discovered glass and to have met her death by being thrown down a waterfall and broken on the rocks. Glass played a key role in the making of Finella the house.

In 1927, Manny leased The Yews from Gonville and Caius College, next door to Clare. Built in 1850, the house was large, dark and run down. It was on Queens Road, on the Backs. Manny began the greatest adventure of his life by renaming it Finella. Having rejected the earlier thought of engaging Harold Tomlinson to design a house for him, he asked Raymond to rehabilitate The Yews.

For Raymond, it was a labour of love and a unique opportunity. Which is just as well, for there is no evidence of his earning any fees for Finella. Otherwise the collaboration is exceptionally well documented. There are Raymond's letters to Manny, six of them, some illustrated, all written in September 1928, when Manny was in Scotland. There are Manny's letters to Jack Pritchard and Pritchard's letters to Manny covering 1929 to 1932, and there are Raymond's occasional letters to Brereton, and to his fiancée and later wife Mary. On top of all this, there is the large corpus of glowing magazine reviews of the house. Between December 1929, and May 1930, major critiques appeared in *Ideal Home, Vogue, Good Housekeeping, The*

Home, The Studio, the *Architectural Review* and the *Architects' Journal,* as well as Swedish and Italian journals and *Country Life,* in which the article, unsigned, was by Manny himself. The most enthusiastic notice was that in the *Architectural Review.* It was written by Albert Frost.

Jack Pritchard, a Cambridge man and a friend of Manny's, was since 1925 director of the Esthonia-based Venesta Plywood Company, the firm that made Plymax, a metal-faced plywood material that was largely used by Raymond in Finella. He and his wife Molly were frequent guests at Queens Road, and any differences about payments or advertising were amicably settled by letter.

In one letter, of January 1929, Manny complained to Jack Pritchard: "No signs of McGrath, who ought to have been here a week ago — I hope he is not ill... he went to Paris before Xmas."

Manny was out of sorts, but still able to express himself in colourful words and with his quirky punctuation:

> It's ghastly here — I'm completely alone (save for College cat, which has arthritis in both hindquarters, and looks genteelly pained when I spit, however disconsolately, into the fire) — I'm also so numbed that I [am] drearily unequal to the very urgent work that has brought me back here, in the hollow nadir of desolate time.

Pritchard responded by suggesting that Manny pack up the College cat and "come up to London for a week-end". He had a very good sofa, plenty of food and some wine. He undertook to have the furniture for Finella (made with copper Plymax) finished by the end of the week.

At the end of some of the September letters, Raymond turned lightly from business to pleasure. Christopher Millett was illustrating a collection of nursery rhymes, and Raymond offered him "a few spares". One, written for Manny, ran:

> Finella, Finella, Finella
> Jumped into a fountain of glass
> All the jaggedy edges
> Like cactusy hedges
> Dissected Finella, Alas!
> Dissected Finella, Alas!

John Beaglehole was torn on the subject of what profession to choose. Raymond offered:

> Can't think *what* I'm to do, observed Beagle
> If I walk in the clouds
> I'll get pecked by the birds,
> If I walk on the ground
> I'll start stepping in turds!
> Can't think *what* I'm to do, observed Beagle.

This letter is subscribed "Smoon" and decorated with stars and a crescent moon.

Meanwhile, Raymond was putting into practice all that he had learned about planning permission, specifications, contracts, insurance, discounts and of course drains. The letters show that his collaboration with Manny was more positive, more authoritative, than his published statements about it. When Brian Hanson[26] asked him in 1977 how much Finella was a design *between* them, Raymond replied:

> Well, it was only designed between us insofar as Manny would say, "Wouldn't it be nice to do this?" or "Wouldn't it be nice to do that?" He had no facility for design himself but he had painted a little. He was a person of ideas. He was the inspiration and I played up to his tastes.

Fred Manderson, an ex-patriate Australian architect and a member of the Ahahlians, helped Raymond with the drawings "which, believe me, take time to think out". As ideas came to him, Raymond wrote to Manny with elaborate descriptions and both useful and comic illustrations, always careful to cost his suggestions and ask for Manny's opinion.

Fred Manderson was highly amused by a dream which Raymond recounted to Manny. It took the form of a playlet and was charmingly illustrated with the figure of Raymond with little angel's wings looking up startled from his drawing board at an enormous God complete with long white beard and haloes, emanating light.

SCENE: Heaven on a Monday morning, all bright and sparkling. I am writing furiously in a colossal room. Enter God (it appears that I am God's architect).

God: (benignantly): Well, how is Gabriel's mirador?

Myself: I am writing the specs now. Everything is splendid (I produce plans etc.).

God: Well, what are the walls made of?

Self: (Proudly, for it is my first job in Heaven) Of beaten gold, God.

God: Beaten gold! To hell with beaten gold. They've done nothing but sing hymns about beaten gold ever since I can remember. What I want's tinfoil or Celotex on two by one battens.

Self: But God, you can't! They've never specified anything but beaten gold in Heaven.

God: I don't care what's been specified in Heaven. Do you remember what you did for Mansfield Forbes? That's what I want.

Self: Very well God. I'll do it. Forbes would be interested. Do you know where he is?

God: Know! Why he's working for me on the Book of Heaven. He's in my combination room now with the floor littered with universal periodicals and leaves out of all the libraries from

God's Architect

87

Saturn to Uranus. I've never seen a happier angel in my life! What are your floors made of?

Self: Of lapis lazuli.

God: To hell with lapis lazuli. What I want's Docker's plevna pink Induroleum on cement screeding. There was an agent here yesterday.

Self: But God!

God: Never mind, and there's a lot more I want too. In another month Mansfield Forbes will be starting his chapter on the Judgement Halls of Glass.

Self: Of glass! But God I didn't know you ever had Judgement Halls of Glass! All the Judgement Halls in Heaven are beaten gold!

God: Perhaps so. But they won't be. You're going to design me a Judgement Hall that is every particle of it glass. There won't be a batten, screw, a nail or a piece of wire in the whole place!

Self: But God, I don't know whether it can be done!

God: What's that to me — whether it can be done or not? Nothing's impossible!

Here endeth the dream.

For his sister Eileen's 21st birthday, Raymond had a leather-bound Volume I of the Book of Clare specially tooled and inscribed with a suitable verse which began:

Be true, my dreams, for she, like Rima now,
Steps from the quiet with a quickening heart,
And lead her where sweet lilies grow apart,
And deftly, with your laurels, touch her brow.

This, post factum, he ventured to push under Manny's critical eye, while in the business part of the letter he "evolved a scheme which is really revolutionary, in fact it will have to be *patented*". The fool-proof scheme involved a constant change of coloured light ranging through the whole spectrum in whatever sequence of colours was desired. "Can you guess how it's done?", asked the excited young architect, his ardour dampened only by the *Architectural Review's* cheque for the first instalment of 'Spanish Moonshine'. Ten guineas he regarded as "rather poor" payment.

Among the many words Manny coined over the years were several relating to Finella. He would talk of matters that were Finellagenda. He invented Pictavian as the adjective from Pict, the Picts coming from his beloved Scotland and Pictish meaning only their (enigmatical) language. It never made the dictionaries. But best loved of Manny was *simple-intime*, meaning simple intimacy, one of the effects for which he strove in the rebuilding of Finella. And magnetic and timely as Finella proved, it was essentially simple. The inventiveness that Raymond showed in creating Finella was not gimmicky; was not a reflection of Manny's whimsicality; *was* a new approach using new materials and new forms of light to make a stimulating house for living in.

Raymond's own account of what he achieved appeared five years later in his book 'Twentieth Century Houses' (Faber 1934), a book which understandably he dedicated to Mansfield Duval Forbes over the words "simple-intime". The reader will detect that this book was written in Basic English, a fashionable form which had a vocabulary of only 850 words. This strangely effective language will be referred to later.

In designing the exterior of Finella, Raymond's object was to produce a house "in pleasing harmony with its beautiful garden and the trees all round":

> Unnecessary woodwork was taken away from its walls, and the yellow-grey bricks coated with a light red wash. The old church doorway gave way to a delicate structure which let the light into the hall. The house was terraced up from the garden and one or two trees cut down. The effect was a house which was light and simple outside and well in keeping with the more unconditioned designs inside.

The interior "was perceived as sumptuous yet interpreted as modern", to use John Warnock's[27] words: an indication perhaps of Raymond's "non-doctrinaire, even evasive, approach to modernism", to quote Warnock again. Raymond said of the interior:

> The hall was roofed with green glass, its walls covered with metal leaf, and the floor done in a polished black mixed substance of wood powder and asbestos. At the far end the wall was completely covered with gold-leaf glass through which there was a door opening into the south of two rooms joined by folding copper doors. Glass of different sorts and colours was used in the room for meals, the coat-room off the hall, and the three bathrooms. All this glass was designed in relation to the lighting, and between them they gave the house a feeling of clear space and delicate colouring by night and by day.

Finella was properly used by its owner as a sort of "country house", where hospitality was constant and abundant: there always were extra places at the dinner table, not so much for the unexpected as for those guests whom Manny suspected he had asked but then forgotten about.

Enjoyable as this life was, it was not the main purpose of Finella, which was designed to attract artists, architects and designers from the wider world outside Cambridge. In this aim, it succeeded beyond the wildest dreams of owner and architect. "The house", Manny wrote to Pritchard, "continues to cause great excitement, tho' I have had no more marchionesses sublimating the offing since you were here."

Lascelles Abercrombie stayed the night and next day told Manny he had dreamt about the house. "So it *is* coming off, as I had hoped, in one

especial capacity — as an Exhilarator or gesture in Exhilaration."

Raymond said the house began at once to be "a kind of Mecca" for anybody interested in anything new in architecture, "or any art for that matter". At Finella he first met the architects Serge Chermayeff and Wells Coates; the "beautiful Charlotte Perriand from Corb's office"; John and Paul Nash the painters; Jacob Epstein the sculptor, of whom it was written: "The world does not forgive talent"; Henry Moore the sculptor; James Wood and Trystan Edwards. Others, good friends of Manny Forbes, were Lance and Natalie Sieveking, "an epic couple", as Manny called them. Sieveking then was at Savoy Hill in charge of drama production at the B.B.C., and was as a result of his visit to Finella to play a major part in the next stage of Raymond's career.

Another visitor was Eric Gill, the typographer and sculptor, whose training was in architecture. Finella made a strong impression on Gill, for whom, "of all the new architecture of the period this building was the ultimate in rationality: a modern glass house". This at least is how Fiona McCarthy[28] interpreted Gill's attitude. "Eric Gill visits Finella!", she exclaims. "It seems such a contradiction, the negation of so much that he believed in. And yet should one be surprised? He was after all one of the oldest of the rationalists..." There is a parallel between this internal argument of Gill's and Raymond's own ambivalence. He was coming round to the modernist point of view: yet there is a sense in which Finella could be seen as his final shuffling off of the art déco style. Manny's perception of Gill was typically responsive:

> He dresses in a long alpaca gown and looks exactly like a Tibetan priest. But he is so natural and whimsical despite the togs. Our ideas of glass sculpture, i.e. tombs of warriors, with themselves laid out on top, excited him quite a lot.

Peter Bicknell, who first visited Finella in 1936, lived there from 1940 to 1980. To be accurate, he lived in half of it, the half that contains the dining-room and the divided drawing-room, North Pink and South Pink. (North Pink is pinker because it gets less light). Bicknell, who was at Jesus College, is an architect and teacher who later became a fellow of Downing. He recalls that Anthony Blunt was a frequent caller at Finella, and I.A. Richards was one of a succession of recipients of Manny's hospitality. Bicknell regarded Manny as "a kind of impresario" and remembers Raymond's visit in the 1970s when Raymond's reaction was: "How nice to see Finella still being enjoyed: Manny would have been pleased to see the garden full of children."

Paul Mellon remembers Finella as a charming concoction of the Victorian and the '20s modern, whereas Alistair Cooke, then on the staff of *The Granta*, had "only one or two furtive glimpses from the outside". Paul Mellon and his father Andrew took part in a unique ceremony at Cambridge when Henry Thirkill, the Master of Clare, arranged that on the day Paul was conferred, Andrew was awarded an honorary degree.

Julian Trevelyan, a constant visitor, says that "many things that have

Facing page:
Finella before Raymond set to work (above), and after completion

91

become commonplace now, I saw for the first time there: tables of glass, lights that switched on by pressing a button, mirrors built into walls…" In his autobiography,[29] Trevelyan speaks of Manny as "the strange little don of Clare in whose home, Finella, could be found ten years too soon all the architectural clichés of the late thirties".

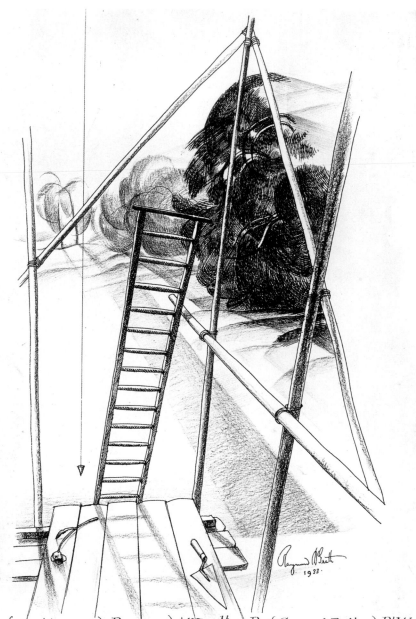

Christmas card, 1933

from Mary and Raymond M'Grath 10 Park Crescent Portland Pl.W1

CHAPTER XIV

inella was a continuing success. One of its attractions for those interested in modern architecture may have been the sheer sunburstry of its delight in new materials. It was far from the functionalism of Adolf Loos, the Moravian architect (1870–1933) who eschewed decorative features or curves, and rabidly preached a total absence of adornment. His article on 'Ornament and Crime' (1908) was hugely influential, yet even he did not practise what he preached.

Raymond's name is irrevocably linked with the modern movement in the 1930s. The term International Modern was, Pevsner[30] tells us, coined in America to refer to the new architectural style of the 20th century, as created before the first World War by such architects as Frank Lloyd Wright, Tony Garnier, Adolf Loos, Josef Hoffmann and Walter Gropius. It was characterised by "asymmetrical composition, unrelievedly cubic general shapes, an absence of mouldings, large windows often in horizontal bands, and a predilection for white rendering". It endured, as we all know, well into the second half of this century (Pevsner shows International Modern houses in Tashkent in 1957).

Raymond resolved what clearly was a dilemma for him by claiming that there were in fact two kinds of architecture. In an article on 'Light Opera' about the reconstruction of the Savoy Theatre, he wrote in the *Architectural Review* (January 1930): "On the one hand there is architecture that is made to last; this architecture is simple and monumental in form and made of permanent material. On the other hand there is architecture which is not made to last; this architecture is decorated and built to be renewed." He makes a plea for "fresh, vital, contemporary decoration everywhere", in today's materials such as stainless steel and neon lighting.

Black glass became a favoured material. Raymond used it at Finella and extensively at the B.B.C. In the lengthy interview he gave Brian Hanson[31] a few months before he died, he declared that Mies van der Rohe was a big influence on him. "I saw his Barcelona Pavilion by accident when I went to Spain. That was the first Mies building I ever saw and it impressed me. I thought his use of black glass was so good, and that influenced me afterwards."

Mies used a wall of polished black glass to reflect the pool, the statue and the foliage of the garden in the German Pavilion for the Barcelona Exhibition of 1929, two years after Raymond's visit to Spain. In his 1927 diary, Raymond ends his day at the bullfight at Barcelona with: "We set off for Montjuic to get the horrible business out of our minds. At

Finella under construction: the plumbline and the rose are missing

Montjuic are the buildings in progress of erection for the Exposition next year [*sic*]. Some excellent work has been done. The lay out and situation is excellent."

There is no mention of Mies here and it is unlikely that such an elaborate pavilion could have reached the stage of installing the black glass wall by then. So one must assume that Raymond's memory played him false in 1977 and that his admiration for Mies was acquired through the continental magazines he constantly studied in his Cambridge years. Ludwig Mies van der Rohe (1886–1969) first displayed his true greatness as an architect in the Barcelona Pavilion, in which, as well as black glass, he used marble, travertine, onyx, polished steel and bottle-green glass in an open plan design. It was one of the high points of the short-lived Weimar Republic. Here too appeared Mies's famous 'Barcelona chair' of leather and stainless steel. It soon became a hallmark of avant-garde interiors in Europe and North America.

Raymond's design for Finella went beyond the physical reshaping of a Victorian house. It was he who "discovered" M.O. Dell and H.L. Wainwright, who went on to become the official photographers to the *Architectural Review*. He found their work at a Royal Photographic Society exhibition and invited them to photograph Finella.

"There weren't all that many obvious people around" in the late '20s, and he needed someone to do work as innovative in their field as he was doing in his. Dell and Wainwright were very conventional photographers until Raymond and Manny Forbes tempted them to become adventurous, suggesting that they "crawl all over the place", look down, look up and make new uses for lighting. They proved willing pupils, "ready to lie on the floor or to climb up a ladder to get a comprehensive view of a space which you normally don't get in a photograph. I was concerned that they should get points of view which gave the quality of the space. And Manny Forbes was always ready with the ladders and things", Raymond told Brian Hanson. In October 1929, Manny wrote to Raymond in a letter from "c/o The Dowager Lady Forbes, Brux Lodge, Forbes-Alford, Aberdeenshire": "The photos, somehow, seem to *clinch* your wondrous achievement, my dear youth…"

At the time he "roped them in for Finella", Raymond was more excited about his find than he would be when he recalled them in 1977. In a letter to his newly acquired fiancée, then in Dallas, he wrote:

> They really are gems. They took prodigious pains with those photographs. They were mightily enthusiastic. All day they pursued shadows over the floors and furniture, all night they made moons rise and created other elusive phenomena with the arc lamps. They competed in style with my lighting effects. It was better than 'Pyramus and Thisbe'… I now yearn for the results.

The results were pictures of such a high standard that they not only served to start Dell and Wainwright on a completely new tack but were very largely the reason why Finella achieved such widespread publicity.

A Dell and Wainwright view of the hall at Finella

Among the many commissions the photographers got as a result, apart from the continuous work they did for the *Architectural Review*, was their appointment as official photographers for Raymond's well-known textbook on 'Glass in Architecture and Decoration' (1937). Regrettably, when Wainwright died in 1976, his widow threw all his negatives away.

Perhaps the warmest, certainly the most informative words on Finella were written by a person with no architectural training. Albert Frost, Raymond's friend and Manny's protégé, summed up his regal discovery in the *Architectural Review* (December 1929):

> Finella, unlike the most of Scottish royalty, has come into her own again. A clean modernity of pure line and plane and clear tones of colour is the sole key of her architecture; light and the overlooked beauty of metal and glass make up the rest. Yet her architect, in an easy stylisation and accord, moves inside the lucid definition of this logic with a self-possessed certainty. Without either trespass into bareness and angularity or exploitation into preciousness, the formal and material possibilities fall into line with a masterly ordination and composed effect. Decoration is not applied: the decorative qualities of pure form and texture are allowed their full rights undeterred. The spacious intervals of rectangular surfaces remain in their unadorned clarity; detail is periodic and not parenthetic; fittings and the details of necessity are in their own candour and conciseness; all is proportionate as in a well-conducted orchestra, or rather as in a quartette where each is a master and none a virtuoso. Little more could be wished of a house.

Major Hubert Corlette, who had been helpful to Raymond from the time he arrived in England, had been working quietly on his behalf with the Board of Architects of New South Wales. Clearly aware that Raymond's Wentworth Travelling Fellowship would come to an end in July 1929, at the same time as his residence at Cambridge finished, Corlette arranged that the Australian Medallion and travelling scholarship for architecture should be awarded to the young expatriate. It was worth £400 a year.

"I was fairly taken off my feet by the news", Raymond told Professor Brereton. Major Corlette advised him to accept the Medallion from July 1929 so that he could "travel extensively and collect very valuable information for the completion of my thesis on Entertainment Architecture". The thesis was due to be presented in July 1930.

"I cabled my acceptance and received a cryptic reply: 'If we award Medallion, when does Fellowship cease?' This was an amazing query. I could not imagine what one had to do with the other and why I should be cabled about the Fellowship when they could consult the University at first hand mystified me. The idea has however grown in my mind that the [Wentworth] Fellowship may not be continued into the third year though of course I have had no warning or inkling of this. Still! Withholding half-

Finella's hallway as it is today.
Photograph by Norman McGrath

The entrance to Finella.
Photograph by Norman McGrath

yearly form until I should have definite knowledge of the third year, I overlooked sending it altogether and the non-arrival of the half-yearly cheque now makes me wonder what the situation is. I have just sent a week-end cable to Professor Holme and am hoping that all my plans can still be carried out as intended."

There was no real hitch. Raymond had amassed influential friends at both ends of the world and his money problem was satisfactorily solved — for the present, at any rate.

His last term of official residence at Cambridge was, he wrote to Brereton in June 1929, "drastically eventful, almost revolutionary". Finella took from February to June and there were innumerable hiccups. A strike in Sweden held up all the decorative glass. The six-foot glass dome which he spent a fortnight engraving with Pictavian designs was accidentally broken in half while it was being taken out of the workshop — "a terrible loss".

"Yesterday Mr. Rizzi, the Italian who is putting down the composition floors, finished the Pictavian snake which I designed for the hall floor. Yesterday afternoon I found it surrounded by an admiring group which consisted of Rizzi, two other Italians, and the local policeman." Amid marvellous and impossible rumours about the house, the stream of visitors was extraordinary. We know about Eric Gill; Raymond mentions also the economist John Maynard Keynes and the ballerina Lopokova (his wife), as well as "hosts of Swedes, some Danes and a great many Americans".

Among the Americans was Mary Catherine Crozier, soon to be Raymond's wife and lifetime companion.

Chapter XV

Into Professor Brereton's sympathetic ear Raymond poured his tale, which began in the summer of 1928. He was too busy working on the drawings for Finella to get away on a holiday.

"At this time of year Clare garden is very beautiful and we sometimes have lunch on the river bank. To one of those luncheons a New Zealander brought Miss Crozier of Texas. I shall remember the day because I fell in love with Miss Crozier.

"I had never encountered a girl before with such natural grace, such an absence of sophistication, such a joyous sense of humour."

Mary, as we shall have to learn to call her, had spent a year at the Sorbonne and was visiting Cambridge for the first time. She was just 19 and was accompanied by her father, Norman Robert Crozier, a former professor of Latin at Texas University and now Superintendent of Schools in Dallas.

On her way back to Paris, "Miss Texas" as Raymond and his friends called her, returned to Cambridge for a few days. She then wrote to him from the Quai de Javel with titbits about the Sorbonne and the personalities of Paris. When he went to see her there she was selling dolls at a charity bazaar. It was a visit quite unlike any other for him. Even Henning, "this respectable French lecturer", might have been observed dancing round the column in the Place Vendôme, under the influence of this American girl.

A tortured homosexual friend of Manny's, taking a cure for tuberculosis at Lake Wanaka in New Zealand, wrote to Manny that sex was still his cruel enemy and gave him hell "in the eternal conflict between my Wesleyan morals and conscience on the one hand and my epiphenomenal wantonness on the other". In a burst of envy that rendered him unable to write more, he cried out: "God, isn't McGrath lucky to win the admirable Miss Texas."

Mary came back to Cambridge with Raymond, audited Spanish and German lectures and acted in a dramatic society. Then her mother, suspecting that the call of Dallas was waning, cabled her home. The two became engaged before Mary sailed on the Cochambeau from Le Havre on 11 May, 1929.

"It is a poor business", lamented Raymond as he saw her off, "to put the Atlantic between oneself and one's love." After the last awful moment of bells and sirens and the terrifying noise of a great ship blowing off steam, he wrote:

Tho' down the Atlantic's path of foam, screw-curled,
Your hard steel ship throbs homeward with persistence…

Dr. Norman Robert Crozier

Mary McGrath – a studio portrait by Dorothy Wilding

And so on for three verses "Written between Dunkerque and Paris." It is a bad poem, made worse by the fact that it was the result of much reworking. A contemporary notebook demonstrates how much labour went into making changes in words and sometimes whole lines. Raymond was in love, but it did not prevent him from pursuing perfection. The pity is that the end product was a classic case of going from bad to verse.

From 2 o'clock that afternoon, when the ship sailed, until the sun went down, he sat drinking coffee in a café. Then he went to see Jean Stempowski, a cotton merchant of Le Havre who did business with the Southern United States. Jean had met Mary in Dallas when he was having an affair with her French teacher, and he remained a lifelong friend to them and to the next generation until he died in 1990. Raymond found him a most lovable person — and he was — but Jean never could relate well to the quiet genius that was Raymond. To Mary, Jean was "the most consistently thoughtful person I nearly ever knew". Jean was a mischievous bon viveur who had spent some time at a minor English public school. He became and remained the compleat Anglophile.

Jean Stempowski

As a "homegoing" gift to Mary Catherine, Raymond had roped in his friends to contribute to one of his manuscript books. He himself included 'Seine Song' ("The Seine ran under its bridges/Like laughter out of my lips"); 'Magician', set to music by an unknown hand; the original version of 'Though down the Atlantic' and a few other verses, none memorable. What *was* memorable were his illustrations of bridges over the Seine and 'The Window over Parker's Piece' (an open space off Regent Street in Cambridge). John Cawte Beaglehole wrote a warm letter of farewell. "Mrs. G." [Mrs. Henry Godwin?] offered a version of 'Pussy-cat' that went: "Mary Cat, Mary Cat, Where have you been?", and "Kristof" Millett did a humorous mock-German illustrated verse.

Albert Frost's untitled poem came nearest to sincerity. It ended:

Then Mary, if you pity me
In rarity and courtesy,
Come ere the winter in a rage
Brings back a second glacial age,
With the glazed air in crystal spars
Precipitated into stars,
Horizons vanished and skies all
Grown vitreous and vertical,
And even your Frost is frozen twice
In dazzling and refractive ice

Mary Catherine Crozier was undoubtedly attractive. She had a lithe grace, a bold handsome face and a figure that suggested the outdoors, Texas and the tennis court. She was good-humoured as well as humorous; intelligent as well as active. It was above all her vivacity that drew people to her and made her the perfect counterpart to Raymond. He was retiring to a fault and too quiet-spoken to make much of a ripple in the conversational pond. In a letter from Finella to 3408 Cole Avenue, Dallas,

101

Norman Robert Crozier junior with his mother, Heart

Aunt Collie Gardner

he tells Mary that a marriage with Pisces is what she needs. (Her sign was Cancer.)

The Croziers and the Gardners (Mary's mother was a Gardner from Missouri) were of good White Anglo-Saxon Protestant stock. Secessionists in the Civil War, one of them was drawn to write 'The Confederate Spy'. R.H. Crozier's novel was set in his own background as a captain in Company 1 of the 33rd Regiment of Mississippi Volunteers. Published in Louisville in 1866, it was into a fifth edition by 1885, and was meant, according to his preface, as an antidote to "the poisonous northern literature which has for many years flooded the South". By the fourth edition, he had been ordained a minister of the gospel and entertained doubts about the propriety of the "profane expressions" used by some of his characters, such as "G-d d—n". He easily persuaded himself that fidelity to the original text and the dark times in which it was written should prevail.

Mary's Aunt Collie (properly Catherine) was a much-loved teacher in Troy, Alabama. She had travelled in Europe in 1900, landing first at Queenstown (Cobh), taking a hotel in Cork and seeing the Lakes of Killarney before visiting Dublin. She was a Daughter of the American Revolution and like her sister Addie Belle (Mrs. J. Hill Guy, who had first married the railroad magnate who gave his name to the town of Opp, Alabama) was a constant support to Mary throughout her long life. (Collie was 105 when she died in 1975.) Mary's mother, Anne Stark Gardner, known to the McGraths as Heart, had three children: Norman Robert junior, who became a lawyer, Isabelle who died at 19 in a particularly horrible motor-car accident at Austin, Texas in 1926; and Mary, who seemed to feel that she did not measure up in her mother's eyes as a replacement for Isabelle. Their relationship was always difficult, not least because Heart could never let go of the parental reins.

It was not surprising then that Heart insisted on Mary's return. Using the excuse that Mary must make her début in Dallas, she worked hard to break off Mary's engagement and only slowly was won over to approval. "Heart", wrote Mary to Raymond, "could have been happy with so many daughters; what a crying shame she had to hit on me! Daddy is just the same sweet man, my familial Rock of Gibraltar...". The engagement of his sister to "a damned Yankee" (the worst insult a Southern gentleman could offer to a man of different background) did not at first endear Raymond to Norman Robert junior.

> Our little affair was a great shock to Heart at first and she was tooth and nail against it. But, Honey, it's surprising what I have accomplished. Now she thinks you're the world's finest. She adores your picture and she gobbles up every word you write... She is proud unto death of my little book.

Professor John Le Gay Brereton
(The Mitchell Library, State Library of New South Wales)

'The Window over Parker's Piece', 1929

Albert Frost (left) with Manny Forbes

But by the next letter, Heart had become "so changeable". There were times — mail days — when she was all in favour of the marriage, when she thought Raymond a wonderful man, "very like Daddy in lots of ways", and she expressed doubt as to whether Mary was worthy of Raymond.

The other times come inevitably. Then she wants her daughter to be "normal", make her début, go over big, fall in love with some wealthy Dallas boy in the set (ahah), have a pretty wedding with a preamble of parties and handsome presents, and then settle down in a cute little home all set for a dinner-party existence for the rest of her life. Her husband will be a golf fiend and love dancing. His friends will be other golf fiends and members of the Idlewild Club. Her friends will be girls she grew up with, also débutantes. All their children will grow up and be in their turns, Idlewilds and Débutantes. Can't you see where we are going to be a disappointment to Mother?…

At luncheons and teas Mary felt stupidly dumb. Her head was full of England: the Dallas women were not interested. And she did not want to be thought "swank".

Telling Brereton all this news, Raymond is thankful for the opportunities and yet "travel besets one's path with a multitude of complications… Morally I want to get back to Sydney soon, yet how hard it is in so many ways, and most of all financially."

John Le Gay Brereton, who died in 1933, received no more letters from Raymond, who had opened his heart to a man of 58. It is some measure of the professor's worth that a former student 32 years his junior could feel so confident of his trust and understanding. We do not possess many of Brereton's replies to Raymond, who in Mary had found another confidante. They are pleasant and chatty enough, but not revealing.

The news from Cambridge was mixed. Raymond went to see "my stupid supervisor", Theodore Fyfe, about his thesis. He did not say, but he was not working on entertainment architecture and the college, which had been very pleased with the arrangement of the thesis, was beginning to get cross with him. It was much more agreeable to go down to London for dinner with Maurice Lambert, not yet his partner on the Anzac memorial scheme but becoming a good friend.

Manny Forbes was marking the final examination papers. For Mary's sake, Raymond picked out three people that he knew would interest her — Tim White, Elsie Phare and Albert Frost. Albert had a first but had not done enough work for it to be a "good" first. Elsie Phare had done the outstanding paper. Manny could not praise it enough and intended to recommend her for a first with distinction and for a fellowship at Newnham. T.H. White's paper tickled Manny quite a lot. It was full of the sort of innuendos and witticisms which invariably appealed to Manny who said White seemed to have done an enormous amount of reading.

T.H. WHITE

If Tim White sounds like just another name to be dropped in the chronicle of Raymond, it would be understandable. But for two reasons, White made an enormous impact on Raymond. When White's biographer, Sylvia Townsend Warner, published her perceptive book in 1968, Raymond wrote to her to "correct a few errors". He told her that at Cambridge "I was absurdly jealous of his charm and good looks because he invited a young American girl to tea in his rooms and inscribed a copy of 'Loved Helen' to her. She subsequently became my wife."

The more important friendship began when White, who had gone to live in Ireland to escape the war in 1939, went from Belmullet, Co. Mayo, to live for five years at Doolistown, Trim, Co. Meath. The first volume of his Arthurian tetralogy, 'The Sword in the Stone', had been an instant success. His Irish years were highly productive in terms of books (and poetry, though he told Seán Glynn: "You know Seán, I'll never make it as a poet. I know all about poetry, its history, its techniques, its forms. But your man Yeats had more poetry in his little finger than I have in my whole body").

'Mistress Masham's Repose' (1946) made him relatively rich, and for this delightful book Raymond, by then married with two children and living in Dublin, prompted by his son Norman, was to design the map that forms the end-papers. White's wealth increased enormously when Lerner and Loewe based their musical 'Camelot' on White's Arthurian cycle, all four books of which were published in 1958 as 'The Once and Future King'.

But all this is more of Manny's "cover-the-groundism". The real Terence Hanbury White was tall, bearded, deeply self-aware, complex, unhappy much of the time, eventually alcoholic and avowedly homosexual. Raymond's view of him as a man of "tremendous imagination and humour which enlivened every encounter with him" is

Norman McGrath with his kestrel

only half the story. Townsend Warner, Sven Eric Molin, Seán Glynn and others have filled in the rest.

"When he came to Dublin he sometimes stayed with us and on one occasion he gave my son a kestrel, made a hood and jesses for it and taught him the elements of falconry", Raymond wrote. White believed what Merlyn said in 'The Sword and the Stone': "The best thing for being sad is to learn something". At Stowe, where he taught until 1936, White took to falconry and became an indefatigable salmon fisher and shooter of wild geese. Walter Allen, the English critic, says: "He did not hide it from himself — he killed these creatures because he loved them."

His fantastic paintings, which Raymond encouraged him to show at the Living Art exhibition in Dublin, were rejected. "In those days glass eyes and tinsel were not acceptable", Raymond noted. White had been tentative about showing — "I don't want to make myself ridiculous" — but had paid Victor Waddington 18 guineas for three frames. At this time too, he flirted with Roman Catholicism, giving Raymond's daughter Jenny a shiny little box containing a rosary beads. His two red setters, she recalls, were called Killie and Slop Slop. When Brownie, his previous bitch, died, he sat up with the corpse for two days and then went by bus to Dublin, where he kept himself as drunk as possible for nine days. His favourite drinking places were O'Mara's on Aston's Quay and the United Arts Club which, curiously, has no memories of him. He liked to eat out at Jammet's and the Dolphin.

When he left Ireland for Richmond in Yorkshire, he wrote the McGrath family a long letter in which he said he and his dogs were "very, very happy". Mary, he thought, would be sorry to hear that he had "a glorious but dumb cock-teaser to wash my floors for two Saturdays — aged 17 — but because I did not lead her to the double bed she got fed up and left".

He also got himself engaged. He was 40: she was 21 "and we are very clumsy about sleeping together". She called it off. "You can imagine how humiliating it is to be turned down by a demirep scarcely out of her 'teens, but there it is. I suppose it's a judgement."

There is a curious inconsistency in Raymond's correspondence with Sylvia Townsend Warner. She replied to Raymond's slightly critical letter ("I was a little sad about the emphasis on White's alcoholism and homosexuality") by saying: "It was on White's own witness that I included the drinking and homosexuality. He made little of them to others but did not blink them, nor his underlying melancholy, to himself."

In the same letter she wrote: "I wish that my letter to you, in late '64 or '65, asking if I could see [White's letters] had reached you. But obviously it did not, for I am sure you would not have left it unanswered." But the letter *did* reach Raymond. It was written on 20 February, 1965 and asked if she could read the letters, especially those about 'Mistress Masham's Repose'; and if she could have Raymond's memories of the Cambridge years. Lamely, Raymond claimed to have given copies of Tim's letters to Sven Eric Molin, "who may have sent them to you". (Molin was an American student who had got a grant to research White's

Facing page:
Raymond McGrath's photograph
of Tim White

*Trim Castle, Co. Meath. This is a
miniature painted by McGrath in
a book of miniatures of the works he
painted in 1944 and 1945.
He was on a visit to Tim White.
The original hangs in the Irish
Embassy in London*

life. He wrote a long article in *The Irish Times* (14 May, 1965) about
'White in Ireland').

Why did Raymond fail to respond to such an explicit and urgent plea?
Why, not to put a tooth in it, did he lie to Sylvia Townsend Warner? His
daughter believes that his innate prudishness prevailed over his instinct to
help; that he did not want his warm memories of Tim White tainted by
some of the phrases in his letters — "You don't know what muddle I am
in with work and dogs and drink…"; "My God, what couldn't I do to a
bottle of Irish!"; "a glorious but dumb cock-teaser"; "I think I did write to
Mary about my new (supposed) son… I have never seen him"; "I feel I
owe you a letter unless I wrote you one last week when too drunk to notice
it". Perhaps even: "Norman exhausts me as I do you" and "To a recluse
like me it is too hard work answering questions for five days on every
available subject including the copulation of bulls…"

From the Channel Island of Alderney — "about 900% nicer than Éire"
— Tim wrote to Raymond in 1948: "Are you, Raymond, willing to
illustrate my whole King Arthur anthology (approx. 250,000 words) with
at least twenty mediaeval pictures?" Raymond heard no more, but the
brooding photograph of White which Raymond took at Trim in 1945 had
pleased White and was used in publicity and in some of the many
obituaries that appeared in 1964. He was 57 when he was found dead in
his cabin during a Mediterranean cruise.

The verse from his diary for 1938 says much, but Raymond is testimony
to the fact that Tim White numbered some hours that were shining:

> Of hapless father hapless son
> My birth was brutally begun
> And all my childhood o'er the pram
> The father and the maniac dam
> Struggled and learned to pierce the knife
> Into each other's bitter life.
> Thus bred without security
> What dared I love, whom did not flee?

CHAPTER XVI

From afar, Raymond's family welcomed Mary into the McGrath fold. Eileen wrote to Professor Brereton: "I am sure she is just the girl to make Ray happy. She is so gay and spirited and I think she is very beautiful." And Raymond's mother Edith wrote to her son: "I love the little extracts from Mary's letters. She writes beautifully. You should both be very happy together… Be happy."

The view from Clare College was different. Chris Millett said in 1983 "Albert and I didn't approve of Raymond's involvement and the accompanying moon-lyrics: we thought that he was being ill-matched and heading for trouble and that it was affecting his concentration, and we did our best to divert him into safer waters, but we were farting into the wind…" At the time Chris, according to Raymond, "painted a grave picture of lost liberties and tried to give me the impression that I was going to gaol… I begin to think he knows damn all — he is too selfish and egocentric to think of anything more than the curbing of his own whims" (sic).

Raymond told Mary that he definitely did not want to marry in Dallas. It would not work. She was not made for Dallas with its elaborate débutante balls and dinners.

"Why", he suggests, "why not be presented at Court instead? You might as well do the thing while you are about it. I'm not joking. Tell Heart I want you to be presented at Court next year (you know our King George?). Mhari Parry, Manny's sister, could, and would, present you. The great thing is to so make your court dress that it can be converted into a wedding dress… Mhari did that.

"The Daily Times Herald can then have a full-page picture and the remark: 'Miss Mary Catherine Crozier… who returned to England recently after her stay in Dallas, has been presented at King George V's court at Buckingham Palace. She is shortly to wed a celebrated young Australian architect and it is thought that, if financially prepared, the romantic couple will tour in Sweden and other remote places.' "

That was the end of Raymond's grandiose notion (Manny said that Mhari was too hard up: try the U.S. Ambassador). Raymond next wrote to confess: "I tried to write to your Daddy and worked myself into a thunderstorm when I got to the financial part… things aren't half as bad as I thought that way. I may have about £500 in hand next Spring, enough to take us to Sweden and California [where he had been asked to design a house for his Los Angeles friend George Yeats] with a bit over, without banking on your allowance…"

His mind was shooting off in all directions. He would accompany

John Beaglehole on the Osterley as far as Egypt, then head for Hungary and Germany. He would go to Sydney for a month. He would fly off to Sweden while Mary went to Japan.

His friend Walter Duncan ("Brother Dunkie") pulled him up short: "The ruthlessness with which you slaughter your own brilliant schemes seems indicative to me of an extraordinarily interesting blend of sadism and masochism."

Manny and Raymond dropped in to Waring and Gillow's the furniture company for a chat with Madame Roni. Waring and Gillow's, like Shoolbred's, had had a few exhibitions which introduced English designers "to a version of art déco" — to use Martin Battersby's[32] words — "diluted with the modernism which was already superseding it on the Continent".

Madame Roni fascinated Manny — "and yours truly". She was Russian — a sister of Serge Chermayeff, who had married into the firm in 1928 and was by 1929 director of the Modern Art Studio. "Lord Waring's belief in the new movement should have important reactions on the furnishing industries in the future" was the unrealised hope of the business, which displayed extravagantly figured veneers not typical of the latest Paris trends. Chermayeff, as we shall see, developed separately into a card-carrying member of the modern movement.

Raymond imagined that Mme. Roni came of some grand pre-Revolution family, and he was nearly right. Serge Chermayeff, an old Harrovian, was a Caucasian jew from Groznyy, whose name was Sergius Ivan Sergeyeff Issakovitch until in 1924 he changed it to Serge Chermayeff, which he thought sounded more acceptably Russian. The family were horse breeders who found oil under their land and by 1900 were very rich. When the revolution came in 1917 they lost everything. Serge, who was then at Harrow, had won a place at Trinity College, Cambridge, but could not take it up because of the drastically changed circumstances.

He is still proud of the title 'The Three Musketeers', which Hubert de Cronin Hastings of the *Architectural Review* bestowed on him, Wells Coates and Raymond McGrath when they were working on the B.B.C. studios. He is as old as the century and quite full still of fond memories of Raymond as a writer, an artist and a designer. He and his wife Barbara, born Maitland May, recall how kind Mary and Raymond were to Serge's aunt Judith Issakovitch. But that is for later on.

Raymond had once admired a necklace that Mme. Roni wore. It had been made in Paris by a friend. She promised to get one for him, and she did. "It seems to me a lovely snakey thing, distinctly in the Finellesque tradition", he told Mary as he sent it to her.

Albert, commissioned by Raymond to submit material to *Lady Clare*, wrote to Mary that his muse would not "write to order". Raymond told him that this was "self-indulgent piffle!" The effect was instantaneous. Albert's "kind heart melted in a moment" and he replied: "I obey. I have started three poems, an essay and a novel… Some time when you have leisure write me on both sides of the sheet in a fine forgiveness of your

"Faithful delinquent

"Albert"

In the long summer of 1929, Lady Stonehaven interested herself in a request from Mansfield Forbes for a transfer to London for Raymond's father. J.M. Bruce was then Prime Minister of Australia and he wrote to Lady Stonehaven to tell her that he had discovered that Raymond's father was manager of the Mental Hospital at Rydalmere, New South Wales, "a State hospital under the jurisdiction of the N.S.W. Government". The Commonwealth Government had no control over Rydalmere or its staff. "In the circumstances I am afraid there is nothing I can do in the matter... but it is possible that the State Government may be able to do something in the direction of transferring him to the Agent-General's Office in London."

Lady Stonehaven, a friend of Manny Forbes and wife of the (unpaid) manager of the Tory Party, pushed the bold endeavour farther and we find the Acting Premier of New South Wales, E.A. Buttershaw, writing to H.E. Sir Dudley de Chair, the Governor of the State, giving two cogent arguments against such a plan.

The first was that Herbert Edgar McGrath had a salary and allowances of £600 per annum. "Only the Secretary in the Agent-General's Office has more than that".

Secondly, the Premier had been thinking of abolishing the Agent-General's Office and having the work done by the High Commissioner's Office.

Writing to Manny from Admiralty House, Sydney, Lady Stonehaven, a daughter of the Countess of Kintore,said she had left no stone unturned but nothing could be done. "It does seem a *thousand* pities that Raymond should have to leave England and I sincerely hope something will turn up to help him remain on at Cambridge." Three years earlier, she had given the departing scholar a letter of introduction to her mother — "I would like you to make his acquaintance", she wrote to Lady Kintore.

The plot thickens. Alfred C. Bossom, M.P., a well-to-do architect friend of both Manny and Raymond, wrote to Manny at the end of July after his visit to Finella:

> I can truthfully say that I have not had such a stimulating experience for quite a long time... I would certainly like to see McGrath have the opportunity of doing a lot more work now that he seems to have found himself...

A week later he wrote again from 5 Carlton Gardens: "Do you know Sir Granville Ryrie, the Australian High Commissioner? It might not do any harm to get in touch with him regarding McGrath's activities?"

And Christian Barman sent a long missive to Manny offering the help of the *Architects' Journal* and the *Architectural Review* under de Cronin Hastings in publicising Finella "complete down to the Orrefors light fittings".

> The more I reflect on Finella, the more I realise what an important achievement McGrath has been enabled — with your

discerning and enthusiastic support — to produce... By getting down to the closest scrutiny of his materials and founding the whole of his scheme on the nature and properties of these materials McGrath has arrived at something which is entirely in accordance with Cambridge's reputation in the exact sciences, and which remains at the same time (or because of this?) quite a conspicuous work of art...

As regards McGrath's future, I agree with you that he could do his country enormous benefit by guiding his many young compatriots in England towards the same aesthetic enthusiasm you have made him embody so brilliantly. One of the most difficult problems we have to face today is surely that of nurturing what is left of the (to our minds) rather valuable Anglo-Saxon mentality in the greater dominions. McGrath will, I feel, be able to hand on to students and other visitors from overseas something which is entirely English, but which they at the same time can take back with them without having to subject it to an arduous process of assimilation before it can be put to some practical use.

Ho hum. But what are they trying to do for/with Raymond? His father is to join him? He is to get help from the Australian Government? He is to imbue his fellow Australian architects with his special Anglo-Saxon attitude towards aesthetics? If Raymond knows anything of these conspiracies he does not reveal them to Mary, or to his father, or to us.

Mary in the meanwhile was bridesmaid at her great friend Anne Craddock's wedding, made her début and, as soon as she decently could, made her exit from Dallas.

When she reached Le Havre, Raymond was there to greet her. Jenny, their daughter, recalls her mother's feelings:

> She looked at Raymond and said to herself: 'Oh God! Have I done the right thing? Who is this man?' It was the worst ten minutes of her life.

They were married on 20 June, 1930 at St. George's, Hanover Square, and flew by Imperial Airways to Paris. It was their first flight. Jean Stempowski had suggested Le Lavandou in the South of France as a honeymoon spot and there they went. Jean had a grand notion that he would like to build a hotel there and that Raymond would design it for him. The scheme remained a notion, but Le Lavandou surfaced again in 1933, when Serge Chermayeff was involved in a greater plan than Jean Stempowski's for Le Lavandou. The ambition of the group was to create an Académie Européenne Méditerranée, a Bauhaus-by-the-sea in which the directors would give a "modern" artistic education. H. Th. Wijdeveld, the Dutch architect who had worked also in England, France and Germany and founded *Wendingen*, the arts magazine, was the prime mover. He was to teach architecture with Serge Chermayeff's future partner Erich Mendelsohn; Amédée Ozenfant the painter and, with Corbusier, the

The honeymoon couple land at Le Bourget

Mary at Le Lavandou

inventor of Purism, would teach art; Paul Hindemith would be in charge of music; Chermayeff of interiors and Eric Gill[33] would lecture on typography.

Gill designed the brochure, which talks of the Mediterranean seaboard as "the historical cradle of and home of the principles of faith, law and order which are necessary for the evolution of a new classical unity". The hand of Gill is in the writing and he also did a splendid wood engraving showing Europe with Le Lavandou as its centre.

Serge Chermayeff says that Wijdeveld was an old friend, as was Eric Gill, whose well-known saying: "Beauty can take care of herself", Serge quotes freely.

The scheme got no further than the prospectus stage and although Raymond must have known of it (Chermayeff and he had shared an office for a couple of years after 1930), his papers make no reference to the place where he spent the first couple of weeks of his marriage.

Mary and he made their first home in Finella. It was a suitable beginning in what Mary called "this English idea of a heatwave… delighting our very souls".

Eric Gill's map of Europe showing Le Lavandou as its centre

'The Labyrinth' from the eponymous book of poems by James W. Mills, 1930

CHAPTER XVII

The summer of 1930 was both warm and eventful. While Mary sent off wedding announcements to what seemed the whole of Dallas society, Raymond worked on the illustrations for James W. Mills' 'The Labyrinth' [34] He produced half-a-dozen of his most successful wood engravings, elegant, delicate, and directly relevant to the subjects of the poems. On a limited edition Mills inscribed: "To Raymond McGrath from the Author":

Though I stand author of 'The Labyrinth'
Whose is the pedestal and whose the plinth?

Heart, who had represented the Croziers at the wedding, went home by way of Spain, preoccupied with the prospect of the next wedding. "Bro. Croz.", as Mary called her lawyer sibling, Norman Robert Crozier junior, had taken it into his head to marry Billie Smith and, Mary told her mother, "there is absolutely no use to dissuade him… I am glad to see he is so determined. Billie is a dear." Billie, properly Mildred Mayrant, had made her debut with Mary. She was the daughter of Frank M. Smith, mayor of Highland Park in the heart of Dallas.

To indicate how happy she herself was, Mary told her brother that she and Raymond daily asked themselves with bated breath: "How long will this last???" Bro. Croz.'s response was: "A new trick: to drink a full bottle of beer fully submerged in a pool." Even then, he was fond of a drink.

"It is a great pity that Manny is so hard up for money just now, for this house deserves nice furniture", Mary wrote to her father in September. She and Raymond successfully scavenged the place for extra furniture and although they now had two "quite nice" extra bedrooms, their "real" dining room still was furnished only with the small glass cocktail table. Harry and Mrs. Godwin (later knighted, he was Professor of Botany at Cambridge) had lived for some time in part of Finella by arrangement with Manny Forbes and their departure left spare furniture which Mary made use of.

G.M. Garcia was once a taxation adviser to the Australian Government and then throughout the 1930s managing director of Aspro Ltd. in England. A Cambridge friend of Manny's, Garcia became a patron of Raymond's and one of the first to give him a commission to design a new house, at Hampstead. Garcia thought to add to the "miraculous amount of publicity" that Finella in Mary's view had enjoyed. He had the hare-brained idea of bringing to Finella the famous Australian cricketer "who has been whipping the socks off the English — one Don Bradman".

"We are planning", Mary told her father, "to get him tight and make him sign his name a dozen times or so, and then sell them [the signatures] at a couple of pounds to some crazy cricket enthusiasts. We are also thinking of concealing several newspaper reporters out in the garden to photograph his every move, and sell them to all the sports papers and magazines, with à propos and praiseworthy remarks re Finella that Mr. Bradman would have made had he thought of it… It would be too bad if he never came after all this elaborate scheming." Bradman came all right, and some of the Australia XI, but only to enjoy Finella quietly.

Serge and Barbara Chermayeff went down to Finella with Manny and the New Zealand architect Amyas Connell. Waring and Gillow's was in terminal decline and Barbara was expecting a baby (who grew up to be Ivan Chermayeff the graphic designer). Manny decided the time had come to tell Serge "about our proposed Company". He meant, not the 20th Century Design Group which he and Raymond had been mulling over and which Manny christened "Modern Movement Ltd.", but a commercial exhibition company which had two backers. Chermayeff was greatly excited.

It was early in Mary's acquaintanceship with Serge and she told her father he was "a most entertaining and amiable person" with an excellent stock of stories that he put over well. Serge had just decorated "a very good modern theatre" (the Cambridge Theatre in London), and Manny had written about it most enthusiastically.

Amyas D. Connell of Connell, Ward and Lucas, went to England about 1924 and when he went down to Finella had just finished High and Over at Amersham, "the most modern house in Britain", for Professor Bernard Ashmole, who held the chair of Classical Archaeology at London University. "High and Over", Raymond wrote later,[35] "is no delicate statement. It is a thundering request for clear thought in all directions."

Mary was very taken with Professor Ashmole, whom "we had pictured as an ancient gent of the more broad-minded order who had generously wished to give a struggling young architect an opportunity to strut his stuff".

We discover, on the contrary, our professor is a young man of thirty-five, brilliant and altogether most unusual. The position he holds in view of his youth is proof of that. He is most distinguished looking. He has a magnificent high forehead and about the best profile I ever saw. He wears a romantic beard, black not blue, and a moustache as well. A deep scar on his cheek completes the picture. I have made him sound silly and posey, but he is not at all that type. He is most intelligent and alert. He and Raymond hit it off beautifully…

"Full of pep and cute as ever", two of Mary's American friends, Mary Elizabeth and Martha Godwyn, arrived mid-week. They had such a good time every minute of their stay that they took off their shoes and stockings and danced on the lawn in the greatest glee. "Everybody broke down and confessed all their secrets", Mary told her father. "I don't believe I have ever had a better time in my life." (This anecdote is revealing because twenty-five years later the McGraths' daughter Jenny was severely ticked off for taking off her shoes on the dance floor). Next morning, Raymond gave the guests personal limericks and sketches of themselves. His shipboard friend Walter Duncan, who had also been staying, was bidden farewell on his journey to Chicago, where he was taking up a three-year Commonwealth Fellowship.

Amid all this excitement, Raymond continued to work. He drew up the memorandum for a society of modern British design, which took shape as the Twentieth Century Group, with Raymond, Wells Coates, Serge Chermayeff, Denham Maclaren, Howard Robertson and Jack Pritchard as its first members. It met first at the Travellers' Club and subsequently at Finella while Raymond and Mary were living there. There of an evening one might meet Maxwell Fry, who in 1934 went into partnership with Walter Gropius; P. Morton Shand, the writer who combined oenology with architectural history, and de Cronin Hastings of the *Architectural Review*. They were a formidable group who but for Mansfield Forbes would have had nothing in common with Cambridge.

While Raymond and Mary lived there rent-free, could entertain as they wished, and enjoyed the services of Manny's dear darling faithful Leonard Strange and the maid, Rose, Manny expected his wishes about the house — his house — to be carried out. On 20 August, 1930, he wrote to Raymond: "Finally, *please* [underlined several times] have Dining Room Fountain once for all fitted up to fount, before Sunday, 24th." There is no mistaking the authority behind that request. Manny (who was staying at Champneys, Tring, Hertfordshire), was bringing important guests and everything must be just so.

Raymond McGrath in Nantes, early 1930s

In a letter to Dr. George Mackaness, Raymond gave a useful synopsis of his academic progress, the ostensible reason for his being at Cambridge in the first place:

> Of my Ph. D. thesis I can only say that I have been pursuing my subject (Modern Entertainment Architecture — Theatres, Cinemas etc.) at intervals, but have had a difference with my architectural supervisors about the methods of my research. My immediate supervisor has been Theodore Fyfe, Director of the Cambridge School of Architecture, a die-hard of the old school. I have completed my residence at Clare.

Raymond's difference with his supervisors was much more serious than he pretended to Mackaness. Theodore Fyfe sent his outline thesis to Mr. E. Bullough, M.A., of Gonville and Caius College in June 1929. To say that Bullough savaged McGrath's work is to understate the case. He did a demolition job. He began with page 2: "This is rubbish… the sort of silly aphorism [that] throws a bad light on the writer's mental background and preparation."

117

In four typed foolscap pages, he dissected the draft thesis of 61 pages with a scholarly scalpel. "Italian information is the weakest spot all through, although fundamental to the whole subject, as both the theatre and the opera originated there" is mild compared with: "The whole section is uninformed and useless." And: "There is a constant confusion between the 'theatre' as an art and the 'Theatre' as a building."

Bullough's rampage through Raymond's china shop was unrelenting. Fyfe thanked him fulsomely "for the care you have taken with it and the thoroughness of your criticisms". He thought the message was "that it is neither possible nor advisable that McGrath should attempt to write a history of the stage".

> I must now inform him, of course, that his final performance will have to undergo the rigid scrutiny of two referees before he can be awarded a doctorate.

Fyfe tried to draw the sting out of Bullough's attack by telling Raymond that Bullough's criticisms might have put the matter too strongly. "At any rate you are fortunate in being able to get into contact with a scholar in the University who makes a pet subject of theatrical history though he does not pretend to know about theatrical buildings." Raymond, Fyfe felt, should do some hard thinking.

Some months later: "Both Bullough and I feel that you are not a suitable candidate for the presentation of the kind of thesis that would be required..." Bullough was more constructive. Raymond should take the Diploma in Architecture and then make out a case to the Faculty Board for the recognition of his work done for Forbes as part of the qualification for the diploma. Thus his years at Cambridge would not be wasted.

By June 1930, matters were still up in the air. Fyfe wrote to Raymond at 2 Kensington Park Gardens, Ladbroke Square: "You will realise that the position is somewhat serious and that it is quite possible to fall between two stools." He should make out a timetable of work and then state his case to Fyfe. By November it "looks as if your practical results combined with your journalistic work would have to be your main, if not your only plank". Fyfe's impatience grew as pressure on him by the Board of Research Studies mounted. He suggested that Raymond should change his subject to modern decoration, about which he knew something. He should go ahead on his own responsibility "on the understanding that it is quite an open question whether the Board of Research Studies would grant you the Ph. D. degree on it or not".

As far as the correspondence and Raymond's inclination or capacity to apply himself to further study in the midst of a busy life went, there the matter rested.

Raymond had not entirely "forgotten the Muse", he informed Mackaness, though he derived more satisfaction from the pictorial arts, and architecture was "so near to realities". As well as the woodcuts for 'The Labyrinth', he has just completed an engraved wrapper for Peter Davies the publisher. The book is 'Highway into Spain' by Marcel

Aurousseau, "a Sydney man who went to Spain with a Texan!" Davies approached him without knowing that he was either Australian or interested in Spain. Davies who paid him £10 liked the wrapper Raymond did for James Jean's 'The Universe Around Us'. Aurousseau was so delighted that he wrote to Raymond: "Your design expresses something that really is in the book, refracted through you, of course, and I thank you for so sensitive an appreciation of it." He told Raymond that he had once been pointed out to Aurousseau in the street in Sydney as a person of whom much was expected; and he invited Raymond to dinner in Soho.

Raymond concluded his letter to Mackaness with a reference to his scheme for the Anzac Memorial. The adjudicators' cool response to the scheme clearly disappointed him, and ungenerously he did not add a congratulatory note to Bruce Dellit or Rayner Hoff.

Raymond was doing the drawings for his entry in the *Architectural Review's* competition for an imaginary Lord Benbow's apartment. The conditions were strict. Lord Benbow, the rules said, was a 60-year-old

Raymond McGrath's prize-winning design in the Architectural Review *competition for Lord Benbow's apartment, 1930*

119

Clydeside shipbuilder with sporting tendencies who needed bachelor quarters in London. The test was to decorate two connecting rooms ("like North and South Pink", Mary observed to her mother). The winner, who would get a generous £100, would have the added kudos of having his or her designs built and exhibited in Waring and Gillow's showrooms. Lord Benbow was discerning enough, so the winner had to keep in mind that his patron knew the work of Charles Rennie Mackintosh, the Scottish architect and exponent of art nouveau, and wished to develop Mackintosh's ideas in a more modern movement context. (Martin Battersby points out that it was unusual in 1930 to consider Mackintosh admirable, although Morton Shand was by this date involved in his rediscovery). Raymond ploughed on.

Mary in the meanwhile offered a glimpse of Manny's enterprise concept. She developed her typewriting skill to the point where she was replying to Mr. Bigge and Mr. Gordon-Dickson, "the men who are planning to float this modern architecture company, with Raymond as their architect at a salary of £1,000 a year". He would be free to do outside work. The "investors" hoped to get various firms interested on the basis that the company would feature their products. The plan was stillborn.

Manny wrote every few days that August, brimming over with ideas, instructions and requests. He suggested that "all of us inaugurators" should be members of *both* the Design and Industries Association and the Royal Society of Arts. Billy (Lord) Sempill or Arthur Bossom would second Raymond. The idea was to form a "spontaneous committee" in the D.I.A. and then appeal to the R.S.A. for help, "especially financial". He wanted his tennis racquet and balls sent to him along with a lot more socks, "all the white duck trousers I have" and one other thick (winter) vest with long sleeves. (Rose was to look after the clothes). Most important: "Please intimate to Barclay's Bank that you can and will transfer *as much as you can spare* from my account to yours [he means it the other way round] — and that it will be, if at all, for a few days only…" He is £6,000 overdrawn and wants to lend £100 to a "big Dane", Professor Brusendorff, who is temporarily embarrassed and going straightway to America.

"I hope", Manny wrote, "you have the *Daily Mail* money by now?" Earlier in the year, Raymond had won two of the principal sections in the *Daily Mail* and General Electric Company's competition in Modern Art and Electric Light. The decoration, furnishing and lighting of a bedroom and a dining-room had netted him 100 guineas each and the designs were to be reproduced in the G.E.C. Pavilion of Light at the *Daily Mail* Ideal Home Exhibition at Olympia, Kensington, in March 1931. An extended account of this, the first of Raymond's succession of exhibition victories, appeared in the *Sydney Morning Herald* (29 May, 1930), as well as in the English papers. One of the assessors was Grey Wornum, soon to design the R.I.B.A. headquarters at Portland Place.

Raymond and Mary's time at Finella was up. It was time to take on the megalopolis. On October 1st, they moved to 179 Hampstead Way, a little house complete with William Morris furniture — "strange surrounding for a supposed-modernist", Raymond observed to Dr. Mackaness. The house, owned by Mrs. Crump, was in what Mary told her father was "a nice section... a block or so away from Hampstead Heath", with a pretty garden separated from its neighbours by a sort of arbour effect. One could have a hot bath only at night, but the little maid, Edith, looked willing and nice and the house was far better than anything you could get for the price in London.

Maid trouble hit Mary early on. Far from being willing and nice, Edith "comes when I need her least, and vice-versa". When she told Mrs. Crump — "very last centuryish and highly respectable" — that she wanted the maid more for cooking than housekeeping, she was crushed by the reply: "*Most* people don't mind turning on the gas."

The McGrath family (Mary already enceinte) was installed at Hampstead when the *Architectural Review* competition results were announced. If that magazine and its enthusiastic editor de Cronin Hastings, had hoped by devising such imaginative conditions to discover new talent, the results must have disappointed them. Raymond, already well known, was in distinguished company. He won first prize with a scheme that included rugs by McKnight Kauffer whose partner, Marion Dorn, was also a carpet and rug designer of distinction; fabrics by Paul Nash the painter; paintings and wallpapers by Edward Bawden, four years away from his first one-man show; and sculpture by Maurice Lambert. Like the other winners, Raymond gave only a token nod to Lord Benbow's desires.

Paul Nash won second prize (£50). His furniture and fittings were by Denham Maclaren, a member of Manny's Twentieth Century Group; the paintings were by Edward Wadsworth, who showed in Unit One in 1933 with Nash, Ben Nicholson, Frances Hodgkins, Henry Moore and Barbara Hepworth. The textiles were by Paul Nash, whose reputation as a painter went back to before the Great War, in which he fought and was wounded. Lance Sieveking, who joined the Artists' Rifles with Paul Nash in 1914, has described Nash as "a small, neatly made, closely knit young man who held himself well".[36] He and Raymond had become closer friends by the middle of the 1930s which, in Battersby's words, "were born prematurely and disastrously on Thursday 24 October 1929, when the New York Stock Exchange closed its doors".

The *A.R.* competition was remarkable for more than the discipline of its regulations (none of which seems to have been obeyed by any of the winners): there is no record of the prizewinning designs' having been built or shown by the dying Waring and Gillow's. While it enhanced Raymond's name and enlarged his purse, the *Architectural Review* competition must have been accounted a failure for the man of whom John Betjeman said: "If anyone asks me who invented modern architecture, I answer 'Obscurity Hastings'."

Raymond's career, piloted though it was by Manny Forbes and crewed by the wide circle of influential friends that he had gathered around him, was nevertheless *his* career. Its best ally was his own glittering array of talents, ably assisted by his dedication to hard work. His disadvantages —

he was a colonial scholarship boy who had not had the benefit of public school education and all that entails by way of accent, access and the old boy network — were outweighed by his early achievements. As the catalogue of his successes expanded, the chances of his receding into the obscurity in which he was bred lessened, and his position in London society became secure. Because he never made real money, he could never be accused of being an arriviste and so largely avoided being the target of envy.

In a letter to her family, undated but certainly written in November, 1930, Mary told them:

> I have epic news to relate. It really is worthy of a cable, but it was so hard to explain in a mere 25 words that we gave it up and decided that it would only serve to arouse your curiosity and put you completely at the postman's mercy.

Raymond had been appointed Decoration Consultant to the British Broadcasting Corporation. It was, in Mary's words, his first Big Job.

CHAPTER XVIII

Broadcasting House was called "the greatest brain centre of the modern world" by the *Daily Express* in 1930. "Will it become the most potent educational factor since Caxton first introduced his printing press into England?", the paper pondered. "London may soon be called on to give programmes that will include every corner of the Empire."

The wireless was the message. The B.B.C. was only eight years old, crawling before it could walk. Under John C.W. Reith, the first general manager of the British Broadcasting Company, the service had been operating since 1922 from Savoy Hill, where only one studio could be used at a time. Reith was an engineer, a Scot, dour and high-principled. He set the B.B.C. into the mould which made it the world's greatest broadcasting service, setting standards to which the rest aspire still.

It seems strange to us now that instruction and education were placed by the print media of the day ahead of entertainment as the aims of broadcasting. What was not strange, but rather fitting, was that the new Broadcasting House should be built at the head of the principal street in London. 'The Palace of the Ether' was designed by Colonel G. Val Myer,

Broadcasting House

Perspective of the Vaudeville Studio of the BBC
(The British Architectural Library, RIBA, London)

123

an architect in private practice, in conjunction with Marmaduke Tudsbery Tudsbery, the Corporation's Civil Engineer. The site had previously been taken for a hotel development, for which Myer was the architect. When the development option was passed to the B.B.C., Myer remained as architect.

And, said *Country Life* in May 1932, "studios [were] under the general direction of Mr. Raymond McGrath, A.R.I.B.A." Only Germany had a purpose-built radio station, the Berlin Rundfunkhaus. The broadcasting of wireless programmes throughout the rest of the world, including the United States where radio, though commercial, became the great national unifier, was done from converted office buildings. (In Ireland, where Raymond McGrath was to submit a design for the first television station, opened in 1961, radio — by then the poor relation — did not get its own building until several years later).

The curved island site at Portland Place, which had been Foley House, presented its own problems. It was Crown property and not therefore subject to the supervision of the Department of Woods and Forests which curiously was the authority responsible for Regent Street as rebuilt. Val Myer and the B.B.C. nevertheless felt that the building should conform in general style to the character of its surroundings. Otherwise a functionalist approach might have been seen as appropriate to a building devoted largely to "delicate mechanical processes", in the phrase used by Christopher Hussey in *Country Life*. The limits set by the site in architectural and engineering terms need not engage our attention except to say that an ingenious solution to most of the problems was employed by creating a building within a building so that the shape emerged rather like a double U:

Thus Val Myer avoided any risk of sound transmission along the girders. Outside decoration was sparingly used. Eric Gill was given the responsibility of designing the sculpture, 'Prospero and Ariel', the best known of all his stone carvings. To do this complicated work, Gill worked on a scaffolding *in situ*, naughtily encouraging the rumour that he wore no underpants under his belted smock by shouting down to a passing friend: "It's all balls, you know!" Then there was what Gill's best biographer Fiona McCarthy calls "the scandal of Ariel's pudenda". After a viewing behind the tarpaulin, the governors of the B.B.C. asked Gill to make the organs smaller. He did: he always obliged in these matters, once the point had been made and the publicity gained.

Gill's model for Ariel was Leslie French the actor, who then was playing Ariel in the Old Vic production of 'The Tempest'. He modelled at Pigotts in the Chilterns, Gill's latest and last property. French remembers:

> At first I was rather embarrassed at standing about so long in the altogether. Mary [Mrs. Gill] used to come into the studio during the sittings bearing a tray with hot soup and since she was the perfect mother figure I was never for one moment embarrassed.

Facing page:
The B.B.C. before Eric Gill's
'Prospero and Ariel' sculpture
was erected

125

Lance Sieveking

As Mary McGrath tells it, Raymond's first Big Job came about in a mysterious way. It began with a "tantalising letter" from Lance Sieveking, who had visited Finella and was so impressed that he later brought down Commander Valentine Goldsmith, Assistant Controller of the B.B.C. Sieveking's letter said simply that there was "something in the wind which we were not to mention". Finella was "rigged out in its holiday best" for the visit of the big man, who with Lance Sieveking enjoyed a pleasant weekend. Sieveking gave the McGraths an outline of what was going on, but when the visitors had gone they had "ample time to forget the project".

They were living in Hampstead when they were told that Mr. Robert Solomon, a big financier, was going with his wife to visit Finella. The McGraths "flew by bus and train" to Cambridge, plundered Clare Gardens for flowers and by tea time when the guests arrived the house was looking as nice as it had ever looked. Manny was there, things went very cheerily and the Solomons, full of admiration for Finella, were persuaded to stay for dinner. No business was discussed, but the Secret Three could hardly breathe with excitement. When the guests departed, they all "fell into a heap and hoped in unison". Robert Solomon was head of the financial syndicate that was responsible for the erection of Broadcasting House.

More delay, hope again abandoned, then Sieveking asked Raymond for his total portfolio, architecture, art, writing and a list of people who would back or recommend him. "The list", says Mary, "was a snap and most impressive, grooggling with titles and all sorts of important [*sic*]." More silence, dinner with Sieveking, silence, then dinner with the Solomons "where we met the remainder of the big noises in a most pleasant and agreeable gathering".

Valentine Goldsmith telephoned the day after dinner and made an appointment with Raymond for the Monday. At this meeting, Raymond was informed that he had been appointed Decoration Consultant for the biggest and most important new building in England, and the largest radio station in the world.

The terms had been drawn up by M.T. Tudsbery and included the following:

2. THE DECORATION CONSULTANT

A gentleman shall be appointed by the B.B.C. on the recommendation of the Decoration Committee, who shall be responsible for instructing Decoration Specialists with regard to the preparation of their Schemes, and who shall cause the Schemes submitted to be amended in detail by those Specialists, as he thinks fit. He shall, throughout, act in close association with the B.B.C.'s Civil Engineer, and shall take instructions only through or from him.

The wording is bureaucratic but the intention is clear. Subject to Tudsbery's agreement, Raymond at 27 years old was to be given wide authority to nominate or approve his team and to supervise their work as well as reserving for himself those studios and offices that he wished to decorate. All fees were to be on a percentage of cost basis and budgets were to be set, approved and adhered to, with provision for exceptional items. It was as near to ideal as anybody could wish — at least in theory. (Val Goldsmith said in the *Architectural Review* (August 1932) that the decorators "were individually selected at a time when the Committee was unaware that they already formed a group working in close harmony".)

He was to get a fee of £500 for supervising all the work, with additional fees for any special work he did himself. (He submitted a design for the Council Room, strictly in Myer's remit. It was thrown out but he received £200 for his work.)

And it was all due to Lancelot de Giberne Sieveking, of whom Raymond wrote 40 years later:

> Lance was unforgettable — around 6 feet 4 inches, handsome, with a fine voice, resounding laugh and twinkling eye.

We do not possess a record of what Raymond thought of V.H. Goldsmith, but Sieveking did mention in a 1962 letter to Raymond: "Remember poor silly old Val Goldsmith!!!"

Sieveking himself, far from silly though not above a little snobbery, was

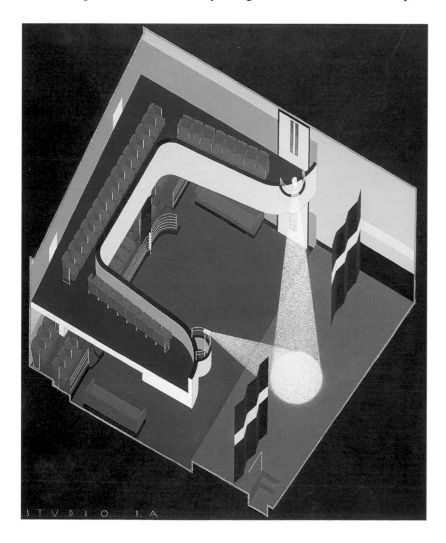

Design for the Vaudeville Studio
(The British Architectural Library, RIBA, London)

127

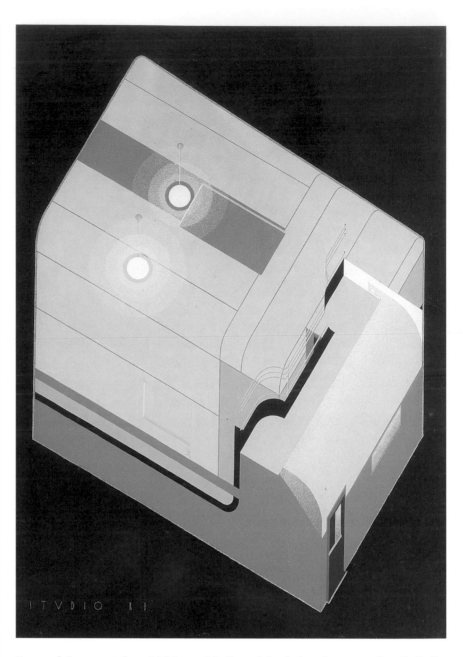

Design for the Dance and
Chamber Music Studio
(The British Architectural Library,
RIBA, London)

"one of the most formidable and influential of the pioneers of radio". So wrote *The Times* when he died in 1972 at the age of 75. "Soldier, sailor, airman — he fought in all three services during the First World War… He was also poet, author, playwright, producer and sometime composer… a rolling stone and jack of all trades." He joined the B.B.C. in 1924 as assistant to the Director of Education and stayed in broadcasting until 1950. He was, to quote *The Times* again, "one of the first broadcasters to understand and make use of the freedom of radio to create a world of its own…".

Raymond told Mary that if he had the choice of any job in England he would have taken the B.B.C. one. It made, she thought, his future career a matter of plain sailing. Sir John (later Lord) Reith, the Director-General, told Raymond that when his name was first brought up, he (Reith) wrote to Sir Giles Gilbert Scott about him and had got a most enthusiastic reply. "Scott had said as nice things about Raymond as anyone could say", Mary told her family, who must have heaved a sigh of relief that the "damned Yankee" had turned out all right in the end.

The confidence that the B.B.C. reposed in Raymond was not misplaced. Nor was the corporation's act of faith in modern architecture to let them down. Raymond made careful if unusual choices for his team. Led by Serge Chermayeff, then aged 29, the group was off to a good start. The other senior figure was the 34-year-old Wells Coates, a Tokyo-born Canadian who first met Raymond at Finella where he was introduced by Jack Pritchard.

Coates had an engineering degree and thought of himself as an architect engineer. He was completely at home in the technological atmosphere of the B.B.C. He had been taught and influenced by his tutor G.E.L. Gauntlett, "the most versatile teacher I have ever known".[37] His outlook, if not specifically modernist, was both practical and unconventional. He had worked and become friendly with Maxwell Fry in the middle 1920s. Because of his initials, he addressed office memos as "A", and he was always intensely aware of the difference between himself and a public-school Englishman in a way that Raymond never was.

Dorothy Warren, director of the Warren Galleries, was married to Philip Trotter. She was the third member of the team and designer of some of the Talks Studios. "She's not a bad designer", Raymond told his wife, "but she simply won't attend to the business side of it". Mary guessed that she was an old flame of Goldsmith's. (There were 22 studios in all. Myer designed the 750-seat concert hall. Chermayeff did the Orchestral and some Talks Studios; Wells Coates designed the Special Effects, News and Gramophone Studios — the more technical rooms).

For the Religious Studio, Raymond picked (later Sir) Edward Maufe, who was 46. The decoration of this small studio produced an ecumenical problem. The signs of the zodiac, tried in an early sketch, were ruled out; and the end product showed a ceiling full of stars, clouds, a sunburst and a suitably amorphous cross. The acoustics were so good that some presenters were believed to prefer the religion studio to the others.

Raymond arrogated to himself the decoration of the Dance Music and Chamber Music Studio and the Vaudeville Studio, thus demonstrating his thetic bias towards entertainment. (Performers in the Vaudeville Studio, which was laid out as a miniature theatre with stage, spotlights and audience, normally wore full evening dress).[38] He also had the right to be "brought in on" Myer's schemes for the entrance hall, the No. 1 Studio and the Council Room.

Decoration specialists were to get a fee of 10 per cent on schemes of £2,000 and over, increasing to 14 per cent for sums as low as £100. The fees covered structural alterations, wall fabrics, and all furniture etc. but an additional 10 percent was to be paid for furniture or fittings not of any standard pattern which had to be specially designed and constructed. Wells Coates, because the fittings in his group of studios entailed special mechanical design, was given a lump sum fee which worked out at 25 per cent. Similar special treatment was accorded to Raymond and the basement group of studios. The only objection came from Serge

129

Chermayeff, who thought the scale of fees too low. Since the Civil Engineer thought the payments too high, an agreed adjudicator was brought in and found in favour of the scale of fees agreed by Raymond with the Decoration Committee. It was an unsurprising decision given that the arbitrator was Raymond's friend Sir Giles Gilbert Scott.

One studio, 3A, was decorated by Randall A. Wells, a survivor from the pre-1914 Arts and Crafts movement. John Seely and Paul Pager, whose drawings were found to be unsuitable and whose responsibilities were handed to Wells Coates, were well known as domestic and church architects with influential connections.

A young group with a younger leader, Raymond's people set to work with a will. Reith did not like Broadcasting House as Myer designed it: there is no evidence that he disliked the interior. But there was potential trouble. Myer's building covered 100,000 square feet and had eight floors upstairs and three below. He claimed that 32 rooms were in his hands for decoration purposes according to his building contract. In an internal memorandum of 18 February, 1931,[39] Myer complained:

> It appears to me that that the Corporation now proposes to relieve me of a still further number of items which were intended to be in my hands. As you know, I have always done everything possible to meet the Corporation's wishes and in this case... I am not proposing to make any difficulty.

Myer did not push the matter further. But when Raymond, who was decorating the Director-General's office, suggested a detailed plan to improve the fenestration, Myer said[40] "this would be most detrimental to the external elevation of the building". He won that round. Reith supported Myer. "Would you [McGrath] like to alter your plans for furnishing accordingly?", asked the Director-General.

Goldsmith early on added the Green Room and dressing rooms to the responsibility of "whoever decorates the Vaudeville Studio". This, of course, was Raymond, who did very well indeed out of the B.B.C. job. He and Chermayeff set up shop at the Pantheon, 173 Oxford Street, and although they went their separate ways after the B.B.C. commission, they shared that office until Chermayeff went into partnership with Erich Mendelsohn in 1933.

The year 1931 saw Britain in a financial crisis. Though there was no talk of retrenchment at the B.B.C., the Depression made a direct impact on Raymond's work. The British Government became acutely aware of the amount of foreign goods coming in and ordered an immediate programme of import substitution. It was greatly to Raymond's credit that he encouraged British manufacturers to design and make materials and products that previously they had left to others, notably the Germans. But it was an added burden to him and to the Decoration Committee to which he was accountable.

The Controller of Programmes, C.D. Carpendale, got a three-page letter[41] from Val Goldsmith, Assistant Controller, and R.H. Eckersley,

Director of Programmes. Both were members of the Decoration Committee. Indeed Goldsmith was chairman.

Their letter was a protest in answer to accusations that the Decoration Committee had "wasted" £4,000 and that the ordering of foreign material appeared to have been uncontrolled by them and that the ordering of particular material through the firm Modern Interiors, "with which one of the decorators is connected", was nothing but 'nest feathering' between the decorators.

The committee also held that the decorators were not receiving full co-operation from the corporation "as, for example, is the Architect for Broadcasting House".

They began to use figures tellingly. The amount of foreign material specified in the schemes was about £820 out of a total of £17,000. The amount ordered through Modern Interiors was £150-odd. As for furniture, the figure was £300 out of over £3,000, that £300 having been spent with Modern Interiors.

> We shall be unable in any case to say that Broadcasting House is "ALL BRITISH"

they declared.

When the committee went on to say they were concerned "that the atmosphere of suspicion, distrust, inaccurate statements and untenable charges" fomented by recent events be dispelled, they invited a reply making the obvious point that they should adduce some particular illustrations of lack of co-operation.

This bickering must have disturbed Raymond, though it also taught him his first lesson in the politics of large organisations. A memo to Tudsbery[42] informed him: "Mr. McGrath has been told by Mr. Dailey [G.C. Dailey, secretary to the Decoration Committee] that he has no further responsibility for the Matron's Room." This was more niggling by the senior staff, but the level of interference was no more than would be found in any corporation and the public was unaware of it.

One of the substitutes for which Raymond himself was responsible was a wall-covering called 'Finella' which replaced trolit, a German product adopted by Walter Gropius. Raymond had it made by Arthur Sanderson and Sons who subsequently sold it on the open market. It may have been this product to which Dailey referred in an internal memo[43] to Raymond in December, 1932:

> Do you think you could find a similar paper of English manufacture? If not there would not appear to be a great deal of harm in making an exception in this case... It is not a case, for instance, where by virtue of our demands we could influence English makers to produce the materials we require.

As with Finella, the publicity given to the decorating of Broadcasting House, as well as to the building itself (they were opened as one), was

Serge Chermayeff

*Studio One at Broadcasting House,
Manchester, 1933*
(Courtesy of the Trustees of the V. & A.)

phenomenal. Even the B.B.C.'s own Year Book for 1933 said:

> A very important, very noticeable and very successful outcome of Mr. McGrath's direction is the standardisation of fittings throughout… [they have] the grace of true functionalism.

"It is no exaggeration to say", Raymond told Brian Hanson in 1977, "that the designs for the B.B.C. gave the first real fillip to industrial design in England, and Wells Coates, Chermayeff and myself were three of the first architects to work in that field in London."

F.R.S. Yorke (1906–1962) was, like Raymond, one of the pioneers in England of the International Modern style of the 1920s and 1930s. He wrote in the same year book:

> I feel the directors of the B.B.C. are to be congratulated for having had the courage to abandon the pursuit of the styles, for having employed Mr. McGrath as Decoration Consultant, and for having given him, within limits imposed by the structure, a free hand and the opportunity to produce an interior that is in harmony with the essentially modern purpose of the buildings.

After all they had been through, Raymond McGrath and Marmaduke Tudsbery Tudsbery did not fall out. It is pleasant to record that 40 years later, when he was enfeebled by a coronary, Tudsbery invited Raymond to the Athenaeum for lunch. "We could each", he wrote, "sandpaper our brains in advance so that we might tell each other how wise we were…" He was 80.

CHAPTER XIX

e sleeps so softly that no signs disclose
　　What transitory shadows fall like leaves
　　Along the shining threshold of his dreams.
　　No thunder of the uneasy world he knows,
　　But quiet Summer, like a spider, weaves
　　A shining web about his shining dreams

— First verse of an untitled poem by Raymond McGrath written
14 June, 1931, four days after Norman's birth.

"Time flies so quickly", Raymond wrote to George Mackaness, "that
your next contributor may be Norman Crozier McGrath." He was sending
some poems for Mackaness's latest anthology[44] and he was full of pride in
his first-born. His banal remark to Manny Forbes — "Mary is doing
splendidly — ditto Norman" — concealed a fierce joy in his son that was
never to leave him. Sixty years on, when Raymond was long dead,
Norman provided a vivid word picture of Somerton Lodge, the house near
Dublin in which Raymond spent his last twenty-five years. Norman was
then as now living and working in New York and on visits home would
bring a fresh eye to the improvement of the house and gardens. "I was
proud", he recalls, "of the fact that Dad with all his experience and talent
valued my views and insights on his own home." So the pride was mutual.

If one dropped in to Raymond's office in the Pantheon, one would
enter a frantically busy scene, "which is supposed to be an absurdity in
these times. London goes on expanding despite the pessimistic
prognostications of its inhabitants", he told Mackaness.

The Pantheon in Oxford Street by then belonged to Gilbeys, the wine
people. It was Anthony Grinling Gibbons, one of Gilbeys' directors, a
sculptor and a convinced modernist, who suggested that Raymond and
Serge Chermayeff take a floor in the building while the B.B.C. job was on.

He and Serge had a staff of six, including a Swiss, a Frenchman and
an Australian. The Australian was Walter Goodesmith, who worked with
Raymond for most of the 1930s and collaborated with him on an hotel-
airport design (unbuilt) and the Pearl Assurance Company's £20,000
building at Bournemouth (1935). Serge and Raymond shared W.L.
Havard, who was Swiss. He was a fine draughtsman, and well worth his
£6 a week, and he stayed on Raymond's staff until the end.

"Raymond and I", recalls Serge Chermayeff, "coincided at a time
when everything seemed to be on the up and up. Everything was new, just
lovely. This produced almost a private euphoria. We were all having a hell

*'Head of a Boy'. Eileen McGrath's
bronze of Norman, 1934*

*Mary pushing the McGrath
pram in Regent's Park, 1937*

of a good time. Jaggers [John Betjeman] and I used to go out to lunch together. We liked particularly the Army and Navy restaurant. I remember once Jaggers' remarking that this was a very full house. 'I bet you', he said, 'that I can make every one of those heads turn.' So he stood up and shouted 'Darjeeling' and every head turned."

Raymond laughed at such mischievous extravagances, but he did not participate in them. Nor was he regarded as a colonial. "For us, Raymond was totally removed from Australia. We did not think of him as Australian, nor indeed did we think of Mary as Texan. We all existed in some kind of fluid of our own, everybody in his own fish bowl. It gave us a chance to work freely. We were never very English. We were eccentrics, outside the mainstream of ordinary life. We fitted into a very narrow spot of history."

We need Gavin Stamp to remind us that: "The 1930s was a decade of crisis and conflict, of the Depression, of Munich, of hunger marches and Fascist-Communist street fights and the darkening shadow of another war."[45] Against that reality, John Betjeman's[46] recollection seems trivial. In the 1930s, he says, he was "a votary of fashion... when I thought that waiting round the corner to burst on us in full glory was a nymph who refused to be caught, called Modern Architecture. She revealed herself in the Lawn Road flats [Wells Coates' major oeuvre] and in some of the white boxes for intellectuals in Hampstead... She was a bit of a disappointment."

While Raymond and Serge were chasing the nymph at the Pantheon, Mary called in to see how the work was going:

> The Pantheon was an old theatre and is a most interesting building in itself. A projecting gallery, supported by two columns, juts out over the noise and tumult of Oxford Street, the only building in sight with a sense of dignity and its own import-ance... A beautiful plywood door, flat with the surface of the wall, bears the names of the two architects, painted in beigey rose. This door leads to a fresh cream-coloured hall. The [second] door opens in to a nice large room with comfortable steel office furniture, three or four rather large rugs, and an efficient stenog. who taps away at a fine typewriter (lent for nothing through friends of Serge). The permanent desks and the bookcases from Germany have not yet arrived... Double doors, their inner side painted the same nice rose colour, lead into the drafting room... I found R. and Miss Mills bending over a floor design for Crowe's shop, and Serge working on a good scheme for his studio at the B.B.C.

The stenographer, also shared, cost £3 a week, and Miss Mills £3.10s.

Through Mary's eyes we get an inside view of what the B.B.C. consultancy involved. Raymond had just finished — this is in late January 1931 — "a really magnificent drawing" of what he believed the entrance hall should look like. It was, Mary thought, most dynamic and appropriate. "It is incredible what he has been able to make out of the dull, prosaic

design of Myer's which was no use at all." (She did praise Myer's exterior.)

Val Goldsmith was most enthusiastic, and Raymond wrote Myer a tactful letter "to assuage his vanity and gain his approval". Raymond was concerned about the design, not who got the credit for it. Myer may have approved of the alterations but as we know he was building up a hefty resentment against those who were eroding his authority.

Raymond and Mary moved house in the spring of 1931. They got a duplex apartment at the top of No. 10 Park Crescent, overlooking Regent's Park. This was a fortunate find, for it was part of John Nash's grand design for Regent's Park and Regent Street. There Norman was born in June and there Jenny was born in 1937. There too, they had room enough to put up not just Manny or Albert but Raymond's parents and sister and later Mary's parents. In the parlance of the day it was "a good address" and it was only five minutes' walk from Raymond's office. They had a Swedish maid (Raymond's word for her) called Märta, the cheapest electricity in London, and altogether were well placed to play Happy Families. At Heart's instigation, Raymond produced one of his best watercolours, done from the balcony.

As well as the B.B.C., Raymond was earning money in a number of

Regent's Park from the balcony of No. 10, Park Crescent, 1931

135

Park Crescent from the balcony of No. 10

The Prince of Wales

ways. He got £8 for a woodcut to be used on the front cover of a novel called 'Each Stands Alone'. He did showrooms and model flats for Easiwork Ltd., a household goods and fitted kitchen firm owned by a Canadian called Crowe. The Prince of Wales dropped in to see the shop one day, talked to Mr. Crowe and ordered a German-style lamp which Raymond then designed for him. ("Pardon us while we burst into royalty!", Mary crowed to her people in Dallas). Raymond also designed a glass trophy and did other work for Austin Reed, the man's shop.

But it was his minor obsession with aeroplanes and his friendship with the Master of Sempill that led to a number of aviation-related commissions. Sempill was a pioneer of civil aviation and chairman of National Flying Services. Raymond first designed a shop for National Flying Services at Trafalgar Square, a design that caused much comment because the awning over the counter area was shaped like an aeroplane wing and was supported by struts. He then designed showrooms in Central London for Imperial Airways, and this commission led to an intriguing offer to take part in the fitting of an aircraft.

The task was to design adjustable chairs and tables for the new four-engined Atalanta airliner made by Armstrong Whitworth and destined for the South Africa and Australia services of Imperial Airways. It was a milestone aircraft, the first monoplane airliner. The cabin furniture was to weigh no more than 252 lbs. in all, so the nine chairs (7lb. 9ozs. each) were cane-bottomed and cane-backed with leather-covered arms. The frames were made of a magnesium alloy called Elektron, the alloy almost certainly containing 6 per cent by weight of aluminium and 1 per cent by weight of zinc.[47] Raymond's use of this alloy was pioneering and demonstrated his eagerness to search for and apply new materials. His fee was £70, out of which the staff had to be paid.

As their social circle widened, the McGraths' confidence grew. Mary still enjoyed dropping names in her letters to Dallas, but she became less gushing and more constructively critical of people such as John Pentland, who "in spite of being one of the youngest peers in the realm", kept at his work as an electrical engineer; Ian Parsons of Chatto and Windus, "not only very wealthy but bright as well"; Arthur Parry ("Pim"), Manny's brother-in-law, who "has gotten heavily into debt, what with drinking etc."; Harold Hemming's new wife Alice: "Manny says she's clever and charming"; Lance Sieveking "a terribly nice man and very genuine. I think she's a little 'social' "; Ray Morell "is going to introduce me to Edith Sitwell"; Wells Coates "tries his best to flirt but somehow misses the boat", and so on. She was an excellent mixer and not above going to boring tea parties on the basis of "you never know where you'll meet a client" [for Raymond].

Raymond put a lot of work into Hyde Park Court, a block of flats at Lowndes Square, Knightsbridge, for the Ainsley brothers, who thought it a good paying proposition. It never happened. But Val Goldsmith offered Raymond a drawing office at Broadcasting House, which much relieved the pressure on space at the Pantheon. Goldsmith also intimated that when the job was completed the B.B.C. would almost certainly appoint Raymond as their permanent Decoration Adviser at £300 a year. He was appointed, at least until 1934, and he was given the Manchester Studios to design. This was a group of five rooms dispersed throughout an existing building. In the studios he used the signal lights, clocks, buzzer and house-phone mountings, microphone stands, mixer desks and chairs and loudspeaker and gramophone cabinets that had been such a succès d'estime at Portland Place. He put his ultimate stamp on the Regional Director's desk, which was of tubular metal and wood with a top of acid-stippled plate glass. The work was finished in 1933, a year after Broadcasting House.

The Garcias, who originally had wanted Raymond to design a house for them, gave him instead the remodelling of their new flat at 14 Bell Moor, East Heath Road, Hampstead. It was to be finished by Christmas Day 1931; otherwise they would have to pay £84 for another quarter's rent on their previous apartment. Raymond had to work himself, his staff and the contractors very hard without knowing how much he would get out of it in the end.

Another difficulty arose through Serge Chermayeff's wanting and Raymond's refusing a full partnership. Serge felt that Raymond had got the better staff and Mary felt that Serge was being unreasonable. The matter was soon settled when Serge went into partnership with Mendelsohn and Raymond moved to 38 Conduit Street. Ruffled feathers were smoothed and the families remained firm friends.

Manny's love for Raymond Mary found really touching. Manny bought Norman an Orrefors loving cup. He had been through a bad time financially and had got no support from his family, who felt that Raymond had caused Manny to spend too much on Finella. It was unfortunate, but it made no difference to Manny's loyalty.

Mary, and presumably Raymond, had been estranged from Mhari Parry to the point where Mary talked of someone also aged 40 as "much more human and attractive" than Mhari. Mary also gave her family an insight into the mores of the times, the era of the Bright Young Thing:

Wells Coates
(Courtesy of Mrs. Laura Cohn)

Perspective of Hyde Park Court
(The British Architectural Library,
RIBA, London)

Yngve Ahlm

This business of inviting wives without husbands and vice versa is all wrong, I think, but it is becoming quite common. It would mean that I'd never see R. at all. If things go like that, you could have such a different set of friends that finally your husband would simply be someone you slept with more than anybody else!

Raymond told Mary that they were "managing" financially, but she said they would be obliged to live "on the margin" until he got a really big job like the Lowndes Square flats. Mary was floating off articles to magazines such as *Britannia and Eve* but without success.

What Raymond had called their "Swedish maid" was Märta, whose position in the household was anomalous. She was in love with the McGraths' good Cambridge friend, Yngve Ahlm, with whom they stayed in touch for the rest of their lives. Märta, who cooked and baked beautifully, kept threatening to return to Sweden until Mary offered her incentives such as a weekend at Finella ("only if Yngve is there too"). Eventually Mary decided she would have to give her wages. Manny, Raymond and Mary did not rate Märta's chances of marrying Yngve very highly, and they were right. His widow Betty still lives in San Clemente, California, where he became a professor of physical education. Märta did not long endure: she was replaced by Dora, a real maid, a German who was perfect for Mary's needs and was calming for the excitable Norman.

The next commission Raymond was offered was to produce no money because, like the flats scheme, it did not materialise. But it did yield a huge harvest of publicity and it appealed to his feeling for the aeroplane as the symbol of a progressive decade.

In 1931, the Hon. Mrs. Victor Bruce commissioned Oliver Hill to design a house. Oliver Hill was "a quintessential figure of the inter-war period"[48] and a friend of the McGraths to the extent of visiting them in Dublin after the war. In January 1932, Hill wrote to Mrs. Bruce: "I am building a new hotel at Morecambe and am arranging a very long flat roof so that you can fly me there without coming to earth." By the end of that month she had told him not to proceed with his design. She cited mounting costs.

Mrs. Bruce was by then a famous aviatrix, infatuated by danger. She held several world records in cars, speedboats and aeroplanes and had flown solo from India to Indo-China, for which feat she was honoured with the Order of the Million Elephants and White Umbrella.[49]

Then, it seems, Manny's friend the Master of Sempill — Commander the Lord Sempill R.N.V.R., as he became — suggested that she should give Raymond a chance to do the house. She interviewed him, told him she wanted to spend only £1,500 ("probably just talk", wrote Mary: "She's wealthy and the whole thing is a whim with her"); and gave him the details of her madcap scheme.

Mrs. Bruce wanted to attempt the world record for endurance in the air. So she would drop the first brick for the house from the plane. Raymond would build at such speed that when she came down she would find the house, Rudderbar, waiting, complete with a hangar in which to park her plane. Rudderbar, which was the subject of an article in the *Architectural Review* (Vol. 81, 1932) was to have been built at Hanworth Airfield, Feltham.

Mrs. Bruce says she did drop the brick but "the house was never built owing to my work for the Government, which suddenly greatly increased, so that I was unable to go on with the project". All that Raymond has left us is his statement: "Why this did not come off is a long story." Which he does not tell. The problem was money. Mary learned that she did not have any money "until she's made this flight and then she'll be worth over a pound a minute".

The owners of the Embassy Club in Clifford Street, off Old Bond Street, saw the photographs of Broadcasting House and decided that they had to be one up on their main competitors, Ciro's. So through Dr. J.O.E. Apthorp, one of the directors, they employed Raymond to refurbish the club in the modern style. It was a huge success, the *Sydney Morning Herald* reporting from London on 12 October, 1932:

> All the best-known people in society seemed to be present at the reopening of the Embassy Club, which has retained its reputation as a favourite meeting place for social celebrities. The Embassy had been done up in a new modernistic scheme that called forth much applause on Tuesday night. Its sky blue ceiling

Oliver Hill visiting the McGraths in Dublin, 1947

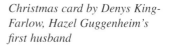

Christmas card by Denys King-Farlow, Hazel Guggenheim's first husband

139

The Embassy Club
(Courtesy of the Trustees of the V & A)

is in striking contrast to its walls of pale green frosted glass, while the door frames and the gallery rails have been painted rose pink to match the velvet flounces finishing the settees. It provided a perfect background for the beautiful frocks of the women dining there on the opening gala night — Lady Furness, in velvet, Lady Queensberry in a blue frock matched by blue gloves, Mrs. Ronald Balfour wearing the latest thing in capes... Lady Edward Hay wore... a deep 'V' decolletage at the back... The young Countess of Dumfries, a recent bride... Lady Georgiana Curzon... Mrs. Ormond Lawson-Johnston... Mrs. Seely and Mrs. Kenelm Lee Guinness were in black. So many well-known people were there, it was difficult to realise that, only a week ago, "nobody was in town".

The McGraths did not frequent the Embassy Club, but Serge Chermayeff did. He was a superb dancer and was quite in tune with

Ambrose and his orchestra.

Mary and less so Raymond, who was working too hard and missed a lot of parties, made a lot of new friends around this time. Eric and Dora Lewenhaupt — he was a Swedish count — joined their set, and Hazel Guggenheim and her newly-wed husband, Denys King-Farlow, became equally good friends. Mary worried about Denys; "I know he loves Hazel but I have a feeling the mode of life she makes him lead is not altogether what he likes. His own flat was informal and homey and now this silly butler dogs his footsteps and their parties go with a mechanical smoothness that could get very dull."

However Mary's friends rated their standing with her (Alice Hemming frankly says she was "probably Mary's second-best friend"), Mary herself regarded Margaret Witt as her best friend. A wealthy American from Connecticut, Margaret was married to John Witt, the lawyer son of Sir Robert Witt. Sir Robert was the eccentric and aristocratic director of the National Gallery. John Witt, Jenny remembers, was "a rather unhappy kind of person, totally different from Margaret".

Alice Hemming tells a revealing story of her year's sojourn in Berlin – Dahlem. When the German Government under Hitler had blocked some Reichsmarks of Harold Hemming's, his response was: "To hell, we'll go to Berlin." He soon returned to London, leaving Alice, the children and her new German Jewish nanny with "that murderous mountebank":

> We were befriended by Frau Züllickmayer, a strong supporter of Hitler's and very aristocratic. She told me that she was Sir Robert Witt's sister. 'No, you can't be', I said, 'Robert Witt is very English'. 'Nevertheless he's my brother', Frau Züllickmayer responded. When I told John Witt this story, he went red as a beetroot and walked away, didn't want to know.

Mary saw Dora off on her three-week holiday to Germany, hoping that there would not be any trouble about her getting back to England. Even then (7 May 1933) Mary was aware that "Hitler seems to be doing such drastic things in his effort to keep the German race pure and holy".

Mary (left) and best friend, Margaret Witt

CHAPTER XX

Not every social event in the McGraths' life was a success. Early in December 1932, Mary gave a dinner party which was such a nightmare that she did not want to tell her folks about it. "I swore never to have anybody else to dinner as long as I lived", she informed them, and went on to tell them all about it.

Here I worked like a slave to have everything smooth and easy, china, glasses, coffee cups, etc. matching reasonably well (not a store in London did I miss and none of them helped much — what trotting!) when at 7 I returned home to find the chickens hadn't come. I frantically phoned the butcher who said the boy had delivered. I said I didn't care a hang, to send some more immediately. They sent the boy to verify if he'd [illegible] got them to the right place — but without chickens. I nearly died. R. came home and found me in tears and was about to dash out to a cooked food place when at 7.30 the chickens were discovered *locked* up in the basement kitchen. Dinner was at 8 and our guests were punctual. I was so shattered by all this I couldn't be natural and make a clean breast of it but tried manfully to fill all conversational gaps… R. had such a headache he didn't speak, and Mrs. Solomon who always looks ill at ease even in her own servanted home, looked more uncomfortable than ever. I won't say any more but how right you were that we shouldn't attempt to entertain until we're fitted for it! Both mentally and materially. We'll have to wait a long long time.

Raymond escaped criticism in that account (his headaches became more frequent and always made him irritable) but when he was doing an article on the Rundfunkhaus in Berlin, Mary carped: "He's so unresponsive when he writes articles, it being very hard work — I'm always glad when the grunting stage is over and he comes back to agreeable life."

Again: "R. of course never turned up at the party, nor to the Hemmings' dinner at the Piccadilly Hotel in honour of *their* baby's christening."

The Hemming child was Louisa, whose head was sculpted by Eileen McGrath when Louisa was seven. Alice Hemming recalls a visit to Finella when she was pregnant. Mary was expecting Norman, and Manny was at home when the doctor called to see the mothers-to-be. The doctor looked at the two large women, then looked at little Manny. "You could see the

Facing page:
Above: McGrath's perspective of Fischer's. Even in a formal drawing he could misspell
(Courtesy of the Trustees of the V & A)

Below:
Interior of Fischer's Restaurant
(The British Architectural Library, RIBA, London)

look on his face. He was thinking: 'Well, he's going it, isn't he?',", says Alice.

At about the same time, Barbara Chermayeff had had Ivan and Margaret Witt brought Christopher into the world. When Margaret was up and about, she and Mary did a little shopping with Lady Witt, who commanded her daughter-in-law's every breath — "terribly well-meant, but irksome", thought Mary. The four besotted mothers were counterbalanced by de Cronin Hastings, who insisted that his children were web-footed and altogether detestable.

One of the most attractive designs Raymond did was Fischer's Restaurant in New Bond Street. The client was the same J.O.E. Apthorp in his personal capacity. Handing Raymond "a shell with columns", he gave his architect a free hand. The owner spent £9,000 on the premises, including the furniture, and the result was not only extensive publicity in English, Continental and American journals, but a satisfied and illustrious clientele. "The finish and completeness of such interiors as Fischer's Restaurant is due in large part to the broad designing experience McGrath has had", wrote the *Architectural Forum* in the United States.

Fischer's made the first extensive use of nitrogen tube lighting. It had a ground-floor cocktail bar (this was the heyday of the Manhattan and the cocktail dress). A curved staircase led down to a basement restaurant with seats for 150 and a dance floor. Subtle lighting and the clever use of colour, patterns and curved forms gave Fischer's the aniconic ambience of one of the large ocean liners then competing for the Blue Riband of the Atlantic.

On a Monday night before Christmas 1932, the McGraths brought a large party to the newly-opened Fischer's. Manny Forbes; Eric and Dora Lewenhaupt; a charming young American couple called Janeway; Rab and Jean Buchanan; a foreign correspondent for Odham's Press called Major Matts; John Layard and others unnamed gathered to celebrate.

Eric Lewenhaupt (later to become Jenny's godfather) was "a bit tight and very charming and amorous", a mood that infected everybody. They danced until the place closed and then returned to the Lewenhaupts until about four o'clock.

"It was an epic evening", said Mary, epic being her favourite adjective at the time, "and I worked off enough surplus frivolity to keep me respectable for several weeks."

> The Lewenhaupts became so attached to me during the course of the evening that they each invited me separately to come and live with them!

As if these ambiguous offers were not bad enough, de Cronin Hastings and Mary at another party made a pact: "We have decided that we are going to have a crush on each other. His wife [Hazel] is leaving town and she promises not to be selfish."

The McGraths meet Aleister Crowley! There's excitement for you. Or was it? Lance Sieveking has left us a whole chapter on Crowley,[50] one of whose books he found was far from being "lovely old pornoggers". Black magic and orgies and satanic rites were attributed to this degenerate man, but Sieveking found it so hard to get the details that at one time he *invented* a rite. It so shocked and revolted his friends that the subject had to be dropped. When Sieveking eventually met 'The Beast' at Cassis in the South of France, they went bathing in the sea and "I noticed that his body was like his face, sunburned all over, but green".

Aleister Crowley was dressed when Raymond and Mary met him at the Lewenhaupts, who thought Crowley's shady reputation unjust, and Mary said that nothing very magical occurred:

> Old Crowley looks rather like a disappointed Mephistopheles. He seems to have just discovered that he is no wickeder than anybody else and is suffering from let-down! Toward 1.30 he suddenly asked me if I'd like a serpent's kiss. He took my wrist near his mouth and made three signs in the air with his left hand, muttering something or other. Then he gave me the most awful bite, leaving two deep dents in my skin. Though the blood didn't come and it's a week old, the marks are still there...

Hendricus Theodorus Wijdeveld, the Dutch architect and lithographer, went with the McGraths to a party at the Howard Robertsons. Mary was impressed by "the *most nicest* man. He's just about everything in Holland — the leading architect, as important in stage designing and producing as Max Reinhardt is in Germany, a well-known writer, a statesman, a painter *and* the father of three grown children. He must be about 60 but he's as fresh and gay and enthusiastic as young people should be but aren't." He told her of his "thrilling scheme" for an international art centre, and mentioned that Mendelsohn and Albert Einstein were involved. Another Dutchman had donated a large site "in no less a place than Le Lavandou, where we spent our honeymoon!"

Although it was Serge Chermayeff who talked to Eric Gill about the Académie Européenne Méditerranée, it is clear from Mary's letter to her family that the *fons et origo* of the scheme was Wijdeveld, who was disappointed by the failure of his seaside school and in 1936 set up an architectural college in Laage Vuursche, near Hilversum. This school, Elkerlyc, was effectively ended by the German invasion of the Netherlands in 1940.

Money never ceased to be a problem. If a sizeable scheme such as the Hyde Park Court flats had come to fruition, the McGraths would not have had to skimp. As it was, the disappearance of a pound in the flat left Mary with tears of prayer in her eyes. The pound did not turn up and she resolved: "I need to be economical to make up for my various fits of carelessness." All the same she did think she had improved a lot. She wanted to try her hand at "those Scottish articles. I shall die if I don't make some money. I don't think it's fair for Raymond to do it all." She was delighted when Lance Sieveking gave her five guineas for a B.B.C. part as "a member of the audience in Panoli's Music Hall in 1902".

145

*Raymond before Mary got to work
on his moustache*

Yet she was conscious that others had less than she and Raymond. Amyas Connell, she reported, had no work and his wife was making the money. "I got 4/11 for the dollar you sent — not bad", she wrote to Dallas.

"And few people seem to be jealous of Raymond except Wells Coates and strangely enough Val Myer... You would think he'd consider himself far beyond R's class, having done two very big jobs, but he has been very petty in several instances." At least the Hemmings, Percy Hume the Editor of *The Sphere*, and John Nisbet were convinced that Raymond was the architectural genius of the present era. This was at dinner in Park Crescent.

While they were living at Finella, Mary had decided to smarten Raymond up, a process which principally involved enlarging his moustache. Three years later, her reforming zeal went farther. While Raymond was in Leeds giving a lecture she wrote: "I want him to make speeches occasionally. It will help him to speak out more." It was a lost cause, as anyone who tried to hear Raymond lecturing will testify.

But things were looking up. His staff had gone up to nine again and he had been given a larger drawing office at the B.B.C. For the David Jones department store in Sydney, modern fabrics were selected by Raymond for the firm's Modern Furnishing Fabric Exhibition held in November 1933. It was Australia's first time to see such fabrics, and *The Home* devoted four pages to this and other work by Raymond. "On Lincrusta, for instance", wrote Madeline Macrae, "he contrived an interesting impressed pattern which has the object of refracting light rays in varying degrees of intensity. This met with such success that the manufacturers decided to adopt it as a standard line under the name of 'Finella Lincrusta'. Again his design for polished woven flax cloth is now put on the market by Edinburgh Weavers."

'Three Sydneysiders go to London' was a handwritten journal kept by Raymond's father Herbert. Leaving Sydney on 1 July, 1933, he, his wife Edith and their daughter Eileen sailed on the S.S. Jervis Bay, which was to meet a heroic end during the Second World War, when she saved a convoy by engaging an attacking German raider, thus ensuring her own destruction.

The senior McGraths spent six months in England, seeing everything, staying with Manny at Finella while they visited Cambridge, and arriving home by the S.S. Moreton Bay by the end of December.

Herbert's journal is long and tedious, intended to be read by those Australians who wanted the details of every bit of the built environment of England from Peter Pan's statue in Kensington Gardens to Tunbridge Wells in Kent (3s. 6d. return by motor coach).

But the three went with Mary to Paris for a week and were much impressed, even in November. Eileen made a little book of her charming drawings and Mary made sure that they saw what was to be seen. They all took photographs.

Eileen, who still had some of her Anzac Memorial money, stayed on at Park Crescent. She soon got a commission doing models for John Gloag, who then worked for the advertising agency that had the Venesta account. She also attended some classes given by John Skeaping the sculptor. Skeaping features in Wilenski's book[51] as a young Englishman who had made experiments in a number of fields. His seated figure of "Akua-ba" had "symbolic sexual meaning; but not the sensual meaning of caressibility because it is not intended to provide the substitute gratification of a pretty-girl ninepin". Raymond, who had given Wilenski's book to Eileen for Christmas 1932, was trying to tell her something.

Brother and sister were together for Christmas 1933. It was like old times. Mary and Norman had left for a visit to Dallas, and only Dora remained to provide them with "the loveliest dinner of really young and tender chicken, spinach and potatoes and… the cutest little pudding… Dora burst into song as she carried it in and we all had some sherry together…".

They would not have been true McGraths if they had not used Christmas Day to write illustrated book-letters — Raymond to all at Cole Avenue, Dallas; Eileen to her parents still on the high seas. Eileen's friend Elaine Haxton, the well-known Australian painter (now Elaine Haxton Foot) contributed a drawing to each little book. She had been staying at Park Crescent but was in Oxford for Christmas.

Raymond's news for Mary included the guests at the Gloags' Christmas Eve party: they included "Miss McGrath, sister of famous architect; Mr. McGrath, brother of famous sculptress [and] Mr. Xian Barman, another famous architect". Albert Frost, who was teaching near London, stayed before Christmas and offered his novel 'High Dudgeon' to Chatto and Windus. They accepted it and gave him an advance of £30 as well as entering it for a humorous novel competition worth £250. Eileen did some little illustrations "in the French manner".

"I suppose, like my magnum opus, it will be published in the Spring", he told her. This is the first intimation we have that his 'Twentieth Century Houses' was ready. Albert's "frequent help and suggestions" are acknowledged in the book, as is the ready interest of Richard de la Mare of Faber and Faber.

(De la Mare's support was sought again forty-three years later when Raymond asked him (he was then president of the firm and still keeping in touch through his son Giles, a director) to consider republishing the book by offset photolithography. "The worst of it", he wrote to Raymond about six weeks before McGrath's death in 1977, "is that the original reproductions were not really satisfactory, at any rate if judged by present standards… [but the idea] is certainly worth considering." He signed himself Dick.)

Eileen's version of Dora, bringing in the Christmas pudding

Elaine Haxton's version of Raymond before Christmas, 1933

TWENTIETH CENTURY HOUSES

Unfortunately 'Twentieth Century Houses' did not appear in the 1934 spring lists, whereas F.R.S. Yorke's 'The Modern House'[52] did. There was inevitably some overlapping and although Raymond's book was much wider in its scope and deeper in its perceptions and historical framework, the fact is that Yorke's being first by six months meant a loss of sales to the Faber book.

Nonetheless, 'Twentieth Century Houses' was very well received, the *Manchester Guardian* calling it "by far the most complete account of the modern house, as it is seen today in all countries, which has yet appeared".

As though Yorke's book did not exist, the *Architectural Review* took Raymond's very seriously indeed:

> Something we have long been patiently waiting for has come to pass. An at once authoritative and comprehensive book on modern architecture has been published in England. And it is better than any foreign book on the subject that has yet appeared; better, even, than the half-dozen best of them rolled into one. For instead of the irascible Continental polemic, which is what *les purs des purs* usually treat us to, or the blatant exploitation of the modern house as a journalistic stunt or publicity 'copy', which is what the English-speaking public has hitherto mostly had fobbed off on it, we encounter a quiet objective sincerity, that never raises its voice, and persuades by reasonableness, common sense and a dryly informing irony.

Through the *Spectator*, the public was informed that the book was not only the best on its subject yet published, "but it is written in Basic English and written beautifully".

Raymond's decision to write in Basic English presumably was influenced by the feeling that Basic was the verbal equivalent of functional in architecture. Purity of word was to match purity of line; the absence of decoration was to be common to literature and architecture.

Basic English, which had a vocabulary of only 850 words, was invented by C.K. Ogden of the Orthological Institute of Cambridge University and I.A. Richards of the Cambridge English School. It was an attempt at "debabelisation", a means of getting the nations to understand one another. It was less successful than Esperanto and it infuriated some of the critics of 'Twentieth Century Houses'.

Christopher Hussey, the architectural editor of *Country Life*, said that in elucidating the aims and values of modernist theory,

> Mr. McGrath has set himself under something of a disadvantage by adopting the colourless and mechanical vocabulary known as "Basic English" which, though clear, is as repellent to the ear as most of his examples are to the eye of the traditionist... The book is not sensuously attractive to read.

In his defence, Ogden said: "We find fully 1500 languages acting as barriers to world understanding. India alone has 200 languages; the Soviet Republic has 20."

Raymond wrote 80,000 words in Basic, a language which allowed him to speak of "living-rooms, music-rooms, libraries, playrooms, terraces and roof-gardens" but denied him the more usual forms for "rooms for meals, the cooking-rooms" and even "layer-wood". And the present writer strongly objects to the abuse of direct quotations involved in rendering them in Basic. Indeed, it used to be said that Churchill's "blood, toil, tears and sweat" came out in Basic as "blood, work, eye-wash and body-water"!

Ogden, who became a friend of Lance Sieveking and of Raymond, was in Sieveking's[53] estimation a man "who gives his friendship with considerable discrimination and seldom allows his heart to get the better of his head". Sieveking says it was "quite an experience to hear Ogden declaiming a Hopkins poem up his resounding stone staircase in Russell Square". Thus Ogden was "showing how the ancient Greeks used always to speak their poetry, in the resounding acoustic which their wonderful scientific achievement had enabled them to construct in their auditoriums". Hopkins always said that his poetry should be read aloud.

(Sieveking's own copy of 'Twentieth Century Houses', he told Raymond in 1962, he had long ago "completely Grangerised by sticking letters from you and drawings into it".)

"Basic", Raymond told Mary, "isn't child's play to write, I fear, not when you're used to squandering words." He asked C.F. Annesley Voysey (1857–1941) to write a foreword to his book and was both excited and disappointed by the great pioneer's reply:

> Many thanks for your letter and the compliments you pay me. As a consistent individualist I am violently anti-international, and against collectivism, mass production of thoughts and sentiments. Regimentation I detest. Also town planning that plays ducks and drakes with private property and vested interests. Any interference with individual privacy is to me quite wrong. All are the outcome of a poisonous socialism and communism.
>
> The way to make quarrels and wars is to become intimate with your neighbours.
>
> Going awhoring with foreign styles has poisoned our architecture.
>
> So now you must perceive I am fundamentally unfit to write anything for your book.
>
> I may be a goat but I am certainly not a sheep. I worship my maker for having made all nations in climate, geological, geographical, moral and spiritual qualities different.
>
> Liberty, equality and fraternity are to me poisonous and impossible lies.

Raymond, who cannot have been surprised that an architect and designer whose distinctive work he knew and admired would so express himself, had to enter a ritual disagreement. Voysey wrote again saying:

> I am sorry you do not see that Inigo Jones and Wren only produced mongrel architecture. And that lovely and purely

English style of Tudor Gothick of which countless churches, cathedrals and baronial halls and great farm houses were bred and born in England. Indeed all great architecture is born out of its native conditions and requirements. Greek, Roman, Spanish, English all come from faithfulness to their own national character, climate, geographical and geological conditions.

Voysey grounds his refusal to write Raymond's foreword on the arguments in these letters. He makes no reference to the plan to use Basic English. Perhaps Raymond did not dare to introduce a second area of controversy when he first wrote to Voysey. The book opens with a preface — 'First Words' — by Raymond himself and ends with a note on Basic English by Ogden. And Voysey's life and achievements are amply covered.

'Twentieth Century Houses' was dedicated to "Mansfield Duval Forbes" with the inscribed motto beneath it: "Simple-intime", which summed up "that quality in a building that was uncomplicated, unaffected, and natural to its own period", to use Hugh Carey's[54] words.

Manny had no idea that the book would be dedicated to him. He went into the Cambridge University Press to see Brooke Crutchley, the assistant University Printer, for a moment. Crutchley, who had the proofs of the book there, said to Manny: "I see it's dedicated to you."

To Raymond, Manny straightway wrote: "My Gawd, boy, what an affecting surprise — and when I saw, below the superscription, the wee, still subscription 'simple intime', I felt like a message from a Ladybird next April… But oui, I hardly know what to do about it…"

FIRST WORDS

The position of the architect is very different from that of any other man of art. A book or a bit of music may be on everyone's lips to-day, and to-morrow be on the shelf, covered with dust. If they are good there is a living force in them which will make them a part of everything which is best in us and in men and women still to come. If they are bad, or designed only for the hour's amusement, they do not, after all, take up much room and may even, with their coloured backs ranged across the wall, give a certain amount of pleasure to the eye. Their material existence is at least short, and the physical damage they may do unimportant. Unhappily this is not so when we come to the equally short-living offspring of the architect. There is no top shelf or dark cupboard for poorly designed buildings. Far from it. They are kept on as a sort of headstone to their early death. Time is no acid-test of building and quality no passport to long existence. A house which is the equal of a third-rate book may have an unpleasing effect on one square mile of country for a hundred years, a house as beautiful as a song of Schubert's be overlooked in the noise of a hundred street-cries or rooted up by a builder to make way for "housing developments".

To a greater or less degree the outside of a house is public property and the most private of architects a public servant. For this reason the architect is in a more responsible position than any other man of art, and when he is so little ready to take his position seriously as he has been for the last hundred years the material effect is far worse than if he had been a writer or a painter. This country of ours is quickly becoming one great waste of badly formed, poorly designed and unhealthy houses simply because the architect has no force of mind, no feeling for his position, no

M H   ix   b

150

CHAPTER XXI

From the time Raymond arrived in England, he had contrived to see every worthwhile film and theatre show in London. He was fascinated by entertainment and frequently commented in letters on the quality of the play or the actor. Mary was equally attracted and, especially when the talkies became universal, they and their friends frequented the cinema, discussed the film and enjoyed the productions flooding in from Germany, Austria, France and the Soviet Union as well as the United States. The British film industry, with some exceptions, was not to be taken too seriously.

While Mary was in Dallas for the first half of 1934, Raymond told her that he and Eileen had seen Noël Coward's 'Design for Living', directed by Ernst Lubitsch — "brilliant and delightful and on no account to be missed". There were "lots of good films" playing just then: 'Prenez Garde à la Peinture' (the original version of 'The Late Christopher Bean'), 'Le Petit Roi' and the Austrian 'Liebelei'. On the stage, Gertrude Lawrence was in 'Nymph Errant'; Elisabeth Bergner in Margaret Kennedy's 'Escape Me Never'; Lynn Fontanne in 'Reunion in Vienna'. 'Fresh Fields', 'Ten Minute Alibi' and 'Richard of Bordeaux' and at least two others indicated how wide was the choice for the cinema- and theatregoer in a couple of weeks.

While he found time for these diversions, Raymond was busy in his new office at 38 Conduit Street, near the R.I.B.A.'s old headquarters.

Frognal House: Georgian to Modern
(The British Architectural Library,
RIBA, London)

Frognal House in the snow. (The British Architectural Library, RIBA, London)

Raymond McGrath , Architect .

Frognal House: Charles de Gaulle's HQ during the Second World War.

Their friend Edith Croll (Mrs. George Croll) left No. 9 Westbourne Street and found herself a very nice little flat at 77 Fitzjohn's Avenue in Hampstead while Raymond refurbished Frognal House (99 Frognal) in Hampstead for her. This job was worth £12,000 and in a sense was another Finella, a Georgian house remodelled in the modern idiom. Edith Croll was a valued client as well as a good friend. Raymond, to whom she showed her wonderful collection of pressed flowering plants gathered in North and Central America and carefully documented, ensured that her rock garden would be "very fine when the plants begin to grow and blossom". (Frognal House became the wartime headquarters of General de Gaulle. After the war Edith Croll sold it for £16,500).

Mrs. Croll was of course another Manny contact. In a letter to Raymond while the newly-weds were living at Finella, Manny had written: "Edie Croll has just promised to guarantee me up to £1,000 or so… Therefore I may have to call *suddenly* on you to put your all, for the space of a *week or so*, to my *credit…* pending fixing with Edie and Bank."

Raymond was, he told Mary, "forging ahead with the new flats" and he might have to cable her to come and lay the foundation stone. There was, he said, a very optimistic feeling in the air of London and a great deal of new work was mooted or afoot. "If only you get this colossal flats job", Manny told him, "I shall push on the Finella booklet fast as possible…"

The new flats did not get built, but Raymond did new showrooms for the Kensington and Knightsbridge Electric Lighting Company; the electrical section of the Building Centre in Bond Street; work on the Plastics Exhibition in the Science Museum in South Kensington, where he also mounted an exhibition for Imperial Airways, and a black glass dining room for the General Electric Company in the exhibition at Olympia.

Towards the latter end of 1932, a young diplomate of the School of Architecture in Regent Street Polytechnic took the train from Paddington Station to Bath. Opposite him sat a man who declared himself a poet and when he learned what the young man did, suggested that he ask Raymond McGrath for a job. The poet turned out to be James Mills and it worked. T. Gordon Cullen for almost two years became a valuable member of the staff at Conduit Street. There were, he recalls, five assistants and Walter Goodesmith, who "acted as though he was a partner". John Earley, whose knowledge of German was to prove useful to Raymond in the preparation of 'Twentieth Century Houses', was one of the assistants. He later worked on Harlow New Town. Another was Arthur Norman Baldwinson who, with his wife Elspeth, was a great friend of Gordon Cullen's. Baldwinson (a Canberra friend of the McGraths wrote to Mary in 1933: "You were so awfully good to Baldwinson") became Senior Lecturer in Architecture at Sydney University in 1951. He had lived in Western Australia and studied architecture at the Geelong Institute of Technology before going abroad for experience. He was, says Allan Gamble,[55] "a modest, rather shy man". In London, he worked with Gropius and Fry, Adams and Thompson between 1932 and 1936.

One day when Raymond was out, Walter Gropius came to have a look around and "that fool Goodesmith, who couldn't speak anything but Australian, tried to explain things in broken English picked up from films: 'Ziss eez zee plan' — that sort of thing".

Cullen is not quite fair to Goodesmith, who between 1914 and 1929 was in Sydney, where he trained as an architect and engineer. He and his wife Una were good friends of the McGraths throughout the 1930s. He designed an interesting modern house overlooking Honolulu Bay, Hawaii, in 1933. It is illustrated in 'Twentieth Century Houses' by two photographs of remarkably poor quality.

Gordon Cullen did some of the interviews for Raymond's book. He met C.F.A. Voysey, who was in a blue shirt and offered him a cigarette. "Then Voysey said: 'Don't smoke — it's bad for you' and I kept the cigarette in my pocket for two years until one day I had to smoke it."

Cullen also talked to F.E. Towndrow, the architect of a house at Hockley, Essex, in 1930. This house, called Forsyte, is, says Gordon Cullen, one of the forgettable houses that should not have been in the book.

As a junior (it was his first job), Cullen did not know the McGraths at home. Indeed he recalls standing at the window in Conduit Street in his first few weeks when a Rolls-Royce pulled up at the street door below. He asked the colleague beside him: "Is that Mr. McGrath's car?" So innocent were they at a time when Raymond probably did not have the price of a motorcycle. Cullen was paid 30 shillings a week and remembers Saturday mornings when there was no money to pay the wages.

"Raymond was incredibly charming and sweet but he could not stand up to hard business people. He needed a manager", Cullen considers. When one reminds Cullen of the work he did for Christopher Tunnard, the landscape architect, and prods him with the remark: "You drew like an angel", his terse response at 75 is: "Still do".

Among the projects he did with Raymond were Frognal House and the glass doors for the fourth floor of the new R.I.B.A. headquarters at 66 Portland Place. Although Gordon Cullen gets no credit in the short history[56] of Grey Wornum's building, his version is interesting: "Raymond

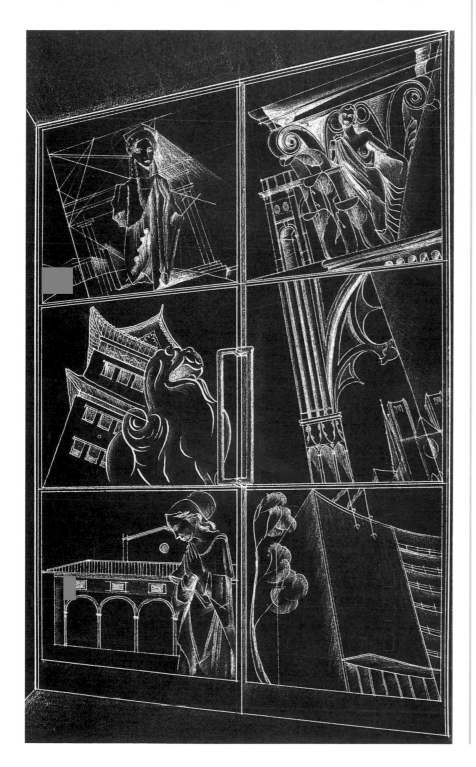

McGrath's design for the glass doors at the RIBA Headquarters, Portland Place

scribbled out some scheme and I drew it. Then it was acid-etched and cut. It's got my name on it too."[57]

Margaret Richardson describes the doors thus:

> [Of] particular interest and very much the treasure of the R.I.B.A. Building are the six acided and sand-blasted glass panels set into the doors opening on to the terrace. They represent the six great periods of architecture, Greek, Roman, Chinese, Gothic, Florentine and Modern, and were designed by the architect Raymond McGrath and executed by James Clark & Son [with whom Raymond had dealt from Finella days]. Each period's contribution to building is noted in the panels; for instance, Greece shows the Golden Section, delineated behind Athena, which is said to have supplied the proportions of the Parthenon. With Modern we are given high-rise building in a form perhaps inspired by Gropius, and the marble bust by Modigliani now in the Tate Gallery...

The office at Conduit Street was very strong on good draughtsmen. Not only Raymond and Gordon Cullen, who says he learned much from Raymond; but W.L. Havard and Derrick Oxley were exceptionally talented, and Baldwinson was, Allan Gamble says, "quite skilled as an artist". John Lawrence and Roy (later Sir Roy) Grounds were other members of Raymond's staff.

The Dorland Hall Exhibition of 1933 was another outlet for the designers of the day. The Depression was at its worst when a committee convened by Christopher Hussey decided to mount an impressive show of British products. Oliver Hill designed it. The Pilkington Bros.' stand demonstrated the potential of new forms of glass. It had a circular floor of glass bricks and bottle-green bedroom pieces. But it was Hill's entrance hall, with sculptures by Eric Gill and Charles Wheeler, that attracted most admiration. It had industrial tools backlit from floor to ceiling and it forced the doubter to look at simple things like saws as the result of designers' intent. The whole exhibition was a cultural and financial success, and Raymond's designs for a bedroom, a kitchen and for glass were critically assessed, one observer noting:

> The interesting experiments by several firms under the direction of Mr. Raymond McGrath towards the effective treatment of walls with engraved and coloured glass have a similar air of expansiveness and of irrelevance as far as the ordinary home is concerned. For gay wall coverings in haunts of pleasure they have already proved themselves.

The next year, the Dorland Hall Exhibition, with Raymond on the committee, lost money. It lost friends too, both Wells Coates and Serge Chermayeff dissociating themselves from what they saw as the elitist nature of some of the exhibits. Oliver Hill again designed it and the committee also contained E. McKnight Kauffer and Dorothy Todd.

"I told you", asked Raymond of his "Prairie Flower from Texas", "that I was designing new radio cabinets for Ekco?" In his book on Wells Coates,[58] Sherban Cantacuzino tells the story of Ekco radio. In a sense, it is the story of industrial design in England. It began in 1930; it was indigenous; it used a new material, and it successfully paralleled and exploited the explosive development of broadcasting as the new medium:

> In 1930 W.S. Verrells and Eric K. Cole, managing directors of Ekco, built the first large moulding plant for plastics in Britain at the Ekco factory in Southend. The wireless industry had grown up with plastics but they were expensive and manufacturers could not afford to take chances on designs. In 1932, Ekco had a competition for wireless cabinets. Among others, there were entries from Serge Chermayeff, Raymond McGrath, Jesse Collins, Misha Black, F.C. Ashford and Wells Coates. Coates won with the only circular design, a shape which not only showed an understanding of the function of the wireless but could not have been produced in any other material.

Because it was circular, Coates' radio conformed with the loudspeaker, itself necessarily round. The use of Bakelite also reduced the number of moulding tools and eliminated sharp corners, with the result that Ekco was able to produce a simple design at less cost. AD65, which was first sold in 1934, became one of the most popular models in Britain.

Raymond followed Wells Coates with another circular design in 1934. Later in the same year, Chermayeff produced another model for Ekco; Jesse Collins did one in 1936 and Misha Black followed in 1938. Raymond's fee was £50 for each design submitted, though not necessarily used.

The fourth Congrès Internationaux d'Architecture Moderne (C.I.A.M.) became famous for two of its aspects. It was held in the summer of 1933 on a boat sailing round the Greek islands; and England was represented by Godfrey Samuel, F.R.S. Yorke, Geoffrey Bomphrey, Morton Shand and Wells Coates. Those whom Wells Coates designated as "popularly and notoriously known as 'modern architects' " were missing — Howard Robertson, Grey Wornum, Oliver Hill, Walmesley Lewis, Oswald Milne and Joseph Emberton. He excluded Raymond McGrath. Le Corbusier was there; Walter Gropius was there, and the organisation was done by Sigfried Giedion, the historian of the modern movement.

There is some evidence of an ideological divide between the left wing, led by Coates and Chermayeff, and enthusiastic about social issues such as public housing; and the rest, including Raymond, who were committed to the evolving international style but were not prepared to extend the role of the architect to a campaign that would have excluded other forms of building. It was not, of course, as simple as that, and personalities as ever obtruded.

The MARS Group (MARS was a loose acronym for Modern

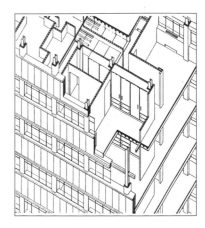

Frame Structure: detail of a building designed by Raymond McGrath, from the book 'Twentieth Century Houses'

Apparatus for the cooking-room. From 'Twentieth Century Houses' (the book was written in in Basic English in 1934)

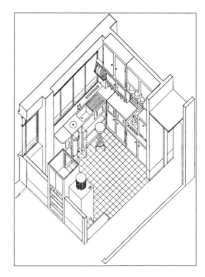

Architectural Research) followed Manny Forbes' Twentieth Century Group,[59] which as we have seen was formed by Forbes and McGrath with Wells Coates, Serge Chermayeff, Jack Pritchard, Frederick Etchells and Howard Robertson. It was short-lived, as was its successor, Unit One.

The MARS Group was the most influential as well as the most enduring of the three. Founded in 1933, it lasted until 1957. It arose because Giedion approached Morton Shand to form a group to represent England at C.I.A.M. congresses.

The first chairman was Wells Coates. Maxwell Fry was vice-chairman, F.R.S. Yorke secretary. Among the founding members were Amyas Connell, Basil Ward and Clive Lucas; Godfrey Samuel and R.T.F. Skinner of Tecton; and David Playdell-Bouverie. Four non-architects, Morton Shand the architectural critic and wine connoisseur, Hubert de Cronin Hastings of the *Architectural Review*, John Gloag the writer and John Betjeman the poet, also were founders. Later Chermayeff, Berthold Lubetkin (of Tecton), Raymond Mortimer the writer, Herbert Read the critic, Commander Val Goldsmith of the B.B.C., R.S. Lambert, editor of the *Listener*, and (Sir) John Summerson, became members. As a pressure group, it lacked cohesion and belied the belligerence of its title, but the coincidence of its emergence and the diaspora from Hitler's Germany of many of the Continent's finest architects brought new life and encouragement to those struggling in England to uphold the modernist banner.

London was the venue for the 1934 C.I.A.M. Congress, to which delegates came from all over Europe. Gropius and Alfred Korn came from Germany; Le Corbusier and André Lurçat from France; J.L. Sert and Torres from Spain; Giedion, Moser and Steiger from Switzerland; Victor Bourgeois from Belgium.

An excited McGrath agreed to put up Bourgeois. (Mary was in America.) Bourgeois spoke no English so when Raymond met him at Victoria Station he wore a white buttonhole and asked Mary to imagine "the limpid French which flowed from my lips".

After the Gropius lecture, Raymond magnanimously asked everybody back to 10 Park Crescent. As well as Gropius, there were Herbert Read, Joseph Emberton and all the people Mary knew. Manny Forbes and Councillor Charles Keene from Leicester were staying overnight.

The Saturday night dinner was amusing. Wells Coates welcomed the delegates; Morton Shand interpreted in French and German. Gropius replied in German and Shand, without making a note, translated.

Le Corbusier had arrived that evening. He is an extremely odd character. Apparently he has gone fascist and is at loggerheads with Lurçat, who is a Communist. But apart from his politics, he is strange. He went off during dinner to buy a map and after dinner we found him sitting on the running board of a taxi trying to explain to the cabman that he wanted to see Limehouse and the grim sights of London.

It was, Raymond told Mary, almost impossible to tell Corb that the East End is not full of gunmen or that nightlife virtually ceases at midnight. Eventually they put Corbusier, Bourgeois, Lubetkin and a few others into a cab bound for Dirty Dick's.

> Can you imagine Corbusier, modernest of all the moderns, drinking beer and studying the dried animals and cobwebs which festoon the ceiling of Dirty Dick's... One very typical Cockney singled out Corbusier and toasted him several times; and then to our great surprise began to talk most fluent French to him...

Wearing a black oilskin, Corbusier himself was the toughest looking object in the streetscape, which was "as gay as a tomb and about as bloodthirsty as Hampstead Way". De Cronin Hastings wound up as the sole custodian of France's greatest architect. It cost him "several quid" in taxi fares to get home.

The congress left Raymond determined that Norman, just turning three, would be able to speak French and German as well as he did English or American. "Break the news to him that hard-hearted poppa's waiting to take him in hand." It did not work.

When the Crystal Palace burned down in 1936, the MARS Group mourned the loss of a mighty symbol of modern materials (glass and iron) and a pioneer showcase of mass-production. Pilkingtons the glass people, already valuable contacts of Raymond's through Finella and the exhibition stands he had designed, organised a competition for a new Crystal Palace. McGrath, Fry and Oliver Bernard were among the competitors. The structure was not built but Pilkingtons heavily sponsored Raymond's next book, 'Glass in Architecture and Decoration'.[60] This seminal tome was to become a reference book for architects and designers

Corb by Corb

McGrath proof-reading 'Glass in Architecture and Decoration'

for decades and was successfully revised and updated in 1961 with a cover photograph by Raymond's son Norman.

For the *Architectural Review* for July 1933, Raymond designed the cover. It was the British Industrial Art number of the magazine. Inside it carried a progress and period chart of English design, covering dress, vehicles and furniture. It was Raymond's work and it was intended to show at a glance the evolution of the design of familiar objects over 433 years. The chart, in two parts, was meant to form the beginning of a series in preparation. In the end, he must have been too busy to do any more work of such an intricate nature. For what was shown, he had done 163 separate drawings.

These elaborate charts, covering ten types of furniture and ten kinds of household equipment on opposite sides of one folded sheet; and eight forms of transport and two forms of costume on another folded sheet, were appended to John Gloag's[61] book on design in 1934. They were objects of beauty in themselves and added greatly to the visual value of the book.

In the meanwhile, Raymond designed a symbol for Gordon England of Mobiloil; a standard clock and sign and standard oil equipment in pressed bronze for the Vacuum Oil Company; a portable electric fire for Belling; moulded furniture for Bakelite; a standard synchronous clock for Smith's Electric Clocks; upholstery and wall fabrics for Edinburgh Weavers; more wallpapers for Sandersons, and a range of Phoenix ovenglass for the British Heat-Resisting Glass Company. This ovenware was designed with Elizabeth Craig and consisted of seven pieces.

He was not the first architect to design almost everything that was to be used in his own buildings, but he was with Chermayeff and Coates a pioneer of the concept of the modern architect as industrial designer. This role he maintained throughout his life and far from diminishing the range of his skills, he was later on to add to them by establishing himself as a painter in Ireland.

Lord Rothermere, the press baron, bought St. Dunstan's in Regent's

Manny Forbes and members of his clan

*One of several wallpaper designs
McGrath produced for Sanderson's*
(Courtesy of the Trustees of the V & A)

Park and commissioned Gerald Warren ("a pretty dull architect", Raymond called him in a letter to Mary in Texas) to build the house. Quite apart from the house, Rothermere planned to spend £15,000 on the garden, and he asked Raymond to submit designs for it. Raymond sketched a grand staircase and a grander terrace, neither of which looked credible for a time of deep depression. At any rate, the scheme did not materialise, any more than did Polyfoto's plans for a chain of 25 photographic shops around Britain. Raymond got final approval for the principal premises in Regent Street next door to the Picadilly Hotel — to be finished by the end of March 1934 — but there is no evidence that the building went ahead.

With another great scheme that got nowhere, Raymond had nothing to do. But he watched with interest and sympathy as his patron and friend Manny Forbes poured the last of his remaining energy into a campaign for "100 New Towns for Britain". Trystan Edwards devised the plan to "Solve the Slum Problem; Give Creative Employment; Save the Countryside; and Make an A1 Population". It was as much political as it was architectural, as can be surmised from the eugenic sound of its fourth aim. Manny was flirting with the Social Credit scheme begun by the Premier of Alberta, Major Douglas, and for the New Towns he tried to enlist the support of his friend, the great economist John Maynard Keynes. By January, 1935, he was distributing, mostly at his own expense, 100,000 brochures about his grand design.

For an Australian developer, Raymond produced prototypes and housing layouts for the Stroud Valley Estate in Gloucestershire. The scheme, on which he was working in 1935, was later built, but Raymond told Peter Varley[62] that he had never seen the result. It was "a nice simple layout" with terraced and semi-detached houses.

161

John Rothenstein and his wife

Raymond's first meeting with Sir William Rothenstein turned out to be instructive. It began with tea at the Mackails, whose daughter Angela Thirkill was there on a visit from Melbourne. Rothenstein, the painter and Principal of the Royal College of Art, was "a very nice old boy" who asked Raymond to call after dinner to meet his son John, director of the Art Gallery at Leeds.

The big William Morris sort of house in Kensington had held two sons and a daughter. John, later to transform the Tate Gallery, was "the ugly duckling", his younger brother good-looking and the daughter *very* good-looking. John's wife was from Kentucky and "very tall and willowy and dark and good-looking... friendly and elflike". Raymond was impressed by her to the point of sending Mary a sketch of her.

It was New Year's Eve and the young people set off for the Notting Hill Sporting Club, where there was a dance:

> The members are chiefly shop-girls (and of course shop-boys) and was it an eye-opener — I'll say it was! In a big room that might have been "chez Florence", a very [*sic*] jazz band was dimly discernible through the fog of tobacco smoke. Tables and onlookers were crowded round the walls — and on the floor a very brown girl in a white lace dress was doing a very wild dance with occasional somersaults. And when the club took the floor, it swayed like a sea and if you missed your turning you were knocked down and killed instantly. Beer flowed and girls were tossed from table to table...

There is unfortunately no record of Mary's reaction to these goings-on. Perhaps she contrasted them with the staid atmosphere of the Idlewild Club in Dallas. Perhaps they hastened her resolve to return to her normally quiet husband.

CHAPTER XXII

ric Lewenhaupt shared Mary McGrath's grief by writing to her: "Yes Manny has left an amazing void in one's life. When I walked through the familiar rooms in Finella after the service... I felt as if M. were quite close, and moreover a gay, happy Manny and not a lugubrious wraith."

At the end of 1935, Mansfield Duval Forbes was a sick man. He was given a year's leave of absence. He had abused his slight body for years, eating the wrong or no foods, drinking too much on occasions, and always uncertain of getting a night's sleep.

To "Dear Remo" he gave more detail: "15 days ago calf of me right leg went foney." The doctor diagnosed thrombosis "and not to be trifled with — i.e. blood-clot in the *blood-stream*. I had to take to bed (in S. Pink) soon as possible and may have to remain 6, 7, 8, 9 weeks — keeping leg still as possibly can for 2–3 weeks at least..."

One night, he disobeyed orders, left his bed and within minutes was dead of pulmonary embolism. It was January 1936 and Manny was 46 years old.

While Raymond's obituary of Manny could not adequately reflect his deep feeling of loss, it spoke feelingly of his adventurous spirit and with understandable and affectionate exaggeration said: "When the Book of Forbes is written it will be as rich in the material of genius as his Book of Clare is."

Unsettled by grief, Raymond made an error of judgement, taking umbrage at de Cronin Hastings' appreciation of Manny in the *Architectural Review*. Worse, he divided Manny's friends and upset his family by soliciting signatures from people who should, he felt, share his abhorrence of Hastings' obituary, which read in part:

> He was a master of a kind of plastic invective which was always at the service of his friends in their battles against pedantry and stupidity; in fact anything he had was at the service of his friends... Any cause as long as it was both lost and picturesque could command his loyalty and labour. But labour with him was not that dull and grudging thing we have learnt to give lip-service to. It was a sort of rake's progress leading up unexplored avenues hung with fantastic situations...

It was not a conventional obituary, but unless Raymond imagined himself as one of Manny's lost causes, it is difficult to discern the source of his anger. *The Scotsman* wrote: "…The brilliant young Australian architect Raymond McGrath, to whom [Forbes] gave a start in this country, has certainly justified Mansfield Forbes' confidence by his subsequent work in London and elsewhere."

What Raymond wanted by way of righting Hastings' perceived wrong was a note of protest against his flippancy signed by as many prominent people as possible. As well as Raymond, it was signed by Trystan Edwards, Lord Pentland, Harry Godwin, Edith Croll, Harold Tomlinson, Jeffrey Mark, Ian Parsons, the Master of Sempill (a cousin of Manny's), F.L. Attenborough, John Layard, Oliver Hill, J. Murray Easton, James Wordie, Lance Sieveking and Albert Frost. A number of people refused, including Clough Williams-Ellis. They felt that no serious injustice had been done.

A bereavement counsellor nowadays would probably say that the organisational energy that Raymond put into this protest gave him a useful outlet for his sorrow. Nor did it permanently sour his good relations with de Cronin Hastings.

As a more enduring way of honouring Manny's name, a memorial volume was suggested by Edwards, McGrath and others. They formally asked Manny's mother, Mrs. A.M. Forbes, to appoint Ian Parsons unofficial literary executor for the book. Parsons *was* asked to look after Manny's papers, but another of Manny's cousins, the influential M.I. Batten (Pud Webb) wrote to Raymond refusing to sign the letter to Mrs. Forbes. She said there was room for only one book on Mansfield Forbes and it should not be rushed into.

"Something which you may have forgotten", she wrote sharply, "Finella and every single paper in it belongs to Mrs. Forbes. In a book about Manny, I want Manny, not just what a dozen or so friends thought about him."

Pud Batten, who was married to Geoffrey Webb, Slade Professor of Fine Arts at Cambridge, got her way. It was 1984, long after nearly all the actors in the drama were dead, before Hugh Carey produced his affectionate tribute,[63] giving himself just enough time to read the proofs before his own premature death. Manny died intestate. The Forbes family, having attended the funeral in Clare College Chapel and the cremation at Golders Green, had to decide what to do with Finella, on which thirteen years of the lease still had to run. They kept the house going until the summer in the hope that Clare College would get a Rockefeller or Carnegie Trust to fund it; but the house was the property of Gonville and Caius and to that college it had eventually to revert. The wonder is that it survived a world war and a succession of tenants to remain worth viewing as the remains of the glittering marvel that Manny and Raymond built more than sixty years ago.

The auctioneers' brochure said that "The Exquisite Modern and Antique Furnishings of Finella" would be sold at auction on 15 July, 1936, along with the remaining thirteen years' lease.

As their personal tribute to Manny, his painting by Ethelbert White, 'Puente san Martín, Toledo' was bought for 25 guineas by his friends whose names are on the back. It was presented to the Mansfield Forbes Library in the summer of 1936. This news was imparted to Raymond by Harry Godwin at Cambridge. In a reference to Mary's recent departure for Texas, "God" added: "You'll be feeling lost without your family. But we hope they will both have loved the Queen Mary".

It was ironic that the Cunard liner Queen Mary had been the subject of a five-page closely-typed letter[64] written by Manny in 1932 to Sir Thomas Royden of the Cunard Line. Manny hoped to interest Royden in commissioning Raymond to decorate "the giant Cunarders which were to wrest for Britain the passenger supremacy of the Atlantic". No reply is to be found, but after Manny's death Raymond was asked to collaborate with Mr. Leech, the permanent architect of the Cunard White Star Line on the decoration of the interiors of the new liner then building. (She was later named the Queen Elizabeth after the new Queen). Although Raymond was prepared to open a Liverpool office for the necessary three years, the job went elsewhere.

Mary was pregnant again and quite convinced that she was going to give birth to a girl. "I know you will have your wish", Raymond assured her, "and I have been thinking what we might call her." Having looked at a large number of Shakespearean, Biblical, Victorian and Hollywood alternatives, he had "become very partial to Jenny". So seven months later, Jenny became the informal name of Jennifer Anne, who like her brother had to wait another fifteen years for baptism. (Mary once asked the three-year-old Norman whom, after Daddy, he liked most in the world. "Jesus", he answered firmly. Mary attributed this response to Raymond's religious instruction; but the parents took their responsibility for spiritual guidance no farther until in Dublin the question of confirmation in the Church of Ireland arose in the 1950s.)

Although he had an uneasy feeling that it was an old chestnut, Raymond asked Mary if she had heard the one about the mother taking her son to be christened. "She hadn't thought of a name and on a pair of opened doors she saw NOSMO KING and called him that".

He was immersed in work. His new client, C.R. Keene, was an old friend of Manny's and Lord Mayor of Leicester, where he commissioned Raymond to build him the new Kingstone store, offices and a warehouse with vitrolite facings. They were steel-frame buildings and their value was £28,000. Keene (later Sir Charles) must have been pleased because he then asked Raymond to design his new house, Land's End, at Galby. This house, now called Carrygate, was worth £6,500, and is of considerable interest, especially since the landscaping was done by Christopher Tunnard. It will be referred to later.

The Pearl Assurance Company offices at Bournemouth, designed with Goodesmith, were nearly finished and so were the estate offices which he did for J.A. Phillips in Pall Mall. "Terrible man, Phillips, who led me a dance in the '30s", said Raymond to Peter Varley in 1976. He had properties all over London, including several in Soho Square which he wanted to develop as a centre for the film industry. Phillips put Raymond in touch with Metro-Goldwyn-Mayer. Raymond and W.L. Havard did sketch schemes for

The Pearl Assurance Company offices at Bournemouth

M.G.M. and other film companies. "They were promotional drawings that I wasn't proud of", Raymond told Varley. Phillips died "owing me thousands and thousands of pounds". Out of the estate Raymond got one halfpenny in the pound and made an uncharacteristically anti-semitic remark about Phillips's partners: "Two of the smartest jew-boys in town."

On the bright side, he wrote to Mary of Miss Minnie Langer who told him from Switzerland that she was "very pleased with my designs for the chauffeur's cottage, garage for four cars, stable group for four horses — a very romantic block of buildings round a courtyard. I designed it more as a challenge than anything else, but it *is* sympathique. The block will cost about £5,000."

The reference here was to Printstile Place, Bidborough, Kent, which McGrath and Tunnard worked on. It involved garden pavilions, a garage and a stable block of brick and timber, and its value in the end was £9,000, not £5,000. It was completed in 1937 and is not only poorly documented but even still access-proof. The clients were Mrs and Miss Langer.

And of course there was St. Ann's Hill, the subject of the next chapter. For the first time, Raymond could talk of "a nice steady flow of work setting in".

He had an interview with the chief architect of the London Passenger Transport Board and "there's no doubt this job will be going on". He designed posters for the L.P.T.B. and he illustrated a book called 'London Adventure' by Elizabeth Montizambert (22 drawings), published by the

St. Paul's Cathedral, one of McGrath's drawings for 'London Adventure'

board. But the job he told Mary about was a building near Peter Jones' new department store: it was to be faced with glass to match the store, and for some reason it fell through. As he wrote, though, he was supremely confident:

> Don't worry your head about finances my dear. It's been slow... but things are really moving now. The fees on the *definite* work which I now have at the office will amount to about £1,950 over the next eight months. So the future hasn't any more financial trials in store for us. Of course if the Yorkshire schools and Leicester College [F.L. Attenborough (Manny's friend Att) was Principal of University College, Leicester] and the Sloane Square flats all come to pass, we ought to arrive, financially. At least we'll be able to teach Norman reading, writing and arithmetic.

A year and some disappointments later, he sent Mary an illustrated letter to Norfolk, where she was on holiday with her small family. He had done some sketches on a visit to Brighton and asked her opinion of them. He himself thought them only adequate, and he extended his doubts about his talent to his poetry:

> I don't know what it is that stimulates the imagination but I know mine is prosaic... I have got into the habit of reproducing what I see, and I am not content unless I am reproducing with accuracy. Something wrong somewhere. Or if I try to write a poem I make a word picture, another kind of reproduction. But very few people seem to get a new angle on anything.

An aspect of Raymond's life which caused him grave anxiety in 1935 and 1936 was the travelling scholarship he had been awarded by the Board of Architects of New South Wales in 1929. Worth £400 a year for three years, the scholarship had its drawbacks. It required him to submit six-monthly reports to the board, and much more importantly it demanded that he return to Australia within a given period to work and give a course of lectures in Sydney.

The penalty for failing to meet these requirements was that his bondsman — in his case his father Herbert McGrath — would be called upon to meet his obligations. The principal obligation was to pay £100 to the board.

The burden of this worry seems not to have fallen on Mary's shoulders. There is no correspondence with her or any of the Croziers to show that he had a care in the world apart from getting and executing commissions. Yet it was a serious matter, one that at the London end he seems to have kept to himself. If it were not for that indefatigable correspondent, his father, we would not know of the concern he was feeling as he faced the prospect of closing his practice and shipping his family to Australia to begin again.

B. J. Waterhouse, whose name already was linked with "The Work of Eileen McGrath', was still president of the Board of Architects of New South Wales and as far as can be judged from the correspondence was willing to bend the rules almost to breaking point for Raymond.

As the McGrath on the spot and the man who had most to lose financially, Herbert extended himself mightily on Raymond's behalf. "Were he", he wrote, "in a stronger financial position he might take the risk of leaving his London practice to enable him to comply with the conditions of his scholarship and incur the expenses incidental to an eighteen months' absence from his office. I cannot see any prospect of my son being able to comply with the board's requirements without severely straining his own and my financial resources…"

Any extension the board could give — and it was a quasi-governmental organisation with rules to keep and red tape to bind them in — was granted to Raymond. The point came when Raymond had to make a final plea — this time for permanent exemption. He designed his long letter carefully.

The Board's final response was crisp: "The Board insists upon your return to Sydney by July next", said Waterhouse. The alternative was outlined by Herbert McGrath in a letter to his son:

> You will think it worth £100 to be free of the importunities of the Board, for it must have been a source of anxiety to you being continually reminded of your obligations. £100 is a lot of money to you and to me but it seems we shall have to part with it. Sorrowfully, I would suggest that you allow me to meet the obligations of the Board and when your ship comes in as it surely will some day, you can recoup me.

So Raymond stayed put. How he had dealt with his similar obligation to Sydney University we do not know. Nor do we know the final outcome of his failure to present his thesis at Cambridge. Many years later, in 1968, he tried through Sir Harry Godwin to get a postgraduate degree from Cambridge. He told Professor Sir Leslie Martin of the School of Architecture that he would like to have "some modest form of recognition", not necessarily a Ph. D., for the three years he had spent at Cambridge. Martin was also chairman of the Faculty Board of Fine Arts (on which Manny had once sat), and Peter Bicknell was a member. When Raymond made a formal application, he was told that under regulation 4(c) the answer was no. It was a sad ending to an academic career that had been so laden with promise. It would have been more fitting in the year of his retirement from the Office of Public Works in Ireland to award an honorary doctorate to one of the pioneers of modern architecture in England.

CHAPTER XXIII

Lance Sieveking describes A.L. Schlesinger as "a short, rather burly, black-haired man of 45 or so". Schlesinger, a wealthy London stockbroker, had seen Raymond's work at one of the Olympia exhibitions and was impressed. He and his friend Christopher Tunnard, the landscape architect, conceived the idea of building a modern house at St. Ann's Hill, Chertsey. They commissioned Raymond to design the house. The gardens would be Tunnard's contribution.

This is the bare outline of the great work that, more than anything he built before or after, made Raymond's name as an architect. Schlesinger, who was fond of music and especially of Sibelius, was married and had an adopted daughter, Pamela. The human story of St. Ann's is incomplete, but while it was being built in 1936 for Schlesinger and Tunnard, Oliver Hill designed and built Hill House, Redlington Road, Hampstead, for the same client. The garden was also laid out by Tunnard. Alan Powers[65] calls this house "one of the best modern houses of its period in natural brick". The Hill House — called after Oliver Hill and sited on the highest point in Hampstead — has echoes of Mies van der Rohe's Tugendhat House at Brno (1930), a design much admired by Raymond in his 'Twentieth Century Houses'.

Because the Hill House (1936–38) was built for Schlesinger, the question must be asked: was he living a double life? He and Tunnard slept in the circular bedroom of St. Ann's Hill. There was no central bed as there is now: there were single beds in open alcoves. There is no record of how long the two lived at St. Ann's Hill, but Tunnard went to America in 1939 to work in the Graduate School of Design at Harvard, and local lore in Chertsey firmly places Schlesinger, his wife and daughter as the occupants of St. Ann's Hill during the war. It may mean nothing or anything that the foreword to Tunnard's 1938 book, 'Gardens in the Modern Landscape', was written from 115 Mount Street, London. For part of Tunnard's time at Chertsey, he lent some accommodation in the outbuildings to his artist brother[66] as a studio. Raymond met him and Tunnard's mother and "quite a pleasant relationship ensued". Raymond often visited the house, where he "was always welcome".

Christopher Tunnard[67] was born in Victoria, British Columbia, in 1910. He went to Victoria College, University of British Columbia, and then to the Royal Horticultural College at Wisley, where he got a diploma in 1930. Two years later, he took building construction courses at the Westminster Technical Institute. From 1932 to 1935, he was a site planner in the London office of Percy S. Cane, the conventional garden designers.

In 1936, the year of St. Ann's Hill, he went into private practice as a landscape architect. Tall, fair and elegant, as Lance Sieveking remembers him, he was then 26.

St. Ann's Hill was the first project in which Tunnard co-operated with McGrath. They went on to do two more designs that were executed and one for which the evidence seems to be confined to one reference in Tunnard's book. This was a weekend house at Cobham, Surrey (again on an elevated site) and Raymond is credited with the design of the house.

Charles James Fox, the Whig leader, was the 18th-century owner of the house and estate at St. Ann's Hill. In 1784 he paid £2,000 for a modest villa and 30 acres on the southern slope of St. Ann's Hill. "The fat, gambling greasy Fox, with smiles too wide to be trusted" as J. Steven Watson has painted him, was out of office at the time. He greatly loved this country retreat.

It was the garden that Fox so carefully made which attracted Christopher Tunnard. It was simple and bereft of what Jane Brown[68] has called the "orgy of awesome grottos, fantastic follies and beautiful walks" that marked some of the surrounding houses in the Surrey countryside.

By the 1930s the house, then of 25 acres, was so run down that McGrath and Tunnard felt no compunction about pulling it down. The planning authorities were surprisingly reasonable. (The stables and walls remain, the stables serving as recording studios for Phil Manzanera of Roxy Music fame. Phil, whose name is Targett-Adams, and his wife Sharon bought St. Ann's Hill in 1977 and were fortunate to find Paul Davis of Davis and Bayne to restore it with a sensitivity and constructive genius that would have gladdened the heart of Raymond McGrath.)

Working to a budget of £14,000, Raymond designed a house that unashamedly was for a rich man. The house was cylindrical in its main form. When Brian Hanson[69] suggested to him that there was a great deal of the aircraft in St. Ann's Hill, Raymond countered with a reply which, with or without attribution, has been used by commentators several times since:

St. Ann's Hill in 1936.
The Wistaria can be seen outside
the drawing-room window.
(Photograph by Raymond McGrath)

Mary (left) and Raymond visiting the building site of St. Ann's Hill, with Eileen, Norman and Toby Hammond, June 1936

That was like a big cheese, with a slice cut for the sunlight to enter the whole house. It was my most ambitious piece of domestic architecture in England.

The cheese simile, it is fair to point out, was originally used in the *Architectural Review's* account of the house in October 1937.

What is important for anyone looking at St. Ann's Hill is that the design is seamless. The house is not just set in parkland: it is an integral part of the space created for it by Christopher Tunnard. It is made to look out from as well as to live in.

Situated on the exact site of at least three earlier houses, it is constructed of reinforced concrete. Externally, because Raymond was not keen on rendering, rough Oregon boarding was used for vertical shuttering and the surface texture of the wood was retained. This shuttering effect was new if not pioneering, and with the pale pinkish grey paint was a remarkable feature of the house. Once Raymond's sketch plans were approved by the clients, not much in the way of change was made, though Raymond recalled that the billiard room, he fancied, was an afterthought.

With a winter garden and large swimming pool, the house is quite sizeable. In a "house within a house" the staff, with their own staircase, were quite cut off. Their service areas, including a butler's pantry, were almost Victorian in concept and have been cleverly remodelled by Paul Davis to suit a young family's needs in the last quarter of the century.

While the 18th century grotto is now gone, the 60-year-old house will stand for a long time. The concealed radiator central heating system still works, but both it and the steel windows are due for replacement. Outside the huge curved drawing-room window is a Wistaria so old that it is protected by order and maintained annually by the man in Kew Gardens who looks after the Wistaria there. (The house itself is now a listed dwelling, one of the few 1930s buildings so protected.) The Wistaria is

now too big and makes maintenance difficult, but its careful tending is a consequence of its age and botanical significance. Some of the ancient oaks and many other old trees on the hill were lost in the severe storms of early 1990.

During building, the Wistaria was severely cut back, and no damage was done to it. Schlesinger's daughter Pamela, when she saw a recent article on the restoration of St. Ann's Hill, made it known that she had a collection of about 100 photographs of the construction work. They were taken by either her father or Tunnard and they form a most valuable record of the work as it progressed.

And progress it did. In the middle of August 1936, Raymond told Mary, who once more was visiting her people, that he had just returned from Chertsey, where "they made me stay to dinner". Ten days later it is clear that the owners were living at St. Ann's Hill well before it was finished:

> I must say the interior is beginning to look exciting now it is plastered out and cleaned up. The railings, balustrades, spiral staircase etc. make a big difference. I have been doing some furniture for the house. The fabrics, curtains etc. so far selected are pretty de luxe, but not too rich. We have found a couple more wells. The hill is honeycombed with them. The garden down there looks lovely, it always does, and now that the scaffolding is down the house fits nicely into the landscape.

A year later, when Mary was staying in Norfolk, Raymond brought back from Chertsey "some super gladioli which I sent around to Mrs. Taylor". (Julian and Margaret Taylor, a surgeon and anaesthetist respectively, lived at Portland Place. Their sons Simon and Jim were playmates of Norman McGrath, and Raymond designed a climbing frame for the Taylor nursery where pre-school classes were held by the governess and Norman had his first schooling. Raymond said later he was

Facing page:
The Winter Garden (above) and a
view showing how McGrath cut a
slice out of the 'big cheese' (below)
(Photographs by Norman McGrath)

Copper-clad columns support a
suspended ceiling in the circular
living-room. The carpet was made by
John French. The occasional tables
(not visible here) and other furniture
including the double bed were by
Fred Baier and Chris Rose
(Photograph by Norman McGrath)

always surprised that Julian Taylor was such a marvellous surgeon and yet could make such a botch of carving a joint of meat.)

"Chertsey", Raymond informed Mary, "is fast becoming a kind of private Whipsnade. Peacocks, pigeons, parrots and now half-a-dozen penguins, all very decorative. Schlesinger walks about with a parrot on each shoulder."

The zoological ambience was not confined to the gardens. On one memorable occasion, Lance Sieveking[70] drove Raymond, Paul Nash and his wife Margaret down to St. Ann's Hill. They had been asked to lunch by the owners, who knew of Paul Nash by reputation and were pleased to show him their wonderful new house. "Paul was enchanted. It was just the sort of house he would have built himself. He was especially delighted at a circular flight of steps made of feathery openwork metal which seemed to have been a moment before flung up into the air. He went up and down it twice…"

The spiral staircase which so delighted Paul Nash that he went up and down twice. The photograph is Raymond's.

The embarrassing moment came while we were seated at luncheon. The whole of one wall of the airy dining room consisted of a vast aviary in which more than a hundred budgerigars disported themselves. Raymond was a quiet, extremely modest Australian and I think it affected him most. Paul was not so much embarrassed as indignant at the folly of the thing. He had quite recovered from his coughing fit [he had the beginning of the asthma which eventually killed him] and was talking with his accustomed wit. Our hosts were obviously stimulated by his conversation and we were all laughing and enjoying the excellent luncheon.

Suddenly, just as Paul was reaching the point of an extremely entertaining anecdote, the budgerigars began to shriek, squeak and chatter all together. Their hundreds of little grating gravelly voices drowned Paul completely as we all leaned forward to hear the point. He repeated it a bit louder, but the noise was so terrific that he gave up with a comic gesture of despair…

It is a pity that Raymond was not in time to insert St. Ann's Hill in his 'Twentieth Century Houses'. But it was well received in books and periodicals in England and on the Continent, including *Nuova Architettura nel Mondo*. It was fully illustrated in the *Journal of the Royal Institute of British Architects, Country Life* and the *Architectural Review*, and in F.R.S. Yorke's book 'Modern Houses in England'. The R.I.B.A. *Journal*, in the nature of things, gave the names of the quantity surveyors (Messrs. Ainsley), the contractors (R. Mansell Ltd.), the swimming pool contractors (Marshall and Co.) and the sub-contractors and suppliers. These latter were too numerous to mention but the reader will be pleased to see among them Pilkington Bros. Ltd, James Clark & Sons Ltd, and Docker Bros., all of whom had begun their relationship with Raymond at Finella seven years before. From Italy Alberto Sartoris wrote to Raymond seeking a photograph of St. Ann's Hill for the latest edition of his book "Gli

Facing page:
The original terrazzo floors have been restored.
(Photograph by Norman McGrath)

elementi dell' Architettura Funzionale", first published in 1932. Raymond MacGrath [*sic*] is given as the sole architect representing Australia.

The greatest boost that St. Ann's Hill got was Christopher Tunnard's book 'Gardens in the Modern Landscape', which was fashioned out of articles in the *Architectural Review*. In a chapter entitled 'Garden into landscape', he included not only the best photographs of the house but seven "aerial" drawings of the life of the hill from the 17th century to 1910, showing the growth of the built area after enclosure. These drawings hang still in the house where on the wall facing the door there is Raymond's engraved map of the garden as remodelled by Tunnard. It is cut on a type of faceted glass called Vitroflex, a new French import.

Elsewhere in the book is an exquisite drawing by Gordon Cullen, showing "an architectural garden, part axial, part asymmetrical... Screen walls frame the distant views". A chimney-like sculpture, now lost, is by Willi Soukop. In the courtyard, with his back to the artist, is what can only be Gerald Schlesinger, a parrot on his left shoulder and three birds feeding at his feet. Cullen at that time had left Tecton and was working on the *Architectural Review*.

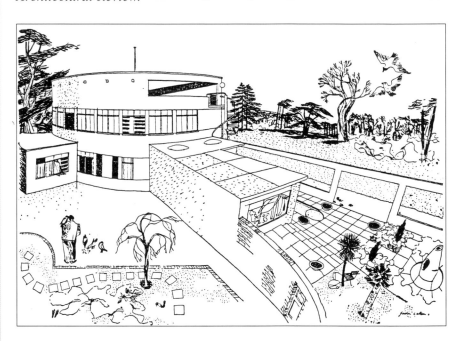

"Schlesinger walks about with a parrot on each shoulder", wrote McGrath. In Gordon Cullen's drawing, one parrot is gone to ground

In 'Twentieth Century Houses', Raymond had written a coda expressing his vision of what was to come:

> The future is in the hollow of our hands. In the wide windows of the twentieth-century house are framed the white towns of tomorrow and the clear-cut buildings of men as awake as ever the Greeks were to the fullest pleasures of living. What other road is there to take but into these surprising distances?

It was the Ctesiphon arch of his modernism, soon modified and tempered by experience and pragmatism, but in St. Ann's Hill reaching the apotheosis of his belief that "where there is no Progress there is no

Land's End at Galby. The house has been renamed Carrygate

Tradition". He gave the New Architecture "a historical pedigree and a standard to aspire to which was also that of the best building of the past".[71]

Already by 1936, Raymond was writing in the *Architectural Review* (January): "Policy surely indicates some slight letting up of our present emphasis on functionalism, for after all we do not practise it with quite the austerity revealed in our preaching."

Not much more than six months earlier, Raymond had made a ringing declaration of his faith in the modern movement. In a letter to the editor of the *Journal* of the R.I.B.A. (13 July, 1935), he castigated the proceedings of the June conference of the R.I.B.A. at Glasgow. They make, he said, "melancholy, almost medieval reading".

> Progress! Was there ever an age and an art in which the real progress was so obscured by petty issues? We do not yet seem to realise what the twentieth century means, or could mean. We wrangle about design. We argue about ornament. We lament tradition, yet it is the social aspect of architecture which matters. England disintegrates while we pursue our politics on the very threshold of a new world. What do we really need? Organisation, co-operation, planning; these living forces which can produce order, order which is the chief meaning of the new architecture.

Practising what he did not preach, Raymond designed the house at Galby, 12 miles from Leicester, that had been commissioned by Councillor Charles Keene. It was Raymond's third successful collaboration with Christopher Tunnard, and like St. Ann's Hill it sat on a commanding site.

Unlike St. Ann's Hill, it used materials of which the purists would not have approved. They were chosen to suit a house that looked across wide

Gordon Cullen's drawing of an early
version of Land's End, Galby

fields dotted with small stands of timber towards the grey tower of the church at King's Norton. The ground floor is clad in Elizabethan bricks from Beaudesert in Yorkshire. The bricks were bought when the manor house was demolished. The first floor is timber-clad, weather-boarded with English elm.

Tunnard's garden is informal, again designed to link the house with the rolling countryside. But the form of the house is curved and modern, and the early plans called for so much glass that the Rural Council, advised by the Council for the Preservation of Rural England, forced their amendment.

The windows were of Swiss pine: otherwise the forests of the British Empire were plundered for Canadian rock elm, Burma teak, gaboon, Indian silver greywood, Tasmanian silky oak, English oak and Raymond's favourite Australian walnut.

Land's End went through more modification, both house and garden, than St. Ann's Hill; and it therefore took much longer to complete. Ian Kitson's recent research[72] shows that, while some of the planting may have begun as early as 1935, the house was finished just as the war began.

Certainly the Gordon Cullen drawing of the proposed gardens, which appeared in the *Architectural Review* (April 1938) and then in Tunnard's book, bears little relation to the gardens as planted. But these discrepancies are for the specialist. The house has an atmosphere that is warm and welcoming. Its present owners, Mr. and Mrs. Nicholas Townsend, have not hesitated to make some internal changes that make the space more gemütlich than it was over fifty years ago. (The house was not listed until 1984, so change was possible. The Thirties Society requested the listing in 1983.) The house is now called Carrygate.

The partnership of McGrath and Tunnard was fruitful. Tunnard was generally recognised as the only pioneer of Modernist garden design in England, and three of the five gardens he did in England were planned as the settings for houses designed by Raymond.

During the war, nobody got excited about new houses, but the *Architectural Review* devoted three pages to Galby in November 1941. The photographs were taken by F.L. Attenborough, to whose college the house was near. He knew C.R. Keene: he was an old friend of Raymond's. *Country Life* too, in the form of Christopher Hussey, reviewed the house and leaving a reference to Tunnard until later in the article said:

> The landscape aspect of modern architecture could not be in more sensitive hands than those of Mr. Raymond McGrath, an artist and draughtsman of great distinction, besides [being] one of the leading contemporary architects.

The *Architects' Journal* (November 1941) gives Tunnard the credit for laying out "the major portion of the garden", whatever that means.

Tunnard said: "The fact that garden making is in part a science does not free it from the duty of performing an aesthetic function; it can no more be turned over to the horticulturist than architecture to the engineer." He was deliberately controversial most of the time, which is why his book, which went into a new edition in 1948, was so influential in both England and America.

The frontispiece shows "the garden terrace of a house near Halland, Sussex". In fact it shows Barbara Chermayeff basking in a low steel chair and enjoying the house that Serge built. Tunnard did the garden. A Henry Moore reclining figure graces the end of the terrace but it was not there for long. Barbara Chermayeff, showing how slack was the architect's grip on security, says that because they had not yet paid for the Moore, it ended up in the Museum of Modern Art in New York.

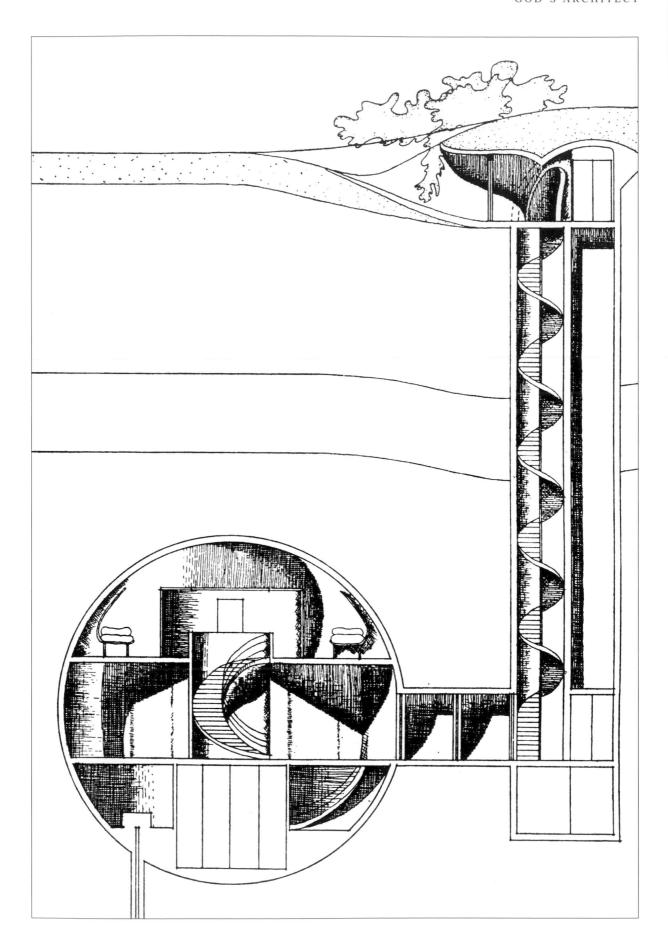

CHAPTER XXIV

enny was born on 7 March, 1937, not long before Eileen and Albert got engaged. But the highlight of the year was the Coronation in May of King George VI and Queen Elizabeth, an event which affected different people in different ways. Serge and Barbara Chermayeff were offered "grandstand" seats at Grosvenor House by Barbara's father. They chose instead to go down to the country. Mary, who did not see the Royal couple either, was chided by her mother for not giving the people of Dallas a blow-by-blow account of the ceremony, but she hit back with unaccustomed anger.

"Pardon the technicality", she wrote to Heart, "but you will remember that my milk supply was with Norman more than abundant and the same is even more true with J. The discomfort of bottling up two feeds with the likelihood of upsetting the works as a consequence put me off as much as anything else and was a risk I did not like to take in view of the baby's being underweight... I may be narrow-minded but I feel she is a great deal more important, to me, at any rate, than any spectacle, however wonderful."

Over thirty years earlier, when Heart was nursing Isabelle in 1905, she had told her own mother: "I don't believe my milk is rich enough for her and am going to begin on a bottle... about once a day."

Woman to woman, talk about breast-feeding was in order, but when Mary spoke to Norman about nursing Jenny, she resorted to "John Dunlap's[73] 'Child's Restaurant' joke". Norman had been down at Battle staying with Hazel Guggenheim (then Mrs Denys King-Farlow), so he knew a lot about farms and cows. "When he empties the baby's bath he likes to pretend he's milking a cow and it's a pretty perfect imitation." He was cutting out a paper doll in a comic one day when he began to look at it critically. After a minute he said: "Her child's restaurant seems to be up higher than yours is, mummie." Mary thought the euphemism "so nice and impersonal".

After the Coronation, the McGraths came back from a holiday near Midhurst in the South Downs. Late at night, taxis were hard to obtain and when they got one, Jenny had to be fed at once. Norman said he "didn't think it looked very nice" to make such a public display.

Albert and Eileen were busy getting their flat ready, Albert discovering that he made a useful carpenter. He had a job beginning on June 1st at a starting salary of £6. Albert too missed the Coronation, but John and Margaret Witt took Eileen to a bank in Whitehall where they had a fine view. She thought the King was most insignificant looking.

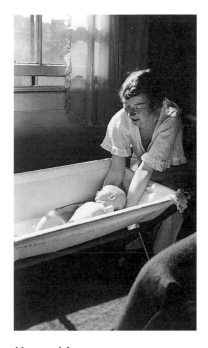

Mary and Jenny

Facing page:
"One possible future" McGrath wrote in 'Twentieth Century Houses', *"for the private house, a structure safe against air attack."*

Alice Hemming, who was settling nicely into 35 Elsworthy Road (where she lived until her death in 1994), gave a very pleasant lunch party at which Mary met Celia Johnson, who had the lead in the long-running play 'The Wind and the Rain'. Celia Johnson had just married "the famous young writer, Peter Fleming, who writes such good travel books and is so very beautiful himself". Mrs. Fleming could not compete with that. She was "very sweet, very slim and frail looking and not particularly impressive, tho' apparently she is a good actress".

Albert had recently finished his work for Raymond on 'Glass in Architecture and Decoration'. His impeccable style is discernible although as an outlet for his wit this weighty volume was less than ideal. His help in "balancing aesthetic, practical and scientific matter and combining them into a satisfactory and readable whole"[74] was invaluable, and Raymond quickly sought Albert's help again when a new edition was mooted 24 years later. It was not forthcoming. Albert and Eileen had been living in Washington since 1941.

The book, all 664 pages of it, was a great critical success and quickly became the standard work on glass in all its aspects. Delany[75] wrote: "…I do not consider it hyperbole to say that no technical book — certainly none written in English — has had so profound and widespread [an] effect on architectural design in these islands and beyond…"

Much praise went to the section on 'The Nature and Properties of Glass' by H.E. Beckett of the Building Research Station. He fortunately was in a position to bring his matter up to date a quarter of a century later.

Raymond's thanks included a tribute to Pilkington Brothers and Chance Brothers for their collaboration, but in fact it was Pilkingtons who made the book economically viable on both occasions. He thanked also Dell and Wainwright, "the book's appointed photographers"; Christopher Tunnard "for valuable data on horticultural building"; his wife Mary for "her free and always charming rendering of it on the typewriter", and finally John Gloag, "the prime instigator and patient accomplice of this

Perhaps the last photograph taken of the Crystal Palace was this, by Dell and Wainwright

collective undertaking". Gloag it was who also urged the preparation of the new edition in 1961.

The book was at the proof-reading stage when the Crystal Palace went on fire, an event which made the picture on the dust-jacket truly topical. Its destruction gave Raymond the opportunity to add only a footnote:

> The destruction of the Crystal Palace overnight... added for us a touch of irony to its end, and gave us the sad necessity of recasting our comments on it into the past tense. On the night of November 30, 1936, a fire broke out in the main transept and in an amazingly short space of time set the whole building ablaze. Nothing had been done to bring the structure into line with modern conceptions of fire-proof construction... It is perhaps fitting that the end of the Crystal Palace should have been as popular a spectacle as its beginning.

Built in seventeen weeks in 1851 to house the Great Exhibition, it was undoubtedly the greatest achievement in glass and iron construction. It was originally designed for Hyde Park, and was later re-erected at Sydenham where it stood, wrote the authors, "a vast judgement seat of brass bands and dogs, overlooking the park and pleasure-grounds designed by its gardener-architect, Joseph Paxton".

In some of this writing one can detect the sardonic humour of Albert Frost, whose contribution to the book seems to have lain in the areas of editing and rewriting.

The Marxist Arthur Korn had just arrived from Germany. He himself had written an important book, 'Glas im Bau', on the use of glass in modern architecture, and he reviewed 'Glass in Architecture and Decoration' in the *Journal* of the R.I.B.A. (10 January, 1938). He stressed the need to carry on the struggle for modern architecture and the rational use of materials "without compromise". He could not always agree with McGrath's and Frost's ideas for the use of coloured and mirrored glass in decoration, though he did hail the production in ringing tones: "They have indeed written a standard book!"

Nikolaus Pevsner, among the most eminent art historians and architectural critics of England (he was knighted in 1969), used an article in the *Architectural Review* (also January 1938) to summarise Raymond's career in terms of his romantic use of the properties of glass:

> Raymond McGrath is one of the outstanding of the romantics. From Finella, which made his fame, to the Embassy Club and his recent house at Chertsey, he dreams, thinks and designs in terms of glass, fascinated as a true romantic by the subtle nuances in the process of the gradual elimination of identity which glass, and only glass, can offer. Nothing is fixed, stable, "classic"; all seems dissolved into an uncertain number of partly transparent, partly solid strata. Brilliant cutting, silvering, acid-embossing, sand-blasting — he takes advantage of any available process, and he

does this scientifically with the thoroughness of a fanatic.

There is a strong contrast here surely between Korn's clinical emphasis on clearly defining the modern movement and Pevsner's belief that Raymond is in pursuit of subtle nuances. Perhaps the link is the word scientifically.

Raymond himself, in the *Architectural Review* (February 1939), wrote: "In the medium of glass, art seldom reaches beyond the humble bounds of decoration. There is certainly an increasing appreciation of the technique demanded by glass processes but, probably because so few serious designers apply themselves to glass, the possibilities are rarely realised. There is still a dearth of good decoration in glass, but fortunately the 'naked quality of the material' has its own beauty."

For the British Pavilion at the great Paris International Exhibition of 1937, he designed a glass mural 24 feet high by 21 feet 9 inches wide. It was built up of 42 panels of quarter-inch plate glass bedded on mastic and supported by corner clips. It had a linear abstract design and was the sort of large-scale wall decoration that formerly might have been done in mosaic. This mural, done for the pavilion designed by Oliver Hill, does not survive.[76] The Embassy Club and Fischer's Restaurant are no more. Indeed apart from the R.I.B.A. windows and the design of Tunnard's garden at St. Ann's Hill, few of Raymond's creations in his favoured medium are still with us.

He was five days in Paris for the exposition, which he said stretched from the Place de la Concorde on both sides of the Seine as far as the Pont Grenelle. The quays had been bridged over and on these structures most of the pavilions were built.

His glass screen, he told Mary modestly, was "about the best thing in the British Pavilion, but elsewhere there are myriads of objects in glass, uses of glass etc. which would fill a book". (He discovered two materials that he had omitted from the glass book.)

Alvar Aalto made a very strong impression on Raymond, who wrote in his 1976 obituary[77] of Aalto:

> I first encountered his work in the Finnish Pavilion which he designed for the Paris Exhibition of 1937, where I acquired one of his free-form glass vases which is one of my prized possessions...
>
> I first met Alvar Aalto in New York, through the good offices of James Johnson Sweeney, when he was travelling with Elissa Makiniemi, an architect from his office whom he was later to marry... Our luncheon in New York was a happy affair which extended well into the afternoon and his modesty and wit enlivened my memory of him when we corresponded afterwards, for, alas, I never met him again... He was an outstanding designer in his own right, a breed of architect nowadays rare.

The vase, still cherished, is in Norman's hands in New York.

Among the ephemeral designs Raymond produced in 1938 was the stand for James Clark and Company, the glass manufacturers, at the

Building Trades Exhibition. On it he made use of glass louvres, glass bricks and vitrolite tiles, as well as backlit engraved glass panels. Among the stand's other features were running water and a pool. Finella rides again.

"In design terms", says Dean[78] of the Women's Fair at Olympia in the same year, "the outstanding display was the electrical industries stand by McGrath, highly characteristic in its transformation of the modest space available to him by means of curved planes and decorative planting schemes." The plants, it is easy to see in Raymond's perspective drawing, featured cacti, forever to him symbols of the Lone Star State and of Mary.

As Europe braced itself for the crisis-ridden summer of 1938, Mary was decorating 10 Park Crescent in the expectation of a visit from her parents. She got a new heater and had the electric current changed to 200/230 volts, which meant that Norman's electric train would not work. Hazel Guggenheim got her favourite toyshop to send him a transformer for his birthday on 10 June, and the day was saved.

By far the biggest commission Raymond got in England then began. The Australian managing director of Aspro Limited, G.M. Garcia, had as we have seen already used Raymond's services to remodel his flat in a mock-Tudor block, Bell Moor in Hampstead. He must have been pleased. The Aspro factory at Slough, on which Derrick Oxley collaborated, was worth £199,000 excluding equipment, and the approval of Raymond's plans was conveyed to Mary's parents at the end of June.

The Aspro factory was called (by the *Architectural Review* September 1939) the first large scale piece of factory planning. It "may well set an example for future industrialists" who set up in the Slough area. It is extraordinary to see the *A.R.*, writing at the outbreak of the Second World War, still referring to "post-war industrial development in the London area" and meaning the war of 20 years earlier.

Raymond's provision of an air-raid shelter for 600 people with a gas infiltration plant was commented on by most critics, yet such was the scale of international tension that trenches were being dug in Hyde Park for shelters and several municipal offices distributed gas masks to residents for use in the expected war. In this atmosphere, Raymond produced, as his and Mary's Christmas card for 1938, the underground house that first

Derrick Oxley and Norman

The electrical industries stand at the Women's Fair at Olympia, 1938
(The British Architectural Library, RIBA, London)

185

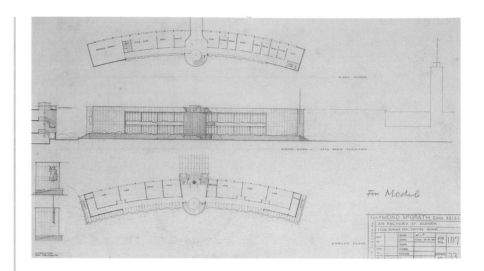

A drawing for a model of the Aspro factory
(The British Architectural Library, RIBA, London)

appeared in his 'Twentieth Century Houses' four years earlier and was captioned: "One possible future for the private house, a structure safe against air attack."

As well as workshops and offices, the Aspro scheme included a circular staff canteen consciously echoing St. Ann's Hill; lounges, a concert hall, gymnasiums, squash courts and a swimming pool. About half of the site was given over to playing fields. It was a progressive project and demonstrated a great deal more compassion and care for the workers than Aspro was to show to its architect.

Raymond put a great deal of work into the factory, concentrating on it to the exclusion of any other architectural work for well over a year. When the war came, very substantial fees were owed to him. There was, as his son Norman relates,

> no pay-as-you-go system. The company did not honour its commitments. The result was that when the construction ceased, he was very considerably in debt. He could not and never did collect those fees and Aspro never came back to him after the war when they decided to build. He never financially recovered from that blow.

CHAPTER XXV

The worst calamity that befell Raymond in 1938 was not financial. It was the first episode of the manic depression which was to dog Mary's life for 40 years. Mary and the two children were staying with Hazel Guggenheim at Battle when, in Hazel's words, "she tried to drown herself in a lake".[79]

The summer had gone well. She had decorated the whole apartment to Raymond's standard of perfection. She was expecting her parents and she had to impress them. When they arrived in July, she and Raymond took Norman to Scotland with Dr. Crozier and Heart. They travelled in style, Mary driving an Isotta-Fraschini which their friend John Pentland had asked her to deliver to his place in Scotland. (Mary, Texas-style, had learned to drive at the age of twelve and never in 55 years at the wheel had an accident. Raymond did not drive until after the war.)

They visited Edinburgh, Inveraray, and Skye on this trip, and Norman aged seven wore a smart Highland kilt with sporran and Glengarry. The Croziers' tour — Mary's last sight of her father as it turned out — seems to have been a success, though there is a dearth of correspondence. They certainly came back to London by ship. Raymond did two successful watercolour sketches of Dr. Crozier and Heart on board and brought home the sketch from which he painted 'Carlton Hill, Edinburgh'.

When the Croziers had gone home to Dallas, Mary took the children to visit Hazel and by then was so depressed that she attempted suicide.

Hazel telephoned Raymond in London. "He dismissed the incident as nothing, but I said he should come at once and bring a doctor. She was committed to Bedlam. It must have been horrible."

Bedlam was the medieval madhouse that became the Royal Bethlehem Hospital in London. In the early 1930s it was moved to Beckenham in Kent, a far cry from the frightening asylum that had sprung from the Priory of St. Mary of Bethlehem in 1246.

As far as Hazel was concerned, Mary's condition came as a bolt from the blue. Raymond may have suspected that something was going wrong. His method of handling Mary's illness always was to avoid confrontation, to delay the necessary action, to hope it would go away, to shut the studio door and devote himself to work.

Neither Hazel nor Raymond knew any more about manic depression than the rest of the world. It had not been studied: it did not even have a name. Nowadays we know the devastating effect of mood swings, not only on the patient but on the family. We know that disorders of mood account for by far the greatest demand for psychiatric consultations and

A Christmas card version of McGrath's painting of Carlton Hill, Edinburgh, 1938

Dr Crozier's Return
from Scotland

that sufferers and their families can rely on strategies of treatment involving medical, social and psychological techniques, as well as successful preventive measures.

When John Cade the Australian psychiatrist first used lithium[81] in 1949, he found it calmed manic patients. Only later was its preventive value realised and accepted as far more important. Lithium is a natural element and therefore not a drug.

Raymond knew none of this. Mary herself, who had written a very bright and breezy letter to her parents at the end of June, went into a classic depression beginning with her encounter at Battle in August and going through several months until in December she felt able to get in touch with Dallas again. Her dominant feeling then, as her letters show, was one of guilt, of having let her parents down, of needing their forgiveness for what she had done. On 13 December, the first letter was posted. It began by dating her breakdown, which coincided with the Munich crisis.

Jenny believes that Mary's collapse had little to do with politics and more to do with a therapeutic abortion which she had had after Jenny was born. We have no documentary evidence to support this belief, but we do know that Mary wanted more children and had several miscarriages over the next number of years, always succeeded by depressions. Her manic episodes, as Jenny says, could sometimes be funny. An anonymous patient has put the feeling well: "I enjoy my highs — don't take them away. Just make sure I don't get depressed again."

In her letter home, Mary began:

> Oh, my *precious* darlings —
>
> How to write this letter? How to explain my horrible silence? I can never forgive myself for causing you to suffer so. I have been in such a queer state. It started at Battle, during the crisis. Something in my mental and emotional make-up went futt and I got so depressed about everything in general and myself in particular that I really couldn't do anything. I couldn't even do the simplest kind of housework. Norman was still whooping and I was worried about him but he made me so nervous I wasn't much good to him. I began to feel I was a completely different person and it's only lately I've begun to feel at all myself again. I read your darling letters and felt so completely unworthy of you and all you are right to expect of me — I got too ashamed to write. And time just went by and the more it went by the more impossible it was to write. I got such moments of panic I had to pretend to myself it wasn't true, I was only dreaming it.

She found everybody so kind. Hazel and her friend Alec returned from Ireland and were lovely. But she could not find anything to say to anybody. "Now would you ever dream that *I'd* lose my gift for gab? Well I have, Heart, and you can't think how painful it is."

Dr. Crozier's return from Scotland to England

189

Raymond has been an angel on earth. He tried to pull me out of it by getting me interested in his electrical stand for the Woman's Fair. I was appalled by how useless I was. He had a puppet show in the exhibition, with a dialogue written by Albert on the benefits of electricity and Eileen made some puppets with wooden heads... Margaret was a darling and helped me make one or two contributions to the show — had to buy a hundred pairs of old spectacles at the Caledonian Market. But all the time I felt so dead.

Raymond was planning a book on Le Corbusier to be written with Morton Shand. He wanted to go to France and Switzerland to see Corbusier and, having obtained a £50 advance from Faber and Faber, he set off on 24 September. He told Mary he would not go without her and "by some miracle off we went" with Shand as their guide and entertainer. The lengthy history of that book belongs in the next chapter, but they took the night boat from Folkestone to Dunkirk.

At Dijon there was a gastronomic fair and Shand the wine expert plied them with food and drink. Mary felt almost herself again. Near Lausanne they went to see the house Corbusier designed for his mother. After a week in Paris, she came home. The children were well but she still could not cope with things, and she had Heart and Daddy on her mind, "feeling I was letting you down so terribly".

Now I feel I'm getting my old grip back and I can honestly write and tell you not to worry. Please try to understand and forgive me, my darlings.

There was no mention anywhere of her stay in Bedlam. Perhaps it was brief and, as Jenny suggests, too upsetting for her parents to hear about. Her next letter, a week later, shed no more light on her hospitalisation, but it did beg forgiveness once more. Mary spent many years in a vain search for her mother's approval:

20 December, 1938

You sweetest people on earth —
I am better, my darlings, but I can't feel happy until I know you have forgiven me for all the anxiety I have caused you. If you knew how tormented I am by that thought you would forgive me.

London was snow-clad, she had left it too late to do something about Christmas, and anyway Barbara and Serge Chermayeff had asked them all to stay over Christmas. The invitation included Hulda, the Swiss girl who was helping with the children; but not Mrs Griffin, the housekeeper, "ever faithful and sweet", who was going to her son's wedding in Ireland.

This letter concluded with a rare note from Raymond "because Mary is very tired and at the moment letter-writing makes her very despondent".

Social attitudes to manic depression were very unforgiving and totally without understanding in the 1930s and for a long time afterwards. Even now, "what relatives find especially difficult to contend with is the patients' changing behaviour, ranging from the withdrawn, listless, depressed phase, where they are possibly bed bound, uncommunicative, clinging and dependent, to the manic turmoil which a family may only be able to manage by arranging compulsory hospitalisation".[81]

Christopher Millett, who lost touch with the McGraths when the war began, reflected the conventional approach when he was asked in 1983 to record his memories of them. "I have the impression", he told Hugh Carey, "that the union did not develop into what you might call plain sailing, she being, I heard, rather a quick hand with the dry martini."

Jenny was an infant when Mary first became ill and she was seven or eight and the family had moved to Ireland, as will be explained later, before she became aware that there was something very wrong:

Jenny as an infant

> I remember being in my parents' large bedroom with my mother. I think she was talking to Dad. She was talking and talking. I have no memory of how she looked or of what she said. The blow for me was that she was not there for me at that time. I had a feeling of total loss and of fear. I knew looking at her that she didn't really know I was there. I felt abandoned, which I was. When she was very depressed she took to her bed. Then I could help her; but certainly not when she was elated.
>
> This elation was to happen many times. All the elations and most of the depressions had to be treated in hospital. Dr. Norman Moore of St. Patrick's Hospital, Dublin, was her psychiatrist, as well as a family friend and counsellor. My mother put up no arguments against going to see him.

Life for Raymond while she was in hospital, often for many weeks, was not easy. He and Jenny shared the domestic chores, shopping and cooking. (There was some help to do the cleaning.) Jenny remembers:

> I think we both enjoyed each other's company at these times. My mother tended to dominate most conversations. I remember people, friends, asking me how Mary was, saying they remembered her as being 'very funny, uproarious'. I felt very uncomfortable because I felt she had been on a high, so I would wonder what she had said or done.

There were times when Mary's elations were really funny. There was the day she bought two grand pianos at auction and a furious Raymond paid the van man to take them away again. They already had a piano. And the time she bought three Aylesbury ducks. Raymond made a pond for them in the garden until one by one they were cooked and eaten. "These stories were funny", says Jenny, "but they were tinged with sadness."

> Good taste came out on top sometimes. Mother bought four lovely glass bowls from a shifty antique dealer in Bray. They are still in use and beautiful. In 1977 she was persuaded to go on lithium therapy and had no further mood swings.

191

Raymond, Jenny recalls, was extremely patient and gentle. He tended to let the course of Mary's illness run well over time before he would take action. It would take a family friend (in later years Birthe Douglas) to tell him firmly to act. Jenny felt unable to force him, so she worked through Birthe:

> In retrospect, I think he was loth to bring her to hospital because he did not want to part with her, whether sick or well.

Raymond's devotion was shown particularly clearly in a letter to his own parents, then living in Wahroonga, New South Wales, in April 1944:

> Mary is in particularly good form which is indeed a blessing seeing that this is the first Easter she has not been in a nursing home since we have been in Ireland. Mary is going to have a baby in September… and I think it is going to make all the difference to her. It has entirely refreshed her outlook on life…

Hope was also the keynote of Mary's letter to the McGrath parents, written a day before Raymond's. She did not share her husband's dismal view of spring in Ireland. "I adore Easter", she wrote. The garden was supplying them with food, as were their ducks, and the neighbours donated flowers, pear blossoms etc.

> I have seen the doctor. He says the new one will arrive the first week in September and I can have the event staged at home, thus saving much expense. I have the layettes, nappies, moses basket and all ready and yet nobody but my own family and the doctor believe I'm pregnant. It's going to be a midget…

It was the middle of the war, so those letters took two months to reach Herbert and Edith. Mary by then had lost that baby, and she was to lose up to four more, according to Norman and Jenny.

The McGraths' closest friends in those Dublin years were Alan and Máirín Hope, both architects. During one bout of elation, Máirín recalls, Mary went missing. Raymond called Alan and the three of them went looking in Mary's usual drinking places. They found her near O'Connell Street in a very excitable and emotional state, and Alan Hope suggested that they all go to the Gresham Hotel for a meal.

As soon as they had ordered, Alan excused himself, ran across the road and up to the Rotunda Hospital, where their friend Ninian Falkiner the gynaecologist was a consulting surgeon. Alan got Falkiner to give him a quick-acting powder, ran straight back to the Gresham kitchens and told the waiter to put the powder in Mary's soup. The ruse worked, but even then, Máirín remembers, Raymond brought his drugged wife, not to St. Patrick's Hospital which was nearby, but home to Monkstown House six miles away.

His state of mind in the spring of 1942 was as bad as at any time since Mary's illness began. In something like despair, he wrote to Aunt Collie

Gardner, Heart's spinster sister in Troy, Alabama:

> Although we have never met and I have never seen your picture, I feel from having read your letters and heard Mary speak about you so often that we really know each other.

He explained a bizarre cable that Mary had sent. "She has been trying to do rather too much as she seems urged to at this time of year." She was arranging an exhibition (presumably of Raymond's paintings and drawings) when Jenny caught whooping cough, so he thought it best to send Jenny to hospital, where she was spending five weeks "quite happily".

At this critical point came a letter from the American Consul saying there was an opportunity for American citizens to sail home on a returning troopship at $1.50 a day. Mary could take one child, but not of course Raymond.

> Mary was so excited by the prospect of seeing you again that she packed her clothes and forgot all about the practical difficulties, not to speak of the danger, and the result was she got quite upset and I have insisted on her going into a nursing home to rest for a few weeks.

Norman and Raymond held the fort until the two were well, when Raymond thought they should have a farmhouse holiday together.

> The trouble is to be able to afford to do the best thing these days and my resources have been sorely taxed I'm afraid.

Aunt Collie had bought some bonds for Mary and "although I know you would probably like them to mature for her", he thought that if the money could be spent on her there and then it would put her on her feet again and "restore her to that state of happiness which sometimes forsakes her".

She seemed to have her heart set on "going back home", a telling phrase which Raymond developed by saying: "…Somehow Mary has never been happy here. Probably it was because the news of her father's death came just at the time when we were settling down… Then came America's entry into the war making it more difficult than ever for her to feel right in a neutral country."

Raymond, while he saw the difficulties, was willing to let Mary go for a year or two. Norman's schooling would be upset if he were to go and he himself would not be able to join Jenny and Mary there unless he had a job and "I have a perfectly good one here, a rare thing these days".

He urged Aunt Collie to be discreet in what she told Heart about these possibilities, "except that Mary has got an idea of travelling home for a holiday by one of the troopships".

In a rare burst of emotion, Raymond ended his letter: "Your love for Mary has been a precious thing to her and I too love you for that."

None of this momentous and distressing news reached Australia, where Herbert was writing a fortnightly report to Dublin about Australia's role in the war and retailing second-hand news from Eileen in Washington. Indeed Aunt Collie seems to have been the sole repository of Raymond's confidence. The mental turmoil he endured in that eventful year inspired him to write what may well be his best poem:

PRAYER AT DONAGHADEE

The stinging Past encrusts my Veins
Like Salt along the tide-swept Wall,
And all the Eyes of Night stare down,
Relentless, hard, accusing all.
        O God of Night
        Release my Tears,
        And hide them, as they fall.
Let Doubts be gone like Shadows dark
Fleeing the Valleys far and wide,
As Hope with all her Angels bright
Rides in with the returning Tide.
        O God of Dawn
        Draw near me now
        Divinely, at my side.
Be tranquil then my aching Heart
For Love steals softly by the Door,
If I am humble will she stay
And smile and leave me nevermore?
        O God of Day
        Lead back my Love,
        Not lost, but gone before.

Why Donaghadee? This town is in Co. Down, in Northern Ireland, an unlikely place for Raymond to be on 10 May, 1942, or any other time during the Emergency. The key may lie in the arrival of American troops in Ireland. They landed first on 26 January, 1942,[82] part of Plan Bolero which was to bring one-and-a-quarter million U.S. soldiers to the United Kingdom in that year. Mary made early contact. It is not surprising that she should have wanted to meet her fellow countrymen. When the American offer of a passage "home" was made to her, it was on one of the very ships which had brought the G.I.s to the United Kingdom that she would have travelled.

She made several visits North that spring. Indeed over the remaining war years she invited several American soldiers to Monkstown House, as extant photographs attest. Raymond, Jenny says, did not like these visits, but he put up with them.

But this poem, so full of pain, came to him at a time when Mary, having been hospitalised in April as a result of her dashed hope of going to Alabama, clearly had made her way to Belfast and been followed by Raymond. "Lead back my Love", he prayed to the God of Day at Donaghadee. And He did.

Mary flanked by American soldiers with Jenny and Norman

CHAPTER XXVI

One of the great might-have-beens of Raymond McGrath's London and later years was the book on Le Corbusier, "the most influential and the most brilliant of 20th century architects", as Pevsner[83] calls him.

The story began in March 1938 with a letter from Raymond to Richard de la Mare, a director of Faber and Faber. Geoffrey Faber was chairman of the company which also had on its board T.S. Eliot the poet. Indeed Fabers, which had published Raymond's 'Twentieth Century Houses' in 1934, was known principally as a publishing house for modern poets, and saw as a corollary of this function the promotion of modern architecture.

Raymond's proposal to de la Mare was the production of a book to which P. Morton Shand would contribute a critical and biographical account; Amédée Ozenfant the painter would write on Le Corbusier as an artist, and Raymond would deal with the architect's town plans and actual buildings and their construction. "Shand", he told de la Mare, "is quite ready to co-operate". He said nothing more of Ozenfant, who disappeared from the scene.

The concept got a warm reception and in June, just as Mary was writing her happy letter to Dallas, de la Mare said he would very much look forward to having "the result of your correspondence with Corbusier…"

Shand was flattered. He thought a book on Corbusier in English — "the whole Corb, writer, painter and architect" — was badly needed. But unless it was critical it would be no use at all. And Shand went on to show that he was your man for criticism:

> Corb is quite incapable of pulling anyone's leg, unless unconsciously his own. He hasn't the vestige of a sense of humour, though a very good medium howitzer fire-control of his enemies with sarcasm — far less often irony.
>
> The great mistake is to think of him as French or representative of the French mind, though he is eager enough to be ranked as both — in fact it is part of his inferiority complex that he knows he is not — in France. No one was ever more essentially Swiss than he, not even J.-J. Rousseau. Many Swiss consider that he is really more 'Schweizer Deutsch' than 'Suisse Romande'. He writes brilliantly in French but what he writes is not French.

This is pure Shand, remorseless, scabrous, and quite compulsive reading. He sees Le Corbusier (born Charles-Edouard Jeanneret in 1887 at La Chaux-de-Fonds in French Switzerland) as a mixture of the sublime and the ridiculous, great and petty, noble and ignoble.

"But nothing can dethrone him from what he has achieved, which is fine and somewhere passably near great." This too, said Shand in intriguing contradiction to Pevsner's view of Corb as "an embarrassingly superb salesman of his own ideas", "this, too, in spite of sometimes rather poor showmanship".

To spare himself trouble, Le Corbusier gives the public what he thinks it wants. "Hence his endless self-repetition on paper. Hence padding out to make books to make money like 'Quand les Cathédrales étaient blanches'."

The reader may think that Shand already was composing the book in his letter to Raymond. And there was more:

An out and out positively brutal egoist, he preaches what he often would not and could not dream of practising: i.e. group work, anonymity. He's a soured man at bottom: soured for not having received the big commissions that might have made a different man of him; soured sexually too. Much as he loves success he hasn't had a quarter of what he thinks (with every right) his due. A man who quarrels with everyone, except such fervent disciples as Giedion who are determined he shan't quarrel with them. A man who can make himself positively abject to the grossest kind of nouveau-riche clients in order to get a little bit of his own way in details. A man always preaching the wider humanity (in so far as it offers scope for *villes radieuses*, etc.), who is himself profoundly inhuman, dehumanised — alcohol apart. An orator always, and never more than, when he writes.

One must remember that Shand, although he was by no means finished with the analysis (some might say demolition) of Le Corbusier, was writing in early 1938, before the United Nations secretariat or the Ronchamps chapel were designed and before Corbusier turned to what Pevsner calls "a new anti-rational, violently sculptural, aggressive style which was soon to be just as influential".[84]

The need to orate, Shand believed, had consequences:

Hence the involved style, the longueurs, the mixed metaphors and the metaphors left stranded and incomplete in the middle of rhetorical paragraphs like broken-down cars in the middle of an unfinished arterial road. A relentless enemy who never forgives a slight méchant comme tout if usually rather too ponderously to be effective. There is little or no nuance in his writing. It's all too holy, too much *une mission*. And vain enough too. Hence that elaborately manufactured name to differentiate himself from his (to him) indispensable cousin [Pierre Jeanneret]. Grudging of praise to others, except to fill out oratorical periods in ingénue acclamation of the — always nameless — "jeunes d'avant garde", who may thus be tacitly roped in as one and all his personal disciples. There are, I believe, no recorded tributes of his to Gropius or any of his own generation, or of the intermediate generation between himself and the "jeunes" like Aalto. Exploits his own pupils to the bone and never puts anything their way. He has never been wrong about anything. All mistakes were due to the stupidity, cupidity, hostility of others. Incredible [*sic*] careless of the accuracy of his facts.

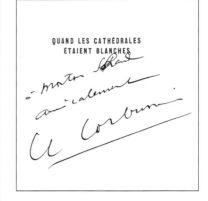

Yet this is the man for whom Corbusier inscribed a copy of 'Quand les Cathédrales étaient blanches': "à Morton Schand [the c is crossed out], amicalement, Le Corbusier". The book, published in 1937, ended up in Raymond's possession.

"What sort of book?", Shand asked McGrath, "The great man is sparing of data, and can't be bothered to fill out the public on known facts except in the most palpably subjective, not to say polemical, spirit. Local research in and round his birthplace might be necessary…"

And that, as we already know, is what the pair, with Mary in tow, did that fateful September. With what result, we are not sure, except that Mme. Jeanneret, that "femme de courage et de foi", lent Morton Shand an album of pictures of the house that Corbusier designed for her, and that Raymond did not return the album and all the pre-war and post-war documents borrowed from Corbusier until 1957.

Corbusier, incidentally, in July 1938 demanded and got agreement on the payment to him of 2 to 3 per cent of the 15 per cent royalty. Raymond noted three cónsecutive meetings with Corbusier in his diary, but they are undated.

Shand wrote to Corbusier in November 1938 looking for information, approval of the project and permissions about pictures. He discussed Mme. Jeanneret's house at La Chaux-de-Fonds and asked Corb to "remember me with respect to your mother" who kindly lent an album of pictures "from which we shall make a selection". Raymond in 1939 promised Faber and Faber: "October 1st should be a reasonable date for delivery of the ms."

There was some correspondence between Corbusier and Raymond before the war, Corb seeking the return of photographs and a fee of 900 guineas, but the opening of hostilities in September 1939 meant that the project had to be postponed, though evidently not shelved permanently. Corbusier sent a note to Shand on 23 November, 1939. It came from Vézelay and it said cheerily: "Bonne chance alors!" Richard de la Mare wrote before Christmas to Raymond saying that he could not plan with confidence until "this beastly war is over. You must be having a wretched time — I am so sorry".

With his gossip-monger's mind, Shand revived the subject once France had been liberated, this time with the added spice that Le Corbusier, he believed, had collaborated with the Germans or at least with the Vichy Government. He wrote to Raymond in Dublin at the end of November 1944:

The question in its simplest form is whether or not de Pierrefeu was a *Vichy* minister… from what I hear it would be most unwise to assume that Sacha Guitry (of *all* people), Albert Chevallier etc. have been definitely cleared... so I am not surprised that Corb has been left in place till now. But the courts will probably be sitting in cases of collaboration with Vichy for years to come.

Anyhow I am most certainly not going to write to Corbusier until I have far more and more definite information and for that I must wait till normal posts are restored with Switzerland. Living in the peaceful remoteness of HOLY Ireland I don't think you've got the angle of all this quite right and living the life of a virtual provincial as I do, I have probably got it a bit a-squint the other way.

He was writing from Bath, Somerset. The war safely over, he agreed with Raymond in mid-June 1945 that he was just as keen on the other kind of collaboration as he had been before the war. Yet he could not leave the Vichy question alone:

But I would like to make a few discreet inquiries about Corbusier's white sheet or otherwise in France first and think I can now manage to get the required information without in any way damaging him. You must keep in mind that the new French Government have been so busy rounding up *active* Vichy collaborators that, as they have several times announced, they are leaving the trial of men whose degrees of collaboration were less heinous, or caused by economic pressure, till right after the big cases are disposed of. (They still seem to be trying and executing batches every week.)

In response to a reminder from Raymond, Richard de la Mare made a fairly firm commitment in March 1946: "Our inclination is certainly to say 'yes', by all means go ahead with the Corbusier book on your own, without Mr. Shand's collaboration — indeed I would very much prefer it that way." Whether the suggestion to dump Shand came from Raymond, we can only surmise.

Whatever happened to Raymond in the next few years, he did not work at the Corbusier book. He had written to Corb at the time of de la Mare's agreement: "I am at the moment finalising my illustration for the Shenval Press book. I would like to have a photograph of the Maison Locative à Alger (1933) Côte Sud, if you have one available."

He devised a title page:

LE CORBUSIER
(Charles-Edouard Jeanneret)
Selected and Introduced by
RAYMOND McGRATH
Edited by Lillian Browse
FABER & FABER
ARIEL BOOKS ON THE ARTS
SHENVAL PRESS

Early in 1947, Richard de la Mare wrote to Mary. He had been expecting to hear from Raymond about the Corbusier book and he asked her to persuade Raymond to get down to finishing it.

Two years passed. For Faber and Faber, P.F. du Sautoy wrote formally on 31 May, 1949:

> You will remember that before the war you signed an agreement with this firm for a book on the work of Corbusier and we paid a sum of £50 to Mr. M. Shand and yourself... We are assuming that this book will not now be completed and... we shall be grateful if you would kindly confirm that this is so.

Raymond replied that in 1946 he had had every intention of completing the book and "have never actually given up my intention". Various factors and his present position as Principal Architect of the Office of Public Works had curtailed his leisure. "I suppose the proper course for me now is to say that your assumption is correct."

Faber and Faber let him down very gently, especially considering that they had been waiting since 1935 for a book on 'Twentieth Century Interiors' to be written by Raymond and Albert Frost. Even after the last exchange, Peter du Sautoy wrote in July 1949: "... if you would really like to complete the book on Corbusier we should be happy to publish it."

So much happened to Raymond after 1939 that, rather than anticipate events, we should regard the Corbusier chapter as just that — a chapter. But it is necessary to set the record straight on Corbusier's activities during the occupation of France. Reviewing two books on Le Corbusier for *The Irish Times* in 1973, Raymond wrote: "During the last war he escaped from Paris with his wife and went first to the Pyrenees and later to Grenoble." That is all he says on the subject.

P. Morton Shand died in 1960, attracting warm words of appreciation from John Betjeman. Those who may have found his dissection of Le Corbusier harsh will find redress in Betjeman's view, expressed in *The Times* (6 May, 1960).

> His fastidiousness, honest expression of opinion and sharp wit isolated him from the crowd. He never liked public relations officers nor those architects who seemed to him to possess their ubiquitous qualities. He invented devastating nicknames for them and used to declare he much preferred quantity surveyors to solemn professional architects... He wrote slowly and thoughtfully, though the result may have seemed racy... Of recent years he... retreated more and more to France, whose people and language he knew so well.

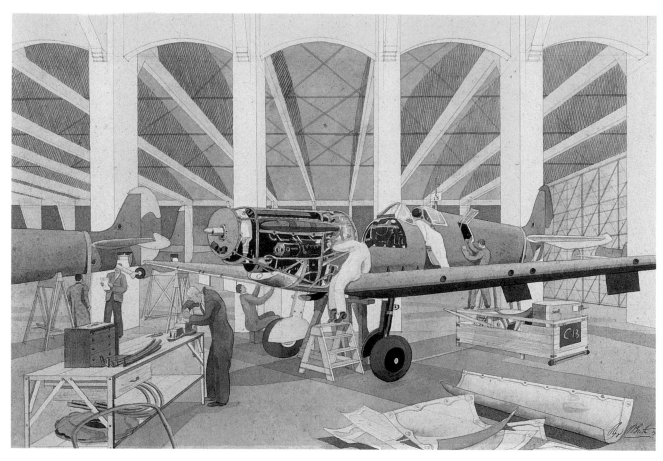

CHAPTER XXVII

I am no longer an artist. I am a messenger who will bring back word from the men who are fighting to those who want the war to go on for ever. Feeble, inarticulate will be my message, but it will have a bitter truth, and may it burn their lousy souls.

Paul Nash wrote that in November 1917. Twenty-two years later, this survivor of the Western Front was a salaried artist in the Royal Air Force, with the difficult task of interpreting the war in the air. He transferred later to the War Artists' Advisory Committee, under the aegis of the Ministry of Information, which also gave work to Raymond McGrath.

Raymond was between a rock and a hard place. The onset of war threatened him with ruin. Work on the Aspro factory closed down. There were no new commissions. The Corbusier book was in suspension. He closed the door of the Conduit Street office for the last time. He had to have employment.

He saw an advertisement in *The Times* for a senior architect in the Board of Works in Dublin, and he applied. The Board was a relic of the old Ascendency, inherited almost untouched from the British régime before 1922, and still staffed by staid and solid architects of the old school.

Joining such an organisation was a counsel of despair. Ireland had firmly declared its neutrality in the European war just begun. Raymond's sense of Irishness, never a thriving plant, had withered in the light of London's lustre as the capital of a great empire and his hard-won place in it.

His success at the successive Dublin interviews was Pyrrhic. It gave him no joy to contemplate giving up all that he had gained in the decade before the conflict, and to transplant his wife and young children to alien earth.

He cast about for alternatives. Sir Kenneth Clark, still in his middle 30s, was director of the National Gallery. When war seemed imminent, he took all the paintings and stored them in caves in Wales. Remembering that in the Great War artists had been commissioned to paint the scene of battle, Clark went to the Treasury on 3 September, 1939, the day Britain declared war on Germany, to ask if he might submit plans for a War Artists' Advisory Committee.

The concept was accepted and the Ministry of Information established the W.A.A.C. on which the Air Ministry, the Admiralty, the War Office and the Home Office represented the Government, and the Royal College of Art and the Slade School also had a voice. Over 5,500 paintings were produced, the criterion being artistic merit and not illustrative accuracy. Clark as chairman boasted later that in over one hundred meetings of the

Facing page (above): Fitters working on a Spitfire, and (below) Whitley Rear Turrets.
(Courtesy of the Imperial War Museum)

committee, not a cross word was said.

Using many of the connections he had made in his London life, Raymond sent off letters in several directions. One was to Kenneth Clark. He told him of the Dublin job worth £700 a year. "Yet I hesitate to remove myself from London and suppose that to many work in Dublin will appear to be a retreat."

> There was a wireless announcement last evening [15 December, 1939] that the selection of Official War Artists was going forward... Would such appointments carry a reasonable remuneration? I know there is a vast number of artists to be considered, yet perhaps I might be eligible for such war work which I should be keen to do.

John Piper the artist and veteran of the first World War, wrote to his father's old friend, Professor John Hilton, on Raymond's behalf. The letter is dated 3 January, 1939. He must have forgotten the New Year. McGrath, said Piper, is "a very good artist and one of the few people in this country who can do a drawing of a building that is at once accurate and beautiful".

About the same time, Raymond enlisted the help of Geoffrey Webb, Slade Professor of Fine Arts at Cambridge and husband of Manny Forbes' cousin Pud Batten. He told Webb too about the Dublin job and his hesitation, and said that Paul Nash had recently urged him to try for an appointment as an official war artist.

Nash himself thought that to advance his own cause, Lord Sempill might be the best possible intermediary "as I once heard by an odd chance that he admired my work in the last war..." In his next letter, he asked Raymond "to put in a word with the Air Ministry from Sempill. I very urgently need to know one way or the other".

In its first sixteen weeks, the War Artists' Advisory Committee considered almost 800 names. It had a budget of £5,000 for its first year of operation. "What a game it is getting to the right quarters", John Piper noted. "I'm sure there must be a job for you, with your talent... I hope to get something to do drawing or painting, but how, or when..."

John Piper did become a war artist — painting an A.R.P. (Air Raid Precautions) control room. His heart was not in it and the result was a poor painting. But, said John Betjeman,[85] "when the bombs fell, when the City churches crashed, when the classic and Perpendicular glory of England was burnt and stark, he produced a series of oil paintings, using his theory of colour to keep the drama of a newly fallen bomb alive".

Paul Nash too was pressed once more into service, and got the same mixed reception for his work. When he died in July 1946, *The Times* obituary noted:

> In the successive exhibitions of war pictures held at the National Gallery he showed many impressions of aircraft and airfields which, though notable for his characteristically tender and lovely colouring, were felt by many to be rather too confused

and indefinite in form to be entirely satisfying. More successful were several large paintings, each simplifying and epitomising some aspect of the combat into an effective poster-like design, such as 'The Dead Sea' — a moonlight view of broken German aeroplanes heaped up like breakers on a sandy shore…

"Art is an instrument of war", said Pablo Picasso; "for use as a weapon of defence and attack against the enemy." The work of the War Artists' Advisory Committee kept the artists at work and out of the services, and it served to maintain national morale in much the same way as Dame Myra Hess's piano concerts did. When no other gallery in London was open, the National Gallery ran a series of exhibitions of war artists' work, a concept probably unique to Britain in that established painters such as Edward Ardizzone, Edward Bawden, Henry Lamb, Eric Ravilious, Stanley Spencer, Graham Sutherland, Feliks Topolski, Mervyn Peake, L.S. Lowry and Henry Moore were employed where other countries resorted to commercial artists. Moore and Sutherland were not representational painters and for that reason Kenneth Clark considered their appointment by the W.A.A.C. as the committee's "boldest stroke". Many of these artists were friends and acquaintances of Raymond McGrath's, people who had more than one string to their artistic bow.

With everybody in the art world jockeying for position, it was surprising and flattering that Raymond, whose reputation had been made in architecture and industrial design, was given a contract as an artist. But he had pulled the strings and Geoffrey Webb had supported his candidature by saying in a backhanded-compliment sort of way: "I have always thought of him much more in [draughtsmanship] than as an architect and decorator."

The secretary of the W.A.A.C. was E.M. O'Rorke Dickey, a man who emerges from the dusty archives as the perfect mandarin. He was much more. He had been a painter of some consequence up to 1924, when he left the Irish art scene to become a teacher and an administrator in England. It is ironic that the two artists, McGrath and Dickey, should have met through Kenneth Clark as one headed for the Ireland which the other had quit.[86]

A native of Belfast, Dickey was born in 1894. He went to Cambridge, where he took part in Manny Forbes' and Archie Don's spoof exhibition, 'Seven Cambridge Expressionists' in 1913; and the Westminster School of Art, where he studied under Harold Gilman. He spent the Great War with the Red Cross and about 1920 returned to Ireland. He joined Paul Henry and a number of others who established the Society of Dublin Painters at 7 St. Stephen's Green. A Post-Expressionist, he was described by the Dublin critic Stephen Gwynn as the most accomplished of the group. He did not exhibit again after his departure for England. His work can be seen in galleries in Dublin, Belfast and Cork and in the autumn of 1991 a number of his works featured in the exhibition 'The European Connection: Irish Art and Modernism' at the Hugh Lane Gallery in Dublin.

Kenneth Clark's first response to Raymond was typically generous and frank. "As you have to make up your mind I will go beyond the bounds of official decency and tell you what is happening about the employment of artists in topographical draughtsmanship, but please keep it entirely to yourself."

The initial plan, to finance 30 artists making pictorial records of scenery and architecture in England, was under the auspices of the Ministry of Labour and the Pilgrims' Trust. Neither the work nor the money — £5 a week for six months — appealed to Raymond, but Clark offered to recommend him and said: "…Unless your Dublin job is very attractive I think it would be worth waiting on until the Pilgrims' Trust have made up their minds one way or the other."

In his desperation Raymond tried another tack. His old Sydney friend R.G. Casey, who had been Minister of Supply in the Commonwealth Government at Canberra, was appointed Australia's first Minister to the United States. Raymond wrote to "Dear Casey", congratulated him, told him how things were as of mid-February 1940, and offered his services if Casey was considering plans for a new Washington legation. He was, he told Casey, "the only Australian architect who has achieved some reputation in private practice on this side of the world." If Casey replied, Raymond does not seem to have kept the letter.

Raymond had used people of influence to press his case with the Civil Service Commissioners in Dublin too. Lord Sempill and Sir Frederick Minter the builder were happy to recommend him. So too was Frank Pick, a friend of long standing, chairman of the London Passenger Transport Board and a member of the MARS Group. "All good luck", he wrote, "though we shall be sorry to lose you from London." Not long after that, Pick was dismissed by Winston Churchill, who described him as "a mere bus conductor".

Hugh Quigley, Chief Economist of the Central Electricity Board, had a reservation about his approach. "I was turning over in my mind the question of whether it would not be better for me to have a talk with [John Dulanty, High Commissioner of Ireland] whom I know very well, and persuade him to use his good offices at Dublin, or take the plunge and do exactly as you suggest."

Julian Huxley, writing as secretary of the Zoological Society of London, enclosed the testimonial sought and asked for the address of Mary's parents in Dallas as he would be in America in the coming weeks and "should like to look them up".

The Civil Service Commissioners, offering Friday the 13 October, 1939 at 3.40 p.m. for an interview, were sharply reminded that "I have not since 1926 used my second Christian name and prefer to be known as Raymond McGrath".

E.M. O'R Dickey gave Raymond McGrath his candid opinion of war art work on 3 January, 1940: "…My own personal view is that if I were in your place I should not hesitate to accept a tempting offer of a full-time job on the chance that you might be missing an opportunity to do some work for war records."

All the same, Dickey wrote to Clark, by then chairman of the

W.A.A.C. of which Dickey was secretary, that notwithstanding, "I shall be sorry if he won't be available for our work".

The upshot of all this was twofold. Raymond was commissioned to do twelve drawings of aircraft production for 100 guineas plus maintenance of £1 a day when he was away from home. And for Faber and Faber he was to write and illustrate a popular account of aircraft production, tentatively entitled 'Blueprint to Blue Sky'.

Dickey wrote to the permanent secretary at the Ministry of Information, Leigh Ashton, on 25 January, 1940:

> I explained to [W.P. Hildred, Secretary of the Air Ministry] that while we have already asked M.I.5 to give us their verdict on Mr. McGrath, we have not yet heard from them… As soon as I know that there is no objection from M.I.5's point of view, I shall let you have a contract letter to him for your signature.

'Farmers in a Train', a woodcut by E.M. O'R. Dickey, 1922–23
(Courtesy of the Hugh Lane Municipal Gallery of Modern Art, Dublin)

While the book project stayed alive until April, when Lord Sempill arranged to lunch with Raymond at the Athenaeum, it did not get farther than a flyer printed by Faber and Faber. It underwent two changes of title before it died and was finally called 'Air and War'. Other books had appeared and obsolescence was a constant risk. Still Richard de la Mare offered Raymond attractive terms — £100 advance on a 10 per cent royalty for the first 1,000 and 15 per cent after that.

The flyer to promote the book said with a fine flourish: "The French were the pioneers of military aviation and today in Saint-Exupéry have produced a writer who does for the air what Conrad did for the sea." The whole cast of the book was to be changed to embrace the human aspect of flying and there were to be no photographs.

For the department of not-many-people-know-this, Raymond noted in handwriting that the woodworking departments in aircraft factories took up 3 per cent of the space: in 1918 the figure was 75 per cent. He told Richard de la Mare that drawings and manuscript would be completed by the end of May.

But on 9 April, 1940, Norway and Denmark were "offered the protection of the Reich", and on 10 May the German Army invaded Belgium and the Netherlands. The *Sitzkrieg* was over: the *Blitzkrieg* had begun, and one of the early victims was Raymond's aircraft book.

His work for the W.A.A.C. went ahead as planned. The artist Henry Rushbury, who had originally been asked to illustrate aircraft production, was told to draw tanks instead. Raymond went by first-class rail (yes, said Ashton, first-class up to a limit of £750 per annum provided the Ministry bought the tickets "as we get a rebate") to all the aircraft factories there were.

His first visit was to Vickers Armstrong at Weybridge, where he drew 'Finishing Touches on the Wellington'. His last work in this series was 'The Spitfire in the Making', which he did at the works at Eastleigh.

On 4 May, Dickey wrote: "…We are prepared to agree that you should make four additional drawings …for which the Ministry will be prepared to pay £50..." Clark's response was warmer: "I am so glad to know that you are doing some more drawings for us. I liked the first lot very much."

Privately Dickey sent a note to Ashton of the Air Ministry: "Sixteen drawings of the kind McGrath does are cheap at £155." Of the 16, five are in the Imperial War Museum catalogue; ten were sent by the Allocations Committee to the Ministry of Defence which gave them to the R.A.F. Museum; and one, 'Wings of the Master. Wings standing ready for fixing and the starboard wing of a Miles Master 1 passing down the assembly line', was lost at sea in 1944, the ship carrying an exhibition of pictures to South America having been torpedoed by a German submarine.

Six of Raymond McGrath's watercolours were sent as part of a Ministry of Information exhibition at the Museum of Modern Art in New York. The others were shown at the National Gallery in London.

The War Artists' Advisory Committee paid for the MOMA exhibition's trans-Atlantic flight, and its arrival gave *Life* magazine an opportunity to reproduce Raymond's drawings. Dickey and McGrath had one of their rare differences of opinion. Raymond knew the rules: — "Property in all original drawings and all rights of reproduction in any form shall be vested in the Crown". But he wanted the right to get a commission from *Life* and he told Dickey that the reproduction of the MOMA drawings might damage his chances.

Dickey told him firmly that they were the Ministry's drawings and he would get no special fee, though he would garner the publicity attendant on their publication.

"But", said Dickey in a memorandum to Ashton, "I think it wiser not to put all this in a letter. We do not want to run any risk of getting a reputation for treating artists meanly."

"Oh! no", replied Ashton, "We can't give him anything unless *Life* pay a very high fee."

Apart from money problems ("finances", he told Dickey, "are always difficult these days"), Raymond had no serious difficulty with his work. His trouble with gaining access to what was in fact private company ground was solved by his getting a special letter from the Air Ministry.

The instruction that all preliminary sketches and studies, as well as finished works, were to be submitted for censorship — "don't show them to your friends beforehand" — was greeted by the reply: "I made no preliminary sketches, so there's nothing to show the censor but the finished works."

With the Bristol Aeroplane Company there was a minor contretemps. The company withdrew permission for Raymond to draw Beauforts on the basis that his original Air Ministry clearance was for Blenheims, and they ceased to be made in December 1939. Dickey smoothed the ruffled feathers of the birdmaker and four of McGrath's original 12 pictures were of Bristol aircraft.

Less than a month before he was due to take up his position in Dublin, Raymond got an offer from Somerville Bros., the makers of K Shoes, to go to the Lake District and do two drawings of the lakes which would be used for publicity. The fee for the two was £50, which emboldened

Raymond to ask £50 for the four extra drawings the W.A.A.C. wanted. As we know, he got his price.

This commission and the K Shoes job meant that Raymond produced at least 18 pictures in four months in different parts of the country. The reception they got from the critics was broadly but not universally favourable. *Country Life* (June 1940) found most impressive in the National Gallery "some of Eric Kennington's portraits and Raymond McGrath's exquisite drawings of aircraft factories" and praised their "admirable design, almost Japanese in its delicacy of colouring".

When the "phoney war" was over, and Dunkirk was evacuated and Britain's cities had crumbled in smoke, Raymond's work was relegated to the morgue in favour of belligerent and artistic action on many fronts. It was only in the calm of a post-war Europe that a real assessment of his work was made by the *Architectural Review*:

> Raymond McGrath's meticulous 1940 watercolours of hangars and the assembly of bombers have the purity and accuracy of architectural drawings, at the same time conveying a lyrical feeling for the beauty of aircraft.

By the last day of May 1940, Raymond was sitting at a desk in a quiet office overlooking St. Stephen's Green in Dublin. For him and his family the golden London years were over, and he thought perhaps of Wordsworth:

> I travelled among unknown men,
> In lands beyond the sea;
> Nor, England! did I know till then
> What love I bore to thee

Treeways, completed

CHAPTER XXVIII

Some time in 1938, Raymond McGrath bought a buff-coloured Austin Seven. He was ten years away from being able to drive, so Mary used it. It was this tiny car that carried her, her two children, a Polish friend called Ernestyna Winkler and Serge Chermayeff's elderly aunt Judith Issakovitch all the way from London to Dublin early in May 1940.

The car, which Nancy Astor earlier had wanted to take in exchange for her Rolls-Royce — precisely because it *was* tiny — ran out of petrol on the way. Mary told the garage attendant in a lordly voice to "fill her up", and made little of his protests when he discovered that she did not have any petrol ration coupons.

Raymond was doing his war pictures and had sent his family ahead. They stayed for a month at the Salthill Hotel in Monkstown, where Raymond joined them. Then they found a ground-floor flat at No. 43 North Circular Road, almost opposite the Dublin cattle markets. From there Norman went to the local Catholic national school.

In England, evacuation fever had caused a great movement out of big cities like London. Eileen took her son Hugh to stay with Albert's people in Carlisle. For six months, until Mary went to Ireland, Eileen also looked after Jenny in Carlisle. Albert was working in the Civil Service in London. When Herbert wrote his weekly letter from Sydney it was to "My dear Raymond and Mary, Eileen and Albert". He was only months from retirement after 50 years in the public service. He bought a site for a house in the Sydney suburb of Wahroonga. He got a Miss McCredie to design it, and Elmo Pye to do the conveyancing. He chose Treeways as its name. Through the war years and until his wife Edith died, the couple laboured hard to make a garden that soon became well known enough to merit inclusion in the gardening magazines.

When Treeways was building, Edith on one of their weekly visits of inspection secretly brought from Parramatta a box of rose petals. "With these", said Herbert, "she christened the foundations, a most graceful and unique act." They both considered Treeways an architectural and artistic triumph.

Every letter of Herbert's talked first of the war and its effect on Australia: "Every fresh act of Nazi bestiality swells the war chest and the military camps..." His children and their children, if they thought of leaving for Australia, would find a ready home. "We shall always have a welcome for you", he wrote. Four months before Pearl Harbour, this stout-hearted Empire loyalist wrote: "...The position has much improved

Edith McGrath

for the enemies of Hitler in the last twelve months, and now that the U.S.A. is thoroughly aroused the defeat of the Axis is assured."

His nephew Tom Sorrell bought *Life* magazine for 15 July, 1940 and saw a drawing by Norman in the section on 'Children's War Art'. It showed a "fabulous British tank firing at small-fry Nazi tanks" while parachutes and airplanes above burst into flames. "But Norman", said the caption, "prefers his war on paper. When one of the first air-raid sirens electrified his household, the young artist could not find his gas mask and sobbed helplessly". He was eight.

Mary sent her father-in-law a photograph of Raymond that reminded Herbert of W.T. Cosgrave, the Leader of the Opposition in the lower house of the Irish Parliament, the Dáil. Both Raymond and Mary, perhaps still starry-eyed, perhaps mendaciously, told him how favourable were their first impressions of Dublin and its people. He was glad they still had their car (they sold it later in the war, known by an extraordinary Irish euphemism as the Emergency); and he was pleased that Raymond not only found the modern architecture of Ireland better than he had expected, but discovered that his intrusion was not resented.

Raymond's fief in the Board of Works was an area covering the Phoenix Park and Kilmainham in Dublin; north County Dublin, and Counties Waterford and Kilkenny, districts that gave him some insight into rural Ireland. The President of Ireland (then the ailing Dr Douglas Hyde) lived in Áras an Uachtaráin, the former Vice-Regal Lodge in the Phoenix Park This house always attracted much of Raymond's interest, especially during the two terms of office of Seán T. O'Kelly (1945–1959), with whom he and Mary became personally friendly. With President de Valera (1959–1973) he did not succeed in establishing the same rapport.

When Raymond first landed in Ireland, it was in a real sense de Valera's Ireland. Éamon de Valera was Taoiseach (Prime Minister) and Minister for External Affairs. He was the only surviving leader of the Easter Rising of 1916, a consummate politician who in 1938 had negotiated such an agreement with the British Prime Minister Neville Chamberlain that Britain went into the most calamitous war in her history without the Irish naval ports that would have helped to ensure the safety of her convoys in the Battle of the Atlantic.

A neutral Ireland — "neutral on England's side" as the Irish cynics put it — was a vital element in de Valera's strategy, but a running sore in the British popular perception of Ireland. Even from Australia, Herbert McGrath could write: "It is a pity the [Irish] Government cannot see the wisdom of joining in with the rest of the Empire in showing a united front to the enemy."

Neutrality implied isolation, spiritual as well as geographical. The people, ignoring the fact that 50,000 Irishmen joined the British Army and twice as many more kept the British economy moving at home, turned in on themselves and, except for a heroic handful in the liberal arts, made a closed society even more tightly locked in. Dublin was a far cry from cosmopolitan London.

Only in Ireland could de Valera have made his famous visionary broadcast on St Patrick's Day, 1943, without being laughed out of office:

> The Ireland which we have dreamed of would be the home of a people who valued material wealth only as a basis of right living, of a people who were satisfied with frugal comfort and devoted their leisure to things of the spirit; and a land whose countryside would be bright with cosy homesteads, whose fields and villages would be joyous with the sounds of industry, with the romping of sturdy children, the contests of athletic youths, the laughter of comely maidens; whose firesides would be forums for the wisdom of serene old age. It would, in a word, be the home of a people living the life that God desires that men should live.

The man who only had to look into his own heart to discover what the Irish people were thinking had no trouble interpreting the desires of the King of Heaven.

"De Valera's 'dream' ", Professor Joe Lee tells us,[87] "has sometimes been derisively dismissed as impossibly 'naïve'. But there was nothing necessarily wrong about it. It is a matter of taste as to how his ideal society compared with rival visions. De Valera realised well enough that the dream deviated widely from existing reality... De Valera's 'dream' Ireland had never existed."

What Raymond, and a fortiori Mary, needed above all in this confusing time was to adopt protective colouring. They did not do so. They made some sound Irish friendships: they made far more among the expatriate colonies of English, French, Danish and American people in Dublin.

In spite of holding an influential position as Principal Architect of the Board of Works (from 1948), Raymond all his life retained his Australian passport. For official purposes, he travelled with an Irish *passeport de service* in which he was described as an "Irish national". His British passport issued in 1950 gives his national status as "Australian citizen by birth and a British subject". The new passport issued in January 1977 made him simply an Australian citizen.

Mary for her part stayed American and seemed most of the time to look on her life in Ireland as a period of enforced exile. She had not felt so in England.

The culture of an Ireland built on an agricultural economy (de Valera himself, in spite of his exotic name, came of farm labourer stock); administered by a lower middle-class 'Establishment'; educated by the Christian Brothers, and dominated by the tacit acceptance that "Home Rule is Rome Rule", was totally alien to a couple accustomed to the intellectual freedom and sophistication of London.

There were artists, actors and writers in Dublin who were worldly wise, travelled and cultivated, but they were outside the mainstream of Irish life. The McGraths were naturally drawn to them but they constituted a barrier to understanding the Plain People of Ireland.

That phrase, the Plain People of Ireland, is not lightly used. It was

R.M. Smyllie
(Courtesy of the National Gallery of Ireland)

minted by Myles na gCopaleen, whose column An Cruiskeen Lawn began its rumbustious, witty and controversial life in *The Irish Times* in the year Raymond and Mary arrived. Myles was Brian O'Nolan, a civil servant. He had in 1939 published 'At Swim-Two-Birds', a novel written at several levels and described by Graham Greene as "a book in a thousand". James Joyce said of Flann O'Brien (another O'Nolan pseudonym): "That's a real writer, with true comic spirit."

Myles wrote equally fluently in Irish and English and was master also of the more important Continental languages, as well as of Latin and Greek. He was, as Tony Gray[88] has called him, a man "of almost frightening erudition". The column began in Irish and was an overnight success. Gray says in his biography of the famous Editor of *The Irish Times*, R.M. Smyllie:

> It probably appealed to Smyllie's impish sense of humour to put one over on the other two daily newspapers and on the various Gaelic-oriented papers and magazines, by running, in the staid, West British, hitherto frantically anti-Irish-language *Irish Times* by far the most literate, intellectual and entertaining column in Gaelic ever published.

Its creator, described by Gray as "a small, shy, taciturn character with teeth like a rabbit and a greasy felt hat", was asked by Smyllie why he had chosen the pseudonym Myles na gCopaleen and the title Cruiskeen Lawn. His reply was typically aggressive and apocryphal: "A Cruiskeen Lawn is a jug full of porter, and Myles na gCopaleen, as you bloody well know, Smyllie, is the archetypal stage Irishman in Boucicault's 'Colleen Bawn'."

Myles's column soon appeared in English as well. In addition to increasing the circulation of *The Irish Times*, it became a regular talking point in any Dublin circle with literary pretensions. For Raymond it provided a useful educational tool, giving him insights into the machinations of Irish society as well as lightening his day. On at least one occasion, Myles had something to say about Raymond's work.

Mary heard from Eileen that she could have the bust of Mary's father Dr Crozier — "I always considered that bust the best portrait I've ever done" — and young Norman in Dublin received a congratulatory letter from his Dallas grandfather addressed "Dearest Boy". Norman's drawing in *Life* and a piece on his 'First Ten Days in Ireland' struck them all dumb. Eileen's head of Norman McGrath had arrived safely in Dallas, and Dr. Crozier said he was gradually getting over his attack of phlebitis.

Within two weeks, he was dead. "Death", said the local Dallas newspaper, "felled Dr. Crozier, superintendent [of schools] in Dallas since 1924 and former consultant for President Hoover's committee for surveying national school finances…" He was full of plans for school expansion when a stroke hit the "whimsical beloved educator with the senatorial poise". He had been born in Sardis, Mississippi, 62 years earlier.

His coffin was given an honour guard of six high school R.O.T.C. cadets in olive uniforms. For three hours they mounted a silent watch at the George A. Brewer funeral chapel and they accompanied the family to Grove Hill Cemetery.

Mary was devastated. Her life, it seemed, was falling apart already. Now "Big Daddy" was gone. She had been in a nursing home, Eden Park, in the spring of 1939 with the same problem that had struck her down so cruelly the year before. But 1940 seemingly spared her, at least until after November, when the family moved into the top floor of Monkstown House near Dublin.

"You are a brave girl, Mary, to want to stick it out with Raymond instead of going to the U.S.A.", Herbert had written just as Norman Robert Crozier was dying. When he heard the sad news from Eileen, Herbert said less than consolingly that Mary "had faced up to the other great anxieties that have beset her and you all for so long, and the end of which is not in sight".

In October, Raymond took time off to go to London, probably to see E.M.O.'R. Dickey and Sir Kenneth Clark about a suggestion of his to Dickey that he should record bomb damage to London in artistic form. He did not succeed, but he did a sketch for a surrealist picture of a clinically damaged house. He called it 'Home Sweet Home' and later tried unsuccessfully to sell the completed picture to the War Artists' Advisory Committee for 12 guineas. He already knew through Eileen that all the glass was broken in Conduit Street and a bomb had fallen on Park

'Home, Sweet Home', inspired by McGrath's visit to London during the blitz

213

Crescent and put a great hole in it. Indeed Nos. 17, 18 and 19 were no more. The new tenant of No. 10 offered to put Raymond up: we do not know if he accepted.

It was not a pleasant visit. Eileen had told him not to go unless he had to. Constant air raids caused him to spend two hours in a stationary train at Euston and a whole night in the Underground. But he did see Albert and discovered that he was enjoying himself. And he talked to Jim (Sir James) Richards of the *Architectural Review* about an article on and photographs of the Keene house at Galby. Richards was very pleased with the idea and a year later the article appeared. McGrath was in Ireland; Tunnard was in America: the *Review* was clutching at architectural straws at a time when nothing new was being built. Richards thought Raymond had "managed very wisely in getting fixed up away from here".

Raymond returned to Ireland on the mailboat Cambria, very soon afterwards to be bombed. His exhibition of watercolours and topographical drawings at the Print Room of Combridge's of Grafton Street had to be organised. He was not six months in Ireland; yet his show contained twelve watercolours of Dublin, Wicklow and Kildare.

'Home, Sweet Home', now in Norman's possession, was shown among the non-Irish pictures in the exhibition, which ran from 4 December to 14 December, 1940. It did not sell and when the following month Raymond offered it to Dickey he told him: "I remember a building near Berkeley square where an old circular stair, beautifully carpeted, rose up unscathed out of a heap of mortar and bricks. That gave me the idea for the picture…" Emptiness and nostalgia were the feelings he sought to portray. The show did not attract a great deal of press notice, but one critic observed that in McGrath, Dublin might have found "our second Malton". This was high praise indeed. James Malton from 1792 had produced a set of 25 engravings of major Dublin buildings. Over the next few years he coloured the engravings and, 200 years on, a set of Malton prints remains a standard adornment of many a Dublin house.

The Combridge catalogue informed potential buyers that McGrath had written two books and that his drawings of modern aircraft had been shown at the National Gallery in London and "are now at the Museum of Modern Art, New York".

In the summer, Raymond had carried on a voluminous correspondence with Councillor C.R. Keene of Leicester and James Clark and Eaton Ltd, the glass merchants. The object was to ensure that the glass in Keene's Kingstone store was in good order and capable of withstanding air raids. It was characteristic of Raymond to look after a client's interests from so far away; but one is bound to ask how much work was being done for the Government that had given him a livelihood. His school and college friend Roy Booth wrote from Sydney commending Raymond's "foresight in entering the Public Works Department" and told him of two mutual friends (one of them Fred Manderson, who had worked with Raymond at Finella before going home to private practice) who had gone into the public service. "I confess that I encouraged Fred to jump the fairly wide ditch as it is obvious that this scrap is going to last a few weeks yet",

*When McGrath had designed Harold
Hemming's dressing-room at 35
Elsworthy Road, London, he painted
this watercolour. On the window, he
and Hemming stuck the regulation
A.R.P. tape in the shape of
Pythagoras' Theorem, which of
course every schoolboy knows*

Booth commented. He himself had just been accepted into the Royal
Australian Air Force as a pilot officer. "Yippee!"

Not one of Raymond's English or Australian friends criticised or even
mildly chided him for not "joining up". To Fiona McCarthy he did in 1968
say: "...As I was still on the reserved list of occupations in England I
decided to take [the job in Dublin] (My grandfather came from Ireland)."
But no jot or tittle of jingoism was directed at Raymond's decision by
Harold Hemming, John Witt, Derrick Oxley or David Renwick, all of
whom were already in uniform.

Many others — and they included Elmo Pye and Roy Booth in
Sydney; Brian O'Rorke, Jim Richards and Jack Pritchard in London;
Morton Shand in Bath, and Barbara Chermayeff (just arrived in America
and staying with Walter and Ise Gropius while Serge looked for a job) —
wished him only well.

The two houses that McGrath lived in during his 37 years in Ireland: Raymond's painting (above) of the balconies of Monkstown House, and (below) the garden front of Somerton Lodge.
(Photograph by Bill Doyle)

CHAPTER XXIX

n January 1941, Eileen fired a New Year's shot across Raymond's bows. Usually the most placid and most philosophical of people, she became angry at the Christmas silence from Dublin:

> I guess you are all very busy — for you never do write, but then you've not written home [to Sydney] for a very long time — which I think is very unfair of you, for naturally they are anxious about you all in times like these — for the peace and love of their souls as well as for the good of their bodily health I think one of you at least could write a little note — simply to say you are well and safe — even Norman could write sometimes, for never have there been more faithful and loving parents than ours — and love is not a thing to be ignored…

Her boldness brought results, though the worsening war was making communication more difficult. In England, the difficulty was compounded by a shortage of writing paper. Some people in Australia were asked to send a few blank sheets with their letters "home".

Albert and Eileen were not for long affected by rationing. What Herbert called "the stroke of fortune that has revolutionised their lives" brought a job for Albert in the British Embassy in Washington. He had been working as an assistant secretary in the Ministry of Economic Warfare and was attached as third secretary to the Washington mission. He set up an economic warfare office, a service which won him a first secretaryship in 1946 and an Order of the British Empire in 1947.

Taking Hugh, the Frosts sailed from Liverpool in April 1941. They were scarcely at sea when they were hit by a tanker and had to return for repairs to the Nerissa. She was a 300-passenger cruise ship doing the Atlantic run to Newfoundland. Although they saw at least two convoys, Eileen says they sailed alone for two weeks, making and breaking contact with only one U-boat. On her return journey the Nerissa was not so fortunate. She was torpedoed and went down with 270 lives lost, including the captain's.

The frequency of Raymond's correspondence with his parents improved, although during the awesome crisis of 1942 (recounted in Chapter 25), he does not seem to have allowed them to share his emotional turbulence.

Wishing Raymond luck in his town-planning examination in July 1943 (we hear no more of this venture), Herbert moved back to "Easter Monday, a truly black Monday for you, Ray. We shared your sadness since

Dr. Le Clerc

we got your cable and we have been longing to hear that Mary was home again, her old self".

Raymond had written with unusual directness: "I'd give a lot to have you with us right now." He told his parents that Dr. and Mrs Le Clerc, the parents of Percy Le Clerc, an expert on national monuments in the Office of Public Works and a dear friend of Raymond's and Mary's, had kindly taken Norman and Jenny to their house. At a critical point in the management of Monkstown House, Lily, their housekeeper, had left for England. Raymond could not continue to work unless he was relieved of the burden of looking after two young children.

His cable to Wahroonga seems to have been a plea for money. At any rate, Herbert told him he could not help. Mary's expenses in hospital added enormously to the debt with which Raymond was already saddled on his arrival in Ireland. In a letter to Mary's mother, he did not ask for support, but he said plaintively: "I haven't any money left for holidays… I have not been able to place any drawings lately, but Constantia Maxwell [the author of 'Dublin under the Georges'] has asked me to do some illustrations for her new book on Trinity College."

This letter, dated 1 June, 1943, told Heart that Mary had been home for a month. She was getting interested in things but she would not write letters. He had taken the family for a cycle to Enniskerry, Co. Wicklow, where Laurence Olivier's film of 'Henry V' was being shot on location. Lord Powerscourt's estate near the village was the scene of the battle of Agincourt and with the help of invitations procured by Alan Hope they were able to see the French, mounted on 200 caparisoned horses, charge down a hill and into battle.

John Betjeman the poet, whom the McGraths had known in England, was posted to the British Representative's office in Dublin. Betjeman was cultural attaché under Sir John Maffey, later Lord Rugby. Although the belief persists in Dublin that Betjeman was a spy, Colonel Dan Bryan of Irish Military Intelligence (G2) could find "nothing more suspicious than an interest in Gaelic poetry and a predisposition 'to go around calling himself Seán O'Betjeman' ".[89] In the middle of 1943, Betjeman got a new job with the Film Section of the Ministry of Information in London. "I wish", wrote Raymond wistfully to Heart, "that we could join him. Mary is very homesick for London, but I wonder if she would be happier there."

During this episode, Mary had been given electric shock treatment, her first. The Cerlette treatment had "put her right very quickly", said Raymond, and the doctor thought that if she had this treatment in the early spring again next year, "we would be saved a recurrent break-down".

With all this going on, Raymond was yet able to give a broadcast entitled 'Dublin Panorama' on Radio Éireann. It was based on an illustrated article in *The Bell* (August 1941). The article — 'An Architectural Review' — took the form of a conspectus of a bombed-out Dublin as viewed from Cruagh in the Dublin mountains in the imagined company of Sean O'Faolain, the famous short story writer and founder editor of *The Bell*. It took up fourteen pages and contained seven of McGrath's most sympathetic and atmospheric drawings. In this issue he was in the company of friends. Louis MacNeice's latest collection of poems was reviewed; Barney Heron, who later built a wardrobe to Raymond's design, contributed a short story, and Maurice Craig the architectural historian published one of his delightful poems.

Mary's lack of interest notwithstanding, Raymond was developing a deep attachment to the city in which he was to live out the rest of his life and to ornament with his double quill. His panorama, in its penultimate paragraph, went over what he had liked amongst that pile of bricks and stone:

"Perhaps", said Sean O'Faolain, "there will rise out of that great waste a city such as we have only dreamed of!" I wondered. I thought of prophets all over the old and new worlds — Aalto, Oud, Gropius, Corbusier, Wright. I thought of town planners burning their midnight oil on the top floors of Baggot Street. I thought of architectural schools bursting with students and ideas. Yes, like its phoenix, Dublin would reappear, new and perfect and beautiful, planned with vision, rebuilt with knowledge. Not quite the same thing of course as Dublin, 1941, in all its magnificent and shoddy detail.

Raymond's acceptance by *The Bell* signalled his joining the lonely and ragged voices prepared to criticise establishment values. They waged war on issues such as the censorship of books and, by publishing the work of most of the banned authors, lent them a stature which without this foolish piece of legislation some of them would not have attained. Founded in October 1940, *The Bell* last rang out in December 1954.

When Raymond wrote: "I thought of architectural schools bursting with students and ideas", he scarcely perceived the daring bid he was to

The Irish House, Winetavern Street

The Irish House, now demolished. This was one of the seven drawings McGrath did to illustrate 'An Architectural Review' in The Bell *of August 1941*

make two years later for the professorship of architecture at University College, Dublin. Rudolph Maximilian Butler, the founding holder of the chair, died in 1943. He had built up the school in the neo-classical style, furnishing U.C.D. with a fitting beginning by designing its grand façade at Earlsfort Terrace.

The façade of the building which now incorporates the National Concert Hall was completed in 1919 and by 1943, when the chair was opened to competition, the students if not the college wanted their school to let in the flood of modern ideas that had built up in France and Germany and even England between the wars.

Raymond decided to have a go. With the knowledge that such students as Paddy Corcoran were behind his application, he compiled an impressive curriculum vitae. In accordance with the rules of the National University, his application had to be printed. His account of his professional career came to nine pages: another ten were taken up with testimonials. He put a lot of work into both sections. He got the application printed by Hely's, who set it in 10 point Gill Sans at his instruction. He chose as frontispiece 'Athena's Parthenon', printed from the original wood engraving.

Like anybody compiling a C.V., Raymond put the best gloss on things. Thus under "Travel", he listed "Australia and the East", the East being stops at Colombo and Port Said on his way to England in the Osterley. He gave his Cambridge research subject, but not the fact that he did not complete his thesis to the satisfaction of the faculty board. And he included "Le Corbusier — Architect, Artist, Author" among his unpublished works although he had not written, and would not write the book.

He had no need to stretch points. His record of achievement was dazzling, and his application was supported by a glittering cast of stars including Lord Sempill; C. Le Maistre of the British Standards Institution; Julian Huxley; Frank Pick, chairman of the London Passenger Transport Board; Henry Thirkill, the Master of Clare, and his superior, J.M. Fairweather, Principal Architect of the Board of Works.

Fairweather's comments are of special interest. They give us an indication of what Raymond was doing when he was not painting, writing or looking after Mary. "...Pure draughtsmanship, planning and design of buildings for State purposes, the development of recreation centres, and keen appraisement of the architectural heritage of the country... such technical matters as factory lay-outs, fire protection, water supplies and drainage problems."

His aesthetic proclivities cover many subjects allied to pure architecture, including trade designs for glass, metal, wood and fabrics applied to furniture and fittings, which have been commercially appreciated. Recently he designed and personally supervised the interior decoration of the principal part of Arus an Uachtaráin [then the correct spelling] for which he received the President's compliments.

Raymond's design for the Ross Williamsons' Christmas card, 1944

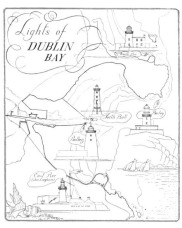

220

The President who complimented Raymond on his work in the Phoenix Park was Douglas Hyde, the first President of Ireland under the new Constitution of 1937. Dr Hyde was a co-founder of the Gaelic League in 1893, a poet in Irish, a professor and a Protestant. Thus, as Professor Lee[90] drily puts it, "he satisfied sundry national self-images and, at the age of seventy-seven, seemed unlikely to be unduly assertive."

Fairweather appreciated the concept of total design, which was a guiding principle in Raymond's work. Raymond had succeeded in persuading the Board to grant him the right to private practice, not as an architect but as an industrial designer. He exercised this right to the full throughout his years of public service, with results that we shall see. J.M. Fairweather's was a generous spirit: he did not have to mention Raymond's private work any more than he had to add: "I must refer to the literary ability with which he conveys his professional reports... an ability which I hold to be a most desirable asset for the post sought."

Sought but not obtained. University College, Dublin, keeps no records of the selection process, so we do not know who else applied or what was said at the meetings. This is in stark contrast to the state of affairs at Sydney University, which has a rich store of archives that we shall plunder later on.

The upshot was that J.V. Downes, a crypto-modernist architect practising in Dublin,[91] was appointed to the chair. It may be that Raymond's application was taken seriously. He may even have been the second choice. Or his alien origin, his modernist outlook, or his lack of a Cambridge doctorate, or all three, may have told against him. We simply do not know, and neither he nor Mary has left us any letters to Australia or America that refer to this important attempt by Raymond to better his own position and widen the doors of perception for Irish students.

With the rejection of some of the best artists working in Ireland in 1943, the Royal Hibernian Academy brought to a head a simmering row between tradition and progress. The result was the establishment by Louis le Brocquy, Mainie Jellett, Norah McGuinness and others of the Irish Exhibition of Living Art to give an annual platform to the avant-garde.

Raymond, who had first shown at the Academy in 1941, could never be accused of being a modern painter, yet he showed two works at the 1944 Exhibition of Living Art; one at the 1945 show and four in 1951. Between 1952 and 1956 he offered one painting a year. It must have pleased him that Stephen Rynne, the art critic of the *Leader*, wrote of the 1945 show:

> We have not been so dumb here at home after all and Neutrality has suited our art as much as it has suited our consciences... It is ... solace and encouragement to know that we here in Ireland have now safely and soundly established our own Living Art... [as] proof of the liveliness of our artists.

Raymond is listed by Kennedy[92] as among the "now familiar names" whose work dominated the Living Art. But the truth is that because he was an architect he was almost by definition an academician. Certainly his artistic future lay in the R.H.A., of which he was to become president before his death.

Louis le Brocquy
(Photograph by Albert Fenton)

221

Achill . September '31 .

Achill Island, Co. Mayo. A similar version of this painting, but with a horse in the field on the left, is in the possession of the Office of Public Works

Theodore Goodman, the art critic of *Commentary* (August 1943), reviewing an exhibition of watercolours at the Contemporary Picture Galleries exhibition, lent weight to the conviction that McGrath was out of place in the Living Art:

> …McGrath's watercolours, where freshness of vision is combined with a fine technique… The drawing of 'Irish Lights Quay, Dun Laoghaire', has a vitality, a dramatic power and sense of light and space which could only be created by an artist who is a master of his medium. 'The Liffey at Straffan' has much of the severity and dignity of the fine English water-colour painters in the early 19th century.

Facing page (above): Roundstone from Mweenish Island, Connemara. McGrath painted two versions in 1944. One, without a cow, went to the Frosts in Washington. This one went to Joseph Connolly, then Chairman of the Office of Public Works.

Below: An untitled fantasy island bought by the Countess of Wicklow at the Royal Hibernian Academy in 1943

If Raymond was only paddling on the riverbank of Irish life, at least he was making a name for himself in the cultural life of the capital. And early in 1944, when his assistant architect was ill, he took Mary touring Cork, Kilkenny and Waterford looking at schools, police stations and other public buildings while they absorbed the rich and sometimes dramatic countryside. They were comforted by a post-Christmas greeting drawn for them by Jack B. Yeats. On a sheet of his writing paper, Yeats had drawn and coloured a circus scene "to wish Jenny, Norman, Mary and Raymond McGrath a Happy and indeed joyful New Year for if you must have post-war plans they needn't be plans for post-war miseries".

Dooega. 10/8/53. (Achill Island)

CHAPTER XXX

Early in 1945, Heart wrote sternly: "Raymond, you must have a thorough examination — there is a cause for your frequent illnesses — so find out at once." Mrs. Crozier was concerned about many things as the war came to an end. She thought of going to Ireland, staying with Mary and Raymond "until you got tired of me", and buying a second-hand Ford car if Irish prices were not too high.

On her way to Ireland, she planned to see Serge and Barbara Chermayeff in New York. She worried about how hard they worked, whether Ivan and Peter had received the $5 she sent them for Christmas, and the fact that their parents never seemed to go out. "I love them really", she added. She had made all her Christmas present money out of radio presentations at $35 for a fifteen-minute programme.

Mary got her usual bagful of instructions in this letter. "Date your letters correctly"; "Please say 'Mr. Huxley' or 'Julian' but *not* 'Huxley'." (Professor Huxley gave a lecture on evolution in Dublin on 31 January, 1945. Mary and Raymond were asked to lunch with Huxley and Professor Erwin Schrödinger of the Dublin School of Cosmic Physics. Heart was not impressed.) She told the McGraths how she wanted to be received at Monkstown House: "Don't dress up the house or anything for me — Raymond, *don't* cut your hair and get new shoes — Meet me casually, all of you…"

Heart worried about the spiritual welfare of Mary's children. "I wish you'd choose a wonderful *minister* and either send or take the children to Service. It is so heathenish not to and that too is where you get the nicest atmosphere and meet the real people."

In March 1945, Mary was nearly 36 years old, yet her mother still wrote "Dearest Child" and wanted to know what Mary meant when she said she had been ill. "What was the matter? Were you 'blue' again? If so, go and have a treatment." In the meanwhile she told Mary in a letter written in May after the war in Europe was over that about fifteen German submarines were still in Atlantic waters. "They are a despicable people and 'twill take several generations to teach them they are not 'superior'. De Valera is a stain on the name of Éire to harbour and fraternise with such fiends… I hope [Raymond] leaves Éire."

It is difficult to reconcile the word-picture painted by this self-willed woman with the kindhearted and considerate grandmother of Jenny's memory. Jenny saw a lot of Heart when she eventually did go to Dublin in 1946, and although Jenny knew that Heart could upset her mother, she recalls more vividly the eccentricity, vivacity, openness and warmth that she felt in

Facing page, above: Dooagh, Achill
Below: Sea Thistle, Mayo, 1963

Heart. The winter of 1946-47 was exceptionally harsh. Heart and Jenny shared a bed over which lay Heart's fur coat. Monkstown House was no exception to the rule that most Irish houses lacked adequate heating systems.

Heart was not the only one on the move. The McGraths and the Frosts also were facing the consequences of peace. Albert and Eileen saw no alternative to returning to England, unless it was emigrating to Australia. Raymond tossed about the notions of going back to private practice (in which case, his father said, he should make sure to have an annual break for his physical and mental health's sake) and of returning to Australia. In June 1946 Nikolaus Pevsner wrote to Raymond: "I was very sorry to hear that you did not succeed in getting a passage to Australia straight away." (Pevsner stayed at Monkstown House in March, "a fairy holiday... beset by whiskey and all too much steak".)

Herbert McGrath's dream was different — a grand family reunion in England. Edith had had operations for melanomas and needed a long holiday. Raymond was off again, this time wondering about building a life in America. His father checked him: "Happiness, contentment and good health are the hardest things in life to obtain and keep and are of much greater value than fame and wealth." Herbert himself was the best example of his own truism. He was 70 in 1946, and celebrated by going to see Bing Crosby and Barry Fitzgerald in 'Going My Way'.

Yngve Ahlm, writing to Mary and Raymond from the University of California at Berkeley, thought America had everything: "Since we took 'refuge' in the land of golden opportunities we have learnt to love and appreciate Amerika and think that it is the only country worth while..."

By the time Albert and Eileen began to make plans to bring their family to Australia, Edith had taken a turn for the worse and Herbert cabled Albert: "Mother dangerously ill — wants Eileen." Herbert would willingly have paid her fare, but how could she travel? There was no way in which she could leave her children.

Edith had cancer; and it had spread to her brain. She lost interest in her garden and her pottery; and she was in pain. Eileen cabled: "Please tell Mother I am with her and love her. I pray for her recovery. I would come if it were possible." Then she and Albert telephoned Herbert from Washington — "a thrilling experience" for him, he said. But Eileen said he was so anxious for her and Raymond to come home. Washington to Sydney by air would cost $700 and the Frosts did not have it; though they could help towards Raymond's flight.

There was little in Edith's face "to show how near death she is", Herbert wrote. "What an awful word to have to write." Raymond said he was coming to be with his mother but Herbert cabled asking him to abandon the idea. The difficulties, he wired, were insurmountable. It was enough for the older McGraths to know the love that he bore for them. Herbert, with some professional help and the support of all their relatives and friends, nursed Edith day and night.

We are both elated with the prospect, Ray, of your getting a job out here with the Irish Ambassador. It would be nothing short

Some of Edith McGrath's pottery displayed at Treeways. The piece on the left is now in Ireland

of a miracle if you could persuade the President [Seán T. O'Kelly] to have the matter fixed up for you.

What had happened to cause Herbert such joy was this.[93] The Australian Labour Party was in office in Canberra. Dr H.V. Evatt, the Minister for External Affairs, wanted to confront Britain, build up Australia as the champion of small nations and exploit support for Ireland within the Australian Labour Party. In April 1946, W.J. Dignam, a Sydney barrister who was a Labour supporter, was appointed Australian High Commissioner to Éire. (Why he was not accredited to "Ireland" is the subject of a different and long-running story).

De Valera in turn appointed Dr. Thomas J. Kiernan Minister Plenipotentiary to Australia. De Valera's motive was the enlisting of overseas Irish opinion against the partition of Ireland. Dr Kiernan interpreted his mission as mainly cultural and he made a significant contribution to Australians' understanding of Ireland. He was aided by the fact that his wife was Delia Murphy, then the country's best-known ballad singer.

Ireland had no legation in Canberra. Raymond seemed to be the ideal architect to design one. He drew up plans for a building that would do justice to the land of his grandfather's birth in the land of his own. He enlisted the support of the newly-elected Seán T. O'Kelly and arranged to travel with the Kiernans. But according to Dr Colm Kiernan, T.J.'s academic son, the Department of Finance in Dublin considered the building too costly and vetoed the design, and the journey. It was to be forty years before Ireland constructed a purpose-built embassy in Canberra. The Australian, Philip Cox, was the architect.

Elmo Pye heard of the possibility of Raymond's going to Australia but told Raymond that Herbert was "wisely not banking too much" on it. Herbert read out the stream of letters coming from Raymond and Eileen to Edith, who wept a little each time. He told his son: "I have still hopes, Ray, that your persuasive powers will work the miracle of getting an official trip to Australia."

Raymond, whose thoughts at this time we can only imagine, sent a note to his father: "Tell Mother we are sending her some special sunshine that will shine into the window when she gets this letter and do her more good than any medicine." Herbert replied to Raymond: "As I read your letter to her a ribbon of sunlight played across her face coming through the space between the side of the blind and the frame. And it may have come from Ireland."

Edith's potter friend, Mrs Chapple, was a devoted companion through her illness. Before she became bedridden, Edith had gone through a few months of intensive pottery-making; and these pieces Mrs Chapple was taking home for glazing and firing. One piece, a table lamp decorated with kangaroos, was glazed in off-white and intended for Raymond. It stands today in Jenny's living room.

Sir Charles Blackburn, Sydney's leading physician, confirmed that Edith had a brain tumour and that nothing could be done for her.

Herbert's sister Alice Lewry in 1956

Sunday morning, August 18, 1946, was bleak and cloudy. The end came peacefully at 10.30. Edith was taken to the funeral parlour at Burwood and cremated next day. Herbert's tribute was a posy of violets with a small red rose in the centre. For the two absent children he made up a bunch of freesias and dark purple anemones. She had planted and loved all these flowers.

At Rookwood Cemetery her ashes lie along with the remains of Herbert's mother Elizabeth Hannah McGrath, and all of Edith's immediate Sorrell family. Apart from Alice, Herbert's sister, and the other relatives, the funeral was attended by a few friends including Roy Booth, Elmo Pye and Fred Manderson. The casket was covered in flowers. Herbert mentioned no clergyman. "Thus", he wrote to Raymond, "closes a long association with a fine woman, wife and chum. Someday I may write her biography to let you know her better than you already do."

Jenny was at home in Monkstown House when the telegram arrived: "Mother passed away Sunday loving sympathy McGrath". She had never seen her father sob before, nor ever again. It was four days short of 20 years since he had left Australia. When his flowers arrived Alice put them on Edith's bed. Herbert read the card — "In loving memory from Raymond and family" — and he too broke down. Both of his children offered financial support, which he declined. He had made provision for this event years ago.

Albert had abandoned the notion of going home to England and was working towards obtaining a transfer within the foreign service to Switzerland. Movement was in the air. Herbert was issued with a passport, but it would be six months before the reconditioned passenger liners could offer a berth. In the meanwhile "I shall know whether and when you are coming out to Sydney". Raymond still hoped to be with the Kiernans when they arrived in October. He was still toying with the notion of going into private practice but he did tell his father that he had the prospect of earning £1,400 a year on promotion with the Board of Works.

Herbert was planning to get to Europe to experience the Irish spring. He was remarkably resilient, sharing the plans and hopes of his son and daughter and quite overcoming the lonely walks around Edith's flower garden that his sister Alice had observed with concern. He still owned Rostella, the house in Gladesville. With his travel plans he had to reckon with letting or selling Rostella and possibly Treeways. And talking of property, he played with friends "a new game called Monopoly. Do you know it? It is an ingenious arrangement of buying and selling railway stations and other property in London... it passed the evening in a new manner for me".

On Christmas Day — "dramatically, essentially Australian" — the hottest for ten years, Herbert went to his sister-in-law at 44 Park Road, Burwood, for dinner. "Millie put on her usual banquet of roast turkey, pickled pork, baked potatoes, beans and peas piping hot. She serves no small helpings." In spite of the heat, they left nothing on their plates and tackled the plum pudding as well. "So you see how hard it is to break with tradition." Millie, Valerie and Tommy, Sorrells all, made Herbert most welcome.

Raymond in 1946 made the first of many working trips abroad. The Irish Government was no better endowed than most with Ministers who possessed cultivated tastes, but it did have P.J. Little. A solicitor and journalist, he was grandson of Cornelius Little (born 1789), who had to flee from Dunshaughlin, Co. Meath and sail for Nova Scotia with a political price on his head. Cornelius' son Philip Francis studied law and became Premier of Newfoundland from 1855 to 1858, and then a judge of the Supreme Court. P.F. Little retired to Ireland in 1867 and later was associated with Charles Stewart Parnell in the national movement. His son Paddy Little (1884–1963) got the best kind of Catholic education at Clongowes Wood ("the cream of the country, rich and thick", mocked those denied a Jesuit schooling), and at University College, Dublin. He had an impeccable record in the movement for independence and edited various magazines from 1916 to 1926, as well as representing the Republic in South Africa and various South American States. As a member of Fianna Fáil (de Valera's party) he was appointed Minister for Posts and Telegraphs in 1939.

This then was, in Dr. Brian Kennedy's words, de Valera's "own art adviser whom he liked and trusted".[94] Little in turn admired de Valera and always referred to him as "the Chief", a term widely used by de Valera's colleagues, for whom it reinforced a direct link with Parnell. As far back as 1936, Little was working towards the establishment of a National Symphony Orchestra and concert hall. He was fortunate in that as well as the patronage of de Valera, he enjoyed the friendship of Seán MacEntee, the Minister for Finance and possibly the most sophisticated of the senior members of the Government.

The politics of such a radical proposal were complex, and there were headstrong civil servants as well as apathetic and even hostile politicians to be manipulated. De Valera's unqualified support was not enough in the face of an obscurantist memorandum such as this one (1937) from the Department of Finance, which flew in the face of its own Minister's views:

> Thirty years ago or more a case might possibly have been made for State subsidisation of public musical performances. At that time a piano in a drawing room or a squeaky phonograph in the parlour supplied satisfaction for the musical yearning of the common man, unless he got a chance to attend an occasional concert. Nowadays musical talking films can be attended every night in the week in all parts of the country; Wireless sets and gramophones are widely distributed; even as he drives abroad a motorist can listen to the best music on his radio set. Accordingly although interest in music must have increased enormously, public attendances at Symphony Concerts, and consequently the necessity for such public concerts, have become smaller and will continue to decline. Is it any part of the State's duty to resuscitate a Victorian form of educational recreation?

In the teeth of such official discouragement, Little battled on. He had no interest in the postal or telephone services, but his portfolio gave him

Paddy Little
(Courtesy of Máirín Hope)

control over broadcasting and this control he exploited "to raise cultural standards". In January 1946 a committee of Ministers was established "to examine the position in regard to the provision of a public Concert Hall and report to the Government". The three Ministers included MacEntee and Little, and Little was authorised to purchase the lease on the Rotunda buildings and refurbish them.

The Rotunda Hospital was the first lying-in hospital in the then British dominions. It was the work of Dr. Bartholomew Mosse, who in Maurice Craig's fine words[95] "combined in a rare degree the love of architectural magnificence with that of his fellow-men". Mosse (1712–1759) had both vision and the will to realise it. He planned to finance his splendid maternity hospital by first constructing a fashionable resort behind it. The gardens were both a social and a financial success.

But that was not the end. After Mosse's death, the Rotunda itself (now the Ambassador Cinema) was built; later the New Assembly Rooms were added. At present, the hospital, the Gate Theatre, the cinema and what was a dance-hall lie under the same roof. It was this complex (without the hospital) that made up Paddy Little's grand scheme.

The Rotunda buildings that made up Paddy Little's grand scheme
(Irish Architectural Archive)

J.M. Fairweather, the Principal Architect of the Board of Works, put the cost at £350,000 and although complications set in, Raymond McGrath was asked to visit Scandinavia to study broadcasting stations and concert halls there. He was there and in Holland and Belgium for most of November 1946.

On the way, Raymond stayed with John and Margaret Witt in London. They made him very comfortable and he saw Eric and Dora Lewenhaupt and their daughter Karin. He sailed for Gothenburg on the Britannia, accompanied by the shadowy Sir John Lyons.

In Gothenburg they saw Eriksson's Opera House in the company of the architect and the town planning officer. Apart from bread and meat, which were rationed, they found the shops full of lovely things. Stockholm had a new broadcasting building at the planning stage, and the

State radio people in Copenhagen got them a hotel there. Copenhagen he found "shabby by Swedish standards" with no hot water but a jug for shaving. But only butter was rationed and they had the first meat they had enjoyed for a week.

"You cannot sit down in the lounge without being told, quite openly, that it is unnecessary to be lonely in Denmark. By contrast there are no flusies [*sic*] anywhere in Sweden", he moralised to Mary.

He saw the radio building and its concert hall. (He had already visited the excellent concert hall in Hälsingborg, Sweden.) Everywhere he went he met architects such as Vilhelm Lauritzen and Arne Jacobsen, who impressed him enormously. His realisation of the dream of seeing the homeland of Iris Wennström must have revived memories of 1927 and Rämon Makra, but the Flower of Åre was among the things he kept hidden from Mary.

From Copenhagen a Swedish Air Lines Dakota flew McGrath and Lyons to Amsterdam. There was one other passenger. The devastation of Kiel below filled Raymond with a feeling of horror. No smoke rose from the burnt-out buildings and the water was littered with warships lying on their sides. A solitary barge moved along the canal. This scene was described in a letter to Norman who at 15 was being addressed as an adult. Raymond had no gift for writing to the younger Jenny yet. She was still being asked how school was.

When he had made his report on the Netherlands, Raymond went to Brussels, where there were no shortages. Why, he wondered, when there was such stringency in Holland? The Institut National Belge de Radiodiffusion involved an intensive day and then they went by train to Paris where Raymond was to meet Kenneth Besson. Besson was an Irish friend, owner of the Royal Hibernian Hotel in Dublin and an admirer of Raymond's work. Much of the decoration and graphic work in both the Hibernian and the Russell hotels was to be done by Raymond in the coming years. Besson booked him into a double room at the Savoy in

The Russell Hotel from the gate of St. Stephen's Green

*Right and below:
McGrath's menus for the Russell*

The Russell Hotel
Dublin

London, where he met Mary for a holiday. He had spent over a month away, but he had written home nearly every day. Among the letters he received on the Continent was one from Paddy Little relieving his mind on the subject of the expenses he was incurring. Little was an uncle of Raymond's friend Máirín Hope (née Cuffe), with whose husband, Alan, Raymond collaborated on the Besson hotels.

Mary wrote to Raymond at Hilversum to say that T.H. White's 'Mistress Masham's Repose' had arrived. The end-papers which Raymond had drawn looked well but were on a chestnut brown background with the lettering in beige. From G.P. Putnam's Sons, Earle H. Balch had promised him "our top fee for a map of this sort", namely $50.

Paddy Little did not succeed in getting his concert hall built. In 1948 the Government changed when the Opposition parties united to "put them out". One of many results was the placing of the concert hall plan on a list of "Projects to be dropped".

When Fianna Fáil was returned to office in 1951, Paddy Little was appointed by de Valera's Government as the first Director of the Arts Council. He was 67. De Valera, who himself had fostered learning at the expense of the liberal arts, had paid his debt to his cultural adviser.

Chapter XXXI

Think! A suite at the Savoy free of charge and meeting all old friends after so long. She needed the change. In fact anyone who lives more than a year in this oppressive climate should be given a free trip by the Government.

Heart wrote thus to Herbert on 8 January, 1947. She was surviving the Irish winter: Herbert awaited a passage from Sydney that would enable him to enjoy his first Irish spring.

Herbert's departure for Ireland was postponed several times by a wharfies' strike at Sydney. Australia had been riddled with industrial unrest since the end of the war. Early in April 1947, the S.S. Monkay, a French cargo vessel carrying wool for Europe and 40 passengers, set sail for Antwerp via Djibouti. Herbert, a long round of farewell dinners under his belt, was as excited as a schoolboy, and every bit as interested in the people with whom he was to spend the next six weeks.

When he arrived at Monkstown House he at last allowed himself to be overwhelmed by "a flood of pent-up emotions". He stayed with Raymond and his family as well as Mary's mother Heart, troubled by "many misgivings, wondering whether I could fit into your home without disorganising it and throwing the shadow of my loneliness across your paths". He need not have worried. He was warmly welcomed and the companionship of Norman and Jenny rejuvenated him.

Welcome as Herbert had felt in Dublin, by September he was anxious to see Eileen. Sailing on the Mauritania, he found a letter from Raymond which he considered another treasure in the long succession of writings from Raymond that had "given me and many others much pleasure" over the years. He had visited the Frosts at Carlisle on the way, had met and stayed with Albert at the Cumberland Hotel in London, and had a drink at Fischer's Restaurant, unchanged in fifteen years.

In Washington, Herbert found the standard of hygiene higher than anything he had encountered before. Since the death of his first-born, Ivor, nearly fifty years before, cleanliness had been an obsession with him. He loved Edith for her many qualities, but for none so much as her devotion to hygiene. In Ireland when he settled there he displayed an abhorrence of insects that Norman never forgot. In America, he told Heart in a letter from 3801 Jocelyn Street, "the screening of windows against flies and mosquitoes is further evidence of the care that is taken against the pollution of food". He congratulated Heart on being an American and was astonished at her modesty when talking about it.

Herbert McGrath leaving Sydney on the Monkay

Albert Frost's job at the British Embassy had been socially useful. He and Eileen met Donald Maclean the Soviet agent, and his wife Melinda when Maclean, with his "exceptional height, good looks and faintly condescending manner,"[96] became First Secretary of the Washington mission in 1944. Albert met Winston Churchill about the same time and took a good photograph of the Prime Minister's departure from the embassy. Then early in 1947, with Elaine Haxton in tow, he and Eileen went to a reception given by President Truman at the White House. They thought it a poor affair, even though they got to shake the President's hand.

By May, Albert's employment problem was solved. He had been kept on at the embassy because Roger Makins and all the others had been posted elsewhere and the new people had to be shown the ropes. When the International Monetary Fund was established, Albert was appointed assistant secretary. So the Frosts stayed in Washington, where Eileen still lives. They did not grudge the money they had expended on travelling trunks intended for the journey to Berne.

Norman's first holiday by himself was a success. Jean Stempowski in Le Havre had suggested a mid-summer exchange between Norman, aged 16, and Marie-José, aged about 20 and studying law. Norman travelled via London — there was then little alternative — and stayed with Alice and Harold Hemming. He was taken out by Margaret Witt and Margaret Taylor, and he charmed all three women. They found him companionable.

Marie-José, who shared Jenny's bed at Monkstown House, had a good sense of humour and was a social success too, especially with Percy Le Clerc who took her around in his motor-car. Her father said she enjoyed her holiday immensely.

Norman too thoroughly enjoyed himself. He had his bicycle with him, and he was fascinated by the bomb-damage the Americans had perpetrated on the town. Even the Stempowski house at 27 rue de l'Alma

Monkstown House

had a wall destroyed and then repaired. The family was not short of food. Jean's American friends sent food parcels; Jean got butter from the country, and Alain his son, just ending his military service in Indo China, sent tea. But milk, although it was rationed, was impossible to obtain, and Norman loved milk.

Perhaps it was the French influence. Jenny wrote to Heart: "...I can swim over my head at full tide at Seapoint and I can do the Brest stroke..." Her godfather, the Swedish Count Eric Lewenhaupt, wondered what a godfather was supposed to do. "Anyway, sending you a broach [*sic*] was, maybe, a good beginning," he thought.

Both McGrath children were at Protestant schools, which in those days meant more or less that the pupils felt more British than Irish. But while Norman's class at Avoca got time off school to listen to the B.B.C. broadcast of the wedding of Princess Elizabeth and Prince Philip on November 20, 1947, Jenny's form at Park House had to miss it. She was allowed to stay up for the repeat broadcast at 8.15.

That other royal-spotter, Mrs Norman Robert Crozier, was well settled back into Dallas by then and listening to the American relay of the programme. Mary, who told Heart that the ceremony had deeply moved Norman, was herself most impressed by the skill of the B.B.C. commentators. "I will certainly take Jenny to the Technicolor film of the event", she promised.

Derrick Oxley, who had been a pre-war member of Raymond's team, visited Monkstown House. "He apologised for taking the Hibernian [Hotel] business so badly", Mary told her mother, "and we all agreed to forget the unpleasantness." Unfortunately we do not know the details of this business. We do know that Mary at the beginning of 1947 was asked by Kenneth Besson to order sheets, blankets, pillowcases and towels for both the Royal Hibernian and the Russell, which Besson and his father had just bought. Linen in Ireland was both rationed and expensive, and she wanted the order to be filled by the Wamsutta Mills of New Bedford, Mass. Payment could be arranged through her mother and the First National Bank of Dallas.

Raymond did some work on the hotels with Oxley, who used an office in Alan Hope's premises. But Oxley had never seen the Russell completed so the McGraths took him to dinner there with Alan and Oxley's "little hunting friend, Mary O'Kelly". Afterward there was a fashion show by Owen Charles, in real life the Marquis MacSweeney, "a beautiful young man...". The dresses, said Mary unkindly, "were mostly hurled together".

Hotels seemed to fascinate Mary. After an October tour of Kerry, Cork and Waterford, she and Raymond had dinner at Shelton Abbey near Arklow, "a first-rate example of Gothic Revival architecture" and the seat of the Earl of Wicklow. This genial and gentle man, known to the literary crowd in Dublin as Billy Wicklow, was a publisher who owned the firm of Clonmore and Reynolds. He later married Eleanor Butler, the architect daughter of the architect R.M. Butler. Lady Wicklow, who lives in the Dun Laoghaire area, recently sold one of Raymond's paintings. She had bought it at the R.H.A. in 1943. She became a Senator in 1948, nominated by the Taoiseach, John A. Costello.

McGrath's painting of Roger Greene's house, Newtown Hill, done as a Christmas card, 1951

Mary seems to have had a good year in 1947. Norman noted in one of his letters to Dallas that she said she "felt really happy and that she really meant it too". Heart wrote to Raymond that she had talked to all the important architectural and planning people at the new United Nations building in New York. The message (the names she mentions are not legible) was that there was plenty of exciting work to do in America, but he should hurry up and get over there. The predictable sting in the tail was: "If you take Mary Catherine out, be *attentive* to her."

Raymond certainly took her out that Christmas. A fancy dress ball at Shelton Abbey on Boxing Day was followed by the architects' dance at which the McGrath party included the Hopes, Ken Besson, Tom Kennedy the architect, and Roger Greene the solicitor. On Christmas night they had dinner at the Le Clercs, and the McGraths took their children to the Royal Institute of the Architects of Ireland annual revue, where Percy Le Clerc over-acted, said Mary. She wrote a skit for them which she called 'Mr and Mrs Triangle and Little Hypotenuse'. She rewrote her 'Cock and Bull' story in the hope that Anthony Gross the painter and Gaumont British cartoon maker would do the drawings for her. Margaret Burke Sheridan, the great Irish soprano, promised to get Mary a pair of gold evening shoes — "Spanish, for *love*. Isn't it sweet of her?"

Raymond delivered an ultimatum to the Board of Works again demanding the right of private practice. Fairweather was retiring in March 1948 and Raymond expected — with good reason: he already was by now Assistant Principal Architect — to succeed him. The Hibernian Hotel job was going ahead; the Bessons had bought the Bailey restaurant on which Raymond and Alan Hope were working together, and the completed Russell Hotel was a social and financial success. Its Robert Emmet grill was the most expensive restaurant in town.

The larger and more ambitious Government building schemes were now being given to Raymond McGrath. His crescent of buildings to enlarge and modernise the inner space of Dublin Castle reached an advanced stage until, like Paddy Little's concert hall, it was axed (though not at once) by the incoming Inter-Party Government. And the work on Áras an Uachtaráin was continuing. A newspaper columnist[97] had written that the President's house was:

McGrath's crescent of buildings for Dublin Castle can be seen on the left of this drawing

now not merely a stately building but a pleasant house to receive the nation. It is spacious and modern… The adviser was the brilliant architect who had the Phoenix Park acres under his care at the Board of Works, Sydney-born Carlow-descended Raymond McGrath, widely travelled author of the most monumental work yet published on 'Twentieth Century Houses'.

But the house was now receiving the constant attention of the Board of Works and of Raymond in particular. He began to feel the need of a motor-car; for most of his journeys were by bicycle. He recorded that in November 1942 he rode seven times to Áras an Uachtaráin, a return journey to St Stephen's Green of about ten miles for which there was no travel allowance. If he went by taxi (when for example there was a fire in the Royal Hospital, Kilmainham), it cost the Board four shillings. He returned by bus for three pence, also chargeable to expenses.

Mary's hope was that the Board would pay him a mileage allowance. They could get a Ford Anglia through Ken Besson but it would cost nearly £500. The final choice was a new Ford Prefect, bought in 1948. On this Raymond learned to drive. He was competent enough, but he lacked Mary's flair and he never enjoyed the actual driving.

The McGraths once again were riding high, but Raymond was still ambitious. He applied to Sydney University for the position of Professor of Architecture. Leslie Wilkinson had held the chair for nearly thirty years. The job was worth £A1,500 and Raymond did not go to much trouble with his application. In fact he took his 1943 brochure for U.C.D. and brought it up to date by scribbling in his later achievements in brown ink. Seen from the Australian side though, the application was elaborate. Sydney does not seem to have regarded printed curricula vitae as obligatory and Allan Gamble, one of the applicants, says that Raymond's document was a surprise to those who submitted typed or handwritten applications. Gamble was a lecturer at the university. Wilkinson said of him that he was "the greatest teacher of architecture we have yet met".

Raymond in his covering letter said that he was not enthusiastic about pushing his application if there was no right of private or consultative practice. The post was advertised twice under different titles. Initially the

Raymond's design for the Ross Williamsons' Christmas card, 1950

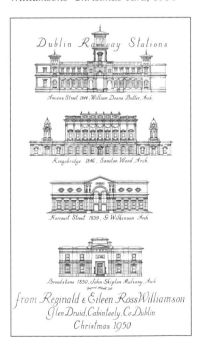

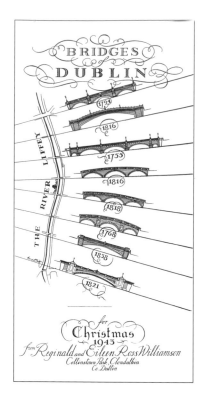

Raymond's design for the Ross Williamsons' Christmas card, 1943

professorship of architecture was offered and twenty-four people applied. When the Senate changed the job to professor of architectural design and history, seven dropped out but new ones applied.

As is not unusual with academic appointments in Dublin or Sydney, there was dirty work at the crossroads.[98] The advisory board, which included the retired Professor Wilkinson, had a member whom we have met before in the pages of McGrath's 'Twentieth Century Houses'. F.E. Towndrow, who in 1930 had designed a house in Essex that was featured in the book, was by 1948 lecturer in charge at the Architectural Department of Sydney Technical College. He told a meeting of the advisory board that H. Ingham Ashworth, one of the applicants, was "more of a businessman associated with [Frank] Scarlett in a large private practice and he would not be suitable". He doubted if Ashworth was at all outstanding.

Towndrow had also met McGrath recently and thought he had declined considerably and become very lazy, and that he was not worthwhile considering for the position.

Other comments at board meetings were that there was no evidence of McGrath's experience in teaching, that McGrath's early promise had petered out, that his present job was small, and that his growth ended before the war.

Leslie Wilkinson on the other hand said he considered Ashworth and McGrath to be the outstanding candidates. McGrath was "an outstanding man, had published a lot, quiet, a remarkable designer. If he would come it would be a great acquisition to the school".

During an advisory board debate about private practice it was pointed out that the R.I.B.A. stated that private practice was vital to good architectural teaching.

From London came more mud to be flung at McGrath. The Vice Chancellor of Sydney University, S.H.A. Roberts, wrote from there to the advisory committee on 30 July 1948:

> I should advise the committee to eliminate McGrath completely. The extent of his decline is greater than we hitherto supposed, and is even physical. ...I talked to Ashworth for three hours last night, in company with Professor Wilkinson. Wilkinson, apart from his many contacts here, has spoken about the chair to many of the leading architects at the recent conference of architects at Zürich, and he strongly feels that Ashworth is the outstanding applicant. [Ashworth's] war record, especially in Burma, was particularly good. In my opinion he is a fully mature man who would mix well with his colleagues...

Raymond's goose was cooked. Roberts had been asked by the committee to make inquiries about Raymond's experience of teaching and his views on private practice. They got more than they had bargained for, and the acting Vice Chancellor presented a report from the Vice Chancellor which contained and reinforced Roberts' view.

Resolved unanimously that the Advisory Committee recommend to the Professorial Board that the Senate be invited to appoint Mr. H. I. Ashworth M.A. (Manchester) F.R.I.B.A. to the chair of Architectural Design and History.

A bald note to Raymond thanked him for his interest "in connection with this chair". It was dated 6 September, 1948. He had first written on 17 June, 1947, before any advertisement appeared.

From the dates on some of his letters to the university it appears that Raymond himself had lost interest, probably because he had in the meantime been appointed Principal Architect in Dublin at £1,275 — without the right of private practice as an architect, though he retained the right to do industrial and other design work. His father was delighted, especially since "what Irish that there is in you [is] greatly diluted".

What made Raymond's old professor change his mind and plump so hard for Ashworth? Did the advisory committee have a hidden agenda, an agenda that tacitly listed black marks against Raymond? He did not have a good war record, nor any. His name was a Roman Catholic Irish one in a university in which at the time Catholics, though taken on as students and for their part encouraged by the Jesuits[99] to aspire to third-level education, were not likely long to saunter through the olive grove of Academe. Raymond told them nothing to dispel any misunderstanding about his religion. He probably did not think in such terms. And his application contained a testimonial from Monsignor D. Enrici, secretary to the Apostolic Nuncio to Ireland, in which Enrici said: "…Not only did I find him most obliging in carrying out all requirements, but he seemed to me to combine sound technical ability with good taste in whatever he did". Again, Raymond made no attempt to explain that the Papal Nunciature was located in the Phoenix Park and therefore was properly under the care of the Office of Public Works and of Raymond as a public servant.

One person at least who was pleased that Raymond had not been appointed was his father, who sensed something of the complexities of academic politics:

There are wheels within wheels in the making of appointments of any kind in Australia and the man who has been chosen in this instance will probably have questions asked about him by the Returned Soldiers' League to ascertain why preference was not given to an Australian with military service. You will probably find that he served in the Imperial Army and that fact would disarm some of the criticism if his professional attainments are outstanding… I think you would be well advised to remain where you are…

In an eventful year, there was to be another incident which in this case upset the constancy of the loving relationship between Raymond and Mary.

Raymond's design for the Ross Williamsons' Christmas card, 1948

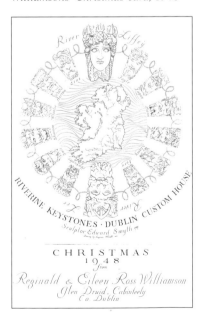

CHAPTER XXXII

Raymond paid Mary's and Jenny's fare to America, so that she could have $250 in travellers' cheques. Exchange control was strictly enforced after the war. Aunt Collie in Troy, Alabama, and Aunt Addie Belle in Andalusia, Alabama, had already offered to pay their passage home. They had money; Heart had money; Raymond at last could say he had no debts. Yet money and what Mary did with it were to figure largely in an angry exchange of letters between Heart and Raymond.

Mother and daughter sailed on the America on 21 February, 1948. They were met on the dock at New York by Hazel Guggenheim McKinley. She was dressed, Jenny vividly recalls, in jade-green satin which astonished an observant eleven-year-old from Ireland.

They had lunch at Schraft's, a meal made memorable for Hazel by Mary's elated state. (Ten years earlier, Hazel had seen the dark side of Mary's manic depression). "Mary shocked the diners", says Hazel, "with stories of all the prostitutes that had been on board the ship." She had brought "masses of baby clothes" for Hazel, then in her 50s and quite beyond reproduction.

Mary was in trouble with her mental health from then until she left Dallas for Alabama. She had annoyed the Frosts and Herbert McGrath in Washington by going on to Dallas from New York without stopping. They had planned a welcome and were in a state of high excitement, easily deflated by what they saw as a snub. In Dallas, Jenny did not take especially to her Crozier cousins Ann and Terry. She was happier in Troy, where she made friends with the postman's daughter Patsy. But Patsy was thought not good enough for Jenny, not because she was black but because she was regarded as "poor white trash".

Mary's views on coloured people and Jews had been formed in childhood and her experience in Europe had done nothing to broaden her horizon. From Andalusia she wrote to Herbert in Washington on 4 April:

> …Of course down south here in Alabama it is heavenly this spring weather and everyone is delightful to me… I am having a swell time driving [Addie Belle's] new Lincoln car… We go up to Montgomery for the day, where Uncle Lucien [Gardner, Chief Justice of the Supreme Court of Alabama] lives…
>
> Alabama has improved a lot. There used to be such poverty here. There is still of course, when you get off the main streets of the towns, white people live in unpainted shacks as bad as the

Facing page:
Cow Parsley by Raymond McGrath

negro families. In fact the niggers live in the prettiest part of this place. They all look happy and well-dressed and behave very politely, but I am scared to go for a walk by myself at night, they hang about the street corners and look restless. The nigger cook of one of my friends in Troy pulled a butcher knife on her husband, severed the main artery in his thigh and he died before he reached hospital... Doris, the Croziers' half Indian cook... has a hangover every day which she describes as appendicitis... Missouri comes two hours a day to clean but spends most of her time picking up A.B.'s things off the floor. I made her wash the windows and I forced A.B. to buy a vacuum cleaner. No dusters, no furniture polish, no windows ever raised — poor rich people, how badly they do live... As many as five heads of lettuce mouldering away in the refrigerator.

Addie Belle's house in Andalusia, Alabama. In the carport is Norman's Jaguar

Herbert with his obsession with cleanliness must have been shocked, though he did not say so. He did not even react to the end of this long letter. Mary said she was not going back to Texas:

It's too hot and they have no space. Anyway I don't want to go back. Too much money in Texas. The place is lousy with Jews and noise. Worse than Jew York.

Jenny briefly went to school in Troy and her father asked inanely if it was anything like Park House, her new Dublin school. Then he confessed to his daughter: "I am feeling quite lonely."

That letter was dated 11 April, 1948. Next day, he wrote out of the

blue to Mary: "Feeling very lonely and strapped for female company…"
He went on:

> Well, feeling as I did, on an impulse I rang up Mary Kiersey
> and asked her to have a meal in town with me… She came
> looking very elegant and was sweet. We had a meal at the Russell
> and I took her home in a taxi and, on another impulse, kissed her.
> Forgive me, Honey. It was no more than that, and it alarmed me.
> I ask myself what sort of a silly ass am I when I have the best wife
> in the world. The only trouble, Honey, is that you are so far away
> (but I'm *not* parting with you again). I hope you won't be cross
> with Mary Kiersey. She'd fall through the floor of the Country
> Shop if you mentioned this. So would I and what would Heart
> think if she read this!!!

Mary Kiersey

Jenny was with Mary when that letter arrived. "Mary was in bits," she
says; "devastated. What Raymond had done was totally out of character
and he wrote to assuage his guilt."

What Mary's response to Raymond was we do not know. But ten days
later, having sent two innocuous and amusing letters in between, he wrote
at the end of a chatty report:

> The American warships are now at anchor in Dublin Bay.
> There was a reception for Admiral Conolly at the Legation last
> night… I couldn't face the party so I asked Mary Kiersey if she
> would substitute for you. She wondered what you would think
> and I hope I interpreted your feelings correctly in telling her you
> would look kindly on the invitation. It was a very super party —
> cars stretched from the legation to the Phoenix Monument,
> dancing in the ballroom and a long marqui (*sic*) on the lawn with
> a view of the Dublin mountains sparkling in the late afternoon
> sunshine. It's the only party I've been to where champagne really
> flowed. There was a varied collection of guests — members of the
> Government, all the diplomats… Had a meal with Mary
> afterwards and saw her home to Belgrave Square.

This time there was no plea for forgiveness. Perhaps he saw no need
for one. But what he did was at best insensitive, and all his letters to "My
Alabama Sweetheart" could not conceal the hurt he had inflicted on Mary.
She had asked him whether Mary Kiersey was happy, and she got this
reply dated 16 April:

> Yes, I found out whether Mary [Kiersey] was happy. She's
> not. Says she can't face going home to her lonely flat. Reads all
> the time and envies her happily married brothers and sister. Paddy
> Corcoran asked her to marry him six years ago and she refused. A
> Belgian baron asked her last year but cooled off when he got back
> to Brussels and thinks she might not be able to bear him healthy

children because her father died of T.B. seven years ago. Her mother is dead too. She learned her French when the family was travelling for his health.

Now I have got that off my chest. Mary Kiersey said she couldn't go to the Country Shop ever again. But she was there the next day and such is the absurdity of this world, nodded with every indication of remoteness. Just the same I realised my danger.

Mary Kiersey married Paddy Corcoran later and in 1957 went with him to Michigan, where Mary died in 1992. They both remembered "the architects' table" at the Country Shop, a restaurant in St Stephen's Green. "It was rather like the round table at the Algonquin. No one else dared to sit there", Paddy recalls, referring to the *New Yorker* immortals and their *Stammtisch* in Manhattan. The Dublin version was born before Raymond arrived in Ireland, and only after he became Principal Architect did he assume any leadership role. But in the 1940s and 1950s there could be found at lunch most days Gerald McNicholl (later to succeed Raymond); Percy Le Clerc, Dermot O'Toole, Desmond FitzGerald, Alan Hope — all architects, most of them working in the nearby Office of Public Works. It was, as Paddy Corcoran says, "not the sort of pasture you would expect to find Paddy Kavanagh [the poet] grazing in". Yet on the spurious ground that " 'tis cheap and 'tis dainty", Kavanagh was a frequent if unlikely visitor. Seán O'Sullivan, R.H.A., Sam Suttle, Andy Devane and sometimes Arthur Douglas dropped in on the group, which could number anything between four and nine.

It was a vociferous gathering, and people at the surrounding tables, such as Paddy Corcoran and Mary Kiersey, could not help but be attracted to it. Mary, who already knew and liked Mary McGrath, later took pottery lessons from Herbert McGrath and helped Mary McGrath in her lampshade business at 19 Merrion square. The two Marys, in spite of Raymond's peccadillo and a considerable age difference, preserved a mutual respect and affection.

On 4 May, 1948, Raymond took Mary Kiersey for a drink at the Shelbourne Hotel. Then they had dinner. She was gloomy and had solved none of her problems. Paddy Corcoran would not speak to her and she asked Raymond to get her a job with UNESCO in Paris:

> I had thought to ask her to go to a reception at the President's
> house next Thursday but we've decided not to meet again. She says
> I might become indispensable to her and it's not fair to you anyway

wrote the lovelorn 45 year old to his wounded wife of 38 about his friend of 25. "It's true", he said, "I shouldn't even have run the risk of upsetting you with the affair. I hope I haven't, Sweetheart, because you know how dearly I love you. *YOU* are all the world to me." Yes. Quite.

Writing from the French Legation where she worked, Mary Kiersey, a week later expressed her gratitude to Raymond.

You are very good to write to Paris for me and draw me a picture which I love very much. Thank you Raymond. Today I have a cold and hate working and I had a row with Michel [Jammet] and Paddy won't speak to me and I hate going to the Country Shop and it's a horrible day and tonight I'm going out with a horrible Spanish man because I don't want to go home by myself.

But soon all this will change and my cold will get better and I'll be able to laugh at what's happening today. So goodbye.

While Raymond was dallying in Dublin, he was having a row with Heart that caused him a great deal of pain. How it began, we do not know, but by 21 April he was writing to her at 4722 Drane Drive, Dallas:

I wrote in anger and of course have regretted it. You know I bear you no ill will — but you have the power of upsetting *me*, just as you do Mary. She wrote: "Heart looks beautiful, but she is not really happy. I wish I could make her happy, but she neither trusts nor admires me and everything I do is wrong to her, even if other people like me and understand me." Of course I know she was very unwell in Dallas — she wrote me about it: "The Ides of March are upon me." I know only too well what that means. March is her dangerous month — it dates from Jennifer's birth. If she gets safely through March I can breathe easier.

Heart had written two letters full of anxieties unnamed by Raymond, who was worried about *her* "as much as anyone". He had had no other letters from anyone in America except from his father who told him Mary seemed to be having an enjoyable time in Alabama but was homesick already; and "a succession of long and delightful letters from Mary which gave *me* no indication of impending breakdown (which *you* fear) or cause for undue alarm".

On 20 April, Raymond got a letter from Mary in which she said: "If only I can get home by August I will have done my duty and cured myself, I believe permanently, of my homesickness." Raymond quoted this letter to Heart and added:

Personally I think you should let things work out as they are doing. And I think it would be much better if *you* did not go to Alabama.

I don't quite see how you could expect Mary to visit America after eleven years and not be tempted to buy some American clothes. I can't see that she has been so extravagant.

He gave Heart a sharp reminder of the impermanence of things: "If you think she has nothing to show for your gifts to her I can only say clothes are like that — they wear out, or lose their original freshness." Part of the money Heart had sent Mary was used to straighten Norman's teeth, which were "improving visibly".

He told Heart that the American Minister, George A. Garrett and his wife had invited him to a reception at the legation to meet Admiral Conolly and he promised to tell her all about it. That was, as we know, one promise he could not keep.

Heart had pushed him hard to join Mary in America and he told her it was "absolutely out of the question". His work load had been increased by the change of Government and he reminded her: "As your family invited Mary and made her trip possible you should see it through and not expect me to be on two sides of the Atlantic at once. But please cheer up."

Heart did not cheer up or let up. An exasperated Raymond wrote on 10 May:

> Heart, I'm sorry I ever mentioned the word "ill-will". All words are dangerous and I am sure you know how much I appreciate all you have done for us and I know your anxiety and advice can only be actuated by your deep feeling for M.C. Rest assured that I will do everything in my power to make her happy when she returns to Dublin... I have always done what I believe to be right. I know you would still like us to try and settle in the U.S.A. If I had an assured commission there I would try it. But I haven't the resources to make any experiments.

By the time Mary and Jenny came home in July, all was forgiven and forgotten between Raymond and Mary. Norman had learned to drive the new car and father and son motored to Southampton to meet the Holland–America liner Veendam.

The car was a surprise for the returning sailors, but Raymond was also bursting to tell Mary the details of Irish Le Klint Lampshades. Mrs Birgit Varming, the wife of Jorgen Varming the Danish consulting engineer, had asked Mary to look after her Dublin business venture. It involved making up and selling an attractive range of paper-pleated Danish lampshades and it gave Mary the kind of outlet for her energy that she had been seeking for a long time. Already Norway and Sweden were taking 60,000 of these shades. She set to work with a will, slowly acquiring the assembly and marketing skills necessary for a successful business.

Seán Mulcahy of the firm Varming Mulcahy Reilly contributes this warm note about that time:

> Michael Scott's offices in a five-storey Irish Georgian house at 19 Merrion Square was a most social and entertaining work-place during the late forties and the fifties. Michael in splendour occupied the first floor *piano nobile*, and his staff the spacious attic and part basement. Ove Arup's office, the first of a now world-encircling chain, was on the second floor. Jorgen Varming's branch of his Copenhagen practice was on the hall level. Mary McGrath and Birgit Varming assembled lampshades also in the basement. Mary was the joker in the pack, warm, witty,

Seán Mulcahy

outrageous. I worked in Varming's at no. 19 from late '47 for four or more years and through Mary rather than architecture first came to know Raymond as a friend. Their hospitality at Somerton Lodge was unlimited and informal. It was the most attractive house, cottage-like in the centre with great two-storey pavilions at each end, with distinctive modern furniture, rare then and even now in Ireland. The company was consistently of architects and designers.

Alan Hope
(Courtesy of Máirín Hope)

BIG HOUSES

In spring 1948 the Architectural Association of Ireland had organised a visit to Carton and Castletown, which are among the most important of Irish "big houses". Raymond and Norman went with Percy Le Clerc, while Alan Hope took Paul and Lisl Campbell, good friends of the McGraths. The Earl of Rosse led the cortège of 20 cars.

Carton stands on the River Liffey in a lovely park. The islands on the river were inhabited by cranes and there were two swans' nests on reedy islets. But inside the grand house at that time "an air of melancholy resides in its empty library and deserted bedrooms", as Raymond wrote to his absent wife in America:

> I was carrying on an involved conversation… with Lady Rosse, trying to be matter-of-fact but aware that, as she was conspicuously and very elegantly dressed, everyone in the party of 70-odd was looking at her. She also talks nearly as loudly as you do (I mean her voice carries). Lisl was very excited about pelmets, as usual. Mrs Leask darted from room to room… like a wasp. No wonder poor old Leask is irritable. She needs smoking out…

This, if not a new Raymond, is a Raymond that showed himself rarely; the social commentator, the gossip, enjoying himself with the recollection as he had with the day.

At Castletown, Lord Carew gave the party tea in the dining room, which fitted the group comfortably. It was a fine room with five great windows overlooking the forecourt, its walls covered with Reynolds and Giorgiones. The long gallery on the first floor was packed with treasures and they wandered about it for some time. "John O'Gorman [the architect] and his wife were holding hands and giggling in corners. He didn't introduce her to anyone. Zita was looking like Lady McNicholl in a very 'new look' creation which much impressed Norman."

> Our wanderings were suddenly interrupted by the terrifying clatter of a piece of falling furniture and Carew darted out like an alarmed midwife. Lisl of all people had dislodged the lid of a spinet. She lifted it to look at the keyboard and it had no hinges. Poor Lisl.

A fine crayon drawing of Oliver Hill the English architect formed the first page of another letter to Mary. Hill, of whom Alan Powers[100] said: "Oliver Hill never forgave Hitler for ruining his career", was staying at Ross's Hotel, Dun Laoghaire, while he looked at the alterations he was doing to Strathmore Hill, Killiney. He went to lunch at Monkstown House, bringing chocolates for Jenny who was in America. The sketch bears the legend: "Oliver's remorse, because Jenny's not here."

In January 1949, Oliver Hill was back, staying this time at Strathmore Hill, bought three years earlier by Sir Richard Brooke, a member of the English branch of the Northern Ireland Brooke family. One of the changes that Hill made was to move the entrance so that it now faces east and not towards Bray Head. The house was bought by the Canadian Government in 1956 as the ambassador's residence. Marion Brooke (Lady Brooke), for whom Puccini wrote 'Madame Butterfly' in 1904, (or so Mary told her mother), wrote to Mary:

> It's like having a tame tornado in the house to have O.H. staying — and not so tame! He hasn't been since August, and then expects one to have the last "period" inkpot in place! let alone the "pelmets from Pilkington…" But it's all great fun.

An untitled picture of trees at dawn, watercolour and pastel, 1941

CHAPTER XXXIII

ichael Scott entered Raymond McGrath's life at about this time. If it is possible metaphorically for a stormy petrel to be a pillar of the establishment, Scott was it. As the focus if not the creator of controversy, Scott so managed his life and so adroitly exploited his talents that he emerged in his later years as the country's leading architect and the doyen of Dublin's cultural life. Mary McGrath wrote of very enjoyable dinner parties at his house around 1950, and her business was in the basement of his practice. When Howard Robertson came to lecture to the Architectural Association (he was not popular with Dublin's young modernists), part of the post-lecture festivities included drinks at the McGraths. There the party danced to Norman's jazz records. Michael Scott, Luan Cuffe and Desmond FitzGerald were among the revellers.

A man of undoubted charm, Scott was also ruthless in the pursuit of power and position in the artistic life of the capital. These characteristics often are married, but to the marriage Michael Scott brought a healthy cynicism, a saving grace. He did not like to be crossed; and for that reason he seldom was. But he had bitter enemies as well as powerful friends, an explosive combination.

From the later 1950s to the early 1980s, he dominated the Arts Council, though Professor Brian Boydell the composer told Brian Kennedy[101]: "The Council members had tremendous integrity and drive to see good things done. Michael Scott, who was reappointed to the Council in 1978, was very surprised at the new régime. At times it was quite clear that he thought things were still done on the 'nod' system where everything was fixed beforehand. Quite the opposite was true…"

From 1960 to 1973, Father Donal O'Sullivan, a Jesuit, was Director of the Arts Council. Michael Scott later told Brian Kennedy: "We ran the Council, Father O'Sullivan and I." Small wonder that he did not find the 1978 Council to his liking.

In architecture too, Scott's personality was magnetic. From small beginnings such as the modification of the Gate Theatre for Mac Liammóir and Edwards he went on to design the Irish Pavilion at the New York World's Fair of 1939, "a frank expression", as Rothery[102] puts it, "of the International Style with an all-glass curved wall". Controversy dogged the pavilion. The Government did nothing for four years after it was first notified of the fair. No competition was held. No list of names was submitted. The plan shape was a shamrock, disliked by the *Architectural Review*. The political dimension — the Government being determined that

Michael Scott
(Photograph by Albert Fenton)

the Irish Pavilion should be as far as possible away from the British and Empire buildings — had nothing to do with Scott; and he netted both kudos and 350 guineas. Scott went on to give Dublin such landmark buildings as the central bus station, Busárus, for C.I.É. (1950), and the television studios at Montrose for R.T.É. He had a gift for picking talented architects and if they did not always get the recognition they deserved, the names of Robin Walker and Ronald Tallon will nonetheless endure.

A revealing vignette of Scott was given to the author by Mervyn Wall,[103] the writer, who was secretary of the Arts Council from 1957 to 1975. Wall says:

> ...Michael Scott, who was a great man for pursuing and finding work for his own firm, had ambitious plans for a concert hall on a site between Harcourt Street Railway station and U.C.D. ...I attended a large meeting which he organised to gain support. My recollection is that he had an elaborate plan prepared...
>
> Michael Scott was a notable courter of people in power, whom he entertained lavishly. He was a man of considerable charm which he knew well how to employ. When... Donal O'Sullivan was appointed Director of the Arts Council, Michael immediately attached himself to him. Michael himself became a member of the twelve-man Arts Council, his membership due to Father O'Sullivan's influence. I was at a reception in the German Ambassador's residence [in 1964], still in the hall, having just arrived, when Father O'Sullivan came in, and most unlike him, he gripped me fiercely by the arm. "A terrible thing has happened", he whispered. "They've given the building of the Concert Hall to Raymond McGrath." At that moment Michael Scott entered and passed us without a glance. I noticed that he was white in the face, and that his face was extraordinarily set. He looked neither to right or left. A few days later he had his first heart attack, and by an extraordinary coincidence, as if out of sympathy, Father O'Sullivan had his first heart attack exactly a week later.

By the same token, when the Government decided to build a television station for the newly established Telefís Éireann, which opened in 1961, Raymond designed a complex for the new station; but Michael Scott's firm was finally commissioned as its architects. The score between Scott and McGrath was even, except that as we shall see the Kennedy Memorial Concert Hall fell foul of another Coalition Government while Scott's Montrose buildings were constructed and later added to. Raymond's colleague Con Manahan has a vivid memory of the Montrose affair:

> I recall Raymond's hurt — near to tears — when he showed me his *privately* prepared scheme for the Montrose T.V. studios and said that Michael Scott had been given the commission that morning.

This leap-frogging saga began with a letter from Raymond to Mary in April 1948. He told her of the Fitzgerald house at Parknasilla, Co. Kerry. "You remember Fitzgerald who fell for you — the South African Butlin magnate with the musical French wife?"

Scott was designing the house, "some sort of Dutch colonial mansion" of cut stone with oak windows which Barney Heron was making, and thatched roofs. Paddy Corcoran was acting as clerk of works while the owners were away in South Africa.

In the Office of Public Works itself, the Dublin Castle reconstruction and development plan was a major project compared with the Rotunda Concert Hall. It took much more time and although it was the subject of much adverse public criticism in 1947 and 1948, it was approved by the Inter-Party Government of 1948 and took longer to die.

Its main feature was the crescent of four storeys and eight radiating blocks, all having a southerly aspect. Senior executives were to have a view over the Castle Lawn — a new amenity — and the blocks (was McGrath intent on replicating the Nash crescent on which he had lived in London?) were divided by two archways.

McGrath with Jim Fairweather

Raymond devoted much study to this scheme and did a great deal of detailed work himself. Jim Fairweather,[104] son of Raymond's predecessor, worked under him on the drawings and remembers Raymond as "an extremely shy man" with very little to say. He had an office to himself and perhaps two or three times a week would slip into the drawing office to see what Fairweather had produced. "Very often [he] just sketched out freehand in pencil his general idea of the whole concept…"

The development was significant enough for Maurice Craig, the architectural historian, to write to the Taoiseach (de Valera was back in office) in 1953:

> …I feel very strongly that the proposal to modernise the buildings, while retaining the historical features in an improved setting, is the right way to deal with the problem. I have no doubt whatever that the architects of the Office of Works will be able to rise to such an opportunity and produce something of which Ireland and Dublin may be proud.

One part of the castle did get its due meed of recognition for Raymond. In January 1941, fire seriously damaged one area of the State Apartments, a range of buildings which effectively consisted of two buildings back to back. That fronting on to the garden was built in the mid-18th century as a continuation of the south-west range designed by Sir William Robinson in 1685. Restoration work on the Upper Castle yard began with the rebuilding in 1961-64 of the cross-block that abutted the burnt-out range. It was decided not to replace the old Presence Chamber next to the Throne Room, but the State Drawing Room was reproduced in facsimile and fitted out with the pier glasses and console tables salvaged from the fire[105].

Oscar Richardson, J.B. Maguire and Raymond McGrath, as the

The Davis Memorial as envisaged by McGrath in 1945
(Courtesy of the Irish Architectural Archive)

architects in charge, shared a silver medal from the R.I.A.I. for this work. But the medal was awarded too late for McGrath to enjoy his share. He had died a few years earlier.

In 1945, a proposal was made to mark the centenary of Thomas Davis's death. Davis, the patriot editor of *The Nation* and co-founder of the Young Ireland movement, had no memorial in the capital city and McGrath was asked to design something grand in his memory. He did. His site was St Stephen's Green, where a central fountain was to spout at the spot where George II's statue had been. Curved pavilions in a neo-classical style would flank the fountain. The formality and the grandiosity of the scheme belied the fact that Adolf Hitler had died in the same year, his party rallies at Nuremberg receding into the collective memory of Europe.

Nuremberg-in-Dublin very quickly and deservedly met a similar fate. "Fortunately never executed", as Nicholas Sheaff[106] puts it. At the site of another foreign monarch's statue, that of William III in College Green, the foundation stone of a Davis memorial was laid by President Seán T. O'Kelly in September 1945. For twenty years, nothing more happened. The present statue by Edward Delaney belongs to the middle 1960s and marked the cultural maturing of the State.

Lennox Robinson (1886–1958) and his wife Dot were friends of the McGraths. Robinson, who was associated with the Abbey Theatre as playwright, producer and director, had a penetrating wit tinged, as Feeney[107] says, "with enough malice to nick the unwary". It is not surprising to find that Raymond was to illustrate 'The Boy from Ballineen' which Robinson described as "an unofficial guidebook to Dublin". Although the book appeared in Michael Joseph's 1949 list, it was not published.

In 1954, Robinson was commended for his foresight in commissioning Raymond McGrath to do the keys, or explanatory captions, to the Beatrice Elvery cartoons that adorn the dining room of the United Arts Club. They provide, as Boylan[108] tells us, "very valuable clues to the club's origins". A ritual dinner was held in February 1954 to thank Robinson as president of the club and McGrath for "their generosity in presenting the keys".

The collapse of Lennox Robinson's book was followed by a decision much more hurtful to Raymond. King Penguin Books had commissioned 'Dublin Panorama' from Raymond after the war. Nikolaus Pevsner, a colleague and friend of long standing, had written several times to Mary in the latter half of the 1940s asking her to use her influence with Raymond to get the drawings out of him. All to no avail.

The final blow fell on February 23, 1951, when Pevsner wrote to McGrath:

> ...The final decision not to publish was caused by the very long delay in the delivery of the material... there has been a complete gap between the end of 1947 and the middle of 1949... I am not only sorry for Mary and sorry for you but also very sorry for the volume.

Raymond took a few days in which to draft a reply, and the draft is all we have:

> Your letter is very sorrowful, but sorrow seems to me inadequate. I have today [28 February] discussed Mr. Harmondsworth's decision with my solicitor, who thinks that the various extensions of time invalidate your Memorandum of Agreement.
>
> In April 1950 you wrote me: "You must not worry about the King Penguin. I can assure you we can wait." In May I told you the drawings would be ready in June. They were, but unfortunately Mary had a serious miscarriage and nearly died. After that distraction I heard no more from you till the "nasty letter" of 7 December.
>
> Will you kindly inform Mr. Harmondsworth that my friendly claim for work done is £50? ['Mr. Harmondsworth' is a sarcastic reference to Allen Lane, the founder of Penguin Books whose headquarters were at Harmondsworth, Middlesex.]

Another book, not Raymond's, featured in the McGraths' life in the late 1940s. In 1947 Raymond and Mary went with a party of friends to a fancy dress ball at Shelton Abbey. Jenny recounts the tale:

Facing page:
Sea Shell and Leaf, 1940

At four in the morning they were still there when a tall dark American in flying jacket and boots began to talk to my mother. She thought he was in fancy dress. As the party broke up she invited Francis Yockey to come and stay with us in Monkstown. I don't know if my father was consulted, but I do remember as the days turned into weeks and Francis was still there, I sensed his irritation and saw his left shoulder twitch a few times.

Francis seemed to have a hypnotic effect on my mother. He totally disapproved of women wearing lipstick and he told my mother as much. Smoking he disapproved of even more. I remember her lighting a cigarette and Francis telling her to throw it in the fire. She did, to my amazement. She liked smoking: it was one of her pleasures. And cigarettes were scarce.

Yockey was far from idle at Monkstown House. By January 1948 he was on the last leg of his book 'Imperium', and had written 180,000 words — "a fine achievement", Mary told her mother. Raymond's irritation notwithstanding, Francis was "great fun to have about". Otherwise, Mary reassured her nagging parent, "we lead a quiet life listening to music, reading books, drinking nothing stronger than tea and smoking very little. I wish you wouldn't worry so about me".

Mary took her children to the Dublin Horse Show, borrowing a member's badge and taking Norman and Jenny into the members' stand for the Aga Khan Trophy. France, Sweden, America, England and Ireland had entered teams for the show jumping competition. America won handsomely.

Luan Cuffe, by then an M.A. in architecture of Harvard, invited the McGraths to a dance next night at the Kilcroney Country Club. It was in honour of Pat Skakel, a small, dark and pretty American, "very natural and unaffected", whom he later married. Pat had been to England with several of Joseph Kennedy's daughters. Her sister Ethel was to marry Bobby Kennedy. Luan and Pat Cuffe reared an artistic family in a house he built in the Dublin mountains, where Pat still lives.

Raymond's first sight of America was in 1949. In Washington he had "a glorious reunion" with his sister Eileen and her husband Albert. Norman Robert Crozier junior (Bro) gave him a ticket to fly to Dallas and he also went to New York and Boston. It was an official visit, mainly to see the Irish Legation in Washington, where Seán Nunan was Minister. As soon as Nunan retired, the status of the mission was raised to that of embassy. This was part of the foreign policy initiated by Seán MacBride, the new Minister for External Affairs.

Mary met MacBride at the opening of the Bailey restaurant, owned by Kenneth Besson and decorated by his sister Pauline Morgan. She found MacBride "a fine looking, very serious type of man" and talked to him about his mother, the legendary Maud Gonne. They spoke too of Maud Gonne's American friend Frau Grabisch, a sister of William Bullitt, who was U.S. Ambassador to France before the war. MacBride told Mary he hated politics, a statement endorsed by his subsequent failure to live up to the enormous reputation which he enjoyed when he entered

Seán MacBride

Doorn's painting of
T.H. White (1950)

Government.[109] Sometimes compared with de Valera, he lacked the Chief's ability to mould an effective working team around him and soon lost his influence in the Cabinet and then the country.

It was MacBride who nominated the members of the first Cultural Relations Committee, although the £10,000 grant-in-aid and the idea had been voted by Fianna Fáil before the Government fell in 1948. One of the committee's projects was to send a touring exhibition of modern Irish art to the United States and Canada in 1950. Raymond designed the catalogue and contributed a picture. He was now an A.R.H.A., much to the delight of architects, who considered his election a great boost for the profession. Michael Scott, who made the first of six attempts in 1941, had to settle for an honorary membership in 1967.

MacBride also appointed Raymond McGrath and Michael Scott as members of an expert committee to select a site in Wexford for the statue of Commodore John Barry, the founder of the United States Navy. America presented the statue on St Patrick's Day, 1951.

Publishers were having a bad time in the McGrath circle. T.H. White wrote to Raymond from Alderney in 1950:

> The publishers are being bloody. *They* want to publish the latest new volume [of the Arthurian cycle] by itself: *I* want them to put all four together in an omnibus, now that the story is finished.
>
> My news from here is little. It's an odd island. Whiskey about £1 a bottle and cigarettes now gone up to 4s. for 50 — as much of either as you want. So everybody is drunk all the time, with occasional flashes of the water waggon, which I am on at present. It won't last.
>
> The enclosed life size picture of me was done by a fellow called Doorn. They say I am saying one of two things: either "I wonder if this fellow knows I am as drunk as I feel" or, "Just say something and I'll contradict it…"
>
> Love from Tim.

The McGraths' Christmas card
for 1950

For Mary, the Ides of March came early in 1951. She fell ill during a visit with Raymond to London. His father, who had returned to Washington after a long stay in Dublin, told Raymond: "We think you have acted very wisely and very promptly in getting Mary into hospital":

> I'm afraid I showed some peevishness on one or two occasions during my last month with you in Dublin for which I have felt sorry since and I ask you all, especially Mary, to forgive me... It was a stroke of good fortune that Hilary Palmer is able to take over Mary's business.

Heart, never one to hold back in a situation, had plenty of advice to offer Raymond from Troy in the beginning of 1951: "If you can do right and have faith, nothing comes that can't be borne. I want you, when you and Mary go out, to *stay with her* and don't leave all the conversational obligations to her."

A month later, when Mary was already in hospital, she berated Raymond for going into some detail "but not the important ones":

> What kind of mood was Mary in? Melancholy? or gay? It seems to me you had a mixed crowd together — maybe she had too much responsibility in entertaining them? She always feels the responsibility more and I wish you'd help her — you go about so much you meet so many people — it would be so easy to tell of those things. Brilliant conversation is not *expected* Mary but everyone is interested in people and places. Try and exert yourself more — Do...
>
> Did others detect her condition? Raymond — I wonder if you could not take her home — put her in your room — close the door, get a long phone and put the phone in the hall?
>
> ...In the meantime you must cut out spending money on drink and cigarettes...

She couldn't keep her fingers even out of Irish politics. Just as they were about to be ejected from office she advised Raymond to make it a point to know John A. Costello, the Taoiseach, and Dr Noël Browne, the Minister for Health. "Costello is brilliant. Spread your friends among such people. I'm so thrilled over the awakening of Ireland. If Costello had only been in power when Norman was growing up."

By April 1951, Heart was so weighed down by the diversity of her admonitions that she could not say much more than: "I do all I can for you all (though I hate to remind any of you of it) ...[Mary] is so wonderful and such an unusual wife."

The remarkable aspect of the marriage of Mary and Raymond was that it was strong enough to take both mental illness and interminable meddling. When Raymond was in America, Mary had written to him: "I'm afraid I nearly worship you, honey." It was mutual, and it was steadfast to the end.

257

Chapter XXXIV

When Raymond McGrath was two years in the post of Principal Architect to the Office of Public Works, he began to feel the need of more space in his home surroundings. His father, having sampled both Washington and Dublin, decided that he preferred Dublin provided his accommodation needs could be met, so Raymond looked at the options.

He could buy a site in Co. Dublin and design and build two houses. He could buy an old house and divide it. Or he could stay where he was, with his father in a flat nearby. His new status and income demanded a radical move. His father came over from Washington and moved into a flat in Vesey Place, Monkstown. Herbert had sold both his houses in the Sydney area, so he and Raymond went site- and house-hunting.

Taking their time, and accepting dollar loans and gifts from Heart, Aunt Collie and Norman Robert Crozier, they eventually settled on Somerton Lodge in Dún Laoghaire. They paid a deposit in July 1952 and had moved in by October. Set in three acres on Rochestown Avenue, the house consisted of a long low two-storey residence to which two tall Regency wings with elaborate wrought-iron balconies had been added. It was an attractive house with a double staircase and a sweeping drive, and Raymond and his father got it from the owners, Dún Laoghaire Borough Corporation, for £4,500. Herbert had his own bedroom and study, but

Herbert McGrath in Dublin

Left:
The garden front of Somerton Lodge

Facing page:
A complicated picture of McGrath's studio. On the easel, a painting of Provence; in the portfolio, a painting by Jenny of the hospital in Maryland where she was ill in 1954

259

what was to appeal to him most was the turreted castellated outbuilding in which he could develop his pottery operation. He delighted in sending his Sydney friends photographs and descriptions of "Mac's Castle".

From 1 March, 1953 to 4 December, 1954, Herbert McGrath kept a diary of events in his pottery studio. Every penny owed to or by him was accounted for, every kiln firing noted, every crack reported and the attendance of every pupil recorded. He advertised several times in *The Irish Times.*

A number of men took part in the classes. A casual list of those learning pottery at this period shows an understandable bias towards architects and their wives; but it covers an interdenominational segment of Dublin middle-class life. Excluding those whose identities have now been lost, the roll — never more than six at a time — goes like this:

> Commander Campbell, Mr. Da Keyne, Mrs. Birthe Douglas, Danish wife of the architect Arthur Douglas; Mrs. Nana Leidersdorff, Miss Garrett, Mrs. Pat Cuffe, Mrs. McKenna, Miss Flanagan, Mrs. Pat Gleeson, Miss Hoctor, Mrs. Coleman, Miss Sinclair, an occupational therapist; Paddy Corcoran the architect; his wife Mary (née Kiersey); Mr. Hoyer, a Danish architect working in Niall Montgomery's office; Mrs. Osborne, Miss Róisín Jammet (now Mrs. David Hood), daughter of the famous restaurateur Louis Jammet and his artist wife Yvonne; Miss Hardy, Miss Cole, Mrs. Norton, Mrs. Beattie, Miss Noelle Cleary, Mrs. Ryan and, occasionally, Jenny and Mary McGrath.

Raymond's father was 74 when he took up pottery in Ireland. He never became as skilled or imaginative as his wife, but he kept at it with some success and was a much-loved teacher up to his death at 87 in 1963.

Before Herbert arrived in Ireland to settle, Raymond set out on the greatest holiday of his married life. Leaving his office in what he regarded as "a satisfactory state", he took Mary and Norman to France in the Ford Prefect for a month.

It was April 1950 and he took his oils and watercolours. Basing himself in Aix-en-Provence, he painted enough pictures to cover, he hoped, "the major expenses of the holiday". Mary paid for herself out of her lampshade business and a handsome cheque from her mother in Troy. Norman, then an engineering student at Trinity College, Dublin, sold a motor-car and enough model aircraft engines to meet most of his costs. They left Jenny at home. Her father thought she was "sweet and unenvious": her mother considered her happy at the prospect of having a school friend to stay every week. In reality, Jenny was angry and deeply disappointed at being excluded from this family holiday.

Jenny nevertheless put the month to good use. She had a burgeoning talent for playing the piano and she bethought herself of Aunt Judith. We left Judith Issakovitch at the port of Dublin in 1940. She stayed for some years with the McGraths looking after Jenny and developing a close bond with her. But two such strong personalities as Mary and Judith were bound

Puimoisson, Provence, 1950

*Les Baux, Provence, one of
McGrath's rare oil paintings, 1951*

to clash and after one clash too many, Judith went to stay in a series of
bed-sitting rooms in the city. In Dublin she had devoted friends such as the
Briscoes, as Barbara Chermayeff discovered during a visit to Ireland.
Daisy McMacken, who was Professor of Russian at Trinity College,
Dublin, was a staunch ally in a strange city. Jenny often went to see Judith,
sometimes unwillingly, and as time went on she became fascinated by
Judith's gift for music. Judith not only played well: she taught well and
she bought music for Jenny. Jenny used the absence of her family in
France to invite Aunt Judith to Monkstown House to teach her more.

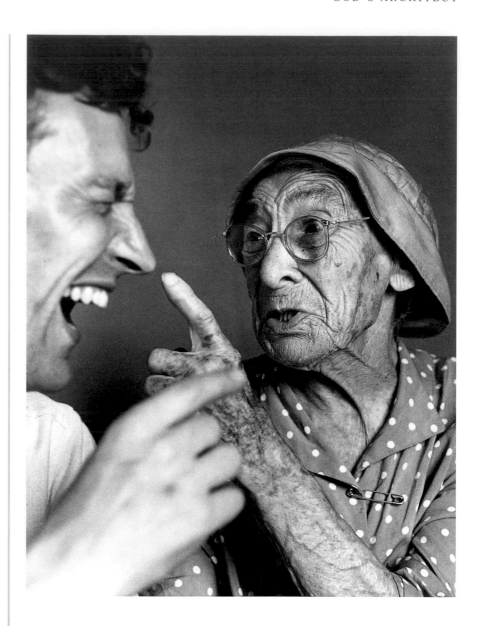

*Norman visits Aunt Judith at
the Tolstoy Foundation*
(Photograph by Francis Keaveny)

"You should see Raymond's face when Jenny plays", wrote Mary to her mother. "She does play beautifully." She went on to study under Miss Lily Huban, who taught many of Dublin's pianists. In 1962, when Serge Chermayeff judged it timely — when he could afford it — he brought his Aunt Judith, by then very old and gnarled, to live at the Tolstoy Foundation in New York. Raymond made the flight arrangements. She was 96 when she died in New Haven late in the following year.

While the musical lady from Groznyy was sharing her love of the piano with Jenny, Raymond was forging another link with the past. The Irish Government needed an impressive house in London for use as an Irish Embassy and residence for the ambassador. Raymond selected and purchased 17 Grosvenor Place, the house of a member of the Guinness brewing family. To do the conveyancing, he employed his old friend Sir John Witt, whose firm was Stephenson, Harwood and Tatham.

This acquisition came ten years after the Earl of Iveagh, the head of the Guinness family, presented Iveagh House in Dublin to the Irish

Government, which converted it for use as the Department of External (now Foreign) Affairs. The department has grown, but Iveagh House remains the office of the Minister and a venue for official banquets and receptions.

Raymond's dedicated work on the major Irish embassies abroad coincided with the rapid expansion of the department under Seán MacBride (1948–51); Frank Aiken (1951–54 and 1957–68), and Liam Cosgrave (1954–57). Apart from the remodelling and furnishing that he did, his fostering of the revived Donegal Carpets industry and the fact that he was free to engage in private industrial design meant that these elegant houses were decorated with McGrath carpets that are still shown off with pride by the incumbent ambassadors in London, Washington, Paris, Rome, the Vatican and Ottawa.

In 1952 and 1953, Raymond did several carpets for Iveagh House, the head office of the Department of Foreign Affairs. On the ballroom carpet, versions of Edward Smyth's riverine heads done in stone for James Gandon's Custom House of 1791, appear. One of Smyth's designs was also used for the Long Gallery carpet at Áras an Uachtaráin in 1955.

What Sheaff[110] calls "one of the most successful of all McGrath's carpets" was the one he did for the *grand salon* of the Paris Embassy in 1954. Here French inspiration from the 18th-century Savonnerie factory is dominant.

McGrath paid so much for this late 19th-century house that a row followed in parliament, where charges of profligacy were levelled against the Government for spending £250,000 at a time of national belt-tightening and haemorrhagic emigration. The Government held the line. This lovely mansion on Avenue Foch is the envy of many other countries which do not possess such central and such beautiful houses in Paris. It was bought from the Princesse de Faucigny-Lucinge. It has splendid 18th-century *boiseries* and *singeries*, taken from older buildings and lovingly restored by Raymond McGrath and Noel de Chenu, who worked together

The Irish Embassy on Avenue Foch, Paris

263

on one of the happiest undertakings of those years.

The new ambassador, William P. Fay, and his wife Lilian, were posted to Paris in 1954 and remained until 1960. Lilian Fay[111] and her husband became very friendly with the McGraths. She recalls Raymond as "an outstandingly talented person, a very encouraging colleague, and very sociable".

McGrath used his contact with Louis Koch of London to furnish the embassy with both original and reproduction pieces. In a moment of doubt about the authenticity of some chairs, Lilian Fay recalls that she was obliged to ask:

Est-ce que ce sont des chaises Louis Quinze ou Louis Koch?

Noel de Chenu, now retired, went on to become Principal Architect of the Office of Public Works. He is an artist of some distinction and has done a head of Raymond McGrath.

The grand rooms of Áras an Uachtaráin and the State Apartments at Dublin Castle are graced with Raymond's work as a carpet designer. On her visit to Dublin in 1980, the British Prime Minister Margaret Thatcher especially admired McGrath's use of colour and design in the carpets to reflect the colour and design of the old ceilings at Dublin Castle.[112]

Raymond worked on carpet designs up to the year before his death in 1977. His successor as Principal Architect, Gerald McNicholl, discussed the renewal of the carpets for the main staircase in the State Apartments with Raymond McGrath in February 1976, though it was clear by June that he was too ill to do much more.

It was lucrative work. One 1972 invoice to the Office of Public Works read: "To design, adaptation, supervision and inspections of 6 Donegal Carpets: 1/2 of 10% on the total cost of £11,892.64p £590 plus V.A.T. @ 10%: £649."

The *Irish Tatler and Sketch* for December 1968 published an article headed: 'Dublin Castle Lives Again: The State Apartments Restored'. The article was by Seymour Leslie: the colour photographs were by Norman McGrath, who by then had forsaken engineering for a meteoric career in architectural photography. Raymond, while he designed the carpets, was not by any means alone in working on the restoration scheme. Oscar Richardson and J.B. Maguire shared the honours with him. Their names, and that of Frank du Berry are linked especially with the work on the Apollo Room, the lobby to the Long Gallery, the Wedgwood Room and the Picture Gallery.

Oscar Richardson[113] recalls the aftermath of a visit he made with Raymond and Mary to Áras an Uachtaráin. Someone suggested going for a drink, so they drove from the President's house to the Hole in the Wall, a pub just outside the Phoenix Park. Mary said that Oscar should give Raymond some advice. Raymond took the hint and asked his subordinate:

"Am I doing anything wrong as Principal Architect?"
"Yes", said Oscar. "You are a distant figure. You should visit

Facing page:
The Old Music Room, Iveagh House
(Photograph by Norman McGrath)

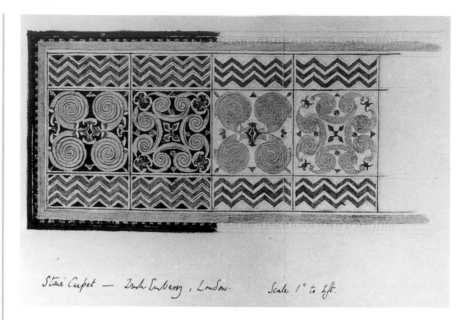

Stair Carpet — Irish Embassy, London. *Scale 1" to ½ft.*

Design for a carpet in the Irish Embassy in London

Carpet for the Grand Salon, Paris Embassy, 1954

every architect's drawing board once a month."

"I think you're right", Raymond replied, "but I've left it too late".

As well as his work for State buildings, Raymond designed commercial carpets and rugs for Donegal, and while the industry began to fail in the mid-1970s, its survival up to that time was greatly enhanced by the commissions it got from the Office of Public Works and its new departure into modern designs with Raymond's encouragement and participation.

The factory at Killybegs was opened in 1898 by the Scottish firm of Alex Morton at the behest of the Congested Districts Board. By November 1972, Raymond was writing to the Minister for Labour and Social Welfare, Joe Brennan, who was a Dáil deputy for Donegal:

> …My original approach to Joe McGrath [the founder of the Irish Hospitals Sweepstake] saved the Donegal Carpet Factory from extinction but the situation is more critical now because neither Paddy McGrath [son of Joseph] nor Dr. [Brian S.] Freeman has much interest in the operation…

And by March 1974 Dr. Freeman was writing in confidence to Raymond:

> …After 21 years of heavy and continuing financial losses (£28,000 in 1972 and £13,000 in 1973) my directors feel that they cannot continue the hand-knotting of carpets at Killybegs after the autumn of this year.

Dr. Freeman gave the causes of Donegal's failure as competition from Hong Kong, China, Portugal, Spain and North Africa; a formidable and growing wage burden, and the fact that every carpet was being made at a loss. He clinched his case with the reasonable statement that:

> ...The 1953 position of grinding poverty and lack of employment in the Killybegs area, which was the original reason for our activities there, now no longer exists. The town is the Republic's major fishing port...

Raymond McGrath and Paul Hogan of the Irish Export Board (both, incidentally, founding members of the Society of Designers in Ireland) did their best to save Donegal. Raymond appealed to W.H. Walsh, chairman of the State-sponsored Kilkenny Design Workshops, to be told:

> I agree that it would be a tragedy if Donegal carpets were to disappear but offhand it is hard to see how we would come into the picture when day-to-day management is of the essence...

Bill Walsh suggested an approach to Gaeltarra Éireann (another State-sponsored agency, covering the development of the Irish-speaking districts on the West Coast); Navan Carpets or Youghal Carpets. Kilkenny would participate if a meeting of interested parties could be held.

Paul Hogan identified potential buyers of carpets by groups. He held a powerful position in the Export Board where he was manager of

The Wedgwood Room in the State Apartments, Dublin Castle
(Photograph by Norman McGrath)

267

*Corner detail of carpet in the Old
Music Room, Iveagh House*
(Photograph by Norman McGrath)

Paul Hogan

the Design and Consumer Products Division. Hogan has acquired a formidable reputation in the design world, especially for his work in Third World countries. (Paul Hogan's first public appearance was more sensational than anything he did later. Sir Hugh Lane, the art collector and nephew of Lady Gregory, was appointed director of the National Gallery of Ireland in 1914. He was returning from America on the liner Lusitania a year later when she was torpedoed and sunk off his native Cork and Lane perished. He already had given his vast collection of pictures to the Tate Gallery, but his will contained an unsigned codicil making a gift of thirty-nine modern paintings to the National Gallery of Ireland. The controversy over the codicil raged until 1956, when Paul Hogan, an art student, and Billy Fogarty, a veterinary student, took Berthe Morisot's 'Jour d'Été' from the walls of the London gallery. It was a carefully planned theft designed to focus the greatest possible publicity on the Lane Pictures debate. The Morisot was returned to the Irish Embassy and under Sir John Rothenstein's directorship an arrangement was made under which the paintings would rotate between Dublin and London.)

The decline of Donegal was in stark contrast to its success in the 1960s. In September 1963, an exhibition of "real hand-knotted rugs" was held by Donegal Carpets at the Aberdeen Hall of the Gresham Hotel in Dublin. The designers included Oliver Messel, the great stage designer, brother-in-law of the Earl of Rosse and uncle of Lord Snowdon; Louis le Brocquy, the distinguished Irish painter; Schwartz-Abrys; W.H. Horsfall, Donegal's chief designer, and Raymond McGrath, who showed four designs called Aurora, Solstice, Eclipse and Palisade. These rugs, the catalogue said, were "geometrical abstractions... in the Abstract Expressionist tradition". (Michael Scott's name had been added to the firm's writing paper, but he showed no rugs at the Gresham.) As a result of this exhibition, Libertys of London selected Raymond's four designs in both colourways. There, Dr. Freeman told Raymond, they were much admired by Elizabeth Arden. Two years later an exhibition at the Munich

The Circular Supper Room at the State Apartments, Dublin Castle
(Photograph by Norman McGrath)

Building Centre resulted in an invitation to show at the Bauschau in Bonn, thus vindicating Raymond's belief that Germany should be a particular market for Donegal rugs.

Joseph McGrath (1888–1966), whose wealth was founded on the worldwide success of the Irish Hospitals Sweepstake, was a native of Dublin. He left school at fourteen and soon made his mark in the Republican movement and in the politics of the Irish Free State until 1924. He established the Sweep in 1930; Waterford Glass in 1951 (a century after its eponymous predecessor died), and Donegal Carpets in 1953. He was an authority on bloodstock and horse racing, in which he achieved international success.

Raymond was proud of the encouragement that he gave to both Waterford and Donegal but that did not prevent him from sharply criticising the glass company's crystal products.

About October 1954, he drafted a letter to Joe McGrath telling him that he had bought the Paris Embassy (12 Avenue Foch) and wanted to put Waterford chandeliers into it. But, he said, "I am quite appalled by the crudity of the design" in a sketch obtained from the firm. At the Ambassador Cinema in Dublin "every piece of glass in [the Waterford chandelier] is cut all over so that the general effect is an agglomeration of barley sugar".

This is a draft letter and we do not know if he went so far in the finished missive. But Raymond McGrath was an expert on glass and on design, and Joe McGrath presumably knew that. Whatever the outcome, the more important Irish embassies are decorated with Waterford chandeliers, there being no native alternative.

The *New Yorker* of December 1971 brought another difference of opinion, this time with Joe's son Paddy. An advertisement showed a 10 inch Waterford vase engraved with 'The Magi' for the Christmas market.

"Surely with its resources", said Raymond, "Waterford could do better than this. I winced when I saw it."

Paddy McGrath replied with the arrogance of success: "We have received enormous praise for the artist and the designer... Needless to say the whole edition is completely sold out." (The edition was of 250 pieces at $1,200 each).

Raymond McGrath's command of all the elements of design in official buildings gave them a recognisable style. He used native carpets, crystal glass and poplin drapes and he incorporated ceilings and fireplaces from other buildings to give an Irishness — whether Celtic or Georgian — to make the State's grander expressions worthy of their function as ambassadors of the new administration.

On the way, he garnered much praise for his co-ordination, supervision and imagination. But not all his critics were favourable. In an important article[114] on McGrath's career and especially on his carpet designs, Nicholas Sheaff, the first director of the Irish Architectural Archive, wrote: "McGrath certainly benefited from American experience in fitting out state rooms which could bear comparison internationally with those of the old monarchies":

> Yet despite being dignified and meaningful as interior schemes, it cannot be said that McGrath's work on the restoration of historical rooms is successful in terms of general atmosphere, the techniques and materials used, or the accuracy of what was done. Moreover, curiously little effort was made to provide genuine Irish furniture for these interiors. Perhaps due to the political function which the rooms were redesigned to serve they have a mechanical and at times harsh effect which compares badly with the sensitive, painterly effects achieved by the English scholar-decorator John Fowler during the 1950s and 1960s, though Fowler, unlike McGrath, was of course working principally for private clients.

As he approached fifty, Raymond's energy showed no sign of abating. His design for the new Cenotaph on Leinster Lawn was executed in 1950 by an Inter-party Government anxious to perpetuate the memory of the three canonised heroes of the foundation of the State — Michael Collins, Arthur Griffith and Kevin O'Higgins. In the circular granite base were inserted bronze plaques by Laurence Campbell, R.H.A., one of the early members of the Irish Exhibition of Living Art committee. The obelisk is capped by a golden flame from which Raymond worked hard but without much success to get a flicker.

In the spring of 1951, Mary had to go to hospital again and although she was home by Easter, Raymond could not get her to write to her mother. She spent a few days at her office in Merrion Square with Hilary Palmer helping her, but business was slack and her presence was in response to a suggestion by her doctor, Norman Moore, that she should have the stimulus of work.

Social life resumed. The Hopes, the Kierseys, Percy Le Clerc (recently appointed Inspector of National Monuments at the Office of

The Cenotaph on Leinster Lawn
(The Irish Architectural Archive)

Public Works), and Paul and Lisl Campbell gave or were given hospitality. Lord Talbot de Malahide, whom Raymond met through the Earl of Rosse, gave a lunch party at Malahide Castle which his family had inhabited since the reign of Edward VI. The Talbot castle benefited from some architectural advice given by Raymond, who hugely enjoyed the lunch. He sat beside the American Ambassador's wife — the Garretts had just returned from Washington — on one side. On the other sat "a very beautiful young Lebanese woman".

The Lebanese was Mrs (later Lady) Cochrane, the wife of Sir Desmond Cochrane, Bt.[115], of Woodbrook, Co. Dublin. He was the Honorary Consul General of Ireland in the Republic of Syria and the Lebanon.

Raymond bought a new car. The Ford was due for replacement and he got a second-hand 1947 Riley for £360. Heart chided Raymond for his reluctance to discuss finances, and he replied: "The truth is, Heart, that I have never had any finances to discuss." His salary was £1,420 after tax. He was not in debt, but he was actively looking for a new place to live. And, although he did not say so to Heart, Mary's recurring illness was a constant drain.

Raymond and the Riley

Mary, who had been in partnership with Mrs. Varming in the Le Klint business, had done so well that she could buy Mrs. Varming out. The agency was, Raymond sharply reminded Heart, much more than just "making lampshades in a basement". Mary was able to design things — mostly light fittings — and get them made. She had made excellent contacts and was much respected as a "businesswoman". She was very well in the autumn of 1951 and looked "years younger".

Raymond had a good talk with Dr. Moore, whose feeling was that "Mary's upset was a glandular disturbance which he thought would disappear with 'the change of life' ". It did not disappear for another twenty-five years.

CHAPTER XXXV

lthough Raymond McGrath was specifically precluded from executing architectural commissions except for the Board of Works, even the Commissioners could not ignore a recommendation from the most powerful Minister in the Government. Seán Lemass was Tánaiste (Deputy Prime Minister) and Minister for Industry and Commerce. Shannon Airport was one of the pet creations of his inventive mind, and by 1953 it was handling a great deal of the traffic from Europe to North America. Lemass, who had seen and admired McGrath's work on the London Embassy, requested that he be put onto the improvement of the passenger areas of the airport.

"I will be allowed special fees for the work", Raymond told Heart, "which will be a great help." As Principal Architect, he already was a member of the Airport Construction Committee, where his contribution was "very positive", according to Dr. T. J. O'Driscoll. Tim O'Driscoll, now retired, was one of a new generation of public servant given their head by Lemass in the 1930s, 1940s and 1950s, when a great network of State-sponsored enterprises was created to fill the voids left by a lacklustre private sector.

O'Driscoll, who served in the Aviation and Marine Branch of the Department of Industry and Commerce (he was a passenger on the first Aer Lingus flight in 1936), went on to become Ambassador to the Netherlands, director-general of the Irish Tourist Board and President of the European Travel Commission. His wife Elizabeth and he were guests at Somerton Lodge on a number of occasions, but Elizabeth's link with the house was closer than that. She recalls:

> For some years up to 1972, I shared a studio in Raymond's former farm-yard with a number of transient silversmiths. It was an ideal setting. We were completely isolated from all unwanted outside influences and the surroundings were beautiful with lovely trees and no houses visible except the main house. Raymond was very quiet and unobtrusive except when we needed him, when he was always most helpful and understanding.

At the same time as Raymond was giving fresh interiors to Shannon Airport, he was commissioned to do three drawings of the old Abbey Theatre, which had been burned to the ground in July 1951. The drawings are in the new Abbey. They were done in pencil, ballpoint and crayon and dated May 1953.

Facing page:
Avocado Plant in Studio at
Somerton Lodge, 1957

Below: Elizabeth O'Driscoll

Séamus Kelly, a.k.a. Quidnunc,
drawn by Robert Pyke
(Courtesy of the National Gallery of Ireland)

The board of the Abbey invited Raymond and Mary to a luncheon at the Russell that month. There were about 30 guests to meet Pierre Sonrel, the well known French architect who was to collaborate with Michael Scott on the new building, to be constructed on the old site. Raymond sat with the legendary Abbey producer Ria Mooney, while Mary was placed beside the equally famous chairman of the Abbey, Ernest Blythe — "a nice chatty old boy", Mary found him.

Sonrel she described as middle aged, rather bald, dignified but amiable. She used her fluent French to help the columnist Séamus Kelly, 'Quidnunc' of *The Irish Times*, who wrote of her next day as "my amusing inventive interpretess". (The new theatre was not opened until July 1966).

Somerton Lodge was proving something of a nuisance. It looked like a big house, so friends from England and America felt free to stay. Yet it had only four bedrooms which, with Herbert occupying one, left no spare bedroom. The Witts, the Frosts and Douglas and Elizabeth Hicks of the Canadian Embassy in Oslo, came in 1953; and were put up somehow. But between long-stay visitors and week-end callers — "Mary always says tea parties are as much trouble as a meal", Raymond told Heart — the strain was beginning to tell. When Norman left for America in the mid-1950s (Jenny already had made her solo flight to America), it became easier and more enjoyable for the McGraths to receive their old friends in comfort.

One visitor in the summer of 1953 was a man who was always welcome. Ove Arup, just made a C.B.E. and later knighted, was the famous Danish structural engineer with a worldwide network of offices (including one in Dublin) and an equally universal reputation. He and his wife Li were friendly with Mary and Raymond in pre-war London, and they never lost touch. Raymond, then designing the Kennedy Memorial Concert Hall, watched with deep interest Arup's pivotal role in the saga of Sydney Opera House.

The fact that Arup did a great deal of work for Michael Scott never endangered the friendship between Raymond and Ove, whose Dublin office was appointed to the Kennedy Hall team. Raymond, after he went into private practice in 1968, continued to use Arup's firm where he could, most usefully at the only house McGrath designed in Dublin, Southwood at Carrickmines.

The concert hall and Southwood lie in the future. In the early 1960s, Arup's daughter Karin (now Mrs Parry) got to know Raymond and Mary well. She was working as a designer in the Anna Livia boutique in Dublin, established by Kay Petersen and Gertrude Hunt, the wife of John Hunt the antiquarian, whose famous collection was presented to the Irish nation.

Ove Arup was not the distant director of an overseas organisation. Michael Scott took the credit for inviting him to set up an office in Dublin in the first place. Indeed John H. ("Jock") Harbison, the first engineer to work for Arup here, not only began the firm in Scott's office but was interviewed for the job by Scott, whose Dublin bus station was then being designed.

In that busy summer, Dublin was host to an international art critics' congress, organised by James White. The James Johnson Sweeneys, old

Jock Harbison

American friends of Manny's and Raymond's, were at a sherry party in the Provost's House at Trinity College. They and Sir Herbert Read came to lunch later at Somerton Lodge with Mme. Sigfried Giedion, the wife of the art and architectural historian and critic. Apart from socialising, Raymond had nothing like the burden he had borne in 1947, when the Royal Institute of British Architects had their annual conference in Dublin. Raymond's contribution as a member of the conference handbook committee and honorary editor of the elaborate conference handbook earned him the council's "cordial thanks for your services... I have heard", wrote C.D. Spragg, the secretary of the R.I.B.A., "nothing but praise for the handbook..." With Raymond on that committee were Eleanor Butler (now the Countess of Wicklow); J.P. Alcock and Harry Allberry, all Dublin architects.

Three weddings in one summer caused Mary to write as many letters to her mother. Ove Arup's son Jens, James Johnson Sweeney's daughter Ann and Cynthia MacWeeney of Michael Scott's office married within weeks of each other, Cynthia causing eyebrows to hit hairlines by marrying Colonel Harry Rice. He was 65; she 26.

James Le Jeune, "an excellent French-English architect of 43" as Mary described him, asked Mary to sit for her portrait. She was very excited at first, but soon got bored with travelling to Delgany for sittings. There is no trace of the portrait, but Le Jeune went on to become one of Ireland's more distinguished painters.

It was Aunt Judith's idea that Jenny should go to America when she left school. It was not a good idea. Jenny's parents did not like it, but Judith's formidable mind was made up. Jenny, thought Judith, needed to get away from her mother and the means to do that would be provided by Barbara Chermayeff. Barbara had discussed the plan with Judith when she was in Dublin in April 1954 and she thought that a job as an au pair girl with the Cuttings was the answer.

Heyward Cutting was Serge Chermayeff's partner in a Boston practice. He and his wife had two young boys and needed help so that Mrs. Cutting could get back to her painting. Jenny, who was only seventeen, flew from Dublin to Gander, where she changed planes for Boston. She was not the placid domesticated Irish colleen that Mrs. Cutting expected and as her housekeeping shortcomings showed up, the relationship deteriorated.

Barbara was called in and after Christmas 1954 arranged that Jenny should visit her aunt Eileen Frost in Washington. The Frosts, who had three children of their own to worry about, sent Jenny to nearby Woodrow Wilson High, where she was miserable. She considered her schooldays were over and resented this extension of them. Her erstwhile employer sent her back pay of $150 to her father, along with $42 which Jenny told Mr. Cutting she wanted to send Raymond. "If you feel like returning to the Cuttings in the Spring you can certainly think about it... but don't commit yourself to such a plan", wrote her father. It was the last thing on her mind.

Nobody noticed that the whole American experience was causing depression in Jenny until she had a sudden appendectomy followed by

Studio photograph of Jenny by Richard Seely

toxaemia at Garfield Memorial Hospital. Her behaviour became erratic and Oscar Legault, a psychiatrist, charged $15 for recommending hospitalisation in Sheppard Pratt.

All this expense worried Albert Frost. "It was a great anxiety to us that we might not be able to give Jenny the best medical care we could get for a long enough period", he wrote to Raymond. "I don't know whether I conveyed adequately to you just how extremely ill Jenny was in the early part of her stay."

Dr. Young, her psychiatrist at Sheppard Pratt, despaired of getting Jenny better in the three months he first spoke of. But Jenny had studied the system. She knew what her stay was costing and she determined to escape. She made such a remarkable recovery that she could leave hospital on 5 March. She and Eileen flew back to Ireland and by 26 April, Albert was able to give Raymond an account of what he had had to spend on Jenny's treatment. The total — appendectomy and depression — came to $1,095, against which he had got $500 from Raymond and $450 from Aunt Collie.

Jenny's recovery at home was slow, and she still was not herself when she entered Trinity College, Dublin, in October 1955. There she read modern languages.

VILLA SPADA

The Villa Spada in Rome houses the Irish Embassy to the Holy See. Raymond, who lavished affection on this building through a succession of ambassadorial reigns, called it "a lovely little seventeenth-century palazzo… purchased after the last war… It stands high on the Janiculum hillside and from its terrace one looks out over the rosy panorama of the city".

Raymond and Mary were staying there in the autumn of 1958 when Pope Pius XII was dying and Raymond painted the scene in an article which he offered to the *New Yorker*. His friend John McCarten conveyed the editors' feeling that it was "really too thin", but the article does contain

The Villa Spada, Rome. This and the photograph on the facing page were taken by Louis McRedmond

276

a warm and sensuous insight into how Raymond viewed his own work at the Villa Spada:

Next day Aristedemo Cotani, a craftsman painter, came to discuss the redecoration of the outside of the villa with me. The finish of the Villa Spada is largely stucco, with terraces and balustrades in peperino, a grey stone speckled like a bird's egg. This stucco has the typical traditional colouring of Roman buildings, which is called tinta Romana, a limewash tinted with natural earth pigments ranging in colour from gold through shades of Etruscan orange to warm, deep reds.

Cotani spread out a sheet in a shaded corner of the terrace and, with the aid of his boy, set out his pot of lime, his package of powder colours and some small brushes. Then he looked intently and for a long time at the walls of the villa which, last painted some twenty years ago and since washed by many rains and baked by a succession of hot summers, have the weathered look of an autumn leaf. Sighing lightly he mixed a pot of colour and, with narrow horizontal brush strokes, began to lay a deep wet terra cotta which dried gradually to a shade of old rose. I nodded approval and he put up a lighter golden colour for the adjoining pilaster. Then with a large sponge dipped in deeper colour he proceeded to patinate both these tints. I watched with pleasure and further nods of approval resulted in a range of half a dozen pairs of colours on walls and pilaster.

I went and looked at these tints from various angles and so did Cotani. As he continued to study the colours from each point of view his expression saddened. At this critical moment of our contemplation Dr. Giuseppi, the Italian secretary of the embassy, appeared. So I said: "Cotani seems to be unhappy about something. Will you talk to him?" They talked seriously for a long time. Then Cotani stepped back deferentially and the Doctor came over to me. "What is the upshot of it all?", I asked. "We

VILLA SPADA, Rome
Baroque wall decorations in Dining-room

3/11/82

The dining-room of the Villa Spada

have been talking", he said, "about many shades of tinte Romane but Aristedemo Cotani says that he can never hope to make the villa more beautiful than it is now!"

The slow, loving pace of life and language at the Villa Spada is conveyed in this unpublished excerpt with a simplicity which matches the quandary that faced the three men in a Roman garden. Raymond's thoughts turned homeward to Somerton Lodge and he saw that "years ago, one of our predecessors in this house had been inspired by the colours of Rome or Tivoli to paint these walls in tinta Romana and to plant our Italian cypresses".

Mary was with her people in Troy, Alabama, and Raymond was very ill with a hernia and being looked after by his father when Jenny, who was working in London, announced her marriage to Derk Kinnane. Norman was leaving engineering and making a career for himself as an architectural photographer in the United States. So no McGrath could attend the wedding, which was in 1961.

Mary wrote to Raymond that Aunt Collie "couldn't be more thrilled over Jen's romantic marriage". The newly weds planned immediately to go to Baghdad, so Mary looked up a map and found that Iraq was not, as she had thought, on the Mediterranean. All the relatives sent gifts of money, but the travel plan fell through and within a couple of years the marriage went the same way. Derk Kinnane, a journalist, lives in Malta. Jenny divorced Derk and she and her son Julian lived for some years at Somerton Lodge, where the boy conceived a total respect for Raymond and his many-branched talents. But Raymond, as we have seen, had no talent for talking to young people. Eileen recalls a drive with Raymond and Julian. When Julian asked Raymond a question, he got a long and detailed reply. Eileen said to Raymond: "The boy is only five. You've given him an answer suitable for a twenty-five year old." Raymond's terse response was: "Well, he asked me, didn't he?"

A year later, Raymond began to grieve for his mother. He had wept when she died in 1946, but the constant presence of his grandson brought back his own childhood. The result is a prosy but touching untitled and unpublished poem, dated 16 November, 1969:

Raymond's photograph of his grandson Julian at Somerton Lodge

> My mother has been dead for many years.
> But now she sometimes comes to me
> And we talk about the times we were together
> When I was a boy of six, like my grandson Julian,
> Standing on the threshold of the world
> In the little town of Parramatta
> On the continent of Australia
> We have been talking about my bicycle
> And remembering things in a motherly way.
> What a flood of memories about little things
> And the great moments in the era of six!
> They say that this is the time in life
> When things are clearly remembered,
> When one should sit down and write an autobiography
> About the world before men landed on the moon
> And about the time before the hippies.
> But if I did that and wrote about my mother
> You would only want to weep for yours.

CHAPTER XXXVI

eath and birth left indelible marks on Raymond in the course of 1963. His father, approaching 87, died in hospital in February, causing a wave of sympathy to wash over Somerton Lodge from America, Australia and England as well as from the dozens of people who had grown to love him in Dublin.

Eileen wrote from Washington reminding Raymond that "it was Dad's wish to be cremated and his ashes placed beside Mum's in Rookwood Cemetery. You have the sad task of making the arrangements..." But Raymond, knowing that the nearest crematoria to Dublin were at Belfast and Liverpool, had made arrangements for Herbert to be buried at Dean's Grange, near Dublin. He learned that to undo his decision would mean applying for an Exhumation Order and he won Eileen around to accepting a *fait accompli*. At the end of February she wrote to her brother:

> Dad had grown so fond of Ireland that I think you have done the right thing in choosing a resting place close to the family and home he loved so well. I can think of nothing better than for him to be buried in the peace and quiet of Irish soil near to the things that meant so much to him.

The Irish Times and the *Sydney Morning Herald* marked Herbert McGrath's passing with obituary notices penned by Raymond and Elmo Pye respectively. He was survived by one sister, the faithful Alice Lewry, then living in Melbourne, who had spent three months at his side while his wife Edith was dying in 1946.

By a matter of months, Herbert missed the birth of Raymond's first grandson, Julian, in whose veins races the blood not only of Ireland, England, Australia, New Zealand and America, but of Friesland in north Holland, whence his father's people the Roelofsmas went to New York.

Death was not done for the McGraths. Later that year, as we have seen, Aunt Judith Issakovitch died. Then, on the day John F. Kennedy's funeral cortège wound its heartbreaking way to Arlington, Albert Frost died of pneumonia at George Washington University Hospital. He was 56 and still assistant secretary of the International Monetary Fund.

Norman was staying with Eileen and her children. He wrote home to Dublin: "There was no sudden crisis: he just quietly stopped living." They planted him in Columbia Gardens Cemetery, a sheaf of white chrysanthemums covering the top of the maroon casket.

Two months later, Raymond was trying hard to sell Faber and Faber a

Facing page: The Pink Nuns

*In the residential quarter of
the Plaka, Athens*

Greek sketchbook and text based on his and Mary's holiday the previous
September. Concentrating on Athens and Mykonos, he first tried the idea
on Richard de la Mare. He had done twenty-four drawings and over 3,000
words. Faber took the concept seriously: then turned it down.

The Irish Times, in the person of the present writer as assistant editor,
ran Raymond's pieces as two feature articles, illustrated by six of his fine
drawings. I also asked Raymond to write an obituary of T.H. White, who
ironically had recently died in the very waters through which Raymond
had travelled. The obituary was illustrated by Raymond's well-known
photograph of Tim.

Using the *Irish Times* cuttings, as he had for Richard de la Mare,
Raymond approached the Architectural Press, but Raymond Philp, while
he liked the articles, suggested a publisher with a more general list. "Don't

On Plati Yialos beach, Greece

Moulin de la Planche, Landreville, Etampes

be put off simply because Faber reject it", he told him.

Much the same fate met a series of 18 elegant little drawings done on a holiday in France. Raymond does not seem to have offered an accompanying text to the six outlets he tried to place the sketches in, but he did draw a blank with the *R.I.B.A. Journal*, the *Architectural Review*, the *Architects' Journal, Country Life, Vogue* and *Holiday*. It began to look as though the time of the quick impressionistic sketch was over, for Raymond Philp of the Architectural Press also told him (22 October, 1965): "We could not succeed with the book [of drawings] you have in mind." Philp suggested he try Hugh Evelyn of 9 Fitzroy Square. From these attempts to get his work published, and from outlets such as *Ireland of the Welcomes* which used articles on castles in use as hotels and on the O'Shea brothers and Deane and Woodward, it is obvious that Raymond

La Collinette, Cap d'Antibes

was still pot-boiling. Mary's chronic mental illness was a constant drain on his salary, so he had to supplement it with journalism. He was also designing Donegal carpets; founder President of the Society of Designers in Ireland; an assessor for various architectural competitions; a member of the Stamp Design Advisory Committee; a member of the W.B. Yeats Memorial Committee with James Johnson Sweeney, Michael Scott, W.H. Walsh and Eavan Boland the poet; and all the time a painter.

When he was elected an associate of the Royal Hibernian Academy[116] in 1949, Raymond McGrath was joined by Mary Swanzy and Grace Henry. At the same time Tom Bodkin, a former Director of the National Gallery and by then Director of the Barber Institute of Fine Arts at Birmingham, was elected an honorary member of the R.H.A. and its Professor of Fine Arts.

It was Raymond's fourth attempt to become an A.R.H.A. Between 1950 and 1967 he put his name forward five times for constituent membership. He was elected an R.H.A. and Professor of Architecture in 1967. (These professorships were both honorary and nominal.)

When Charles Haughey was Minister for Finance he startled the art world with his 1969 Budget proposal to exempt from income tax painters, sculptors, writers and composers living and working in Ireland. He caused a storm of controversy. Maurice MacGonigal, the President of the Royal Hibernian Academy, foresaw the innovative concession's being abused by

Mountain Landscape with Shells, Jawbone and Bog Oak, 1946

"the Art Nits of Dublin" and the "Art Parasites of Europe".

Brigid Ganly R.H.A. called publicly for the resignation of MacGonigal. At the academy meeting called to discuss the affair, Brigid Ganly did not attend and Raymond, a regular attender, left the building before that point was reached on the agenda. It would not, presumably, have been seemly for the Principal Architect of the Office of Public Works to become involved in a row centred on criticism of the man who was not only his political head but the key to the success of his architectural monument, the Kennedy Memorial Concert Hall. The ten-year tale of this vast project will be the subject of the next chapter. Brigid Ganly's resignation from the Academy was accepted and a number of other artists resigned in protest with her. Kennedy says of Haughey's initiative:[117]

> The introduction of tax-free status for creative artists was without doubt the most important political gesture towards the arts in Ireland since independence. Charles Haughey deserved every credit for his enthusiastic support for the measure.

The difficulty of implementing this radical scheme need not concern us here. Suffice it to state that the Minister foresaw, if not MacGonigal's intemperate outburst, something of the looming problems. In his speech on the Finance Bill, 1969, he said:

> This is something completely new in this country and, indeed, as far as I am aware, anywhere in the world. We are entering a field in which there is no precedent of experience to guide us. It is a difficult undertaking because there are bound to be differences of opinion as to what constitutes a creative work and what has or has not cultural or artistic merit.

Although Mary McGrath's episodes of manic depression continued to plague the lives of those around her, Raymond preserved his steely determination to do things and make a life for his family. A great deal of the financial pressure came off when, within a year or so of each other, Heart and Addie Belle died, leaving substantial legacies to Mary. By 1967, the lack of money ceased to control his actions and he began to look forward to his formal retirement.

Another death to affect Raymond was that of the architect Fred Manderson in September 1966. Roy Booth wrote: "The ranks are thinning and it is later than we think." Manderson, who had assisted Raymond on the Finella project in 1929, had joined the New South Wales public service on the outbreak of war and in later years had become an accomplished watercolourist.

At the other end of the architectural spectrum was the Bauhaus. Inspired by the Bauhaus exhibition at the Royal Academy of Arts held in London in 1968, Raymond wrote two long and well-illustrated articles for *The Irish Times* (January 2–3, 1969). He managed to convey the meaning and enthusiasm of Dessau and its teachers without personalising his own relationship with Walter Gropius, Marcel Breuer and Moholy Nagy. Mies van der Rohe, whose strong imprint is on Ronald Tallon's R.T.É. studios and, more impressively, on his Bank of Ireland head office in Baggot Street, Dublin, figured largely in Raymond's articles but was not, so far as we know, a friend or even an acquaintance. Serge Chermayeff, who induced Breuer to build a house like his own in the strange, forested lakeland near Wellfleet on Cape Cod, still chuckles at Moholy Nagy whose mastery of English in the 1930s led him to thank his host most warmly for his hostility!

The general title of the *Irish Times* articles was 'The New Architecture and the Bauhaus', a title taken from Gropius' little book published in England in 1935. One of the rare personal comments Raymond allowed to intrude into the text was a reference to Gropius, "who went to Harvard after Cambridge had lost the opportunity of appointing him to its School of Architecture. Cambridge dons were deterred by the look of Dessau. Now they vie with each other to be the *avant garde*".

From The Mead, Wantage, Berkshire, came a funny note from John Betjeman, dated 18.7.69:

> Penelope and I salute you from G.E. Street's first practice and Alfred's Birthplace and thank you for your greeting from across the monkey puzzle and yews. Was Harbury Hunt greater than Butterfield? Is Blacket later than Blore? To the second question the answer is yes. To the first it's fifty-fifty. — Love to Francis Johnston, the Morrisons, Semple and other old friends, including Tommy Drew, le meas mór do chara [illegible] Seán Ó B.

The subscription in Irish is in the old Gaelic script as is the word England in the address. The people that Betjeman mentions were all 19th century architects.

Another voice from the past was that of John Beaglehole the historian from Wellington, New Zealand. He and his wife Elsie visited the McGraths after a lecture tour which included the Royal Society and the Society for Nautical Research and a visit to Achill Island.

In 1962, Professor Beaglehole edited the massive two-volume *Endeavour* Journal of Sir Joseph Banks,[118] a task that included a 126-page essay on 'The Young Banks'. Banks, for over 40 years president of the Royal Society, had sailed with Captain Cook as a natural historian, thus beginning the scientific exploration of the Pacific Ocean.

By a strange coincidence, Raymond's old English master at Fort Street, Dr. George Mackaness, had died a few months before Beaglehole made his visit to Ireland. And among the 98 books that Mackaness wrote was a small volume on Joseph Banks and his links with Australia. He had kept up a steady correspondence with Raymond — much more regular than Beaglehole's — and this in spite of his prodigious output and his assiduous collecting of 15,000 books, one of the best private collections in the Commonwealth.

For Raymond, there suddenly was a spate of reminders of the

antipodes. Fred Manderson's death was followed by Arthur Baldwinson's: John Beaglehole's visit was followed by Roy Grounds'. (Grounds told McGrath that after he had received his knighthood from Queen Elizabeth, he found himself in an ante-room of Buckingham Palace and asked a footman what he was supposed to do now. "Piss off", said the flunkey). Grounds had built up a thriving practice in Melbourne, and it was from that city that Robin Boyd of Romberg and Boyd wrote to Raymond in search of material for an article on "Australia's most famous architect overseas".

The Victorian Chapter of the Royal Australian Institute of Architects published *Architect*, and Boyd in 1969 was its editor. He shared an interest in Herbert Bayer and the Bauhaus with Raymond, and he sought plans, models, photographs and sketches of Raymond's present and future projects. He also wanted brief thoughts on such questions as:

> How does Australia look to you now from afar? Do you consider yourself Australian still? How do you see the Modern Movement now? Have you ever thought of updating my bible of earlier days, 'Twentieth Century Houses'? Do you still ever practise Basic English?

Intentionally or not, Boyd was stirring it up so that when the Irish Government eventually decided in 1975 to erect a purpose-built embassy in Canberra, Raymond wrote to Martin Burke, then Assistant Principal Architect of the Office of Public Works. He indicated his aspiration clearly:

> …Would you keep in mind that *I* would very much like to act as associate architect for a residence in Canberra? The association would mean a lot to me…

He reminded Burke (the letter is a draft) that apart from his birth and training in Australia, he had included Leslie Wilkinson's house Greenway at Vaucluse, Sydney, in his 'Twentieth Century Houses'. ("Very good for its time (1922)"). In his 'Glass in Architecture and Decoration' (1961) he had illustrated Sir Roy Grounds' own house at Toorak, Victoria, and Harry Seidler's house at Kurrajong Heights, New South Wales. ("Seidler is probably one of the best modern architects in New South Wales.")

> I have a rather special interest in domestic architecture — which of course was not fostered here — and had hoped to have some association with the residence on the original Canberra plot.

Whatever Martin Burke thought, Raymond was already ailing and his second stab at an Irish building in the Australian capital was no more successful than his first.

CHAPTER XXXVII

Nothing that Raymond McGrath designed would have given him more universal recognition than the Kennedy Memorial Concert Hall. Conversely, nothing could have inflicted on him more long-drawn-out anguish than the cat and mouse games played with the project by successive Governments over ten years.

The concert hall story began, as we have seen, with the Rotunda scheme propounded by Paddy Little, designed by Raymond McGrath, and axed by the 1948 Inter-party Government. The return of Fianna Fáil to office in 1951 injected new life into the Rotunda plan. The new Minister for Posts and Telegraphs, Erskine Childers, asking and receiving the Government's permission to revive the project, pointed to the fact that Dublin was "the only capital city of the European Continent without a proper Concert Hall".

Little, as Director of the Arts Council, had lost none of his old energy. He got his old ally Seán MacEntee, now back in Finance, to reactivate the Rotunda purchase and Raymond was asked to draw up revised plans. "For a few weeks", says Kennedy,[119] "Little believed that Dublin would finally have its oft-promised concert hall." And so did McGrath.

The Tourist Board, the Arts Council, Dublin Corporation, the Royal Dublin Society — all were involved in what was becoming a ritual dance of death. There was no political will to provide the Irish people with a national concert hall. There were, to put it crudely, no votes in it. In the 1950s there was a national mood of deepening despair. It was answered by a number of positive economic signals, but the signals were not interpreted until the end of the decade, when they were embodied in the reforms of T.K. Whitaker, the new secretary of the hitherto opaque Department of Finance.

Concert and Assembly Hall Ltd. was established by the Music Association of Ireland in 1953 to campaign for a national concert hall. It limped on with intermittent unfulfilled promises of assistance from the State until, in the new climate of economic self-confidence of the 1960s, the company was offered a grant of £100,000 provided Dublin Corporation offered it a suitable site. There was a site at Christchurch Place, but the scheme foundered because the Government's offer of money fell so short of the £650,000 needed to build the concert hall.[120]

A.P. Reynolds, a former chairman of C.I.É., the State transport company, was chairman of Concert and Assembly Hall. Other directors were Sir Alfred Beit, Edgar Deale, L.P. Kennedy, Dr. John F. Larchet, Lord Moyne and Michael Scott. The secretary was Olive Smith.

Facing page (above): One site suggested for the Kennedy Hall was St. Ann's estate, Raheny.
Below: A model of the Concert Hall

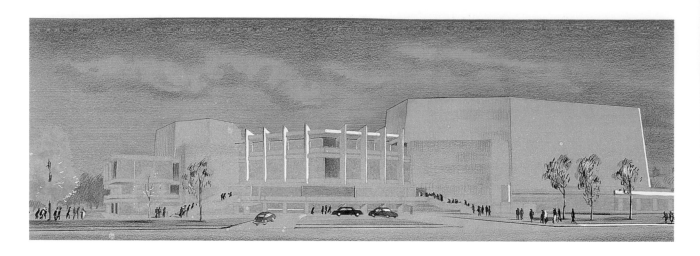

McGrath's perspective of the Kennedy Hall as it would have looked on Haddington Road

President John Fitzgerald Kennedy's assassination changed everything. The Irish Catholic Playboy of the Western World was dead, and the Dublin Government under Seán Lemass saw that out of this tragedy and the universal shock it caused, there could be a convenient marriage of sentiment and culture. When the Arts Council in January 1964 suggested that the Irish people's memorial to Kennedy should take the form of a concert hall, the Government swallowed the bait and formed an All-Party Committee to advance the concept.

The committee consisted of Dr. James Ryan, Minister for Finance (chairman); Dr. Patrick Hillery, Minister for Education, and Donogh O'Malley, Parliamentary Secretary to the Minister for Finance (in charge of the Office of Public Works) — all Fianna Fáil; Liam Cosgrave, leader of Fine Gael; Maurice Dockrell and Gerard Sweetman (both F.G.); Brendan Corish, leader of the Labour Party; Dr. Noël Browne and Seán Dunne (both Labour).

The committee's first action was to select Beggar's Bush Barracks on Haddington Road as the site for the new centre. Then, without giving any serious thought to holding an international competition for the design, the committee recommended Raymond McGrath as the architect in charge. He was appointed by the Government.

There was a widespread welcome for Raymond's appointment. It was not, as we have seen, shared by Michael Scott, or Donal O'Sullivan, but letters of congratulation poured in from his architect friends in England, the European mainland and the United States. In Sydney, the *Morning Herald* ran a headline which proclaimed: "Australian Architect to Plan Kennedy Memorial."

Dr. George Mackaness said it was unfortunate that Raymond had not been invited to enter the design competition for the Sydney Opera House. "In a sense the Dublin memorial to the American President will rival our Opera House", he said.

It seems to me that we have lost the opportunity to get one of the world's great architects — and an Australian, which I would underline — an opportunity that will never come again.

290

Phillis Bean Uí Cheallaigh, wife of the former President of Ireland Seán T. O'Kelly, wrote to Raymond: "We were literally charmed and delighted that you have been given the President Kennedy Memorial Concert Hall. We know that no man in Ireland could do it better…"

The *Irish Architect and Contractor* added its voice: "We salute Raymond McGrath; we wish him well; we realise that his task will be a heavy one in any event, will perhaps be an unrewarding one if he is subjected to an excess of sage advice or polite offers of help, or detailed admonitions from the lunatic fringe about the detailed form which the hall should take…"

The Government announcement recalled that Raymond had been responsible for the design of the National Concert Hall which the Government was planning in 1946 for the Radio Éireann Symphony Orchestra and at that time, visited the outstanding concert halls on the Continent and in America. His career was given in some detail and the fact that he was a fellow of the Society of Industrial Artists was highlighted, as was his work as an assessor for the Trinity College Library competition with Sir Hugh Casson and for the headquarters of the Antrim Council Council with Sir Basil Spence.

McGrath was relieved of his administrative duties as Principal Architect and the staff of the Special Projects Section of the Office of Public Works was retained and augmented for the project with an office at Merrion Row and, after Raymond's official retirement, at 18 Lansdowne Road.

In May and June 1964, with the help and guidance of the Goethe Institut, the All-Party Committee visited concert halls in Germany. Early in 1965 they went to England. Not many members could spare the time or indeed had enough interest to make these musical pilgrimages, and Raymond soon made friends of those who did travel with him: Dr. Jim Ryan, Liam Cosgrave, Donogh O'Malley, Maurice Dockrell, who had a personal interest in music and Seán Dunne, a maverick socialist of unusual charm.

The Kennedy Hall as it would have looked in the Phoenix Park

291

O'Malley, while not a maverick, was *sui generis*, a rumbustious Limerick man with a quirky sense of humour and a joie de vivre that distinguished him from the grey men in grey suits that fill the ranks of most Governments. He had a special relationship with Éamon de Valera and delighted in telling the author the story of his summons to the President's house for a scolding:

> "They tell me, O'Malley, that you broke a plate-glass window in Limerick last night."
>
> "I did, Chief."
>
> "And what's more, O'Malley, they tell me you were drunk at the time."
>
> "Yerra Jasus Chief, do you think I'd have done it if I wasn't? And what's more, Chief, they tell *me* that you slept with Mary MacSwiney." [A notable member of the Republican movement.]
>
> "Well you can tell them that's a lie!" roared de Valera, thumping the study table.

When Donogh O'Malley, for whom the phrase "tall, handsome and debonair" might have been minted, was promoted Minister for Education in 1966, he initiated a radical programme of reform. He established free secondary education for all, closed small rural schools, bussed children to larger schools and proposed a controversial merger between Trinity College, Dublin, and University College, Dublin. He died suddenly at the age of 47.

It did not follow that a retiring Raymond McGrath and a larger-than-life Minister of O'Malley's stature would achieve instant or any rapport. But they liked each other and O'Malley's support was readily offered when the Kennedy Hall project began to encounter problems.

Con Manahan, a senior architect in the O.P.W., was on the pre-planning visit to German concert halls. He recalls:

> We were in a superb village outside Stuttgart, I think it was Sindelfingen... and had been entertained to a very large Germanic lunch in an edge-of-forest tavern. As the party trailed out the door, the jovial wife of the owner wished each guest the traditional farewell. Raymond was struggling into his topcoat, with me assisting him, when she loudly addressed him with *"Guten Fahrt!"* Raymond went bright pink with embarrassment and shot out the door...

Myles na gCopaleen, in one of his less witty outbursts,[121] wrote:

> The Plain People of Ireland were so taken personally with John Fitzgerald Kennedy that they would gladly have found the money for [the memorial hall] voluntarily there and then from their own pockets, but the Feeny Fayl outfit decreed that it must come from tax-nourished "public funds" so that it would look like a present from themselves...

At the launch in Iveagh House,
Raymond shows the model to Mary

The design[122] that Raymond devised featured two prominent hexagonal masses linked by a central four-storey foyer. The large hall seated 1,840 with the choir providing seats for 200 more. One unusual feature for the time was a box for the disabled catering for 37 and having ramped approaches. No member of the audience was seated more than 130 feet from the conductor. The organ had four manuals and 50/60 stops.

Seats for 464 were provided in the small hall and it had a chamber organ. Both halls were flexible enough to suit many purposes, orchestral concerts, conferences, ballet, dramatic performances and, in the case of the smaller hall, dancing.

The cost Raymond put at £2.5 million, which was not high by world standards but did not please the mandarins at the Department of Finance.

Ove Arup's firm in the form of Jock Harbison were the structural engineers. J.A. Kenny and Partners looked after services and Desmond MacGreevy and Partners were the surveyors. The special consultants were Professor Lothar Cremer (acoustics) and Ralph Downes (organ).

Cremer, who was originally employed for the Sydney Opera House but fell out with Utzon, was acoustics consultant for the Philharmonie and Deutsches Oper in Berlin and the concert hall of Sender Freies Berlin, as well as for the Liederhalle in Stuttgart, the Residenz Theater and National Theater in Munich and the Meistersingerhalle in Nuremberg. Ralph Downes designed the organs for the Royal Festival Hall, the Fairfield Halls, Croydon, and Buckfast Abbey. A large scale (1:16) acoustic model was built for the scientific testing of this most important aspect of a concert hall. The tests were carried out in the University of Berlin.

The principal members of Raymond's team were Oscar Leach, an acoustics expert with a knowledge of broadcasting, and Con Manahan; and 1968 was the target date for completion. Raymond knew that public

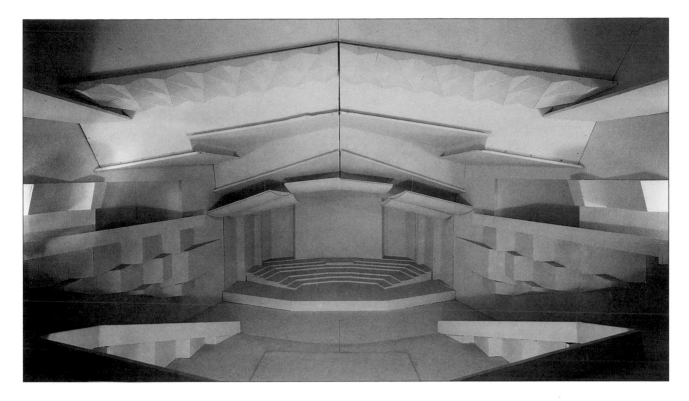

*The acoustic model, looking
towards the organ*

interest in the hall would be great, so early in 1965 he asked Patrick
Delany to undertake some public relations work for him for the official
press conference and "unveiling" of the model of the projected building.
Delany was architectural correspondent of *The Irish Times* and one of its
second-string music critics. He saw no conflict of interest in the roles of
public relations consultant and journalist, and indeed where criticism was
needed he provided it.

Delany's brief was written by McGrath, who paid special attention to
his views on acoustics and on Cremer: "Was he the sort of man I could
work with?" For Delany, Raymond described the plan shape succinctly:

> The plan shape, an eight faceted oval not primarily dictated
> [by] but nevertheless not inimical to good acoustics had been
> developed out of a desire to create as intimate an atmosphere as
> possible in an amphitheatrical auditorium, with good sight lines,
> satisfactory blocks of seating and good gangways and exits.

From Greece he got a heart-warming letter. Patricia (Lady) Jenkins, a
fellow artist and friend, said of the design: "I really like it very much —
the elevation looks simple and interestingly sculptural — the plan a feat
of imagination… What made you hit on the hexagonal form for the small
and large halls? It seems so obvious and yet is so rarely used. It's
incredibly architectural…"

The first anxiety betrayed by Raymond was that he should have
enough staff. Jack Lynch, who took over as Minister for Finance in 1965,
assured him in March 1966 that he would "make enquiries" into the
possibility of diverting some staff to the Special Projects Office.

Facing page:
The model viewed from above

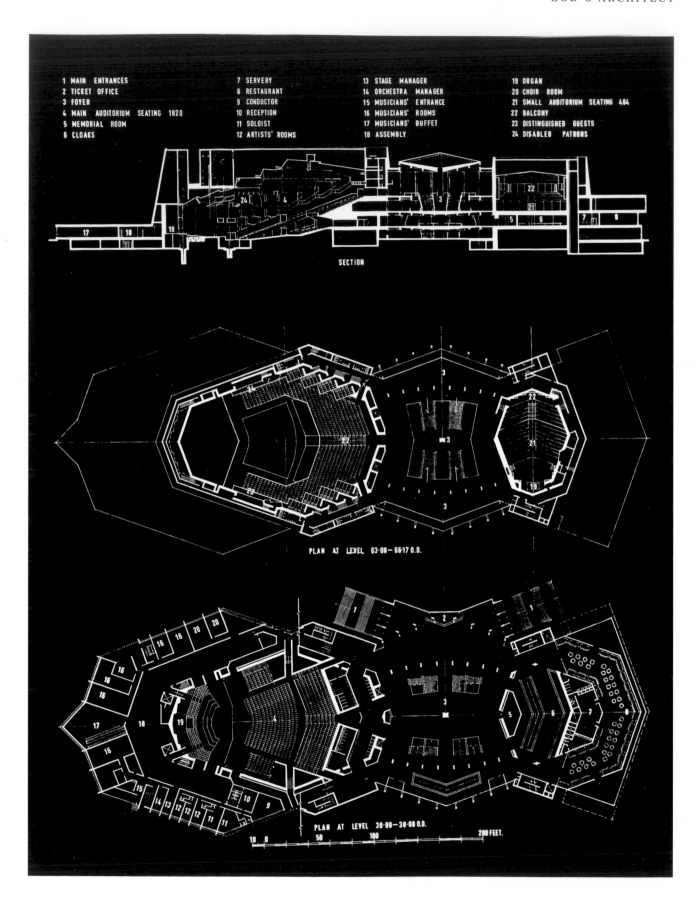

The plan of the Kennedy Hall

But Raymond had more personal concerns to lay before Lynch. "May I take this opportunity of referring to my own position as the appointed Architect for the building and to the assurance given me by Dr. Ryan that I would be retained to supervise and carry the work to completion?", he asked the Minister in March 1966. "As you are aware I am due to retire from the Public Service on 7 March, 1968. I would like to have an agreement, similar to the agreements with the consultants, covering my services after that date."

On staff, Lynch replied in September that he was "glad to note" from Raymond's recent letters that "you will now be able to make do without additional architectural staff". The Minister regarded Raymond's request for an agreement as premature. "I think you should... take this matter up with the Secretary of the Office of Public Works in the first instance".

When Seán Lemass resigned as Taoiseach in November, Lynch succeeded him and Raymond had to get used to another Minister for Finance, Charles J. Haughey. The dead hand of the Civil Service can be seen in Haughey's reply to Raymond's repeated demand for clarification of his position "...Difficult and premature at this stage to determine the conditions of retaining you... after 7 March, 1968."

Raymond was becoming frantic and resented Haughey's further letter of January 1967 in which the Minister said: "I do not think it would be good administrative practice to decide this matter so far in advance." It was all of fourteen months before Raymond would retire. In the heel of the hunt, it was less than one month before his retirement that his retention for the Kennedy Hall job was firmly decided on.

With the approval of the Chairman of the O.P.W., Raymond applied for the position of architect of the proposed hospital at Wilton in Cork, associating himself, as he told Haughey, with Anders Tengbom, "probably the most outstanding architect in the hospital field in Scandinavia". Tengbom, whose father Ivar Raymond knew, had seen the Kennedy Hall design in Dublin and been impressed. Raymond wanted to know if he (Raymond) would be free to devote time to Wilton if he were chosen.

In the end, an English architect designed Wilton Hospital and his design was used ten years later for Beaumont Hospital in Dublin.

The All-Party Committee's choice of a site for the memorial had always been controversial. Charles Acton, the eminent music critic of *The Irish Times*, had fought tenaciously for a change to the Central Model Schools, in the heart of the city. The site was available, adequate and accessible to everybody. Beggar's Bush was south of the Grand Canal and thus outside the inner city's boundary. Sporadically the choice was contested. Then somebody moved the goalposts.

In a major story in the front page of *The Irish Times* on 15 September, 1967, the architectural correspondent (Paddy Delany) told the paper's readers that a firm decision had been taken to build the Kennedy Hall in the Phoenix Park, Dublin's green lung of 1,760 acres, protected by an Act of 1925. To build there required the approval of both Houses of the Oireachtas.

Delany was not in favour of the change, but in the interests of open public debate he devoted a long article to the pros and cons, noting that a

Charles Haughey with Paddy Heffernan of the Bank of Ireland. The author can be seen behind them

perspective drawing (Raymond's, now in Norman's possession) of the building substantially unaltered in its new setting graced the top of the page. He did not know why the change had been made, but as it was only the first of several it does not now matter. Broadstone, Bachelors' Walk, and St. Ann's Raheny; all were canvassed until poor Raymond's brain was addled.

In the *Evening Press*, a reader (Rory Cowan) asked: "…What better place and more appropriate location for a white elephant than with all the other animals housed in that area?" (The Phoenix Park contains Dublin's Zoological Gardens).

Raymond had a major row with Wilfrid Cantwell, the President of the Royal Institute of the Architects of Ireland, who had written to Tomás Ó Laidhin, the secretary of the All-Party Committee, on 4 August, 1967 saying: "It is the view of this Institute that the Phoenix Park should not be selected." Raymond contended that "this is not the considered view of many members of the Institute", and he objected to Cantwell's going public before the All-Party Committee had had an opportunity to consider the letter.

"Some may take the view that the Phoenix Park should be preserved as a kind of glorious cow-pasture. Others may see more imaginative possibilities… The modern concert halls in West Berlin, Nürnberg, Bonn, Bad Godesberg, Stuttgart and Sindelfingen are all sited in parks", McGrath told Cantwell in a closely-argued but clearly angry letter.

He was fighting a losing battle, a battle that was not about fields but about strategy. The Government clearly was not as anxious to honour J.F.K. as it had been four years earlier and the morale of the Special Projects Office was sagging.

At a consultants' meeting, Raymond reported to the Minister, "the pessimists gave it as their opinion that it [the memorial] would 'never get off the ground' ". In a spirited defence of his life's work, he said to Haughey:

> I wonder how many realise that in the Kennedy Hall this country could have one of the half-dozen best halls in Europe? The design of the building has been illustrated in the leading architectural journals abroad. Here the interest in the building has been largely lugubrious, chiefly because of the All-Party Committee's complete lack of public relations since the Taoiseach launched the project at the reception in Iveagh House in March 1965.

Haughey's reply was withering: "…I am afraid that I am not in a position to say anything definite to you about this matter at the present time."

Raymond drafted a reply two days later, on 8 February, 1968. He called for an early meeting of the committee so that

> I can give an account of the state of the job and offer my resignation as architect.

He moderated this reply and sent merely a further plea for his status to be clarified.

Donogh O'Malley promised to "do what I can to help you", but of course O'Malley was close to Haughey and even closer (less than a month) to death, so his offer came to nothing. At least Raymond's terms of employment were settled. He was to get £10 for each full day's work subject to a maximum of £50 a week. He did his sums. His salary was £3,850. His pension would be £1,347.10s. Forty-four weeks at £10 per diem or £50 a week: £2,200. R.I.A.I. standard charges: 18 guineas for a six-hour day or 90 guineas for a 30-hour week. The terms offered did not seem over-generous, and he got the daily fee increased to £11, plus of course his pension and a lump sum of £3,593.6.8d. That per diem fee of £11 also applied to his work on the casting of Oisín Kelly's massive sculpture, the Children of Lir, to be placed in the Garden of Remembrance. He also got an extension to his official passport so that he could do some more work on the Villa Spada.

A contemporary publication[123] recalled the earlier disappointments that Raymond had undergone and said:

> We ardently hope he will not have to suffer further frustration over the long-awaited concert hall planned for Dublin and the nation and that this artistic, kind hearted man will yet enjoy his favourite relaxation within the auditorium of his own building — listening to music.

Donogh O'Malley's successor in the Office of Public Works was Noel Lemass. Padraig Faulkner, as the new Minister for Education, was another ex-officio member of the committee. Sean Dunne was dead. Lemass said in the Dáil that the contract drawings would be ready at the end of the year or early next year. That is how matters stood when Northern Ireland blew apart on 5 October, 1969. Civil rights agitation spread throughout the North, the British Army was called in, the I.R.A. split and the Republic became deeply involved, its Government promising money for arms to the more militant, less socialist wing of the Republican group. Professor Joe Lee[124] tells the story admirably:

> Following a series of murky manoeuvres, [the Taoiseach, Jack] Lynch dismissed Haughey and [Neil] Blaney on 6 May, 1970 on the grounds that they failed to fully subscribe to Government policy on the North.
> …On 28 May, Haughey and Blaney were arrested and charged with conspiring to import arms and ammunition.

Blaney and Haughey were acquitted. Haughey was banished to the political wilderness, and Raymond had lost another Chairman of the All-Party Committee. He had to accommodate himself to George Colley. Haughey's reputation as patron of the arts and cultural commissar had not served Raymond's cause especially well; but Colley had no such high-flown pretensions and was even less helpful in furthering the concert hall concept.

Donogh O'Malley
(Lensmen)

299

Chapter XXXVIII

ormal retirement from the Office of Public Works did not relieve Raymond of the burden of contending with bureaucracy. The Board read a newspaper report on 10 January, 1970 which, wrote T. Ó Conghalaigh three days later, implied that Raymond had been appointed architect for the proposed R.H.A. administrative block and art galleries. "It is noted that work will be commenced this year and will extend over eighteen months or two years."

Worse was to come. The Board had noted earlier that Raymond was undertaking the planning and reconstruction of the King's Hospital for the Incorporated Law Society.

> The question arises of how these commissions — there may be others of which the Board is not aware — impinge upon your duties as Architect of the John Fitzgerald Kennedy Memorial Hall. Your attendance returns show virtually full-time attendance at Lansdowne Road.
>
> Your observations are requested.

In other words, explain yourself. And Raymond did, quoting chapter and verse. He replied to T. Ó Conghalaigh on 15 January, 1970:

> The attendance returns are correct. Up to now constant attendance and regular meetings have been necessary... The Specification and Bill No. 1 are now ready. Other contract documents will follow.
>
> The implication that I have been appointed as architect for the R.H.A. building is correct. The announcement came as a surprise to me as I was in the process of completing sketch plans for the project. I had prepared a perspective drawing, which you have seen, over the December holidays. The sponsor has said that building will commence in June, but planning permission has still not yet been applied for and no one can say, at this stage, how long the project will take. I was appointed as architect for the reconstruction of the King's Hospital over a year ago... The Law Society does not expect to get possession until the school has moved to Lucan...
>
> I have no desire to become involved in any other important projects, although other commissions have been offered to me, and I am satisfied that I am sufficiently on top of the J.F.K. job to

Facing page (above):
Capri from Monte Tiberio, an oil painting of 1972.
Below: Venice with St. Mark's in the distance, 1971

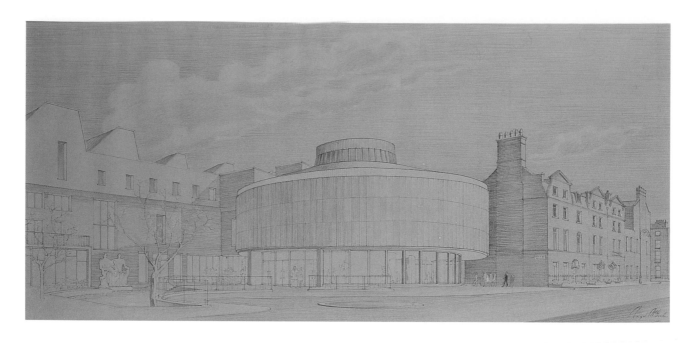

*An early perspective of the
R.H.A. Gallagher Gallery*

do justice to it, *if it proceeds*, as well as to carry out the Academy and King's Hospital projects, if they proceed.

The R.H.A. Gallagher Gallery project came about in this wise. John Healy was a journalist with *The Irish Times*. He had revolutionised political commentary in Ireland, first in the *Sunday Review* and then in its parent *Irish Times*, as well as on television which in Ireland had been born as late as 1961. It was widely believed that Donogh O'Malley was the source of much of Healy's political information. At any rate, Healy's political influence was at its height in the middle and late 1960s, a period of unprecedented prosperity in which developers and builders became important national figures.

One such figure was Matthew Gallagher, one of a family who already had made reputation and fortune in England. Like the Wentworths of Sydney and the Kennedys of Boston, Matt Gallagher sought respectability and standing in society, and when John Healy suggested to him that the building and donation of a headquarters and gallery for the Royal Hibernian Academy would confer both, he seized the opportunity with both hands.

The original Royal Hibernian Academy of Arts building was built and paid for by Francis Johnston, the great architect whose most conspicuous work in Dublin is the General Post Office of 1818. His academy building — he was the second president and was elected in 1824 — was on Middle Abbey Street. It was completely destroyed during the 1916 Rising and never rebuilt. The Academy, having lost its records, art collection and library, had no home until 1938, when it bought the former house of Oliver St. John Gogarty at Ely Place. It was on this site that the Gallagher gallery was to be built. Its architect, by general consent, was to be Raymond McGrath, the Academy's Professor of Architecture since 1967.

Raymond's first thoughts on a design were inspired by Frank Lloyd

Wright's Guggenheim Gallery and then dismissed in favour of the rectangular galleries of the Museum of Modern Art and the Whitney. In view of the protracted and frustrating history of the Dublin building, it is pointless to describe the plan shape that came to an end with Matt Gallagher's sudden death in January 1974. Arthur Gibney, R.H.A., who was appointed in 1987 to complete the unfinished gallery, says simply:[125] "…The main gallery spaces are much as Raymond McGrath envisaged them and their immense success as exhibition facilities is a tribute to his considerable skills."

Gogarty's house was demolished in September, 1971 and work on the half-acre site began. On 7 January, 1974, the Council of the R.H.A. noted:[126] "Matthew Gallagher, generous donor of the new building, died this day."

Within a year, work had ceased on the site, though the building was assessed as 70 per cent constructed. Raymond in 1976 was optimistic that building would proceed. But he was whistling in the wind.

For his "great services to artists working in Ireland", Charles J. Haughey was elected an honorary member of the Academy in 1973. His exile from the corridors of power was still in force, and Jack Lynch was able to say patronisingly: "Deputy Haughey is working well within the party." Within two years Haughey was back on the front bench.

At the same meeting, the Academy elected Terence de Vere White Professor of Literature. White, who died in June 1994, was a remarkable figure in Irish letters. Lovable, irascible and always inventive, he was a solicitor when about 1961 he became the literary editor of *The Irish Times*. He was a prolific novelist with a waspish wit; a biographer, notably of Kevin O'Higgins, and a historian.

In response to a leading article that Terence de Vere White wrote in 1967, Raymond retaliated. A curious couple of letters from White is extant,[127] addressed to "Dear Raymond".

> I don't often do leaders now and my responsibility for the one you mention I can only acknowledge to the extent that I on several occasions told the paper that Michael Scott had complained to me bitterly and *at great length* about the concert hall. Whenever he is confronted with what he says he always denies it.
>
> As for the rest: we were told officially that there would be a tripartite building at Ballsbridge and that Morehampton Road was out. I am on the board of the National Library.
>
> It is a quibble that the library is not going out to the [Phoenix] Park. The Concert Hall is — evidently, and a scheme to wrap up all three has been dropped. But we are not told about these things; and someone who met you lately, said you had remarked that you had no word yet to go ahead.
>
> If there were to be a tripartite building and now the Board of Works is going back on all that, I can well understand why you have to write to me in the hurt way which is becoming the hallmark of Board of Works communications.

Matt Gallagher, from the portrait by John Kelly RHA

*Terence de Vere White by
Robert Pyke*
(Courtesy of the National Gallery of Ireland)

Lack of humility or humour in high places.

However, you have to write officially and not as your natural charming self.

I feel that I am addressing a faceless dignitary looking over your shoulder.

Personally I would like to see the National Library housed first; and I don't give a damn where the Concert Hall is put so long as it is beautiful and practical.

In your hands it can hardly be less than both.

White reread Raymond's letter and wrote to apologise for his own reply:

I was feeling very ill when it came in and — to be frank — the name of Michael Scott sent blood to my head. I have resigned from the Municipal Gallery at his suggestion as he was going to do also. He then decided to take the City Manager out to lunch instead.

He spoke to Eleanor Wicklow about his horror at what the E.S.B. was doing [demolishing a Georgian terrace and replacing it with a new building by Stephenson Gibney and Associates. McGrath was an assessor and favoured this winning design] and then told them [the Electricity Supply Board] that the Arts Council would not interfere.

He gave similar assurances to the Nitrogen Gas Co. [Nitrigín Éireann Teo.] about Shelton Abbey.

When I am aware of how he went on about the Concert Hall, I am sickened to see that once again he is at his strange two-faced game.

So please forgive my rudeness and intemperance.

I have been working too hard.

This letter is vintage White, incisive and honest, yet generous and fair. Like Michael Scott, he was a board member of most of Ireland's art and cultural institutions; but he was modest, self-deprecating and dedicated to public service.

By 1972, Raymond McGrath was once again in a quandary. He was hoping against hope that the Kennedy Hall would go ahead. He was pressing ahead with the R.H.A. Gallery. At the end of the year he wrote to the Minister for Finance, George Colley, to say that "a group interested in the Kennedy Hall had drawn his attention to the impending sale of the Masonic Girls' School at Ballsbridge". The site area was about the same, nine acres. The interested group was aware of "the pressure on the Beggar's Bush site and the Government's indecision about the use of the Phoenix Park site. I would regard the [Girls School site] as an attractive alternative…"

He prepared a modified scheme omitting the small hall — "the Royal Dublin Society has a small hall" — and costing around the £2.6 million sanctioned for the project by the Department of Finance in 1965.

Co-operation with the R.D.S. offered, he thought, "the most likely opportunity of ever getting a concert hall".

In 1968 and again in 1971, newspaper stories had indicated that the concert hall project had been "axed". McGrath wrote to Colley claiming that the "axing" seemed somewhat premature:

> ...I cannot conceive that the pledge of a memorial to President Kennedy in the form of a concert hall in the capital city could be abandoned without due consideration by the Committee set up to further it...

The Minister was not listening. The whispering campaign being continued by Michael Scott and the dawning discovery that John Fitzgerald Kennedy had feet of clay were probably enough to kill the grand plan. But a change of Government and the oil crisis of 1973 hammered the last nails into the coffin of the Kennedy Hall.

In the columns of *Hibernia*,[128] the music critic Fanny Feehan, having praised Raymond and his "brilliant team of architects", went on:

> It is suspected by a good many people that a fair amount of finagling has gone on behind the scenes between the various rival interests. Some people also feel that certain influential persons have succeeded in blocking the project by arguing over the site...

In the Dáil,[129] Dr. Noël Browne was told by George Colley that the All-Party Committee last met on 15 June, 1967. He proposed to call another meeting at "an early convenient date". After further dialogue:

> Dr. Browne — May we take it that this scheme is shelved? Kennedy is dead.
> Mr. Colley — If that is what the Deputy wishes to think I cannot stop him.

After the general election of March 1973, there was a change of Government. George Colley was succeeded by Richie Ryan as Minister for Finance. Up to 1994 a member of the Court of Auditors of the European Union, Ryan then was a young, thrusting, ambitious politician who had been given a senior ministry that Garret FitzGerald had been expected to get. The new Taoiseach, Liam Cosgrave (an original member of the All-Party Committee), was a conservative who preferred Ryan's orthodoxy to what he suspected might be FitzGerald's radicalism.

As 1973 dragged on and Raymond waited, the author took a hand and privately wrote to the Minister:

> This is a cri de coeur... You know that the Concert Hall is [Raymond's] masterpiece, the culmination of a long and distinguished career, the justification for over thirty years spent in a strange country with a wife who never settled down, and the

Richie Ryan

consolation for other schemes thwarted and stillborn.

I do not ask that you build the hall. I believe you should but I can see the difficulties and the decision is yours.

What I do ask is that you see Raymond soon, and talk to him and let him talk. (He doesn't articulate easily.)

The worst part of the last nine years for him has been the non-communication, the messing, the rumours and counter-rumours, the punching at sponges. Almost a touch of Kafka.

He is a great and good man who has served us well and I know that you will not allow his spirit and his talent to go on being eroded just because he is perhaps a political innocent.

And I know you will not add to the string of broken promises that he carries around like a rosary beads.

Richie Ryan met Raymond McGrath on 6 September, 1973. The world oil price increases had not yet taken place. Ryan does not remember any details but says:[130] "I doubt if it assuaged Mr. McGrath's anger that I told him that I would have been delighted to launch his project if financial resources permitted. That was a time when it was unpopular in Ireland to preach living beyond one's means... Raymond and I were looking at his dream from different angles." On a more personal level, Richie Ryan says:

I believe I met Raymond McGrath more often in your hospitable home than when wearing my ministerial hat. He struck me as an urbane, imaginative, cultured gentleman who did not suffer fools gladly and did not pretend that he did.

He was very disappointed that his great design for a super John F. Kennedy Concert Hall was never built. I feel he did not quite accept my decision to put the grand plan into cold storage in favour of the Earlsfort Terrace compromise. He was not alone in disapproving. The most hostile press conference I ever had was the one to announce the Earlsfort Terrace project [9 May, 1974]. But God and time have been good to me and every one of my critics whom I have since met have apologised for their mistake and are fulsome in their praise of the National Concert Hall.

Raymond had managed to put the Kennedy Hall fiasco behind him, and was concentrating on the R.H.A. building and the design of Southwood for Bobbie Mitchell. But in January 1974 Matt Gallagher died, leaving no structured provision for the completion of the galleries. The gods had conspired to leave a great architect without an Irish monument.

Facing page (above): McGrath's drawing of mills on Mykonos with their sails down, c.1964
Below: The Monastery of Tourliane at Anomera, Mykonos (Greece)

Monastery of Tourliani, Ano Mera

Above: Aoife and the Children of Lir, 1963

Right: Lilies

Chapter XXXIX

lmo Pye's view of Raymond McGrath's career was expressed succinctly in a letter of 1970:

> Ray has never complained... to me, but I would have thought he had suffered more than his share of frustrations and disappointments in delays and failure to carry out work for which he has prepared the preliminary plans.

Norman says that Raymond in 1940 could never have guessed how unproductive his career would be from then on. Yet was it so unproductive? In his Irish years Raymond knew many consolations. He made a parallel career as a painter, ending his days as President of the Royal Hibernian Academy. This distinction made him the first Principal Architect of the Board of Works since Francis Johnston in 1824 to become president of the Academy. More than that, he emulated Johnston by designing the academy's galleries and offices.

McGrath made a singular contribution to design in Ireland, not only by his work for Donegal Carpets and Waterford Glass and on the Stamp Design Advisory Committee, but by his founding and presidency of the new Society of Designers in Ireland in 1973. The story of the establishment of the S.D.I. is well told by Paul Hogan of the then Córas Tráchtála:

> From my side, once I had embarked on the design development road there were three mountains to climb: promotion – relatively easy; education – an intractable problem which had beaten better men than I; and the organisation of the profession – impossible. What made the last named so difficult was that while I knew exactly how an Irish professional society of designers should be constituted, I could not solve the problem of an acceptable leader. Every candidate I considered was unacceptable to this faction or that. Raymond was my brainwave and it is a matter of history that of 100 people invited to the inaugural meeting (on personal letters typed in C.T.T. and individually signed by Raymond), 99 accepted. (The exception was the designer Len Deighton, then living in Co. Louth, who wished the venture well but said that he intended to concentrate on the writing!)
>
> I am sure that only Raymond could have brought about this

Francis Johnston
(Courtesy of the Irish Architectural Archive)

result. As it was, there were some sticky moments at the meeting with some of the attendees clearly feeling that others should not be there. Raymond was, I think, oblivious to these undercurrents and that disarming "innocence" seemed to me his greatest strength then and during the first year of the Society. Anyway, the fact is that the S.D.I. was so soundly established (Raymond helped me write the Constitution) that it has survived where other ventures have passed into memory. As Kevin Fox put it in a splendid obituary notice he wrote for the S.D.I., it was somehow fitting that at the end of his career Raymond should be elected to lead the oldest (the R.H.A.) and the youngest Irish design societies.

He was elected a Fellow of the Society of Industrial Artists in 1961. Since the publication of the Scandinavian experts' report on 'Design in Ireland' in 1961, in which McGrath's work was acknowledged, standards had risen dramatically and the Government had established Kilkenny Design Workshops. To all these changes, Raymond McGrath brought his keen sense of form and colour, his deep knowledge of materials and the vast experience of his ten years' pioneering work in London.

His grand building designs may not have been implemented, but his work as Principal Architect involved more than executing his own plans. Indeed these schemes were subsidiary to the setting and maintaining of high standards in all the Office of Public Works' architectural operations. In this work, unseen and unheralded, he was assisted by a team of great distinction, though it was known that at least two of them, Basil Boyd Barrett and Sidney Maskell, harboured a grudge against Raymond from the time he was appointed Principal Architect in 1948, a post they felt rightly belonged to one of them.

Boyd Barrett, who was Assistant Principal Architect in charge of school building, "ran an empire within the Board of Works", in the words of Oscar Richardson.[131] Known as "B.B.", Boyd Barrett was a very powerful man who "had the ear of every parish priest and bishop in the country".

When the Kennedy Memorial Concert Hall was mooted, *The Irish Times* in a leading article (unsigned of course, but bearing the acerbic hallmark of Terence de Vere White) said:

> Happy for England that she had a Christopher Wren after the Great Fire of London, happy that it did not take place in the period of Christopher Robin. But we have no Wren — at the moment. It is not insulting anyone to say so. Or, if we have, his presence has not been made known. The Kennedy Memorial might — if anything could — show him to us. Let us not rule out the miraculous possibility.

Quick to retaliate, the paper's architectural correspondent (Patrick Delany in disguise) used the letters column to praise the All-Party

Committee's choice of Raymond McGrath, and to defend the architects of the Office of Public Works who as public servants could not defend themselves:

> You draw an implicitly unflattering comparison between the age of Christopher Wren and that of Christopher Robin; but, as you yourself admit, we have at the moment no Wren, and surely a live Robin is better than a dead Wren; especially as the Robin in question has for many years led a design department at the Office of Works whose level of excellence many a larger country might envy.
>
> Faraway architects, too, have long horns. Let us be glad that we have locally… a man of the calibre of Raymond McGrath, who had an international reputation before ever he came to Ireland…

In *Corridor*,[132] an internal O.P.W. publication, "A.S.R." (Angela Rolfe) wrote: "One must look at the total output of the Office of Public Works during [Raymond McGrath's] term of office to appreciate the influence he exerted on standards and quality throughout those years. Indeed it is extraordinary that despite his commitment to management of a large Architectural Branch he could still give attention to such a wide range of individual projects."

> He carefully watched the output of design work and in many cases rejected work that he considered below standard in the most circumspect manner. He was dedicated to encouraging native industries…

Once the Coalition Government and its Minister for Finance Richie Ryan had firmly decided to convert the Great Hall of University College Dublin at Earlsfort Terrace into a concert hall, the flames of controversy raged anew. Raymond would have been well advised to steer clear of it, but he jumped in, displaying the labels of anger and disappointment.

> Adaptation of the Great Hall would be a misguided operation which would be bound to postpone indefinitely the consideration of the city's real need for a hall of an adequate size…

Inevitably, the headline over *The Irish Times* report read: "Concert Hall Architect Raps New Project." And while Richie Ryan attacked the Fianna Fáil Opposition for its "ten years of make-believe and procrastination", the indomitable Charles Acton wrote to the Editor:

> We are now to be saddled with what will only be a makeshift radio orchestra performing studio, completely inadequate for most other purposes.

An important voice raised against the McGrath project was that of Anthony Cronin the writer, some years later to become the powerful

Patrick Delany
(Courtesy of Joan Delany)

Michael O'Doherty

cultural adviser to Charles Haughey. Writing in *The Irish Times*, where he had an occasional column entitled 'Viewpoint', Cronin argued:

> There are enough gleaming sepulchres around already which contribute nothing to the creative life of the nation... no more contributions to the grand illusion should be encouraged until the reality begins to keep pace... You could do wonders in Ireland with far less than the sum the concert hall would have cost.

Suffice it here to say that a 1,250-seat National Concert Hall, designed by Michael O'Doherty, now Principal Architect of the Office of Public Works, was opened to the public in September 1981. It serves also as a home for the National Symphony Orchestra. Acton's successor, Michael Dervan, has said[133] that while its capacity "militates against the commercial viability of concerts", in the circumstances it "has fared remarkably well".

About 50 years after he designed St Ann's Hill, Raymond was retained as the architect for the only house he did in Ireland. The client was Bobbie Mitchell of the wine merchants in Kildare Street. He and his wife Sheila held their first party at Southwood, Carrickmines, on 4 October, 1974. Southwood was a fictitious name given to the house by Raymond eighteen months earlier. But the Mitchells liked it and retained it.

The house has echoes of St Ann's Hill, with which Gerry Byrne[134] compared it:

> Southwood is a more modest house of around 3,000 square feet with cavity block walls and suspended pre-cast concrete floor and roof. The external finish is Tyrolean render... The house is sited beside a pine copse on the sloping side of the valley.

Ove Arup's firm was of course the structural engineer on the job, which cost £48,600. Varming and Mulcahy provided the engineering

Southwood, Carrickmines

services and Seán Mulcahy recalled that this was the second time he worked with Raymond.

In the year of his death, Raymond was still owed £762.30 by Bobbie Mitchell. He suggested:

> What I should like to do would be to have some goods on account of these fees as my cellar is getting low… If you agree you could credit me with the balance towards some future transaction.

He ordered, inter alia, twelve bottles of Mitchell's Green Spot (a twelve-year-old Jameson whiskey); a case each of Cutty Sark and Club Gin and some Château Courbet and Château de Langel — £328 worth in all.

"No difficulty", said Mitchell. "Congratulations on your maths. You have however overcharged yourself for Green Spot. The price is £4.50, not £5: it actually came down." Most of this order was in the cellar at Somerton Lodge when Raymond died in December 1977.

Norman was 36 when he married Molly Wade in 1967. The wedding, with Jenny as matron of honour, was in Princeton, Molly's birthplace. When they arrived in Ireland, Molly faced a second reception at Somerton Lodge. She felt well prepared to meet "these distinguished people who had come to wish us well".[135]

> I don't know if anyone can understand my chagrin when I realised after being introduced several times that every conversation was going to begin with some comment by the other person about how tall I was. How surprised they were! How extraordinary, they thought! No-one had mentioned that I was SO tall! Although I had had some practice in fielding comments regarding my height, I found I was exhausting my resources for dealing with all these. I was terribly troubled that so many conversations never proceeded beyond observations about my size.
>
> Finally I decided that these people must think Norman had married a giraffe. I ran from the room in tears, and who was right there, immediately, to find out what was wrong but Raymond. I told him tearfully of my distress and he knew exactly what to do and say. He put his arms around me and said: "But Norman is tall too. And you look beautiful together." That, above all, was what I wanted to hear.

Raymond and Mary were forty years married in 1970. They invited 75 people to Somerton Lodge and "himself", Mary told Elmo Pye, was "fine, sunburned, distinguished-looking *and* acting."

Sir Robert and Lady Mayer (he was then 91) were guests. He and Dorothy Moulton Mayer — a native of Cork — placed hundreds of thousands of people in their debt for giving them an opportunity to enjoy the boon of music. Concerts for children were the legacy of this

Molly Wade McGrath

remarkable pair, to whom the world of music from Bernstein to Barbirolli paid tribute in a privately-printed 90th birthday book.[136] In a truly banal contribution whose only merit is its author's famous name, Pádraic Colum the poet wrote:

> Pitched to affection's note,
> Our greetings for this day,
> To you who dowered us
> With music's lilt and swell

There are two more verses in that watery vein.

Another member of the McGraths' circle was feeling her age more than was Robert Mayer. To Aunt Collie, nearly old enough to have seen the American Civil War, Mary wrote on 25 August, 1974:

> I know life is dull when you can't see or hear but I know you are thinking and feeling and I know *you* know how loved you are. It is surely a responsibility to be 105 years old. I am going to pay you a visit in November if I can fix up a suitable person to look after Raymond… I am by no means indispensable at home…
>
> I have vivid dreams about you and Heart and Aunt Addie Belle and Raymond and Norman and Jenny nearly every night. I almost hate to wake up…

Raymond, Mary and Norman on Lac d'Annecy, 1971

McGrath's drawing of the living-room of Peter Dunlop's house at Patterson, New York

In 1971 and again in 1973, the Raymond McGraths and the Norman McGraths took long holidays in France together. To Norman it was a source of wonder that his wife and his parents should travel in harmony on such long journeys. To Molly it was a rare opportunity to get to know Raymond. She observed him carefully as he used his trained eye to register the colours and shapes that appealed to him.

What sights would have met his eyes if two proposed lecture tours of Australia had come off! That the first failed to happen he ascribed to the parsimony of the host institutions, but it is quite as likely that in 1972 he needed an excuse to shield him from the light of memories that such a visit would have let in to his head. Perhaps too the sight of the completed Sydney Opera House would have been too painful a reminder of what might have been in Dublin.

There was a good reason why the second opportunity of "going home" after nearly fifty years did not materialise. Raymond had been invited as a visiting lecturer to the Power Institute of Fine Arts at the University of Sydney, arriving probably in September 1975. He also was preparing for publication 'An Expatriate's Sketchbook', which was to consist of a collection of his drawings with text. And he had some buildings on hand, including the rebuilding of some blocks at Dublin Castle.

Over all this activity was cast the shadow of illness, the terminal cancer of the bile duct that was to kill him. It came slowly and it offered remissions. Elmo Pye and Roy Booth in Sydney were disappointed not to see him. So too were Norman and Molly in New York, for Raymond and Mary were toying with the idea of retiring to upstate New York where Norman was building a house designed by Myron Goldfinger. Eileen on the other hand cautioned her brother to "think well before you make any decisions".

CHAPTER XL

Raymond was quite as deliberately blind to his own condition as for forty years he had been to Mary's. Right to the end he used the word cist as a euphemism for tumour. After a prolonged stay in hospital around Christmas 1976, he affected to believe that his "pneumonia" was quite cured and that he could finish the set of definitive stamps he had begun with drawings of Conolly's Folly, Gallarus Oratory and Clonfert Cathedral. He had left the Stamp Design Advisory Committee in order to design this set, which in the result was done superbly by Michael Craig.

The Minister for Post and Telegraphs, the tergiversational Dr. Conor Cruise O'Brien, marked Raymond's departure from the committee in 1976 with a presentation book containing all the stamps with whose design Raymond had been concerned.

Mary tape-recorded a letter to Elmo Pye. She said haltingly that she and Raymond had had a long year of bad experiences at the end of which Dr. Gordon Mullins had "cured Raymond of cancer of the liver". She was unable to go on, and she did not send Elmo the unfinished cassette.

Not Gordon Mullins, not Brian Mayne, not the cleverest doctor in the world could reverse Raymond's illness; but he did have an opportunity in the early summer of Seventy-seven to go on a Greek cruise with Mary. He did only one drawing, at Mykonos which he already knew well. There he spent three hours working: he ended up cold and stiff.

Their ship was the Orpheus and among their fellow-passengers were Tom Stoppard the playwright and his wife. The cruise ended at Venice. Back in London the McGraths were met by George Giri, who is married to Karin the daughter of Eric and Dora Lewenhaupt. They saw John and Margaret Witt and Natalie Bevan, Lance Sieveking's ex-wife, who had a dying John Nash staying with her. It was a touching farewell to old friends.

London, Raymond said, "was just too hectic for us". But at home in Dublin, the news was also bad. Hilary Heron the sculptor had died. Leo Smith of the Dawson Gallery had had a heart attack in Pat Scott's car and died. (Scott is a well-known Irish artist.)

When Raymond had his penultimate spell in hospital, he learned from Norman how to use a tape-recorder. In a taped message to Molly, he told her that her husband was on the way home to her and that she should look after him "because he's a very precious person". As he spoke that phrase, he broke down.

When he recovered he told Molly of a young English engineer in the

Facing page (above): St. Werburgh's Church, Dublin.
Below: Two of McGrath's stamp designs, used a year after his death

Open University who had stayed at Somerton Lodge two months before and planned to write a book on Raymond's work in the thirties. He had been to see the buildings, including the house at Galby.

This was Peter Varley, who gave a lecture on McGrath in April 1978, but did not do a book. He had seen Finella and St. Ann's Hill, which had then for three years been empty and dilapidated. Raymond took comfort from the news Varley gave him that a successful young musician, Phil Manzanera, and his wife, had just bought St. Ann's Hill, realised what they had, and intended to restore it even to the furniture. Raymond gave Peter Varley drawings and photographs which would act as references in the restoration scheme, which was carried out by Paul Davis. Varley was to work with Keith Hilton of the University of Newcastle on Tyne, whose interest was in writing about McGrath's work in Ireland. "Such as it is", Raymond drily remarked to the tape-recorder.

Urged by Mary, Raymond began his memoirs. He used a pen. "The difficulty", he wrote, "is, if one has a job to do, and an architect always seems to have a job to do, to relax sufficiently to do a little looking back instead of planning ahead. Conscience prods the attention to all sorts of footling details, footling in themselves, though perhaps important in the overall picture."

> Many people imagine that architecture is a kind of inspirational occupation like painting. It is anything but that. The architect has his inspirations but they are soon swallowed up in a mass of detailed drudgery. The tragic moment in Jørn Utzon's career was when his flight of fancy was chosen as the concrete project for a real building, the Sydney Opera House. But at least it materialised. Most of the architectural projects which I have embarked upon have not. They have only a paper existence. It is a moot point whether they and I are happier that way.

In a clear reference to Matt Gallagher and the R.H.A. Gallery, Raymond continued:

> As a client of mine said sagely when he embarked on an ambitious building: "Neither you nor I will get any thanks for it."
> As he died before he could finish the building, he was probably right.

Raymond could not type, and he shied away from dictation, so his recollections would be "writing the old-fashioned way, the hard way". He began at eight o'clock on 18 January, 1975, when there was "a rim of warm light on Killiney Hill, the promise of sunshine and a continuation of this premature spring. It was cold. Around the arbutus a halo of white frost spread across the grass. Cold brought tears to the eyes but it was a day one wanted to enjoy".

He drove to Marlfield Nurseries in Cabinteely and home by way of Kill o' the Grange. He wanted to see what had become of Kill Abbey and its old garden since Louis Jammet died.

Kill Abbey was still there, rising gauntly from the remnants of its decimated garden, hidden away behind the new housing, a stone's throw from the ruins of [the original] Kill Abbey. Yvonne Jammet's garden studio was gone. A road ran where the old garden had been, but the house was still there, that strange curiously French house, French because of its furnishings and the family, after a lifetime in Dublin, remained superbly gallic — Yvonne and Louis, the daughters Raymonde [now Kiersey] and Roisín [now Hood], the sons Michel and Patrick. One remembers Louis's now legendary restaurant in Nassau street. One remembers the studio parties when architect Michel came back from London with his sculptress wife, Elizabeth Frink…

Houses and gardens played a pivotal role in the few pages that Raymond managed to gather together. He described Monkstown House "in wooded grounds with beautiful trees… owned by a Jew in George's Street who wanted to exact the last ounce of profit out of the development of its surroundings. As the trees came down and the menace spread we became more and more unhappy…"

And Somerton Lodge, "a curious, beautiful and in many ways a unique house. It began life as a modest early 18th century cottage… at a later stage Regency style wings, balconies and staircases were added and it became the long picturesque house which it is today…"

Of himself, this fragment tells us nothing new. We already know of his feeling and intuitive touch where rooms and buildings were involved. Apart from his public work, he did decoration and a carpet for Trinity College Dublin. There is a warm letter from Professor David Webb dated 24 September, 1962:

The carpet of the Common Room of Trinity College, Dublin, destroyed by fire in 1986
(Photograph by Norman McGrath)

319

Front Square, Trinity College
Dublin, 1958

Now that your part of the Common Room is finished I must send you a note of thanks for all your good work… I would like to say how grateful I am to you, in the first place for undertaking the job at all; in the second place for having taken so much trouble over details; and in the third place for having displayed such a judicious blend of flexibility over some points and firmness over others, which is just what we wanted.

In 1973, the Agent for Trinity, Colonel J.M. Walsh, asked McGrath whether the college should repeat the colour scheme which he had devised "about twelve years ago". It was generally considered to be a great success so "the question arises, should we just repeat it exactly… or do something different?" Raymond suggested discreet changes and agreed a fee of £200. The Dining Hall and the Examination Hall also benefited from his guidance, his fee for advice on the redecoration of the Dining Hall in 1976 being £100.

J.V. Luce later wrote to *The Irish Times*: "It should not be forgotten that Raymond McGrath was one of the five assessors who judged the entries for the new T.C.D. Library competition [which] attracted 216 entries from countries as diverse as the Argentine, Turkey and Japan." Luce was secretary of the organising committee. He said the final result – the design entered by the then unknown Paul Koralek – "owed much to [McGrath's] experience, taste and good judgement."

These commissions, and the myriad other ways in which Raymond McGrath ranged outside the core of his work for the State, make it fruitful to ponder on Serge Chermayeff's considered view of McGrath's stature:[137]

Raymond was fundamentally not an architect; he was an artist and in architecture a decorator. He was not interested in solving problems but in making shapes. He was a very fine draughtsman, far finer than I. So in Ireland he got the wrong job.

A radically opposing view of McGrath has come from John O'Gorman. A partner in Buckley and O'Gorman, O'Gorman has been described by Seán Rothery[138] as "the most prolific and possibly the most important Irish writer on architecture from the mid-1930s to the early 1940s". Rothery sees O'Gorman as playing in Ireland the role played in England by Morton Shand — propagandist for the Modern Movement. Born in 1908 at Wisbech in Cambridgeshire, O'Gorman used the pen-name Wisbech for most of his articles in the *Irish Builder*.

He wrote for other periodicals including *Ireland Today*, and for *The Irish Times* and *The Irish Press*. In 1990 O'Gorman, who had spent seventeen years in North America, observed to the author[139] that:

> If McGrath had gone to the United States, the world would not now be talking of Mies but of McGrath.

Ove Arup wrote some verses to Raymond in January 1977. He sent them to Mary, telling her to "consider carefully" whether to show them to Raymond. We may be sure she did not:

We all must die	You have some chapters	Then you will win —
but don't start hurrying	still to write	of that I'm certain
For that would really	So don't give up	It's my turn next
set me worrying!	without a fight	to take the curtain

On 19 October, 1977, Raymond McGrath was elected President of the Royal Hibernian Academy of Arts in succession to Dr. Maurice MacGonigal, who retired. Raymond was present and at the council meeting on 7 November took the chair. He reported[140] that Charles Haughey, then Minister for Health and Social Welfare, was "actively pursuing the completion and maintenance" of the unfinished galleries. Haughey was taking a welcome interest in the R.H.A. Gallagher Gallery, as it became known. His concern, which contrasted sharply with his uncaring attitude to the Kennedy Hall earlier, was of little practical use to Raymond. While this was the first opportunity he had to preside over the Royal Hibernian Academy, it was also his last.

Chemotherapy having failed, the Meath Hospital discharged him finally towards the end of November. He was home in Somerton Lodge for four or five days when, on the morning of Friday December 2nd, Mary awoke to find that he was dead in the bed beside her. He had died sometime between one and four o'clock in the night. In the studio below him, on his antiquated drawing board, were the finished drawings he had just been working on for the rebuilding of Blocks 8 to 10 of Dublin Castle.

Raymond McGrath's funeral service was a large affair, conducted by the Rev. Billy Wynne, the rector of Monkstown. He was a family friend and he asked Jenny to write a short tribute to her father which he read to the congregation. It spoke of "many things I remember... He seemed to

321

Maurice Craig
(Photograph by Albert Fenton)

spread beauty around us…"

He was buried with his father in Dean's Grange Cemetery beneath a headstone that describes him as "architect, artist, poet: Sydney, London, Dublin."

The Irish Times[141] asked Maurice Craig, the architectural historian, to write an appreciation. It was a masterly summary of Raymond's career and it ended:

> In truth Raymond McGrath could have distinguished himself in any of several careers. He was a fine writer and he could draw like an angel. He loved travel, and his holidays produced a crop of drawings and paintings in a great range of styles and treatments. He loved "all trades, their gear and tackle and trim", and the poet in him never died. The gentleness and fortitude of his temperament enabled him to surmount disappointments which must have been bitter indeed…
>
> If he had a fault, it was a want of self-assertiveness, the most likeable of faults, which in his case concealed a heroic determination; as when, a few weeks before his death and in the grip of mortal illness, he presided over a two-and-a-half hour meeting of the Academy, founded and first presided over, by his great predecessor, Francis Johnston…

The Times[142] was less kind, remarking that while he was one of "the small band — for the most part members of the Modern Architectural Research group — who propagated in England the new notions about architecture then recently established on the Continent", in Ireland

> he achieved little of note and appeared to have lost his interest in the new movements, or at least his will to contribute to them.

It was a major obituary, almost certainly written by J.M. Richards. It did justice to McGrath's academic and English achievements — Finella's "sparklingly original and mildly Expressionist interiors" which "became something of a landmark for students of the new architecture" — but the obituarist considered that, "either through a loss of intellectual stamina or simply through the absence of the right kind of opportunity", his Irish work "never developed in the direction his London career had promised".

Harsh, partly true, ill-informed yet affectionate, *The Times* obituary was an ideogram for Raymond's time in Ireland, which at 37 years formed exactly half of his life.

What influence did Raymond McGrath wield? His buildings are few and in England significant. His drawings, woodcuts and paintings are many and in Australia and Ireland treasured. His books are two and seminal; his other writings pure and accurate and sometimes romantic. His poems, for the most part juvenilia, once or twice scale the heights of true feeling. His design, whether of clocks or glass, or carpets or stamps, shows a rare sympathy for materials and forms.

If all that is not enough to earn McGrath a place in the general burial ground of the great dead of his century, how can one explain the fact that when this book was begun, at least three writers, two in Australia and one in Ireland, already were working on a similar task?

"Be sure that you go to the author to get at *his* meaning, not to find yours", said John Ruskin in 'Sesame and Lilies'. To get at McGrath's meaning, it is useful to end on an unpublished, undated but certainly pre-Modern verse in which he twisted the title of Ruskin's most famous book to give us:

THE FIFTY SEVEN LAMPS OF ARCHITECTURE

When I decided to build me a house
I felt just a little afraid
That plan and design were not quite in my line,
So I sought Architectural aid;
And I said: Show me, pray, something most recherché;
For I'm weary of hanging my hat
In an early Victorian
Pre-Montessorian,
Plain two-by-fourteen flat.

The Architect puffed at his period pipe,
As he sat in his Renaissance chair,
And he gave me a smile in the pure Gothic style,
Though he spoke with a Romanesque air
Said he: If your taste is not wholly debased,
The best you are certain to find
Is the later Colonial
Pseudo Baronial
G. Washingtonian Style

I thanked him politely and paid him his fee,
But sundry acquaintances cried:
"That stuff you should shun for it hasn't been done
Since Benjamin Harrison died".
And they took me direct to a new Architect
Who argued with Logic compelling
For a Quasi-Delsartean
Post Bonapartean,
Wholly Beaux-Artean dwelling

My downfall had started; I groped in a maze
Of traces, transitions and trends,
And I laboured anew over prints that were blue,
With the aid of my numerous friends.
But I don't knit my brow about building plans now,
For all my money he spent,
And my home's an Arcadian
Second-Crusadean
Pink-Lemonadean Tent.

Above: The Kingstone Store, Leicester, 1937, in which "remarkable materials are treated in a polite and restrained manner"

Right: The New River at Canonbury Grove, Islington, 1938. Evidence of McGrath's interest in the history and conservation of Georgian architecture

The Architecture of Raymond McGrath

Alan Powers

The 'Modern Movement' in British Architecture of the 1930s has long been accepted as a self-sufficient phenomenon. Raymond McGrath's obituarist in *The Times* could hardly see the individual architect apart from the group and its shared values. Anonymity was one of the watchwords of the movement, so that an architect like McGrath, who was so evidently an artist and individualist, is hard to place in this idealised picture of a movement in which he played a part, composed though it was of other equally distinct individuals.

The truth is that his career cannot be seen only as a phenomenon of the 1930s, although it was during this period that he produced virtually all the work by which he is remembered and, from force of circumstances, his best work. By looking also at the lesser-known periods of his student work in the 1920s, leading up to Finella, and the last thirty-five years of his work in Ireland, a different and ultimately more consistent picture emerges, albeit modified by the very different environments in which he found himself.

Raymond McGrath's graphic ability comes across strongly from his earliest drawings. His etchings and other early prints are remarkably accomplished, derivative though they may be. The element of fantasy in them is not uncommon in adolescent work, influenced in his generation by the illustrators of the late Victorian romantic movement.

McGrath's architectural formation was attributed by him first to the Macquarie buildings designed from 1816 by the convict architect Francis Greenway, to which he developed a natural affinity, recognising, as did "that strange architect and writer" Hardy Wilson, their Chinese character. China was accounted by McGrath his second formative influence, and one clearly visible in his student work.

The third influence was Leslie Wilkinson, McGrath's professor at Sydney University. A good draughtsman and, by all accounts, an engaging character, he was the product of the Edwardian period in England, who had been absorbed in the burgeoning demand for architectural education in the British Empire after the First World War. He had travelled in Italy to imbibe the newly fashionable classical architecture at source. One of Wilkinson's published drawings from this period (Arthur Cates Prize, *RIBA Journal* 3rd Series XVII 1909) shows the Palazzo Tarugi in Montepulciano in Tuscany, a fascinating mannerist composition by Antonio Sangallo the elder, an unusual and inspired choice of study for its period, although a building with links to the contemporary use of classicism by Sir Edwin Lutyens or Sir J.J. Burnet. Wilkinson also imbibed the latest fashion in Britain for the Regency period, which he was to reproduce to good effect in Sydney in his domestic work. His architecture at Sydney University is partly Tudor Gothic and partly Classical, a combination of tastes shared by American university buildings at this period. While the Gothic buildings speak of provincialism, the columnar entrance to the physics building, with its Italianate overhanging eaves and sudden monumental scale, is as good of its kind as anything in Britain in the 1920s.

Wilkinson's own work, generously illustrated in a monograph of 1982, was conservative and traditional in its picturesqueness, but as McGrath wrote (in the Basic English of 'Twentieth Century Houses') of his own house in 1921, Greenway at Vaucluse, Sydney, "...unhappily, the public only saw the little bits of Spanish ironwork in these designs, the highly coloured coats-of-arms and such-like details" rather than the adaptation to climate in the plan and structure which Wilkinson's work displayed. Compared with the over-formal neo-Georgian common in England in the 1920s, these asymmetrical courtyard houses are subtle and understated, with a strong relationship to nature which was to typify McGrath's mature work.

McGrath's surviving student drawings show the exercises in Tudor and Gothic necessary for the exams, which were controlled with a standard syllabus from London, but also his development of the Chinese theme, which introduced colour and decoration into his designs without achieving any synthesis. They are more like the Chinoiserie efforts of the late Georgian and Regency period. All are more beautifully drawn and rendered than was common even in this period of high graphic attainment.

It was not surprising that Wilkinson's influence should have led McGrath to the Tuscan Renaissance and Brunelleschi. This phase of the Renaissance had been given widespread additional popularity in Geoffrey Scott's book 'The Architecture of Humanism', first published in 1914 and reprinted in 1924. Although Scott's book is sometimes taken too simply as a shorthand for English architectural theory of the 1920s, it was widely read and provided grounds for rejecting the unfashionable legacy of Ruskin, while further weakening English architecture's already tenuous links with constructional reality and social responsibility in favour of a hedonistic 'Art for Art's Sake'. Its philosophy was certainly prevalent in the Cambridge School of Architecture, as revealed in the publications of one of its lecturers, T.H. Lyon.

The architectural scene in England on which McGrath arrived in 1926 seems in retrospect a peculiar one. Although the work of the more extreme modern architects of the continent was known from books and journals, it had made no impact on anything built in Britain apart from the house designed for W. Basset-Lowke by Peter Behrens in Northampton.

All of this was to change within three or four years, partly as a result of McGrath's work with Mansfield Forbes, and partly through the efforts of other outsiders, non-architects who wrote books and articles and commissioned buildings. Joining McGrath among the outsiders by nationality were the New Zealanders Amyas Connell, Basil Ward and George Checkley and the Canadian Wells Coates.

There was nothing inevitable about the importation of the 'Modern Movement' into England, although by the time that McGrath wrote 'Twentieth Century Houses' in 1934, it had become an accepted commonplace to trace its evolution from William Morris, C.F.A. Voysey and Charles Rennie Mackintosh and treat it as a native product re-acclimatised, Mansfield Forbes was unique as an architectural patron at this period, not only granting liberty to develop new ideas, but leading with a highly informed knowledge of architecture and building. His circle provided opportunities for the interaction of architecture with a more general culture, something that isolated architects in the 1920s desperately needed. One can imagine the effect on the unsystematic critical thought of architects of meeting at Finella such incisive minds as I.A. Richards.

Although unlike anything seen in England before, Finella was hardly part of the Modern Movement at all. It appears to owe much to the architecture of exhibition displays, something to the French 'Style Moderne' which followed after the 1925

Paris Exhibition, and something to the lightweight decorative classicism and whimsical iconography popular in Sweden before 1930. None of this adds up to what is usually defined as 'Art Deco'. McGrath found outlets for his drawing skill in the ornamentation of this and later buildings, but here, as nowhere else, he did have the opportunity to develop a literary iconography.

Anyone interested in the meaning of the interiors at Finella must read Hugh Carey's 'Mansfield Forbes and his Cambridge', but even this gives no definite key to the iconography. It is as individual as the Tempio Malatestiana in Rimini, another building which was a clothing or fitting out of an earlier shell by an impoverished patron. McGrath's achievement was to respond to Forbes's fey and whimsical notions about Pictish (or Pictavian) myth with an appropriate visual form. No other architect or decorator in England at the time could have done it, and its success is not surprising. At the end of the 1920s, the decade had suddenly found its own style in a house typically given over to the holding of parties. It was a building of child-like innocence and naughtiness – a temporary release from the pressures of real life.

At Finella, the exterior was lightly adapted, lacking the totem-pole at the entrance which McGrath intended. The metal-framed doors led beneath a Swedish-style porch to the hall, which was probably always the most dramatic moment in the design, with glass linings to the vault, reflective walls, concealed lighting in the thresholds and niches, and inlaid decoration in the floors. Beyond this was relative calm, with the twin pink drawing rooms, divided by copper plymax folding doors, and the dining room with its acid-etched dome, decorative floor and niche hollowed out of the chimney-breast.

Compared with Finella, imaginary projects like Lord Benbow's drawing room lack the charm of real personality. The Broadcasting House interiors lead on from Finella, and place McGrath in context with two of his major contemporaries – both, like him, misfits in the conventional world of English architecture. Wells Coates had no architectural training, and was only beginning to change career from journalist to designer. Serge Chermayeff had picked up an unconventional training, and was not to complete a building until 1934, although in 1930 he was already an accomplished interior designer.

Coates was given non-public technical areas in Broadcasting House for which his austere functionalist approach was suitable. Chermayeff revealed a subdued softness in his interiors, the style of visual and psychological comfort which he was to develop throughout his career. McGrath's interiors are the boldest and most dynamic in use of colour, with directional banding on the floors. He was inclined to streamlining effects, but they are always bold and held in balance. The smaller-scale, Swedish-inspired detail of Finella temporarily disappears from view. The whole group of interiors represents an important transitional stage in English Modernism, with a growing consciousness of maturity. McGrath's design for the entrance, had it been chosen instead of the more conventional version by Val Myer, would have given the passing public more of an idea of what was concealed behind the solid façades.

As a designer of interiors, McGrath's next major opportunities were to come with the Embassy Club and Fischer's Restaurant, where the experience of providing party settings, learnt at Finella, came into play. At Fischer's, inlaid patterns, reflective surfaces, metals and glass, all have roles in the drama, and all are brought together by lighting, reputedly flattering to the complexion. The repetitive horizontal banding of the floor suggests an influence from the later Amsterdam School. The Embassy appears to have been more reserved and aristocratic in tone, with a greater emphasis on textiles and incised mirrors. Also widely published was the flat at Bell Moor, a rather dreary neo-Tudor block overlooking Hampstead Heath, designed by McGrath for Mr. Garcia, the director of Aspro who was later to offer him the tempting prize of a complete factory to design.

Among the opportunities for young designers at this time, exhibition stands offered possibilities for publicity and for the extravagant use of materials for the benefit of different manufacturers. The only works of Le Corbusier erected on British soil took the form of exhibition stands. McGrath's Black Glass dining room for the General Electric Co. at Olympia, 1931, is a successor to Finella with a niche over the door holding a Maurice Lambert sculpture and a frieze of what appear to be Pictavian warriors. The black polished plate glass walls and ceiling are illustrated in the *Architectural Review* for January 1932 opposite an introductory text by McGrath, 'Looking into Glass', which contains one of the earliest discussions in England of the work of Mies van der Rohe. It is worth quoting at length for its crystallisation of a moment of discovery:

> The architecture of symmetry, axes, vistas and shapely plans has been superseded by an architecture of spaces and asymmetry. This architecture remains imperfect and incomplete and as yet vulnerable to classical criticism. Yet it is beyond this criticism and constitutes for many of us an inspiration and a portent.
>
> To Mies van der Rohe belongs the credit of imbuing modern architectural forms with the genuine spiritual qualities of great design. His magnificent simplicity, his sensitiveness to form and his understanding of spatial relationships, combine to make his rare works outstanding. He is known particularly by his interiors at the Plate Glass Exhibition at Stuttgart, by his German Pavilion at the Barcelona Exhibition, and most recently by his Haus Tugendhat at Brunn.
>
> At Stuttgart, he discovered the value of black glass in creating depth and space. At Barcelona, the black glass wall of his terrace reflected in dark tones the foliage of the whole garden. This pavilion was clean and empty, in a strange contrast to the other exhibition stands. Its rooms and patios were uninhabited. Sudden encounter with metaphysical architecture brought home its quality.
>
> The House at Brunn is an arrangement of connected and related spaces. The living room with its screens of waxed wood and honey-coloured onyx, is divided only by plate glass walls from the garden, and along one side of it, as in a glass avenue, runs the Winter Garden.

Seen against this knowledge and sophisticated insight, McGrath's work for subsequent exhibitions fails to climb out of English modernist provincialism, enjoyable though it may have been. He played a part in the two successive exhibitions, in 1933 and 1934 at the Dorland Hall, for which Oliver Hill was the chief designer. The experience of Finella seems to have played an important part in Hill's conversion to Modernism. Both he and McGrath were natural exhibition designers, enjoying dramatic effects which pointed up the inherent physical and decorative qualities of the materials. They were selflessly dedicated to the promotion of modern design and enjoyed a cordial relationship, even though Chermayeff and Coates were among a group which publicly repudiated Hill's extravagant stunts such as snakeskin furniture in the 1934 show. McGrath's devotion to glass was shared by Hill, and the 1933 exhibition may have taken some inspiration from Finella in its theme of deriving modern forms of design from the nature of different materials.

For the highly successful 1933 exhibition, McGrath designed some engraved glass, but principally a specimen bedroom, with built-in furniture in ash, in a colour scheme of lemon yellow and chartreuse with a black and vermilion carpet. McGrath stayed faithfully in the team for the 1934 exhibition, a less well funded and more problematic affair, designing the catalogue cover and Snack Bar. For Hill's British Pavilion at the 1937 exhibition in Paris, McGrath also designed decorative glass panels for the entrance lobby. His last major exhibition work was the Electrical Section of the Women's Exhibition, Olympia in 1938, which shows his adoption of the style common at the end of the decade, much concerned with framing motifs, condensed lettering and tilted angles. Some of the displays enjoy touches of surrealism.

McGrath's personality as an architect rather than as an interior designer took longer to emerge. Viewed critically, the Rudderbar design of 1932 is incoherent. Some charming coloured sketches for a seaside hotel by the Mediterranean, which may date from this time, are more inspired. His need was to find a way to channel his fertile imagination into built forms of a sufficient maturity and simplicity. To have written as he did on Mies van der Rohe in 1932, McGrath showed that he was clearly aware of the possibilities that Modernism had opened.

From the year 1934, England had two other leading German émigré architects as short-term guests, Walter Gropius and Erich Mendelsohn. While McGrath expressed his admiration for Gropius then and later in life, it is likely that Mendelsohn, who became the partner to Serge Chermayeff that McGrath might have been, should have had an effect on his work. Mendelsohn is quoted in 'Twentieth Century Houses' on the need for discipline in house design. The phrase "rigorously limited" is applied by Mendelsohn to the overuse of architectural details. His poetic intention in architecture and his desire to express philosophical ideas in built form would have been close to McGrath's instincts, although Mendelsohn's accumulated wisdom and experience gave his designs an authority McGrath could not yet possess.

Two unbuilt projects of McGrath from 1934 would support this theory. The house for A.M. Garcia at Coombe, Surrey, one of the first modern designs to be rejected by a local council on aesthetic grounds under the 1932 Town and Country Planning Act, is not a brilliant plan, but in McGrath's low level perspective view expresses a dynamic quality in its curves and a search for unity.

The Hyde Park Court flats of the same year are unusual in their geometry and boldness. With the toned surface materials seen in the drawings, and the smoothed corners, they have some of the qualities of Frank Lloyd Wright's Johnson Research Tower of 1944-50, the neighbour and successor to the famous office building, but Mendelsohn may be the common source. As a plan form, they are quite unlike any of the modern flats built in England during the 1930s, which are all relentlessly orthogonal, apart from the circular Lowndes Court by Burnet, Tait and Lorne of 1937. McGrath's design seems to anticipate ideas of the 1950s about grouping around stairways and service cores. It had the distinction of being illustrated in Alberto Sartoris's international survey of modern architecture.

From 1935 came another unexecuted project, the Hotel-Airport (with Walter Goodesmith), with its curved and strongly banded hotel overlooking a large swimming pool, the back of whose grandstand forms the hangar for the adjoining airfield. Mendelsohn comes once more to mind. As a compendium of 1930s ideas of speed in the air, the water and in transitory dwelling, it would be hard to beat.

Similarly speculative is the design by McGrath for a replacement for the Crystal

Palace, which had burnt down in November, 1936. Pilkingtons also invited Maxwell Fry and Oliver Bernard to submit designs, and McGrath's, although only existing in the form of perspective, is the boldest of the three. Its glass is supported only on the thinnest framework, and the design is presented in the form of an extruded section, with north light glazing above and a sweeping horizontal frontage. It was something even to have dreamed so pure and glassy an architecture in 1937.

It was not in Sydenham but at St. Ann's Hill, Chertsey, however, that McGrath's architecture came of age, and with no exceptional pyrotechnics in glass. It is still the most surprising, daring and satisfying of the modern houses of the thirties, suggesting the potential for formal development which modernism seldom explored. A genealogy for the circular form can be constructed from the café at Canvey Island, Essex, by Ove Arup, built as part of the sea wall defences by Christiani and Nielsen in 1932 and still existing, via the Gorilla House at London Zoo by Lubetkin and Tecton, 1933, to the project for a circular house by Raymond Mysercough Walker published in September 1934. This bearded and eccentric architect and perspectivist once danced Mary McGrath off her feet.

Neither Myerscough Walker's ideal project, nor his realisation of it at Chilwall in Nottinghamshire in 1937 bears much relation to St. Ann's in plan. One realises that part of McGrath's skill in planning the house was not to create a central circular staircase, as Myerscough did, however tempting that may have been. The stairs are in a conventional position near the entrance door, but the hall is the most exciting room in the house with its balance of curved forms extending upwards through the double height. By cutting away a segment of the garden side, the living room can be composed entirely from concave forms, with a calm and restful effect.

Externally, the overall geometry of concentric cylinders remains clear but McGrath was able to introduce the complexity of detail which fascinated him, without loss of clarity. This applies particularly to the extension of the building into the garden as a segmental architectural framework struck from the same centre as the house. Here, if anywhere, the influence of Paul Nash's mysterious evocations of Platonic geometry in landscape achieves an architectural reality.

As in the neo-classical period, which produced circular houses like John Plaw's Belle Isle on Windermere, so in the 1930s houses related to their surroundings by deliberate contrast. Here the relationship, no doubt also the product of Christopher Tunnard's thinking on the subject, seems perfect. The interlocking beams of the roof terrace act as crisp frames for the view and for the leafy background. From the roof terrace, one looks down onto the simple curve of the swimming pool, itself leading into the Augustan landscape.

The board-marked concrete of St. Ann's Hill comes as a surprise. Although not unique in 1930s Modernism, it is suited to the cylindrical form and suggests a desire for more texture than the more popular use of render. Texture appears more frequently in English Modernism after 1937, and McGrath played his part in this shift. Given his strong concern from the time of Finella with materials, he would have been sensitive to their contribution to architectural form and appreciated the new tendency, which produced timber houses by Maxwell Fry, Connell Ward and Lucas, and, most notably, Serge Chermayeff's own house, Bentley Wood at Halland, clad in Canadian red cedar and built with a frame of jarrah wood. F.R.S. Yorke and Marcel Breuer followed Le Corbusier's lead in the use of rubble stone walling.

In 1938, McGrath worked on plans for a house at Chislehurst, Kent, for H. Marsham-Townsend. This was to become another unrealised scheme, although two alternative versions are shown in perspectives. The plan-form is a segment of a circle, with a two-sided entrance court formed by a single storey service wing extending from the body of the house. Neither version is particularly elegant and, unless the design had progressed further, there is no loss to be regretted.

During the years 1937 to 1939, Frank Lloyd Wright began to have a renewed impact in English modernism, finding a welcome reception among architects who had already tired of pure white geometry. His work of the later 1930s like Falling Water, coming after the publication of McGrath's 'Twentieth Century Houses', offered a more exciting model than anything Wright had done since 1914.

Carrygate at Galby was McGrath's built contribution to this genre, although designs exist for other houses in the same style. As with St. Ann's Hill, the geometry of the plan is one of the most remarkable aspects of the house. In the illustration by Gordon Cullen of an earlier scheme for the house, published in Christopher Tunnard's 'Gardens in the Modern Landscape', the centre of the house is cranked, but as built, the curved end containing the drawing room and master bedroom merges into a straight run of rooms, with a series of emphatic horizontals. A peculiarity is that the narrow upstairs corridor faces the landscape, rather than the bedrooms, but since this is the area most used in daylight, it is a rational solution. The monopitch roofs occur in a number of designs of this period, not all of them built. McGrath himself made a pleasing design for a timber house at Cobham in 1937, also illustrated in Tunnard's book, with broad overhang on the upper storey, which is recessed itself to form a balcony.

Compared with the obvious architectural drama of St. Ann's Hill, Carrygate is modest and retiring, yet it has Christopher Tunnard's hand in landscaping as a common link. In spite of recent interest in Tunnard's work, his contribution is still hard to assess. At Carrygate, any kind of formal gardening is kept close to the house and confined to planters on a terrace, all architecturally planned. The landscape flows freely up to the house. It may be, however, that McGrath, like the Regency architects he admired, found in attention to landscape the key to stylistic liberation and greater freedom of form, which for many architects immediately after the war was to lead away from the rigid geometry of Modernism towards a picturesque revival.

It was McGrath's earlier building for the same client (Charles Keene), the Kingstone Store in Leicester, which took the aesthetic of Finella onto the streets in 1937, with shell pink vitrolite banded with copper cover strips. As a stirring but virtually forgotten building, it deserves more attention, although the remarkable materials are treated in a polite and restrained manner, with overhanging eaves. These eaves, used again at Carrygate, were an unusual feature for modern architecture in England. Do they suggest an Australian's instinctive desire for a hat-brim, or a classically articulated termination with cast shadow? The board room, with the same fabric covering walls and bench seating, seems a restful solution to a small space.

Only at Leicester was McGrath able to use glass extensively as a facing material. The design for the Aspro factory, a much larger concern published in 1938, and ready to start on site that year, would have been no English equivalent of the Brinkmann's Van der Nelle factory in Rotterdam, with gleaming curtain walls of glass. The design is difficult to discuss, as it exists in so many versions, and would doubtless have changed again had it proceeded to construction.

The factory floor itself forms a large square on plan (wedge shaped in the last version), fronted by a long row of offices covered with rows of windows flush to the facing of precast slabs. A shallow curved block of directors' offices, standing forward from these on the front lawn of the factory, remains a constant feature of all the schemes. From the variety of elevational treatments tried out for this, it appears to have been a problem. Although this description suggests the type of plan used by Wallis Gilbert and Partners for their factories which were a byword of contempt among progressive architects, the Aspro factory had a broad-fronted site, allowing the flank of the factory to be occupied by extensive social buildings. With a circular canteen, concert hall, gymnasium and swimming pool, as well as generous circulation spaces, this would have been the best-equipped factory in Britain. The outdoor facilities would have included playing fields, a bowling green and kitchen garden. All that was built was the pavilion for the bowling green, the sketches for which suggest a great attention to detail in the manner of Berthold Lubetkin, another of the architectural influences absorbed by McGrath's receptive eye.

The account does not include every work, built or unbuilt. Some in each category failed to measure up to the highest standard that McGrath had set himself, but one most regrets the loss or non-realisation of the smaller designs such as shop interiors and shop fronts. The Easiwork Shopfront in Tottenham Court Road was admired by contemporaries, and the Polyfoto shop is presented in such enticing graphics that the reality, had it been achieved, could not have failed to be stimulating and memorable.

Of the London architects connected with the Modern Movement in the later 1930s, Raymond McGrath appears to have taken the greatest interest in the history and conservation of Georgian architecture. This is evident in his support of the Londoner's League, run by his former colleague on the Broadcasting House commission, Dorothy Trotter. It is clearer still in his intriguing research and publication on the New River in Islington. From the evidence of his student years, these historical interests should come as no surprise; neither should the wiry line drawings and the exquisite water-colours, such as the Paul Nash-like vision of a climbing frame on snowy ground by night. There is a subtle suggestion of a new poetics of urban history in the New River article. While comparable with the revival of picturesque antiquarianism undertaken by John Piper in these years, McGrath's approach is that of a working architect and planner.

The water-colours were to fill part of the gap left in McGrath's creative life after he left London. Raymond McGrath's move to Ireland in 1940 made a decisive break in his career. Not only was his geographical position different, but as a State employee, so was his professional one. Such changes were common in careers at the time, and often involved even greater shifts. Serge Chermayeff went to America, and although he designed a number of houses, achieved his ambition of becoming a teacher. Wells Coates went to Canada, although he returned to England. Amyas Connell went to Kenya after the war, only to return to England on retirement, and his former partner Colin Lucas joined the LCC Architects' Department and remained in salaried employment for the rest of his career. There were relatively few architects eminent as Modernists before the war who like Maxwell Fry or F.R.S. Yorke survived to re-establish their practices and thrived.

It is against this background that McGrath's Irish work must be assessed. Although Ireland was far from being a backwater in modernist terms, the opportunities for building were limited by circumstances and by the presence of rivals such as Michael Scott, as Donal O'Donovan describes. In the circumstances, the work which McGrath was able to accomplish is interesting in its indication of tendencies not necessarily compatible with the text-book model of a modernist.

The Cenotaph on Leinster Lawn (1950), for example, is a piece of official architecture in the full sense of the word, such as modernists had little or no vocabulary to cope with. In adapting and refining a neo-classical precedent, the Obelisk, McGrath provided an object which adorned its sensitive setting and could be registered either as part of a classical continuum, or as a piece of abstract geometry. Less ambivalent, certainly, would have been the Davis Memorial in St. Stephen's Green (1945), had it been carried out in the stripped classical style shown in McGrath's elegant perspective.

Among the larger unexecuted projects, drawings exist for Television Studios at Montrose, Dublin, in 1960, evidently taken only to sketch stage. The curving front block, with a slender link to the main building ranged axially behind, is a clear reminiscence of the Aspro factory. Behind this rises a production studio with a two-way stretch shell-concrete dome, lit from the segmental spangles, in the manner of the Brynmawr Rubber Factory by Architects Co-partnership of 1951. The elevational treatment of simple regular bays is symptomatic of the age that began to see great virtues in Mies van der Rohe.

Before the war, McGrath had anticipated aspects of the sculptural, would-be-baroque quality of many 1950s buildings. There is no evidence that he would have developed this way, since he seems to have become more serenely classical in temperament, but then the decade which should have found him at his creative peak produced fewer opportunities than any in his career. Those opportunities he had did enable him to play a part in the spirit of the decade, with the design of Donegal carpets for Irish Embassies and for the restoration of Dublin Castle. Although historical sensitivity and a skill in pattern design are not necessarily attributes of a great modern architect, McGrath was able to fulfil some of the promise in interior design shown in the 1930s. Translating a classical vocabulary at Dublin Castle into the large-scale weave of the Donegal workshops prevented over-attention to small details and provided a fine means of re-interpreting tradition. Here, too, a painter's sense of colour was needed and McGrath responded with a full range of strong colours. The Dublin Castle project consisted of more than carpets, however. McGrath's sensitive and scholarly eye was a fortunate find for his adopted country.

Had the National Concert Hall proposed as an extension of the Rotunda Hospital in Dublin materialised in its first manifestation in 1946, McGrath's whole career might have widened. It is not clear what form it would have taken, but McGrath's sketches made on his tour of Sweden, Denmark and other countries at the time shows his enjoyment of the lightweight Modernist style found in the Malmö Concert Hall by Sven Markelius and the Broadcasting House in Copenhagen by Villem Lauritzen.

When the concert hall project was revived in 1964, as a national memorial to John F. Kennedy, it carried forward elements of the former plan, but the world of architecture had by then changed significantly. A further study tour was made, now including the new Philharmonie in Berlin, designed by another veteran of the 1930s, Hans Scharoun. McGrath's formation of his own scheme can be interpreted in the light of his characteristically self-effacing comment in a report on the genesis of the project written in 1967:

> Stuttgart and Berlin each made their particular impressions and it was surprising that when queried about his reaction to the very dynamic 'Philharmonie', the Chairman of the Committee said: "If I had been an architect that is the sort of building I would like to have designed." His remark gave the architect courage in his task.

McGrath's approach to the concert hall design is described in the same document, with some insight into his own position in the post-war architectural world:

A tempting approach to the building was from what I might call the *classical Miesian grid*, good examples of which are Nürnberg, Rotterdam and Tel Aviv. In this Miesian concept, the hall or halls emerge in their true shapes, or else struggle to emerge, from a rectangular cage which accommodates all the ancillary accommodation – the foyers, artists' rooms, administration, restaurants, etc... The Miesian grid is a tidy solution to the planning problem with a certain structural simplicity about it, but I was not satisfied that this was really enough. I felt that it was the main hall itself which should express itself clearly in the exterior of the building, as in the Liederhalle in Stuttgart and the Philharmonie in Berlin, both of which may be described as *organic plans*. But whereas these two buildings are romantic in character, my own feeling was for a *classical organic plan*, a plan developed symmetrically on its axes.

Given the relatively open site proposed on Haddington Road, in the southern suburbs of Dublin, where the building was to be approached from both sides, this seemed particularly fitting. The genesis of McGrath's design in Scharoun's hall is apparent in the irregular polygon of the exterior, and the linking of large and small halls with a 'waist' in the form of a foyer. The main hall, however, never realised the radicalism of Scharoun's surrounding the platform with terraces of seating, with its implied breaking down of distinctions of price, and hence of class. To criticise McGrath for not being Scharoun would, however, be unproductive. The Berlin Philharmonie was an exceptional work in every way, and the problems in Dublin were different and acute.

Not only was the source of funding a perennial and ultimately fatal source of uncertainty, but the multiple function of the building was continually in dispute and several essentially incompatible uses had to be accommodated, including stage performances and conferences. A multitude of experts in acoustics, organs and structure had to provide their views, still leaving room for premature criticism of the unbuilt building in the press.

As the head of the firm of consulting engineers to be employed, Ove Arup wrote enthusiastically to McGrath about the design in December 1965: "I was very pleased indeed about the new look of the Kennedy Hall. I think this is absolutely right. Now the two massive blocks are shown and the connection and auxiliary structures are very strong and simple and this is much better than anything I have seen before."

In its various versions, the Kennedy Memorial Concert Hall is surprisingly massive by contrast to any earlier works by McGrath. This was partly in the nature of the brief, requiring no external windows, and acknowledging the need to exclude sound. Yet the form of the hall also seems to reflect the international architectural currents of its time. In London terms, it corresponds to the Queen Elizabeth Hall rather than the Royal Festival Hall. McGrath visited the former on its opening in 1965 and collected cuttings criticising and praising its acoustics. Yet the Kennedy Hall, in its balance of the classical and organic, avoids the randomness introduced to the South Bank by the young team of GLC architects. The balance struck is reminiscent, rather than imitative, of the later work of Marcel Breuer with its development of faceted non-rectilinear forms. It was Breuer's design for the IBM Research Centre at La Gaule in France (1961) that McGrath illustrated in his report for the *Irish Times* on the London Bauhaus exhibition of 1968, with evident approval.

The exploration of unusual angles in the organic manner of Scharoun is the theme of the Mitchell house at Carrickmines, 1972, the fruit of McGrath's early years of retirement. It displays all the expertise in house planning he had developed before the war with a cranked plan descended from Carrygate at Galby. The scale is small, and the opportunities restricted, but it achieves character with its Italianate chimneys and moon window in a spur wall, framing the view as one moves round towards the garden.

More engaging as a concept, though, is the sketch design for the Patterson Guest House in New York State, dated 6th February 1976, a square turned through 45 degrees, presenting a symmetrical elevation with a cut-off corner shaded beneath an overhanging roof, capped by a central chimney. The single bedroom interior is neatly planned within the geometry. Although not built, this design could provide any number of distinguished holiday chalets today.

However ingenious a solution the Kennedy Memorial Concert Hall design may have been to a complex series of problems, neither the surviving drawings nor memories of contemporaries can raise it to the level of a great unbuilt work. The reasons for this may not be hard to find. Was McGrath, who for so long had no chances to build in the later modern idiom, unpractised in the forms he adopted? Was the creative tension between architect and client, so valuable from the time of Finella onwards, lacking, since he was almost in effect his own client? Although criticism is strangely silent about the actual appearance of the design, it may be that lack of enthusiasm in the architectural community was the deciding factor in the ultimate failure to get a building started, let alone finished. For once, McGrath was playing Modernism strictly by the rules. The quality of delight which he had so often in the past managed to smuggle past the guardians of moral rectitude and strict functionalism seems never to have come anywhere near the concert hall design.

The feeling that one may have today that, whatever the personal tribulations in the architect's own life from this failure, it was better for his reputation that the concert hall was not built may be the temporary reaction of a generation for whom this manner of architecture is still hard to swallow. One can only hope that had it been built, some special quality not evident in the drawings would have lifted the fortress-like polygons into poetry.

Without this concrete example of a late McGrath style, the historian is left to appraise the Matthew Gallagher Galleries for the Royal Hibernian Academy. This building owes its completion to McGrath's colleague and successor as Professor of Architecture in the R.H.A., Arthur Gibney, and does not represent a finished design by McGrath. Nonetheless, the concept of a brick gallery 'box' mounted on a recessed and largely transparent plinth derives from McGrath's second scheme, the first having been for a cylindrical gallery, more exciting perhaps, but disruptive of the street frontage and less economical in land use.

It is a well-resolved scheme, providing two clearly contrasted spaces for exhibitions of different character. The central stair provides a formality suitable to an august institution, and one arrives into the high, lit space of the upper gallery with a sense of occasion. The columns of the lower gallery are once more from the stable of Marcel Breuer, but they are neatly detailed and scaled. The total effect, however, in the management of light and simplicity of overall form, can be compared to Louis Kahn. The galleries will stand as proof that McGrath had found it possible, in the words of the psalm, to sing "in a strange land".

REFERENCES

1. Fort Street: The School. By Ronald S. Horan. Honeysett Publications. Leichhardt, New South Wales. 1989.
2. Interview, May 1990.
3. M.L.S.L.N.S.W.
4. Letter from Black to Andrew Metcalf, architect and lecturer in the University of Newcastle, New South Wales.
5. "Rhapsody in black glass". Raymond McGrath interviewed by Brian Hanson. *Architectural Review*, July 1977.
6. Old Colonial Architecture in New South Wales and Tasmania. By Hardy Wilson. Published by the author at Union House, Sydney, in an edition of 1,000. 1924.
7. Hanson. Op. cit.
8. M.L.S.L.N.S.W.
9. *The Home*, September 1930.
10. View of Deborah Edwards, Curator of Sculpture and Decorative Arts, Australian Art Department, Art Gallery of New South Wales, expressed to the author in February 1992.
11. M.L.S.L.N.S.W.
12. Letter supplied by Professor T.H. Beaglehole of the Victoria University of Wellington, New Zealand, May 1991.
13. The Muse Unchained. E.M.W. Tillyard. London. 1958.
14. A History of Western Architecture. By David Watkin. Barrie and Jenkins. London. 1986.
15. Mansfield Forbes and his Cambridge. By Hugh Carey. Cambridge University Press. 1984.
16. C.C.C.A.
17. Rima (Riolama) is the child-heroine of W.H. Hudson's book "Green Mansions" (1904). McGrath's reference is to Jacob Epstein's sculpture of Rima.
18. M.L.S.L.N.S.W.
19. The Eye of the Beholder. By Lance Sieveking. Hulton. London. 1957.
20. Mansfield Forbes and his Cambridge. By Hugh Carey. Cambridge University Press. 1984.
21. The Surnames of Ireland. By Edward MacLysaght. Irish Academic Press, Dublin. 1985 (sixth edition).
22. Volume II 1923–50. Angus and Robertson. London, Sydney, Melbourne. 1985.
23. Indigo Days. By Julian Trevelyan. MacGibbon and Kee. London. 1957.
24. The Eye of the Beholder. By Lance Sieveking. Hulton. London. 1957.
25. Guide to Western Architecture. John Gloag. Allen and Unwin. London 1958.
26. "Rhapsody in Black Glass": Raymond McGrath interviewed by Brian Hanson, *Architectural Review*, July 1977.
27. John Warnock was working on a life of Raymond McGrath when he died in February, 1990. He was 45 and a well-known and much-loved Australian writer and broadcaster.
28. Eric Gill. Fiona McCarthy. Faber and Faber. London 1989.
29. Indigo Days. By Julian Trevelyan. MacGibbon and Kee. London. 1957.
30. A Dictionary of Architecture. Nikolaus Pevsner, John Fleming, Hugh Honour. Allen Lane, London 1957 (Revised edition).
31. Rhapsody in Black Glass. Brian Hanson. *Architectural Review*. July 1977.
32. The Decorative Thirties. Martin Battersby. Studio Vista. London 1976.
33. Eric Gill. By Fiona McCarthy. Faber and Faber. London 1990. This lively biography tells the story of Le Lavandou.
34. The Labyrinth and other poems. By James W. Mills. Williams and Norgate. London, 1930.
35. Twentieth Century Houses. By Raymond McGrath. Faber and Faber. London. 1934.

36. The Eye of the Beholder. By Lance Sieveking. Hulton. London. 1957.
37. Quoted in 'Wells Coates: A Monograph.' By Sherban Cantacuzino. Gordon Fraser. London. 1978.
38. Architecture of the 1930s. By David Dean. Trefoil, London and Rizzoli, New York. 1983.
39. B.B.C. Written Archives Centre. R35/247 18.2.31.
40. B.B.C. Written Archives Centre. R35/247 17.9.31
41. B.B.C. W.A.C. R35/247 13.10.31
42. B.B.C. W.A.C. R35/247 2.2.32
43. Ibid. 8.12.32.
44. The Wide Brown Land: A new Anthology of Australian Verse for Schools. By George Mackaness (with Joan S. Mackaness) Angus and Robertson. Sydney. 1934.
45. Britain in the 1930s. By Gavin Stamp. Academy Editions. London. 1979.
46. Ibid.
47. Information from Professor Kenneth Entwistle and Dr. D.E.H. Edgerton of Manchester University and Paul Lyon of Magnesium Elektron of Manchester.
48. Oliver Hill: Architect and Lover of Life 1887–1968. By Alan Powers. Mouton. London. 1989.
49. Architecture of the 1930s. by David Dean. Trefoil, London and Rizzoli, New York. 1983.
50. The Eye of the Beholder. By Lance Sieveking. Hulton. London 1957.
51. The Meaning of Modern Sculpture. By R.H. Wilenski. Faber and Faber. London. 1932.
52. The Modern House. By F.R.S. Yorke. Architectural Press. London. 1934.
53. The Eye of the Beholder. By Lance Sieveking. Hulton. London 1957.
54. Mansfield Forbes and His Cambridge. By Hugh Carey. Cambridge University Press. 1984.
55. Allan Gamble, who preceded Baldwinson as Senior Lecturer at Sydney, wrote 'The University of Sydney' (1952) and five other books as well as collaborating on a number of sketchbooks. His latest work is 'Down from Barranjoey: Sketch Impressions of the Peninsula'. Gamble. 1987
56. 66 Portland Place. By Margaret Richardson. R.I.B.A. Publications. London. 1984.
57. Alan Powers in 'Simple Intime — the Work of Raymond McGrath' (*Thirties Society Journal*, 1983) says the door was "designed by McGrath with Gordon Cullen".
58. Wells Coates: A Monograph. By Sherban Cantacuzino. Gordon Fraser. London. 1978.
59. Information from Architecture of the 1930s. By David Dean. Trefoil, London, and Rizzoli, New York. 1983.
60. Glass in Architecture and Decoration. By Raymond McGrath and A.C. Frost. Architectural Press. London. 1937. New revised edition 1961.
61. Design in Modern Life. Ed. John Gloag. George Allen and Unwin, London, 1934
62. Interview with McGrath, November 1976.
63. Mansfield Forbes and his Cambridge. By Hugh Carey. Cambridge University Press. 1984.
64. G.C.C.C.A.
65. Oliver Hill: Architect and Lover of Life. By Alan Powers. Mouton. London. 1989.
66. McGrath interview with Peter Varley, November, 1976. This was not John Tunnard the well-known painter
67. 'Strident modernism/ambivalent reconsiderations: Christopher Tunnard's "Gardens in the Modern Landscape" ' *Journal of Garden History*. 1990 Vol. 10 No. 4 By Lance M. Neckar Pp 237 – 246.

68. '20th Century Fox'. By Jane Brown. *The Times Saturday Review.* June 15 1991.
69. 'Rhapsody in Black Glass'. Raymond McGrath interviewed by Brian Hanson. *Architectural Review.* July 1977.
70. The Eye of the Beholder. By Lance Sieveking. Hutton. London 1957.
71. John Warnock's unpublished manuscript. Sydney. 1990.
72. 'A Country House near Leicester', by Ian Kitson. *Landscape Design*, September 1990. pp 22–26.
73. John Dunlap was a family friend.
74. 'Window on the World', by the Architectural Correspondent of *The Irish Times*, November 30, 1961 (Patrick Delany then held the position.)
75. Ibid.
76. Alan Powers in 'Oliver Hill: Architect and Lover of Life' says that Gertrude Hermes' and Raymond McGrath's glass works were to have been reused in the Newbury Park Underground station which Frank Pick commissioned in 1937. It did not happen. David Regan, who is writing a history of London Underground station architecture, has found a letter in Oliver Hill's papers written by McGrath and indicating that the reuse idea was his.
77. *The Irish Times* 21 May, 1976.
78. Architecture of the 1930s. By David Dean. Trefoil, London, and Rizzoli, New York. 1983.
79. Interview, New Orleans, November 1990.
80. Coping with Depression and Elation, By Dr. Patrick McKeon. Sheldon Press. London. 1986.
81. 'Living with Manic Depression', by Gillian Corcoran and Patrick McKeon. The *Irish Doctor,* October 1990.
82. Ireland in the War Years: 1939–1945. By Joseph T. Carroll. David and Charles, Newton Abbot, and Crane, Russak and Company, New York. 1975.
83. A Dictionary of Architecture. By Nikolaus Pevsner, John Fleming and Hugh Honour. Penguin Books. London 1975.
84. Ibid.
85. John Piper. By John Betjeman. Penguin Books. London. 1944.
86. Information about Dickey as painter comes from a letter to *The Irish Times* (31 December 1990) from S.B. Kennedy, Curator of Twentieth Century Art in the Ulster Museum; and from Irish Art and Modernism 1880–1950, by S.B. Kennedy, published by the Institute of Irish Studies at the Queen's University of Belfast. 1991.
87. Ireland 1912–1985: Politics and Society. By J. J. Lee. Cambridge University Press. 1989.
88. Mr Smyllie, Sir. By Tony Gray. Gill and Macmillan. Dublin 1991.
89. In Time of War. By Robert Fisk. Paladin. London. 1985.
90. Ireland 1912–1985. By J.J. Lee. Cambridge University Press. 1989.
91. This description of Professor Downes of the firm of Downes and Meehan was offered to the author by the present holder of the chair, Professor Cathal O'Neill.
92. Irish Art and Modernism: 1880–1950. By S.B. Kennedy. Institute of Irish Studies at the Queen's University of Belfast, 1991.
93. The Irish in Australia. By Patrick O'Farrell. New South Wales University Press. 1987.
94. Dreams and Responsibilities: The State and the Arts in Independent Ireland. By Brian P. Kennedy. The Arts Council. Dublin. 1990.
95. Dublin 1660–1860. By Maurice Craig. Allen Figgis. Dublin. 1969. (Second Edition.)
96. The Climate of Treason. By Andrew Boyle. Coronet. London. 1980.
97. 'Spectator' in the *Irish Independent* 28 May 1945. Kees van Hoek was the columnist.
98. The author is greatly indebted to Kenneth Smith, Sydney University's archivist, for his help with the university's records of this appointment.
99. To the Greater Glory: A History of the Irish Jesuits. By Louis McRedmond. Gill and Macmillan, Dublin. 1991.
100. Oliver Hill: Architect and Lover of Life 1887–1968. By Alan Powers. Mouton Publications. London, 1989.
101. Dreams and Responsibilities: The State and the Arts in Independent Ireland. By Brian P. Kennedy. The Arts Council. Dublin. 1990
102. Ireland and the New Architecture. By Seán Rothery. Lilliput, Dublin 1991.
103. Letter to the author, 25 February 1990.
104. The story of the Dublin Castle project is told in *Corridor Supplement 2* by A.S.R., February 1985
105. Information supplied by Frederick O'Dwyer of the Office of Public Works.
106. 'The Harp Restrung', *Irish Arts Review*, Vol. I No. 3, Autumn 1984, by Nicholas Sheaff.
107. William J. Feeney in the Dictionary of Irish Literature. Ed. Robert Hogan. Gill and Macmillan. Dublin. 1980.
108. All Cultivated People: A History of the United Arts Club, Dublin. By Patricia Boylan, Colin Smythe. Gerrards Cross. 1988.
109. Ireland 1912–1985. By J.J. Lee. Cambridge University Press. 1989.
110. 'The Harp Re-strung' by Nicholas Sheaff. *Irish Arts Review* Vol. 1 no. 3 Autumn 1984.
111. Ibid.
112. Statement by Charles J. Haughey, then Taoiseach, to the author in December 1980.
113. Interview 23 February 1990.
114. 'The Harp Re-strung', an article by Nicholas Sheaff in the *Irish Arts Review*, Vol. 1, No. 3, Autumn 1984.
115. Thom's Directory Ireland. 1955.
116. R.H.A. records.
117. Dreams and Responsibilities: The State and the Arts in Independent Ireland. By Brian P. Kennedy. The Arts Council. 1990.
118. The *Endeavour* Journal of Joseph Banks 1768–1771. Ed. J.C. Beaglehole. Public Library of New South Wales and Angus and Robertson. Sydney. 1962.
119. Dreams and responsibilities: The State and the Arts in Independent Ireland. By Brian P. Kennedy. The Arts Council. Dublin. 1990.
120. Ibid.
121. *The Irish Times* 4 October 1965.
122. The Kennedy Memorial Hall, *Oibre* No. 3. February 1966. Office of Public Works.
123. *The Irish Builder and Engineer*. 15 June 1968.
124. Ireland 1912–1985: Politics and Society. By J.J. Lee. Cambridge University Press. 1989.
125. *Martello*: Royal Hibernian Academy of Arts special issue 1991.
126. R.H.A. records.
127. I.A.A.
128. *Hibernia* 15 May 1970.
129. *Irish Times* 29 January 1971.
130. Letters to the author, 28 February 1990 and 15 March 1990.
131. Interview 23 February 1990.
132. *Corridor Supplement 2*, February 1985.
133. *The Irish Times* 12 September 1991.
134. *Business Press of Ireland*, May 1975.
135. Memoir to author, April 1991.
136. Tributes to Sir Robert Mayer. Privately printed at the Dolmen Press, Dublin. 1969.
137. Interview with the author November 1990.
138. Ireland and the New Architecture 1900–1940. By Seán Rothery. Lilliput Dublin. 1991.
139. Conversation Dublin 17 September 1990
140. R.H.A. records.
141. *The Irish Times* 6 December 1977.
142. *The Times* 23 December 1977.

CATALOGUE OF WORKS

The Black Fort, Aranmore. Inscribed as above, lower left and signed and dated lower right. 1944. Watercolour. 42 x 58cm. Derrick Oxley Contemporary Irish Art 1950, School of Design Museum, Rhode Island; Symphony Hall, Boston, Mass.; Canadian National Gallery, Ottawa. Irish Exhibition of Living Art, 1950, No.44. Country Life, 1950 p.3.

Fragments of Prose and Verse. Illustrated Book/Album 1917 water-colour 32.3 x 20cm. Jenny and Donal O'Donovan. Neptune Gallery, Dublin, l979.

Summer Sunshine. Inscribed, signed and dated. Probably an illustration. 1918. Pen and ink on an ochre wash. 19.5 x 33.5cm. Nevill Keating .

Rain Prince and Fire Demon. Illustrated Book/Album 1918 Water-colour 38.1 x 28.5cm. Mitchell Library, Sydney. Neptune Gallery, Dublin, No.45, 1975.

River Scene. Signed c.1919. Water-colour 23.6cm x 33cm. Nevill Keating.

He Spurred his Horse Faster Right to the Brink. Frontispiece to chapter II of a book, probably never published. c.1919 Water-colour 23.7 x 34 cm 4 Nevill Keating.

Kookaburra on a Branch. Signed and dated August 1918. Water-colour 21 x 30.3 cm. Nevill Keating.

Untitled. Illustrative Decoration, signed. c.1920. Water-colour 24.4 x 37.1cm. Nevill Keating.

Sydney House. Sketch. Signed and dated 1920. 1920. Pen and ink. 8.2 x 11cm. Nevill Keating.

Where Aurora's Gleaming Arches Shine. 1920-1929. Pen and brush on ink and pencil. 21.2 x 11.8cm on 42.7. Nevill Keating.

Haunted Castle. Inscribed, signed and dated l920. Probably an illustration. 1920. Pen and ink on blue wash. 13.2 x 24.2cm. Nevill Keating.

A Ti-Tree Silhouette. Inscribed, signed and dated '20. Probably an illustration. l920. Pen and ink on lilac wash. 24.2 x 33.3cm. Nevill Keating.

Moonrise. After Ida Rentoul Outhwaite. Signed and dated. 1920. Water-colour 30.5 x 24cm. Nevill Keating.

Pierrot's Song. Inscribed, signed and dated. Probably an illustration. 1920. Pen and ink on pink wash. 24.2 x 33.8cm. Nevill Keating.

The Rising Moon. Adapted from Ida Rentoul Outhwaite. Signed. c.1920. Water-colour. 24 x 32.8cm. Australian National Gallery, Canberra. Deutscher Gallery, Armadale, Victoria, l979.

St. John's Parramatta. c.1922. Water-colour. 17.7 x 12.7cm. Ken Pye.

Untitled. [Jester dancing with a ballerina.] Signed and dated. 1925 watercolour on pen and ink and brush on pencil. 29.0 x 20.4cm. Australian National Gallery, Canberra.

W. Nagle's Wagon. Signed and dated '21. 1921. Pen and ink. 24.5 x 22.2cm. Nevill Keating.

Illustration to Erinore – an Australian Legend of the Fairies. Similar Version bound in Dreams of the Orient. c.1921. Water-colour. 24 x 23.2cm. Nevill Keating.

Conversation. Signed and dated '21. 1921. Pen and ink 24.5 x 22.2cm. Nevill Keating.

Trees. Signed. c.1921. Water-colour 37.7 x 23.1cm. Nevill Keating.

Viaducts on Laptone Hill. 1921. Water-colour.

Government House, Sydney. No signed or numbered edition known. c.1921. Etching printed on wove paper 6.3 x 12.7cm. Deutscher Gallery, Armadale, Victoria, 1979 no.2.

Self Portrait. Signed and dated 1921. Pencil with slight beige wash. 34.5 x 24.2cm. Nevill Keating.

Glenbrook Creek. 1921. Water-colour.

Untitled. [Landscape]. Undated. c. 1920s. Unknown. Oil 42 x 30cm. Sydney University.

Two Songs of Albatross. Hermes, Vol.XXVIII, p.122; 1922.

The Art Gallery, Sydney. No signed and numbered edition known. Drawing of subject bound in manuscript book 'Dreams of the Orient and Other Poems, 1921. 1922. Etching printed on wove paper 17.8 x 18.8cm. Deutscher Gallery, Armadale, Victoria, 1979. No.3.

The Deserted Farmhouse, Ermington. Signed and numbered edition of 10, Title inscribed lower left. 1922. Etching-printed in sepia on wove paper. 7.5 x 13.9cm. Deutscher Gallery, Armadale, Victoria, 1979. no. 14.

The Hayshed, Windsor. Signed and numbered edition of 30. Inscribed in plate lower right R.H. McGrath/22, and with the title, lower left. 1922. Etching printed in sepia on Japanese vellum 8.9 x 18cm. Deutscher Gallery, Armadale, Victoria, 1979. No.15.

Looking for Work. Signed and numbered edition of 10. Sketch drawing in sepia on paper mounted on card exists in possession of Jenny and Donal O'Donovan. 1922 Drypoint. Unknown. Deutscher Gallery, Armadale, Victoria, l979. No.11 Art in Australia, September 1925 [listed in].

The Medical School. Signed and numbered of 20. Inscribed with title and R.H. McGrath l922. 1922. Etching printed in sepia on wove paper. 20 x 12.6cm. Deutscher Gallery, Armadale, Victoria, 1979. No.9.

Early Morning, Sydney Harbour. Signed and numbered edition of 10. 1922. Etching printed on laid paper 5.8 x 8.9cm. Deutscher Gallery, Armadale, Victoria, 1979, No.8; Neptune Gallery, Dublin, 1979.

Lennox Bridge, Parramatta. Signed and numbered edition of 5. Inscribed in plate R.H. McGrath 1922. 1922. Etching printed in sepia on wove paper 8.7 x 13.7cm. Deutscher Gallery, 1979, Armadale, Victoria No.13.

Killcare Wharf. Signed edition of 8. Inscribed lower left R McG 1922. Water-colour of above subject in 'Dreams of the Orient',1921. 1922. Etching printed in sepia on wove paper 12.9 x 21cm. Deutscher Gallery, Armadale, Victoria, 1979, No.4.

Untitled. Sketch of a child's head. Signed and dated 1922. 1922. Pencil on card 24.9 x 19.1cm. Jenny and Donal O'Donovan.

The Gargoyle, Sydney University. Signed and numbered edition of 14. Inscribed on plate R.H. McGrath. 1922. Drypoint printed in sepia on wove paper. 24 x 16.2cm. Deutscher Gallery, Armadale, Victoria, 1979, No.7.

Tiptoe Wrapper design 1. 1923. Pen, ink and water-colour 43.2 x 26.7cm. Australian National Gallery.

Tiptoe 'Contents' design and vignette IV. 1923. Pen, ink and water-colour. 43.2 x 26.7cm. Nevill Keating.

Tiptoe Frontispiece V. Signed. Illustration for poem 'By pools, where, under a moon forlorn/The Marsh maid melts into a pallid form.' 1923. Water-colour 43.2 x 26.7cm. Nevill Keating.

Tiptoe VI. Signed with initials. Illustration for 'Over the creeks and pebbled streams/Into that strange deep land of dreams'. 1923. Pen, ink and water-colour 43.2 x 26.7cm. Nevill Keating.

The Charm of Ettalong. Signed. Illustration for 'I Shall not sound for rapture/My syrinx in the rain/Or build my amber castles/Upon her hills again'. 1922. Pen and ink. 43.2 x 26.7cm. Sydney University, presented by Sir Victor Windeyer, Editor of Hermes. Hermes, Vol.XXVIII, New Series, No.1, May 1922, p.19; Vol.29, p.19, 1922.

Tiptoe (The Rubbish Bin). XII. Signed. Illustration for 'Such windy berylled, rubied boughs/As clasp Pomona's lovely brows' (The Rubbish Bin). 1923. Pen and ink 26.7 x 43.2cm. Nevill Keating.

Tiptoe (The Death of Shackleton). XIII. Illustration for 'Among the crankled mountains of the Horn' (The Death of Shackleton). Signed and dated '23. 1923. Pen and ink 43.2 x 26.7cm. Nevill Keating.

Tiptoe (The Death of Shackleton). XV. Signed, Illustration for 'And Ocean took the ship they sailed upon/Cresting a mighty wave heaped Helicon'. 1923. Water-colour on pen and ink and pencil 28.8 x 20.5cm. Australian National Gallery, Canberra.

Tiptoe XVI. Signed with initials. Illustration for first verse of 'Nineveh'. 1923. Pen and ink 43.2 x 26.7cm. Nevill Keating.

Tiptoe (A Song of Windsor across the River). XXI. Signed. Illustration for 'Girl Clouds, tossing their skirts of mirth/In scorn it seems of this sweet brown earth'. 1923. Pen and brush and ink and pencil. 29.0 x 20.5cm. Australian National Gallery, Canberra.

Tiptoe (To the native Thrush). XVII. Signed. Illustration for 'White the moon-light clear the flute'. 1923. Water-colour 43.2 x 26.7cm. Nevill Keating.

Tiptoe Epilogue XXII. Signed with initials. 1923. Pen and ink 43.2x26.7cm. Nevill Keating.

Parramatta. Signed and dated. A sketch of this subject exists in a sketchbook of c. 1922 in the possession of Jenny and Donal O'Donovan, pencil with notes for colour. 1923. Pencil 15.2 x 33cm. Donated by Jenny and Donal O'Donovan to the Mitchell Library, State Library of New South Wales. Neptune Gallery, Dublin, l979, No.1.

Lansdown Bridge from the Garden of Eden. Signed and numbered edition of 15. 1923. Etching printed in sepia on wove paper. 16.6 x 27.9cm. Deutscher

Gallery, Armadale, Victoria, l979, No.16.

Windsor across the River. Signed and numbered edition of 10. Inscribed in plate top right R McG, and lower right with the title. Illustration for poem *A Song of Windsor Across the River,* 'The tranquil sleep of this clean wide plain/ Where long boughs rustle and drowse again/And the river winds in purple haze/Crooning the rapture of halycon days'. 1923. Etching printed in sepia on laid paper 9 x 20.2cm. Deutscher Gallery ,Armadale, Victoria, 1979, No.17. Art in Australia, October, 1924, p.60.

The Tower, Sydney University. Signed and numbered edition of 25. 1923. Linocut printed on thin wove paper 30.6 x 19.4cm. Deutscher Gallery, Armadale, Victoria, 1979, No.23.

The Great Hall. Signed lower left. c.1923. Water-colour on card 17.5 x 9cm. Jenny and Donal O'Donovan.

Great Expectations. Signed and numbered edition of 25. Also entitled **The Fisherman.** 1924. Etching, printed in sepia on Japanese vellum. 17.8 x 18.4cm. Deutscher Gallery, Armadale, Victoria, 1979, No.20; Neptune Gallery, Dublin, 1979. Art in Australia, etching no. September 1925, pl.42.

The Isthmus. Signed and numbered edition of 25. 1924. Etching, printed on Japanese vellum. 22.3 x 18.3cm. Trial proof in possession of Ib Jorgenson. Deutscher Gallery, Armadale, Victoria, 1979, No.19; Neptune Gallery, Dublin, 1979, No.22.

The Women's College, Sydney University. Signed and numbered edition of 10. 1924. Woodengraving printed on Japanese vellum. 10.2 x 14.7cm. Deutscher Gallery, Armadale, Victoria, 1979, No.34. Included in 'Twenty Four Woodcuts'.

(Moonlight). No signed and numbered edition known. 1924. Wood engraving printed in a folded sheet of paper. Probably for use as a greeting card. 7 x 8.5cm. Deutscher Gallery, Armadale,Victoria, 1979, No.45. As a greeting card to George Mackaness, 1924.

Night, Sydney University. No signed or numbered edition known. c.1924. Aquatint printed on wove paper 13 x 18.7cm. Deutscher Gallery, Sydney, 1979, No.22.

Will You Set the Bells Ringing? Three colour poster for the war memorial of bells to hang in the Great Tower of Sydney University. 1924. Pencil on card 4.6 x 13.5cm. Australian National Gallery, Canberra.

The Seven Songs of Meadow Lane. Book of Poetry and Woodcuts by Raymond McGrath, 1924, Sydney. Limited edition of 30. 1924. Woodcuts 30 x 17.7cm. Neptune Gallery, Dublin, 1979, No.7.

Seven Songs of Meadow Lane. Cover-Piece. No signed and numbered edition known. 1924. Wood engraving printed on thin grey paper. 6.4 x 4.8cm. Deutscher Gallery, Armadale, Victoria, 1979, No.24.

The Seven Songs of Meadow Lane (The Haberdasher). Signed and numbered edition of 30 of which 25 were bound in Seven Songs. Decoration for the 1st song, *The Haberdasher,* 'Ben Button heard the cuckoo sing/From his dim haberdashery shop;/ Paused in his dogged book-keeping/Harkened the echoes thin, and stop/Awhile he stood; the pale shop light/Scarce filtering through the moted gloom;/For Youth came by him in the room!' 1924. Wood engraving printed on Japanese vellum. 9.6 x 7.7cm. Deutscher Gallery, Armadale, Victoria, 1979, No.27.

The Seven Songs of Meadow Lane (The Sunflower). Signed and numbered edition of 30, of which 25 were bound in 'Seven Songs'. Decoration for the 3rd Song, 'But if I in sadness/Have my heart cast down,/She will stand beside me/in her radiant gown,/With the golden sunflower/Fashioned for her crown!'. 1924. Wood engraving, printed on Japanese vellum. 12.1 x 6.4cm. Deutscher Gallery, Armadale, Victoria, 1979, No.29.

The Seven Songs of Meadow Lane, (Ice Cream Vendor). Signed and numbered edition of 30, of which 25 were bound in 'The Seven Songs'. Decoration for the 5th Song, 'The little children run/From every woken lane/With dusty feet and bare/To hear him wind again'. 1924. Wood engraving printed on Japanese vellum. 9 x 6.5cm. Deutscher Gallery, Armadale, Victoria, 1979, No.30. *Architecture,* Vol.XV, No. V. May 1926.

The Seven Songs of Meadow Lane (Pomona). Signed and numbered edition of 30, of which 25 were bound in Seven Songs. Decoration for 5th song, *The Rubbish Bin,* 'Such windy, berylled rubied boughs/As clasp Pomona's lovely brows'. 1924. Wood engraving, printed on Japanese vellum 9 x 6.5cm. Deutscher Gallery, Armadale, Victoria, 1979, No.31.

The Seven Songs of Meadow Lane (The Dustman). No signed and numbered edition known. Decoration for the 5th song, The Rubbish Bin, 'A dustman, brown as city smoke/My sense to present fact awoke/He brushed me by and seized the bin/With all its store of dreams therein.' 1924. Wood engraving, printed on Japanese vellum. 2.6 x 6.5cm. Deutscher Gallery, Armadale, Victoria, 1979, no.26.

The Seven Songs of Meadow Lane (I Smelled Blossoms in the Rain). No signed and numbered edition known. Title page vignette for 'Seven Songs'. Decoration for the 5th song, 'I smelled blossoms in the rain/Among the apple boughs again/And cider-tubs, and glowing store of /quinces, golden to the core. 1924. Wood engraving, printed on Japanese vellum. 5.6 x 3.7cm. Deutscher Gallery, Armadale, Victoria, 1979, No.25.

The Seven Songs of Meadow Lane. (The Organ Grinder). Signed and numbered edition of 30, of which 25 were bound in 'Seven Songs'. Decoration for 6th song, *The Organ Grinder,* 'Pico, the organ-grinder,/In the dusty hours/Plays his best to the alley children/And the calm, grey towers!' 1924. Wood engraving 14.7 x 7.5cm. Deutscher Gallery, Armadale, Victoria, 1979, No.33. *Architecture,* Vol.XV, No.V, May 1926.

Among the Blithe Trees. No signed and numbered edition known. Rejected design for 'The Seven Songs', originally intended to be decoration for the 5th song, 'The Rubbish Bin'. The poem was also rewritten 'The happy flies flew up and sang; But I was where the apples hang,/For dirt and drain forgetting, these/Bore me among the blithe green trees'. 1924. Wood engraving 8.3 x 6.4cm. Deutscher Gallery, Armadale, Victoria, 1979, No.32.

The Paleolithic Bone. Original drawing for the conclusion of *The Romantic History of Australia* by Walter La Rue, Sydney, 1924. 1924. Pen and ink. 18 x 25.5cm. Nevill Keating. *Hermes,* Vol XXXI, 1925.

View under the Bridge. Signed and dated 1924. Water-colour laid down on a board 12 x 19.6cm. Nevill Keating.

Nevermore Sailor. Signed and numbered edition of 25. Decoration for *Nevermore Sailor* by Walter de la Mare, 'Nevermore sailor/Shalt thou be/Tossed on the Wind Ridden/ Restless Sea.' 1924. Wood engraving, printed on Japanese vellum. 6.4 x 15.3cm. Society of Artists, 1924; Farmers Exhibition Hall, 1924, No.61; Deutscher Gallery, Armadale, Victoria, 1979, No.35.

Nevermore Sailor. Preparatory drawing for the wood engraving of the same title. 1924. Pen and ink 21 x 26.5cm. Nevill Keating.

Dark Château. No signed or numbered edition known. Decoration for *Dark Château* by Walter de la Mare, 'In dreams a dark château/Stands ever open to me,/In far ravines dream-waters flow/Descending soundlessly'. 1924. Wood engraving printed on Japanese vellum. 12.8 x 6.5cm. Society of Artists Annual Exhibition, 1924, No.63; Farmers Exhibition Hall, 1924, No.63; Deutscher Gallery, Armadale, Victoria, 1979, No.36.

"Is there Anybody there?" Said the Traveller. No Signed or numbered edition known. Illustration for *The Listeners* by Walter de la Mare. 1924. Wood engraving printed on Japanese vellum. Society of Artists Annual Exhibition, 1924; Farmers Exhibition Hall, 1924, No.62; Deutscher Gallery, Armadale, Victoria, 1979, No.38. Art in Australia, December 1925.

Come Hither Child to Me. No signed and numbered edition known. Decoration for *Keys of the Morning* by Walter de la Mare, 'While at her bedroom window once,/Learning her tasks for school,/Little Louisa lonely sat/In the morning clear and cool/She slanted her small bead brown eyes/Across the empty street,/And saw Death softly watching her/in the sunshine pale and sweet'. 1924. Wood engraving printed on Japanese vellum. 9 x 9.6cm. Society of Artists Annual Exhibition, 1924, No.60; Farmers Exhibition Hall, Sydney, 1924, No.60; Deutscher Gallery, Armadale, Victoria, 1979, No.37. Art in Australia, December 1925.

Who is it Calling by the Darkened River. No Signed or numbered edition known. Decoration for *Voices* by Walter de la Mare, 'Who is it calling by the darkened river/Where the moss lies smooth and deep./And the dark trees lean unmoving arms,/Silent and vague in sleep. 1924. Wood engraving, printed on Japanese vellum. 14 x 14.6. Deutscher Gallery, Armadale, Victoria, 1979, No.40.

(Yea, in my Mind these Mountains rise). No signed or numbered edition known. Decoration for poem by Walter de la Mare. 'Yea in my mind these mountains rise,/Their perils dyed with evening's rose;/and still my ghost sits at my eyes/And thirsts for their untroubled snows'. 1925. Wood engraving, printed on Japanese vellum. 5.2 x 12.2cm. Deutscher Gallery, Armadale, Victoria, 1979, No.39. Art in Australia, December 1925.

The Bells. Frontispiece decoration for *Hermes* Magazine, Vol. XXX, No.3, 1924. Inverted monogram R McG, dated. 1924. Ink on card. 50.8 x 28.2cm. National Gallery of Ireland, Dublin. *Hermes,* Vol.XXX, No.3, 1924.

John of Paris 'Ah Quel Plaisir d'être en voyage'. Signed and dated. 1924. *Hermes,* Vol.XXX, June 1924, p.75.

If the Bugles Blow. Decoration for a poem published in *Hermes,* June 1924. Printing instructions in pencil evident, c.1924. Pen and ink 18.1 x 12cm. Nevill Keating 1983. *Hermes,* Vol. XXX, June 1924.

The Pantheon, Rome. No signed and numbered edition known. 1924. Etching and aquatint printed in sepia wove paper. 14.9 x 18.9cm. Deutscher Gallery, Armadale, Victoria, 1979, No.21.

Matthewtown. Illustrated essay, winner of the Knyvett Prize. Originally to have been printed. Signed. 7 MS pages in pen and ink, with title page and 3 full page illustrations, forming a booklet of 12 pages. 1924. Pen and ink. 25.5 x 19.4cm. Mitchell Library, New South Wales. Hermes, Vol.XXX, No.3, 1924.

Matthewtown. Verso of title page of essay. A View of a township in the distance. 1924. Pen and blue/black ink and water-colour 5.6 x 7.9cm on 25.5 x 19.4cm. Mitchell Library. *Hermes,* Vol. XXX, No.3, 1924.

St. Matthew-of-the-firs, Matthewtown, New South Wales. Illustration in essay 'Matthewtown' 1924. Pen and blue/black ink with wash 21.4 x 12.3cm on 25.5 x 19.4cm. Mitchell Library, New South Wales. *Hermes,* Vol.XXX, No.3, 1924.

Inigo, Matthewtown, New South Wales. Illustration to essay 'Matthewtown' 1924. Pen and blue/black ink with wash 17.2 x 11.4cm on 25.5 x 19.4cm. Mitchell Library, New South Wales.

The Sunflower. Signed. Possibly a study for wood engraving of same subject. c.1924. Black Indian ink with water-colour. 25.4 x 17.7cm. David Newman Johnson. Neptune Gallery, 1979.

Prehistoric Skeleton. Drawing for title page of the 'Romantic History of Australia' by Walter la Rue. Published Sydney, 1924. Inscribed and marked with printing instructions. 1924. Pen and ink 16 x 14cm. Nevill Keating. *Hermes,* Vol.XXXI, May 1925.

The Romantic History of Australia. Illustration for frontispiece of 'The Romantic History of Australia' by Walter la Rue, published in Sydney, 1924. Signed. 1924. Pen and ink 33.6 x 23.7cm. Nevill Keating. *Hermes,* Vol.XXXI, May 1925.

Richmond River Lands. Signed and dated 1924. Pen and ink 27.7 x 26.5cm. Nevill Keating.

(The Wind and the Rain). No signed or numbered edition known. Illustration for 'Twelfth Night' – 'When that I was a little king boy,/With hey, ho, the wind and rain./A foolish thing was but a toy,/for the rain it raineth every day'. 1925. Wood engraving printed on Japanese vellum. 10.5 x 8.5cm. Deutscher Gallery, Armadale, Victoria, 1979, No.46.

Techelles, Draw thy Sword. Signed and numbered edition. Decoration for Marlowe by J. le Gay Brereton, '...Techelles, draw thy sword,/And wound the earth, that it may cleave in twaine,/And descend into th'infernall vaults/To haile the fatall sisters by the haire/And throw them in the triple mote of hell,/For taking hence my faire Zinocrate.' 1925. Wood engraving printed on Japanese vellum. 11.2 x 8.3cm. Deutscher Gallery, Armadale, Victoria, 1979, No.49.

The Royal Mint, Maquarie Street. Signed and numbered edition of 50. 1925. Wood engraving, printed on Japanese vellum. 15.1 x 18.3cm. Deutscher Gallery, Armadale, Victoria, 1979, no.41.

The Skeleton of a City. No signed or numbered edition known. Inscribed in block- RAYMOND McGRATH 1925. 1925. Wood engraving printed on Japanese vellum 15.3 x 12.5cm. Artists Annual Exhibition, Sydney, 1925; Deutscher Gallery, Armadale, Victoria, 1979, No. 42. The Annual Brochure and Catalogue of the Institute of Architects, New South Wales, 1925, in an advertisement for reinforced concrete.

Bookplate for Heather McDonald Sutherland. No signed or numbered edition known. Inscribed in block- EX LIBRIS – HEATHER McDONALD SUTHER-LAND 1925. Wood engraving printed on laid paper 10.3 x 7.1cm. Deutscher Gallery, Armadale, Victoria, 1979, no.51. Pictorial Book Plates: Their Origin and Use in Australia by P. Neville Barnett, Sydney, 1931, p.65.

Tamburlaine. 1925. Wood engraving. Unknown. Society of Artists Annual Exhibition, Sydney, September-October 1925, no.104. (Proceeds to go to the Marlow Memorial Fund); Deutscher Gallery, Armadale, Victoria, 1979, no.48.

Landscape and Seascape. Inscribed on reverse. Signed and dated. 1925. Water-colour. 27.2 x 29cm. Nevill Keating.

St. Simeon Stylites. Signed and numbered edition of 30. Illustration to St. Simeon Stylites by Tennyson, 'A sign betwixt the meadow and the cloud,/Patient on this tall pillar I have borne/Rain, wind, frost, heat, hail, damp, sleet ,and snow;/And I have hoped that ere this period closed/Thou wouldst have caught me up into thy rest,/Denying not these weather-beaten limbs/The need of saints, the white robe and the palm.' 1925. Wood engraving printed on Japanese vellum. 22.5 x 18.6cm. Engraved wood block in the Mitchell Library, New South Wales. Society of Artists, Sydney, 1925; Deutscher Gallery, Armadale, Victoria, 1979, no.47.

St. Simeon Stylites. Preliminary design (one of three) for the wood engraving. 1925. Pencil 22.5 x 18.8cm. Mitchell Library, New South Wales.

St. Simeon Stylites. Preliminary design for wood engraving of the same subject. 1925. Ink on butter paper 22.5 x 18cm. Mitchell Library, New South Wales.

In Memoriam (To John Irving Hunter). Decoration to poem of the same title. 1925. Pen and ink. *Hermes,* Vol.XXXI, 1925, pp.16-17.

Joie de vivre. Illustration in *Hermes.* Vol. XXXI, No.2, 1925.

Juno's Bird. Illustration in *Hermes.* Vol.XXXI, 1925, pp.82-3.

Mill on the Cove. Inscribed on reverse. Signed and dated. 1925. Water-colour 27.2 x 29cm. Nevill Keating.

Pied Piper. 1925. Water-colour 40.6 x 38.1cm. Ken Pye.

Purple Weeds on the Shallows. Signed and dated 1925. Water-colour and pencil 38.1 x 17.7cm. David Newman Johnson.

Callan Park. Perspective sketch of Callan Park War Memorial, showing colour scheme and planting details. Signed and dated in block capitals. 1925. Water-colour 45.7 x 63.5cm. Aidan Powell.

College Chapel in Gothic Style. Elevation of west porch of the chapel of Sydney University and a half plan of the porch door. Signed and dated 1925, Sydney. 1925. Graphite and wash on paper 77 x 56cm. Irish Architectural Archive. *The*

Architect and the Drawing, Royal Institute of Architects in Ireland, 1989.

Gum Trees. Wood engraving of the same subject exists. 1925. Water-colour 33 x 19cm. W. Henningham.

House of Professor E.R. Holme. The House is in Shellcore Road, Neutral Bay, Sydney. Signed and dated. Lower right. 1926. Water-colour 38.7 x 31.1cm. Dr. J.L. Holme.

The Architecture of China and its Adaptation to Japan. Bound thesis 1926. Water-colour, pen and ink on paper. 26.6 x 21.5cm. Australian National Gallery, Canberra. Neptune Gallery, Dublin, 1979, No.52. 'The Classic Architecture of the Orient' by Tristan Edwards, *Architectural Review,* January–June 1930. p.113–118.

Richmond River Art Gallery. Front elevation and roof plan. 1926. Pencil with blue-green wash. 57 x 77cm. Irish Architectural Archive.

Richmond River Art Gallery. Ground plan and longitudinal section. 1926. Pencil and colour wash. 77 x 56cm. Irish Architectural Archive.

Richmond River Art Gallery. Sketch of ground plan and longtitudinal section. 1926. Water-colour. 77 x 56cm. Jenny and Donal O'Donovan.

Richmond River Art Gallery. Plan and elevation of door. 1926. Pencil and coloured wash. 77 x 56.5cm. Irish Architectural Archive.

Lorannaleah – Some Pieces in Prose and Verse. Leather-bound album MCMXX-MCMXVI by Raymond McGrath at Sydney, Australia. With decoration by Eileen and Raymond McGrath. Collected and bound together in the month of July MCMXXVI. 1926. Water-colour and ink 29.8 x 24.1cm. Mitchell Library, Sydney. Neptune Gallery, Dublin, 1979, No.46.

Town Club, Elizabeth Street, Sydney. Title inscribed lower left. Signed lower right. c.1926. *Architecture,* Vol.XV, No.V, May, 1926.

(St. Paul's). No signed or numbered edition known. Same block used for a 1926 Christmas card, with minor alterations. 1926-8. Wood engraving 8.3 x 6.4cm. Deutscher Gallery, Armadale, Victoria, 1979, No.73. *Lady Clare Magazine,* Vol. xxiii, No.1, 1928, p.11.

Ex Libris. No signed or numbered edition known. Title inscribed in block. A copy of this in 24 Woodcuts has the name James S. Gardiner penned into the blank space. 1926. Wood engraving printed on Japanese vellum. 7.7 x 5.8cm. Deutscher Gallery, Armadale, Victoria, 1979, No.52.

Macbeth and the Witches. Numbered edition on rice paper pulled but few signed, numbered, or issued. Illustration for Act 1, Scene 1 of Macbeth, 'When shall we three meet again/In thunder, lightning, or in rain?/When the hurlyburly's done,/When the battle's lost and won/that will be ere the set of sun/.Where's the place? Upon the heath./There to meet Macbeth./I come, Graymalkin!/Paddock calls, Anon? Fair is foul and foul is fair,/Hover through the fog and filthy air.' 1926. Wood engraving 11.1 x 8.7cm. Society of Artists Annual Exhibition, Sydney, 1926, No.43; Deutscher Gallery, Armadale, Victoria, 1979, No.53. *Lady Clare Magazine,* Vol.xxii, No.1, Michaelmas Term, 1927, p.6.

Casa del Marques, Valencia. Inscribed as above in pencil. 1927. Water-colour 29 x 22.2cm. Irish Architectural Archive.

Valladolid. Signed and dated 1927. Valladolid written below mount but described as the Casa del Marques in *Architect's Journal* of 1928. 1927. Water-colour 29 x 23cm. Irish Architectural Archive. *The Architect's Journal,* January 11th, 1928.

Interior of a vaulted building (probably Spanish), with figures carrying paintings. c.1927. Sepia and wash. 25.4 x 18.4cm. Irish Architectural Archive.

Santa Cruz, Toledo. Unsigned, undated. 1927-8. Ink and grey wash. 20 x 15cm. Irish Architectural Archive. *The Architect's Journal,* January 11th 1928.

San Francisco, Palma de Mallorca. Signed R.McG and dated. 1927. Water-colour 19.6 x 13.9cm. Charles Henry de Gale Price. Neptune Gallery, Dublin, 1979, No.23.

Paris Windowscape (or Montparnasse). Inscribed with title lower left, signed and dated. 1927. Ink and grey wash 29 x 19cm. Irish Architectural Archive. Reproduced as a card.

Tours. c.1927. Ink and water-colour 20.7 x 15cm. Irish Architectural Archive.

Angoulême. c.1927. Ink and water-colour 20.5 x 15cm. Irish Architectural Archive.

A Prospect from the Air: Clare, Old and New. c.1929. Tempera. As a Frontispiece to Vol.II of Clare College 1326-1926, Cambridge University Press, 1928-1930.

Escalls, Cornwall. Inscribed with title lower right. Signed and dated. 1927. Water-colour 24.1 x 34.2cm. Jenny and Donal O'Donovan. The Neptune Gallery, Dublin, 1979, No. 2.

An Old Man's Song. Full page illustration for Albert Frost's poem published in the *Lady Clare Magazine,* 1927. 1927. *Lady Clare Magazine,* Michaelmas Term, Vol. XXII No.1, 1927.

Alberto Hielo. (Albert Frost). No signed and numbered edition known. Decoration for 'In a corner of a Red Cupboard' by Ramón Majraz (Raymond

McGrath). Published in the *Lady Clare Magazine,* Lent, 1928. Illustrated the following lines 'Years ago Alberto Hielo plucked from this his deft music/Valencia, O Valencia, he sang softly as he played/Curanto mas la vee hermosa, mas le crece su pesar!/He used to sit on a blue seat among the thick lime trees/Singing, though young as men remembered, an old man's song'. 1927. Wood engraving 3.4 x 3.3cm. Deutscher Gallery, Armadale, Victoria, 1979, No.59. *Lady Clare Magazine,* Vol. xxii, No.2, Lent Term, 1928, p.65.

Untitled. No signed and numbered edition known. c.1927. Wood engraving. 6.4 x 5.1cm. Deutscher Gallery, Armadale, Victoria, 1979, No.57. *Lady Clare Magazine,* Vol.XXII, No.1, Michaelmas Term, 1927, p.5.

Montserrat. No signed or numbered edition known. 1927. Wood engraving 7.5 x 5cm. Deutscher Gallery, Armadale, Victoria, 1979, No.58. Printed as a decoration in the *Lady Clare Magazine,* Vol. xxii, No.1, Michaelmas Term, 1927, p.25. Also reproduced as a Christmas card.

I Cannot See What Flowers are at thy Feet. No signed or numbered edition known. Decoration for Keats 'I cannot see what flowers are at thy feet/Nor what soft incense hangs upon the boughs./But, in embalmed darkness, guess each sweet/ Wherewith the seasonable month endows/The grass, the thicket and the fruit tree-wild'. c.1927. Wood engraving printed on Japanese vellum. 8.9 x 6.4cm. Deutscher Gallery, Armadale, Victoria, 1979, No.55.

Untitled. No signed or numbered edition known. Same block as 'I cannot see what flowers are at thy feet' but with space inscribed JANET FREW WATERHOUSE. Probably used as a bookplate. c.1927. Wood engraving printed on Japanese vellum. 8.9 x 6.4cm. Deutscher Gallery, Armadale, Victoria, 1979, No.56.

El Riguelete: The Belltower of Valencia. Issued in a signed and numbered edition of 30. 1928. Wood engraving, printed on Abbey Mills paper. 12.7 x 10cm. The Macquarie Galleries, Sydney, 1928; Deutscher Gallery, Armadale, Victoria, 1979, No.61 *Lady Clare Magazine,* Vol. xxii, No.2, Lent Term, 1928, p.64.

Flying the Stroke of Dawn. Signed and numbered edition of 30. Decoration to poem by Raymond McGrath, published in the *Lady Clare Magazine,* Lent term, 1928, 'I clasped her little finger/ and whispered to her ear;/"You are too sweet to linger/Except by stars, my dear./Dreams are foredoomed to vanish,/Flying the stroke of dawn,/The castles of the Spanish/And the dew-flowers on the lawn,/The fire flowers in the ember/And the rock flowers in the sea;/Dear, 'ere you go, remember/How dearly I loved thee"'. 1928. Wood engraving, printed on Abbey Mills paper. 7.8 x 7.7cm. Macquarie Gallery, Sydney, 1928; Deutscher Gallery, Armadale, Victoria, 1979, No.63. *Lady Clare Magazine,* Vol. xxii, No.2, Lent Term, 1928, p.111; *The Cambridge Review,* 6th June, 1928, under the title 'Andalusian Dancers'.

The Meeting. Signed and numbered edition of 30. Illustration to *The Meeting* by George Meredith 'The Light in a thin blue veil peered sick/The sheep grazed close and still'. 1928. Wood engraving, printed on Abbey Mills paper. 9 x 7.8cm. Macquarie Gallery, Sydney, October, 1928; Deutscher Gallery, Armadale, Victoria, 1979, No.70. *Lady Clare Magazine,* Vol. xxii, No.2, Lent Term, 1928, p.126; *The Cambridge Review,* 6th June, 1928, p.495.

La Vie en Rouille Laquée ('Babette s'en va'). Signed and numbered edition of 30. Illustration for poem 'La Vie en Rouille Laquée' by Ian Hemingway, published in the *Lady Clare Magazine,* Lent term, 1928: 'babette s'en va;/babette sera/bientôt de retour/surement, car/le but du tour/c'est le point de départ'. 1928. Wood engraving, printed on Abbey Mills paper. 10.3 x 12.7cm. Macquarie Gallery, Sydney, October 1928; The Deutscher Gallery, Armadale, Victoria, 1979, No.64 under the title 'La Vie en Rouille Laquee'. *The Lady Clare Magazine,* Vol. xxii, No.2, Lent term, 1928, p.123; Nicholas Draffin, *Australian Wooodcuts and linocuts of the 1920's and 1930's,* Melbourne, 1976, p.65.

Pericles. Signed and numbered edition of 30. Illustration for Pericles Act III, Scene 1 'Thou God of this vast, rebuke these surges;/Which wash both heaven and hell;' 1928. Wood engraving printed on Abbey Mills paper 8.8 x 7.5cm. Macquarie Gallery, Sydney, October 1928; Deutscher Gallery, Armadale, Victoria, 1979, No.69. *Lady Clare Magazine,* Vol. xxii, Lent term 1928 p.75; Vol. xxiv, No.1, 1930.

Soft Shadows like Birds. Signed and numbered edition of 30. Decoration to McGrath's love poem to Iris Wennstrom, published in *The Venture,* 1928, illustrating the following lines 'And the sign crosses my fancy, again and again/Of the showery haloes of lamps and soft shadows like birds.' 1928. Wood engraving printed on Abbey Mills paper. 7.8 x 5.2cm. Macquarie Gallery, Sydney, October 1928; Deutscher Gallery, Armadale, Victoria, 1979, no.66. *The Venture,* No.1, 1928, p.44.

Paradise Lost. Signed and numbered edition of 30. Illustration for *Paradise Lost, Book xi* by Milton 'Oh, unexpected stroke, worse than of death/Must I leave thee, Paradise? thus leave/Thee, native soil, these happy walks and shades,/Fit haunt of gods? Where I had hope to spend,/Quiet, though sad, the respite of that day/That must be mortal to us both'. 1928. Wood engraving printed on Abbey Mills paper. 9.1 x 7.7cm. Macquarie Gallery, Sydney, October 1928; Deutscher Gallery, Armadale, Victoria, 1979, No.67. *Lady Clare Magazine,* Vol. xxii, No.2, 1928, p.12.

Hark , All You Ladies. Signed and numbered edition of 30. 1928. Wood engraving printed on Abbey Mills paper. 7.6 x 6.4cm. Macquarie Gallery, Sydney, October 1928; Deutscher Gallery, Armadale, Victoria, 1979, No.65.

(Arterio Scelerosis). No signed or numbered edition known. Illustration for 'Arterio Scelerosis...a playlet in the Russian Manner' by E.L.C., published in the *Lady Clare Magazine,* 1928 '...Old man, you must come off this shooting/it affects the heart.' 1928. Wood engraving 6.3 x 6.3cm. Deutscher Gallery, Armadale, Victoria, 1979, No.72. *Lady Clare Magazine,* Vol. xxii, No.1, 1928, p.10.

Thames Barges at Hammersmith. No signed and numbered edition known. 1928. Wood engraving. 9.3 x 10.7. Deutscher Gallery, Armadale, Victoria, 1979, No.71. *The Lady Clare Magazine,* Vol. xxii, No.1, 1928, p.45.

The Towers of San Gimignano. Signed and numbered edition of 30. Illustration for the poem 'The Fair Lady of San Gimignano' by Ramon Majraz (Raymond McGrath). 1928. Wood engraving printed on Abbey Mills paper. 3.5 x 3.3cm. Macquarie Gallery, Sydney, October 1928; Deutscher Gallery, Armadale, Victoria, 1979, No.62. *The Lady Clare Magazine,* Vol. xxii, No.3 Easter Term, 1928, p.108.

The Woods of Westermain. Signed and numbered edition of 30. Illustration for 'The Woods of Westermain' by George Meredith. 'Only at the dread of dark/Quaver, and they quit their form;/Thousand eyeballs under hoods/Have you by the hair./Enter these enchanted woods/You who dare.' 1928. Wood engraving printed on Abbey Mills paper. 9 x 7.7cm. The Macquarie Gallery, Sydney, October 1928; Deutscher Gallery, Armadale, Victoria, 1979, No.68. *The Lady Clare Magazine,* Vol. xxii, No.2, Lent term, 1928, p.115; *The Cambridge Review,* 6 June, 1928.

(Workmann! Spahir θot Treeh). No signed or numbered edition known. Illustration for poem by Mansfield Forbes, published in the *Lady Clare Magazine,* 1928. 'Workmann! Spahir θot Treeh!/Poir Knot tse wooky woohd!/Twazeffer weet t'mch/Zinz s'Rarebit ohphtly sooed/S'luvsplight tso's penderly/Wat taime wei hai wei s'tud/Lipshtuck unnpseperablee,/ Wroohted imp ulssluge bluhd.' 1928. Wood engraving. 10.3 x 10.1cm. Deutscher Gallery, Armadale, Victoria, 1979, No.75. *The Lady Clare Magazine,* Vol. xxii, No.1, 1928, p.16; Hugh Carey, *Mansfield Forbes and His Cambridge,* Cambridge, 1984, p.101.

Untitled. No signed or numbered edition known. Illustration to McGrath's poem 'The Magician' published in *The Lady Clare Magazine.* 'A sudden peace invaded me/Like moonlight in the still black nights/Where lonely ships with searching lights/move slowly on the ariel sea'. 1928. Wood engraving 5.3 x 7.6cm. Deutscher Gallery, Armadale, Victoria, 1979, No.74. *The Lady Clare Magazine,* Vol. xxiii, No.1, 1928, p.26; *The Venture,* No.1, 1928; as a greeting card with poem 'Winter Solstice' by Mansfield Forbes.

Avenue. [In Granmont?] c.1928. *The Cambridge Drawing Society,* 1928, No.65.

Seine Bridges. c.1927-8. George Checkley 1928. *The Cambridge Drawing Society,* 1928, No.61.

East End Landscape. Signed lower right and dated. 1928. Pen and wash 31.5 x40.5cm. Tim Beaglehole. *The Cambridge Drawing Society,* 1928, No.57.

Inveraray. Sketch – similar to a photograph illustrating McGrath's article 'The Crown of Scotland' published in the *Architects Journal,* 6th June, 1928, p.788. 1928. Sepia and crayon 17.8 x 22.7cm. The Irish Architectural Archive.

One or Two Little Forget-Me-Nots for Dear Mary Catherine's Homecoming. Album. May, 1929. Water-colour 29.8 x 22.8cm. Jenny and Donal O'Donovan. The Neptune Gallery, Dublin, 1979, No.50.

Perspective of Hotel at Le Lavandou for Jean Stempowski. Signed. 'From Ray McGrath, Clare College, Cambridge' inscribed on reverse. 1930. Ink with coloured wash 39 x 52cm. The Irish Architectural Archive. The Irish Exhibition of Living Art, 1951, No.89, [possibly]; 1953, No.99.

The Rising Moon. c.1930. Pen and brush on ink and water-colour 23.4 x 32.3cm. Nevill Keating.

Untitled. Drawing in praise of glass: showing a woman on a balcony with still life. Signed. A similar drawing by McGrath was reproduced in the article by Brian Hanson, 'Rhapsody in Black Glass', Architectural Review, July, 1977. 1930's. Ink and crayon 58.5 x 41.5cm. The Irish Architectural Archive.

Sketch of Living Room, Park Crescent. 1930's. Ink 25.6 x 20.3cm. Jenny and Donal O'Donovan.

Thro' Dumb Infinity. No signed and numbered edition known. Frontispiece to *The Labyrinth and Other Poems* by J. W. Mills, published in 1930. 1930. Wood engraving 10.1 x 8.2cm. Deutscher Gallery, Armadale, Victoria, 1979, No.78. *The Labyrinth and Other Poems,* by J. W. Mills.

The Labyrinth. No signed and numbered edition known. Illustration for 'The Labyrinth' in *The Labyrinth and Other Poems.* 1930. Wood engraving 9.7 x 9cm. The Deutscher Gallery, Armadale, Victoria, 1979, No.79; The Neptune Gallery, Dublin, 1979, No.51. J. W. Mills, *The Labyrinth and Other Poems,* 1930, p.3; *Lady Clare Magazine,* Vol.xxv, No.1, 1930, p.13.

Ars Alandae. No signed and numbered edition known. Decoration for *The Labyrinth and Other Poems.* 1930. Wood engraving 9.5 x 9.6cm. The Deutscher Gallery, Armadale, Victoria, 1979, No.80; The Neptune Gallery, Dublin, 1979, No.51. J.W. Mills, *The Labyrinth and Other Poems,* 1930, p.23; *The Lady Clare*

Magazine, Vol.xxvi, No.3, 1932, p.119, as 'He Sings for Singings Sake. Then Why Not You?'

Untitled. No signed or numbered edition known. 1930. Wood engraving 9 x 6.6cm. The Deutscher Gallery, Armadale, Victoria, No.82, 1979; The Neptune Gallery, Dublin, 1979, No.51. J.W. Mills, *The Labyrinth and Other Poems,* 1930, p.55.

Kedington Church, Suffolk. No signed and numbered edition known. 'St. Peter and St. Paul, Kedington' inscribed in the block. Illustration for *The Labyrinth and Other Poems.* 1930. Wood engraving 11.4 x 9.1cm. The Deutscher Gallery, Armadale, Victoria, 1979, No.83; The Neptune Gallery, Dublin, 1979, No.51. J.W. Mills, *The Labyrinth and Other Poems,* 1930, p.65.

Sequence. No signed and numbered edition known. Illustration for *The Labyrinth.* 1930. Wood engraving 12.1 x 8.8cm. The Deutscher Gallery, Armadale, Victoria, 1979, No.84. J.W. Mills, *The Labyrinth and Other Poems,* 1930, p.77.

Untitled. No signed or numbered edition known. 1930. Wood engraving 7.7 x 5.3cm. The Deutscher Gallery, Armadale, Victoria, 1979, No.7. *The Lady Clare Magazine,* Vol. xxv, No.1, 1930, p.7.

Park Crescent. Signed and dated 1931. Pencil and water-colour 45.7 x 58.4cm. Jenny and Donal O'Donovan. The Neptune Gallery, Dublin, 1979, No.35.

Regents Park. Inscribed top left 'Regents Park', signed and dated. 1931. Ink, pencil and water-colour. Unknown. Unknown.

Fischer's Restaurant. c.1932. Pencil on tracing paper 24.2 x 30.7cm. The Irish Architectural Archive.

BBC Studio, Manchester. Signed and dated. 1933. Crayon 340 x 430cm. RIBA.

Untitled. View of scaffolding, a ladder and trees. Signed and dated. Possibly designed as a card. Mounted print exists in the Irish Architectural Archive with 'Finella' inscribed below the mount. 1933. Sepia, black ink and crayon. The Irish Architectural Archive. As a greeting card; An advertisement in the Greyfield Building Co. Ltd., Stroud Valley Development Brochure.

Frognal House in Snow. Exterior perspective sketch. Alterations to the Georgian house executed by McGrath. 1933-4. 210 x 180cm. RIBA.

Design for wallpaper: Monoplanes and Clouds. Intended for use in projected house, 'Rudderbar' for woman aviator, the Hon. Mrs. Victor Bruce. The house was never built. c.1933. Victoria and Albert Museum.

99 Frognal House, Hampstead. View of terrace and entrance. 1933. Pencil on paper. 390 x 480cm. RIBA.

Casino at Goodwood. Signed and dated. Painted from a photograph published in *Country Life,* 1938 of the grounds of Goodwood House, Sussex. 1938-1941. Water-colour 43.8 x 31.1cm. Julian O'Donovan. The Neptune Gallery, Dublin, 1979, No.41.

Dr. Crozier's Return from Scotland. Signed and dated, lower right, August 1938. 1938. Water-colour 23 x 14cm. Jenny and Donal O'Donovan.

Barton's Farm. Signed and dated 17th April 1938. 1938. Water-colour 42 x 29cm. Nuala and Sean Rothery. Cambridge's Fine Art Ltd., Dublin, 1940, No.18. Royal Institute of the Architects of Ireland, 'The Architect and the Drawing', Dublin, 1989. No. 273.

The Meadows near Cheddar. Dated 2nd of April, and inscribed with title. 1938. Sepia ink. 19 x 25.4cm. Jenny and Donal O'Donovan.

Cheddar Cows. Dated 3 April 1938, and inscribed lower right with title. 1938. Sepia 19 x 25.4cm. Jenny and Donal O'Donovan.

Cathedral Green, Wells. Dated 3 April, 1938, and inscribed as above. 1938. Sepia 19 x 25.4cm. Jenny and Donal O'Donovan.

2-14 Duncan Terrace. Inscribed top left 'built 1790-1800 Clerkenwell Corner Court, Corner of Duncan St. and Duncan terrace'. Lower right signed and inscribed 'Duncan Terrace and Colebrook Row looking north.' 1938. Sepia ink. 13 x 18cm. Irish Architectural Archive. *Architectural Review,* 1940, p. 69.

The New River. Architectural Review, September 1940. [House in Duncan Terrace]. Marked with initials. Inscribed 'Charles Lamb's House in our time and his.' 1938. Sepia ink 25.3 x 19.3cm. Jenny and Donal O'Donovan. 'The New River', *Architectural Review,* September, 1940, p. 70.

Calton Hill, Edinburgh. Signed and dated. 1938. Watercolour 38.1 x 31.1cm. T.V. Murray. Combridge's Fine Art Ltd., Dublin, 1940, No.14; The Neptune Gallery, Dublin, 1979, No.24. O.P.W. *Corridor* Supplement 1.

The New River at Canonbury Grove. Signed and dated. 1938. Sepia ink 19 x 25.4cm. Jenny and Donal O'Donovan. 'The New River', *Architectural Review,* September 1940, p. 67.

[Big Ben] Captioned in the *Irish Times,* 13th May, 1941 as 'Mr. Raymond McGrath's Drawing of the Houses of Parliament and Westminster Abbey'. Signed lower right and dated. 1938. Pen and ink. 13th May, 1941, *Irish Times.*

Furlong Road. Inscribed 'Numbers 8-28, Furlong Road, West Islington N.7. Measured and Drawn by Raymond McGrath. B. Arch., A.R.I.B.A. 1938.' 1938. Pen and ink on tracing paper. Irish Architectural Archive. *Architectural Review,*

April, 1938, p.214; *Country Life,* 9th April, 1938.

Top of the 'Spire' of St. John's Bermondsey. Inscribed as above. c. 1938. Sepia 8 x 6cm on 25.4 x 19cm. Jenny and Donal O'Donovan.

Cheddar Gorge. Probably part of the series of drawings executed in April 1938. c.1938. Probably sepia. Stolen. Neptune Gallery, Dublin, 1979.

Untitled. [Landscape]. c. 1938. Sepia, coloured crayon and water-colour. 19 x 25.4cm. Jenny and Donal O'Donovan.

Street Scene in Stratford on Avon. 1938. Oil.

The Crescent, Portland Place. Signed and dated. 1939. Graphite and water-colour on board. 38 x 55cm. The Irish Architectural Archive. The Royal Institute of the Architects of Ireland, 'The Architect and the Drawing', Dublin, 1989, No.275.

Athena. Sandblast and brilliant cut panel. One of 6 executed by Messrs. James Clark and Eaton, 1936. 1936. Glass – Sandblast and brilliant cut. R.I.B.A. Raymond McGrath, *Glass in Architecture and Design,* p.418, ill.259.

Austin Reed Sales Trophy. Made for Austin Reed Ltd., and awarded annually to the branch achieving the highest sales. 1935 Plate Glass and metal 64.7cm. Austin Reed Ltd. The Hayward Gallery, London, October 1979 – January, 1980, No.7.

The Swale at Faversham. Signed, dated and insribed as above. 1935 Water-colour. Formerly in the collection of John C. Witt; sold at Sotheby's, 1983.

Church of St. Mary and Gabriel, Harting, Sussex. Signed. Inscribed as above and 'Drawn 2 days in situ, July, 1936'. 1936. Ink and Wash. Karen Giri. Combridge's Fine Art Ltd, Dublin, 1940, No.19. Reproduced as a card.

The Burrow. Design for a Christmas Card. Shows house designed to be safe against air attack. Inscribed top left 'Seasonal Greetings from Mary and Raymond McGrath' and lower right 'The Burrow 2648 East 59th Subway, Deeper London'. c.1934. Ink and line on tracing paper. 31.0 x 20.5cm. Royal Institute of British Architects. Raymond McGrath, *Twentieth Century Houses,* 1934; David Dean, p.141, No.25.; O.P.W. *Corridor* Supplement 1; Alan Powers, 'Simple Intime – the Work of Raymond McGrath', *Thirties Society Journal,* No.3, 1982, p.3.

Athene. Signed and dated. 1937. Rectangular etched glass panel raised on revolving platform on black table. 55.8 x 60.9cm. Private Collection.

Clovelly Harbour, North Devon. Signed and dated. 1939 Water-colour 40 x 55cm. Nuala and Sean Rothery. Combridge's Fine Art Ltd., Dublin, 1940, No. 17; The Royal Institute of The Architects of Ireland, 'The Architect and the Drawing', Dublin, 1989, No. 274.

Park Crescent, Portland Place during a Night Air Raid. Signed and dated 30th September 1939. 1939. Water-colour on board 38 x 54.5cm. The Irish Architectural Archive.

A Sandy Day at Trevose Head, Cornwall. Signed and dated 1939. Water-colour 37.5 x 54.6cm. Jenny and Donal O'Donovan. Combridge's Fine Art Ltd., Dublin, 1940, No.16.

Mooring Pool at Portobello. Signed and dated lower right. To be used as a colour illustration for the planned King Penguin volume, *Dublin Panorama.* 1939. Water-colour 38 x 53.3cm. Private Collection. Combridge's Fine Art Ltd., Dublin, 1940, No. 1. *The Irish Times,* 9th April, 1962.

Rear Turrets of a Whitley Aircraft. Inscribed as above and dated. 1940. Water-colour 57.7 x 73.9cm. The Imperial War Museum. Alan Ross, *The Colours of War: War Art 1939-45,* London, 1983, p.35; S.E. Veale, *Achievements in British Aircraft,* n.d. pp. 18, 194.

Training Aircraft under Construction. Signed and dated 1940. Water-colour 38.1 x 55.8cm. The Imperial War Museum.

Hangars. Signed and dated, lower right. 1940. Water-colour 36.5 x 54.6cm. The Imperial War Museum. Alan Ross, *Colours of War,* 1983, p.32.

Assembling the Wing of a Blenheim Bomber. Signed and dated. 1940. Water-colour 36.5 x 52.2cm. The Imperial War Museum. Museum of Modern Art, New York, 1941.

Fitters Working on a Spitfire. Signed and dated. 1940. Water-colour 36.5 x 54.6cm. The Imperial War Museum. S.E. Veale, *Achievement in British Aircraft.* n.d. p. 18.

Beaufort Bombers. Signed and dated, lower right. 1940. Water-colour on canvas-board. 35.5 x 53.3cm. R.A.F. Museum. Museum of Modern Art, New York, 1941. *The Studio,* Vol.120, 1940, p.154; Herbert Read in *Britain at War,* Museum of Modern Art, New York. 1941. Edited by Munroe Wheeler. Text by T.S. Eliot, Herbert Read, E.J. Corker and Carlos Dyer. n.d., S.E. Veale, *Achievement in British Aircraft,* n.d.

Wing Section Awaiting Assembly. Signed, lower right. 1940. Water-colour on canvas board 76.2 x 53.3cm. R.A.F. Museum. Museum of Modern Art, New York, 1941. H.E. Bates, *War Pictures by British Artists,* R.A.F., 1942.

Wellington Bombers Nearing Completion. Signed, lower left. 1940. Water-colour 38.1 x 55.8cm. R.A.F. Museum. S.E. Veale, *Achievement in British Aircraft,* p. 18.

Wings. Lost at sea, 1944, while being shipped to South America. Ship sunk by a German torpedo. 1940. Water-colour 38.1 x 55.8cm. Lost. Alan Ross, *Colours of War,* 1983, p.172.

Walrus Amphibian Aircraft. Signed and dated, lower left. 1940. Water-colour 35.5 x 55.8cm. Imperial War Museum.

Assembling a Sunderland Flying Boat. Signed and dated. 1940. Water-colour 38.1 x 55.8cm. R.A.F. Museum.

Assembling Beaufort Bombers. Signed and dated. 1940. Water-colour 73.6 x 55.8cm. R.A.F. Museum.

Wellington Front Turrets. Signed and dated. 1940. Water-colour 38.1 x 55.8cm. R.A.F. Museum.

Blenheim Bomber. Signed and dated. 1940. Water-colour 35.5 x 53.3cm. R.A.F. Museum.

Bombers Mainplane under Construction. Signed and dated. 1940. Water-colour 35.5 x 53.3cm. R.A.F. Museum.

Aircraft Wings in Store. Signed and dated. 1940. Water-colour 38.1 x 55.8cm. R.A.F. Museum.

Summer Day on the River at Straffan. To be used in *Dublin Panorama.* c.1940. Water-colour. Cambridge's Fine Arts Ltd, Dublin. 1940, No. 3. Contemporary Pictures, Dublin, 1943.

Home, Sweet Home. Signed and dated. Painted on a visit to London in 1940 to see E.M.O'R Dickey and Kenneth Clark about his suggestion to record London bomb damage in artistic form. He failed to sell the painting to The War Artists Advisory Committee. 1940. Water-colour 39.3 x 54.6cm. Norman McGrath. Cambridge's Fine Arts Ltd., Dublin, 1940; Neptune Gallery, Dublin, 1979, No.42.

Howth Harbour. Signed and dated. To have been used in *Dublin Panorama.* 1940. Water-colour. Private Collection. Cambridge's Fine Arts Ltd., Dublin, 1940, No. 4.

Prospect of the Castle, Edinburgh. 1938-40. Probably water-colour. Cambridge's Fine Arts Ltd., Dublin, 1940, No.13.

River Landscape with Bridge. Signed and dated 1940. Water-colour 40.6 x 55.8cm. Unknown, sold at Adam's, Dec.11th, No.174, 1990.

A Steep Street in Bath. c.1938-40. Cambridge's Fine Arts Ltd., Dublin, 1940, No.20.

Shells from My Voyages. c.1938-40. May be the same as **Shells**, in a private collection, dated 1940. Cambridge's Fine Arts Ltd., Dublin, 1940, No.21.

Untitled. [Avoca – the Meeting of the Waters]. Signed and dated 1940. Water-colour 38.1 x 55.8cm. Cornelia Hope. The Neptune Gallery, Dublin, 1979, No.25.

Sea Shell and Leaf. Signed and dated. Two sketches exist, both close to the finished painting. One is a water-colour, which differs from the painting in that the clouds are more stylised and that there are no birds. The other is a sepia sketch, with a pier instead of a cliff. 1940. Water-colour 58.4 x 45cm. Jenny and Donal O'Donovan.

Untitled. Signed and dated 12 April 1940. 1940. Water-colour 24.1 x 34.2cm. Jenny and Donal O'Donovan. Neptune Gallery, Dublin, 1979, No.3.

Glenmacnass River and Mall Hill, Co. Wicklow. Signed and dated. 1940 Water-colour 39.3 x 53.3cm. Jim Kenny. Cambridge's Fine Arts Ltd., Dublin, 1940, No.12, as 'Footbridge over Glenmacnass'.

Avonmore at Laragh. c. 1940 Water-colour. 54.6 x 39.3cm. Ken Pye. Cambridge's Fine Arts Ltd., Dublin, 1940, No. 6.

The Liffey at Ballysmuttan. 1940. Cambridge's Fine Arts Ltd., Dublin, 1940, No. 8.

August in a Wicklow Pinewood. c.1940. Cambridge's Fine Arts Ltd., Dublin, 1940, No.10.

In the Valley of the Avonmore. c. 1940. Cambridge's Fine Arts Ltd., Dublin, 1940, No.11.

Afternoon on the Grand Canal. c.1940. Cambridge's Fine Arts Ltd., Dublin, 1940, No.7.

The Seacoast at Rush. c.1940. Cambridge's Fine Arts Ltd., 1940. No.5.

Untitled. [Winter Scene]. Signed and dated. 1940. Water-colour. Architectural Review, Vol. XXXVIII, July-December 1940, p.69.

Shells. Signed and dated. 1940. Water-colour 54.6 x 55.8cm. Private Collection. May have been exhibited as **Shells from my Voyages**, in Cambridge's, 1940, No.21.

Rainy Morning at McKee Barracks. Signed and dated. To have been used in *Dublin Panorama.* 1940. Water-colour 55.8 x 40.6cm. Bruce Arnold. Cambridge's Fine Arts Ltd., Dublin, 1940; Neptune Gallery, Dublin, 1979.

Untitled. [Seascape]. Signed and dated. 1940. Water-colour on board 38.1 x 40.6cm. Cornelia Hope. Neptune Gallery, Dublin, 1979.

Untitled. [Sketch]. c.1940. Sepia 20x25.4cm. The Irish Architectural Archive.

View of the Custom House. Signed RMcG. To have been used for *Dublin Panorama.* 1941. Ink 25 x 30cm. The Irish Architectural Archive.

Untitled. Signed and dated 1941. Water-colour and pastel 55.8 x 40.6cm. Clodagh Studdert.

College of Surgeons. Signed and dated, lower right. November, 1941. Water-colour 55x40cm. David Apthorp. R.H.A., 1942, No.249.

Back View of a House and Garden. Signed and dated. 1941. Water-colour 40.6 x 55.8cm. Private Collection.

Interior of O'Neill's Pub. Signed and dated. 1941. Ink 32x39cm. The Irish Architectural Archive. *The Bell,* Vol.2, No.5, August 1941, p.45.

The Lying In Hospital [Rotunda Hospital], **Dublin.** Signed and dated, lower right. Shows Rotunda gardens. 1941. Water-colour 54x39cm. David Apthorp.

Sir Patrick Dun's Hospital. Signed and dated. To have been included in *Dublin Panorama.* Preliminary water-colour sketch in possession of Dr. J. Kirker. 1941. Water-colour 53.3 x 76.2cm. Frank Foley.

View of Four Courts with Fr. Mathew Bridge. 1941. Sepia ink and coloured wash 14.5 x 18.5cm. The Irish Architectural Archive.

Spring Landscape near Delgany. Signed and dated. Spring, 1941. Water-colour on Board 38.1 x 55.8cm. Bill Doyle. Neptune Gallery, Dublin, 1979, No.26.

Longford Terrace, Monkstown. Signed and dated. To have been used in *Dublin Panorama.* 1941. Sepia ink 19 x 25cm. The Irish Architectural Archive; *The Bell,* Vol.2, No.5, August, 1941, p.38.

O'Neill's of Aungier Street: A Conversation Piece. Signed and dated. 1941. Sepia 19 x 25.5cm. The Irish Architectural Archive.

O'Neill's of Aungier Street. Signed and dated 1941. Ink 32 x 39cm. The Irish Architectural Archive; *The Bell,* Vol.2, No.5, August 1941, p.45.

The Irish House, Winetavern Street. Signed and dated. To have been included in *Dublin Panorama.* 1941. Sepia and ink. 19 x 26.5cm. The Irish Architectural Archive; *The Bell,* Vol.2, No.5, August 1941, p.41; O.P.W. *Corridor* Supplement 2.

Salthill Railway Station. Signed. Another sepia sketch of the same subject is also in the collection of the Irish Architectural Archive. 1941. Sepia 19 x 25cm The Irish Architectural Archive; *The Bell,* Vol.2, No.5, August 1941, p.47.

Shrine of St. Anne's. [St. Audoen's]. Signed and dated, lower left. 1941. Sepia ink 19.5 x 26.5cm. The Irish Architectural Archive; *The Bell,* Vol.2, No.5, August 1941, p.43.

The Custom House across the Liffey. Signed and dated, lower left. 1941. *The Bell,* Vol.2, No.5, August 1941, p.34.

Autumn. c.1941. Oil. The R.H.A., 1941, No.271.

Black Church in Parnell Square. Signed and dated. To have been included in *Dublin Panorama.* 1941. Ink and wash 38.1 x 33cm. Mrs. E. Ticher. *The Irish Times,* 27th September, 1941.

Reverie. c.1941. Oil. R.H.A., 1941, No.240.

Kings Inns. Signed and dated. To have been included in *Dublin Panorama.* 1941. Water-colour. Waddington Gallery, Dublin, 1945?

Leixlip Castle. Signed and dated. To have been included in *Dublin Panorama.* 1940. Water-colour. Cambridge's Fine Arts Ltd., Dublin, 1940, No.9 as 'A Still Reach by Leixlip Castle'; Victor Waddington Gallery, Dublin, 1945. Reproduced as a card.

Snowscape from Knockmaroon. c.1941. Oil. R.H.A., 1941, No. 317.

Untitled. [Study of Ivy Leaves/Trees]. Signed and dated. 1941. Water-colour 66 x 80cm.

'The Castle', Blackrock College. Signed and dated. To have been included in *Dublin Panorama.* Preliminary sketch of the same subject in the possession of Niall Meagher. 1941. Water-colour 60.9 x 40.6cm. Blackrock College. Blackrock College Annual.

Guinness and the Grand Canal Harbour. Signed and dated. 1941. Ink 32 x 39cm. The Irish Architectural Archive.

Newcomen's Bank and Castle Hill. Signed and dated. To have been included in *Dublin Panorama.* 1941. Pen, ink and water-colour. 38.7 x 31.7cm. George Redmond. R.H.A., 1962; The Neptune Gallery, Dublin, 1979, No.36; *The Bell,* Vol.2 No.5, August 1941, p.40, under title 'The Ivory Tower, Dublin Castle'. R.I.B.A. Handbook, 1947, pl. xv.

Customs House, Dublin. Signed and dated. On McGrath's list for *Dublin Panorama* under title 'Liffey Sunset from the Custom House'. 1942 Water-colour 40.6 x 55.8cm. Private Collection.

Regent's Canal, Islington. Signed and dated 1942. Pen, ink and water-colour. 38.1 x 121.9cm. Robert Jacob. R.H.A., 1978, No.30; The Neptune Gallery, Dublin, 1979, No.4. Alan Powers, 'Simple Intime – the Work of Raymond

The Rotunda [Lying in Hospital]. Signed and dated, lower right. 1942. Water-colour 55 x 37.5cm. David Apthorp. Victor Waddington Gallery, Dublin, 1945?

The Rotunda Hospital and the Parnell Monument. Signed and dated, lower left. 1942. Water-colour 54 x 39cm. David Apthorp.

The Chapel, Rotunda Hospital. Signed and dated, lower left. 1942. Water-colour 53 x 37cm. David Apthorp.

Dalkey Sound. To have been included in *Dublin Panorama*. 1942. Wood engraving. Reproduced as a Christmas Card.

Trinity College and the Bank of Ireland. Signed and dated. To have been included in *Dublin Panorama*. 1942. Water-colour 53.3 x 38.1cm. Lyal Collen. R.H.A., 1943, No.273; Victor Waddington Gallery, Dublin, 1945? *R.I.B.A. Journal*, Vol.54, No.10, July, 1947, New Series, p.449.

Untitled. [Fantasy Landscape with House at Goodwood.] Signed and dated. Study of the same subject in the Irish Architectural Archive. 1943. Water-colour 38.4 x 35.1cm. Alan Powers.

Harbour Scene – Breakwater. 1943. Water-colour 45.7 x 27.9cm. W. Henningham.

Pacific. Signed and dated 1943. Water-colour 44.4 x 52.7cm. The Contemporary Picture Galleries, Dublin, 1943; R.H.A., 1950, No.228.

Navigation Buoys Stacked on the Hard at Dún Laoghaire. Signed and dated. To have been included in *Dublin Panorama*. 1943. Water-colour 37 x 54cm. Mrs. Margaret Smythe. Contemporary Pictures Galleries, Dublin, 1943?

Shandon Church and Buttermarket. c.1943. Sepia ink 27.9 x 19.5cm. Robert McKinstry. *The Bell*, Vol.VI, No.1, April 1943, p.43.

The Avonmore near the meeting of the Waters. Signed and dated. 1943. Monochrome wash 35.5 x 49.5cm. Cornelia Hope. The Neptune Gallery, Dublin, 1979.

Bridges of Dublin. Christmas card designed for Reginald Ross Williamson. Signed lower left and inscribed as above. 1943. Pen and ink on tracing paper. 26.5 x 17.5cm. The Irish Architectural Archive. Reproduced as a Christmas card.

A Still Life of Flowers in a Glass Vase with Shells. Signed and dated 1943. Water-colour 37 x 26cm. Mrs. Margaret Smythe.

A View into the Demesne from the Balcony of Monkstown House. 1943. Ink. Reproduced as a Christmas Card.

Deserted Cottage, Glenmalure, Co. Wicklow. Signed and dated, inscribed with title, lower right. 1943. Water-colour 36.1 x 48.2cm. Bruce Arnold. Neptune Gallery, Dublin, 1979.

Untitled. [Castle Howard, Co. Wicklow]. 1943. Water-colour 31.7 x 43.1cm. Private Collection.

Untitled. [View of Enniskerry]. Signed and dated 1943. Water-colour 30 x 44cm. Mrs. N.Baker.

Oisin Approaching Tir na Nog. Signed and dated lower right. 1944. Water-colour 75 x 134.5cm. Jenny and Donal O'Donovan.

Freshwater Lodge. Signed and dated lower right. 1944 [1940 ?]. Water-colour 31.5 x 45cm. Jenny and Donal O'Donovan.

The Twelve Pins and the Killary from Bundorragha. Signed lower right and dated, there is a miniature water-colour sketch of this in a sketch-book in the possession of Jenny and Donal O'Donovan. 1944. Water-colour 32 x 46cm. Paul O'Toole.

Roundstone from Mweenish Island. Two versions exist; this one with a cow, the other without. Miniature water-colour sketch exists in a sketch-book in tne posession of Jenny and Donal O'Donovan. 1944. Water-colour 45.7 x 32.3cm. Fr. Brian Connolly.

Roundstone from Mweenish Island. Version without cow. 1944. Water-colour 45.7 x 32.3cm. Eileen Frost.

Untitled. [Derelict bog in Sligo]. Signed and dated 1944. Water-colour 37 x 74cm. Mrs. Joan Godwin. Reproduced as the cover of *The History of British Flora: A Factual Basis for Phytogeography*, by Sir Harry Godwin, Cambridge University Press, 1975.

Looking Down the Killary from Leenane. Water-colour miniature sketch exists in a sketch-book owned by Jenny and Donal O'Donovan. 1944. Water-colour 45.7 x 32.3cm.

Looking up the Killary to Leenane. Water-colour sketch exists in a sketchbook owned by Jenny and Donal O'Donovan. 1944. Water-colour 45.7 x 32.3cm.

Lights of Dublin Bay. Christmas card designed for Reginald and Eileen Ross Williamson. Signed and dated lower right. 1944. Ink.

The Camp on Inishdegil. Water-colour miniature exists in a sketch-book owned by Jenny and Donal O'Donovan. 1944. Water-colour 45.7 x 32.3cm.

Ben Gorm from Glenmalure. Water-colour miniature exists in a sketch-book owned by Jenny and Donal O'Donovan. 1944. Water-colour 45.7 x 32.3cm.

Aoife and the Children of Lir. 1944. Water-colour. R.H.A., 1944, No.315.

Temple Lake. c. 1944. Irish Exhibition of Living Art, 1944, No.146.

Trim Castle on the Boyne. Water-colour miniature exists in a sketch-book owned by Jenny and Donal O'Donovan. 1945. Water-colour 53.3 x 38.1cm. Irish Embassy in London. Oireachtas, 1945.

Wexford Bridge. Inscribed 'The middle arch of the New Slaney Bridge, Wexford and a general view of bridge seen through this arch'. 1945. Pencil and grey wash 18 x 26cm. The Irish Architectural Archive. R.H.A., 1945, No.238.

The Davis Memorial. Perspective view, plan and section. Inscribed 'Ray McGrath Inv. et Delt. Presentation drawing'. 1945. Ink and grey wash on board 38 x 53.5cm. The Irish Architectural Archive; R.I.A.I. 'The Architect and the Drawing', 1989, No.132; O.P.W. *Corridor* Supplement 2.

Some Towers, Spires and Domes of Dublin. Signed and dated. Used as a card for Reginald Ross Williamson. 1945. Reproduced as a card; R.I.B.A. handbook, 1947; *Journal of the R.I.B.A.*, 3rd Series, Vol.54, No.10, July, 1947, p.450. Maurice Craig, *Dublin 1660-1860*, Dublin 1952.

Alderman's Stairs. c. 1945. The Irish Exhibition of Living Art, 1945.

Ochre Berth, Arklow. c. 1945. Victor Waddington Gallery, Dublin, 1945.

Four Courts. Signed and dated, lower right. Ink and wash sketch also exists in the Irish Architectural Archive and another is in the posession of Jenny and Donal O'Donovan. 1945. Water-colour 63.5 x 86.3cm. Private Collection. Victor Waddington Gallery, Dublin, 1945. R.I.B.A. Handbook, 1947, pl.XVI.; Alan Powers, 'Simple Intime – The Work of Raymond McGrath', *Thirties Society Journal*, No.3, 1982, p.10.

Glencree Valley, Co. Wicklow. Signed and dated 1948. Water-colour 28.5 x 46.3cm. John Ross. Possibly R.H.A., 1949, No.190; The Neptune Gallery, Dublin, 1979, No.5.

Croscombe Churchyard, Somerset. Dated, lower right, 4 April 1948. Sepia 19 x 25.4cm. Robert McKinstry. The Neptune Gallery, Dublin, 1979.

Untitled. [Riverine keystones from the Custom House]. Inscribed 'Dublin Custom House – Sculptor Edward Smyth 1787. Drawing by Raymond McGrath 1948'. Designed as a card for Reginald and Eileen Ross Williamson. 1948.

Rustle of Spring. c.1948. Water-colour. R.H.A., 1948, No.169.

Dialogue between Shells. c. 1946 Water-colour. R.H.A., 1946.

Mountain Landscape with Shells, Jawbone and Bog Oak. 1946. Water-colour on board 49.5 x 69.8cm. Norman McGrath.

Newtown Hill. Signed and dated 1946. Water-colour 45.7 x 38.8cm. Mrs. Robin O'Brien. Oireachtas 1945. Reproduced as a Christmas card, 1951.

Bridge at Boyle, Co. Roscommon. Signed and dated 1949. Water-colour 45.7 x 60.9cm. The Royal Hotel, Boyle. R.H.A., 1949, No.196.

Untitled. [Stamp Design]. Inscribed 'Poblacht na h-Éireann 2 p 1949'. 1949. Pencil on tracing paper 21.7 x 32.6cm. The Irish Architectural Archive.

Untitled. [Four Heads in Profile, of McGrath and family]. Signed as a Christmas Card. 1949. Ink 21 x 15cm. Jenny and Donal O'Donovan.

Maretimo, Dublin Bay. 1949. Sepia 14 x 23cm. Dr. D.J. Meagher.

Avenue in Monkstown. Signed and dated 1949. Pen, ink and water-colour 52 x 76.2cm. R.H.A., 1949, No.212; The Neptune Gallery, Dublin, 1979, No.6.

Glencree River and Sugarloaf. c.1949. Water-colour. R.H.A., 1949, No.190.

Industrial Administration Building. c. 1949. R.H.A., 1949, No.240.

Russell Hotel Brochure Design. Front design shows elevation of the Russell Hotel from St. Stephen's Green, the back shows a chef. Designs are on a fold out sheet. 1950's. Water-colour and ink 22.5 x 20.7cm. The Irish Architectural Archive.

Russell Menu Design. Shows a man and a butterfly. Unsigned, Undated. 1950's Water-colour and ink 21 x 22.7cm. The Irish Architectural Archive.

Russell Hotel Menu Design. Shows a feather and two leaves. Signed with initials. Undated. 1950's. Water-colour and ink 20.2 x 16.5cm. The Irish Architectural Archive.

Russell Hotel Menu Design. Shows a fish. 1950's. Sepia 28.2 x 22cm. The Irish Architectural Archive.

Russell Hotel – Design for a Christmas card. Shows Hotel entrance in the snow. Signed. 1950's. Ink 27 x 38.5cm. The Irish Architectural Archive.

Oceanides. Signed and dated 1950. Oil on canvas 48.8 x 59cm. R.H.A., 1950, No.87; The Neptune Gallery, Dublin, 1979, No.38.

Untitled. [Railway Station Façades]. Inscribed 'Ray McGrath del'. 1950. Ink.

Untitled. [Riverine Head]. Design for a catalogue cover for the Exhibition of Contemporary Irish Painting in North America, 1950. A pencil sketch also exists in the Irish Architectural Archive. 1950 Ink 36.5 x 26.5cm. The Irish Architectural Archive.

Royal Hibernian Hotel Menu Design. Shows the Custom House from the bridge. Design for front of menu. 1950's Pencil 28.3 x 22cm. The Irish Architectural Archive.

Ambert – Puy de Dôme. Dated 1950. Sepia 8.8 x 14cm. Jenny and Donal O'Donovan.

Crestet, Provence. Inscribed as above and dated 22 April, 1950. Sepia on card 9 x 14cm. Jenny and Donal O'Donovan.

Top View from Norman's Window at Digne. Inscribed as above and dated 25/4/50. Sepia 14 x 9cm. Jenny and Donal O'Donovan.

Mountain Flower – Gorge du Tarn. Scale and colour notes indicated. c.1950. Sepia 14 x 8.8cm. Jenny and Donal O'Donovan.

Marlborough from Norman's Bedroom Window, Ailesbury Hotel. Inscribed as above, lower right, and dated 13/4/50. Sepia on card 9 x 14cm. Jenny and Donal O'Donovan.

Chenonceau. Inscribed as above and dated, lower left. 1950. Sepia on card 9 x 14cm. Jenny and Donal O'Donovan.

View from Norman's Window in the Hostellerie de la Reine Jeanne, Les Baux. Inscribed as above. c.1950. Sepia on card 9 x14cm. Jenny and Donal O'Donovan. Basis of 'Les Baux'. Oil painting. 1951 q.v.

Cours Mirabeau, Aix en Provence. Signed and dated. Preparatory sketch owned by Jenny and Donal O'Donovan. 1950. Sepia. Suzanne Stempowski.

Puimoisson, Alpes de Provence. Signed and dated 1950. Oil on canvas 29.8 x 40cm. Jenny and Donal O'Donovan. R.H.A., 1951, No.34; The Neptune Gallery, Dublin, 1979, No.39.

The Basses – Alpes at Digne. 1950. Water-colour 45 x 26cm. Nuala and Sean Rothery. The Irish Exhibition of Living Art, 1951, No.95.

Burial on Mweenish Island. Signed 1950 Water-colour 12.5 x 18cm. Noel deChenu. R.H.A., 1950. No.202; The Neptune Gallery, Dublin, 1979, No.31.

The Cenotaph, Leinster Lawn. Inscribed with title and RAYMOND McGRATH, ARCHITECT 1950-1951. Water-colour 55 x 75cm. Charles Henry de Gale Price. The Neptune Gallery, Dublin, 1979, No.33.

Les Baux from the Hostellerie de la Reine-Jeanne. Dated 1951. Black ink and water-colour 55.8 x 39.3cm. Mr. and Mrs. Cremins. The Irish Exhibition of Living Art, 1951, No.53; 1956, No.103.

Corrymine House, Achill. Inscribed as above and dated 13/9/51. Pen and blue ink 15.4 x 27cm. Jenny and Donal O'Donovan.

View of the Main Façade of Áras an Uachtaráin. To have been included in *Dublin Panorama.* c.1951. Pencil 25 x 32.5cm. The Irish Architectural Archive.

Achill Island. Signed and dated, September 1951. 1951. Water-colour on board 35.5 x 53.3cm. Norman McGrath. The Neptune Gallery, Dublin, 1979, No.7. Used for the Royal Hibernian Hotel menu design.

Glencree River. Sketch, dated 14/5/51. 1951. Coloured pencil 25 x 14cm. Nuala and Sean Rothery. The Neptune Gallery, Dublin, 1979.

Umbelliserae. Signed and dated 1951. Pastel-gouache 71.1 x 53.3cm. David Newman Johnson.

Vaison-La-Romaine. c. 1951. Water-colour. R.H.A., 1951, No.211.

Trinity College and the Bank of Ireland. Signed, lower left and inscribed as above lower right. 1951. Water-colour 38.1 x 25.4cm. Dr. J. Kirker.

The Chapel and Dining Hall, Trinity College, Dublin. Signed and dated lower right. Inscribed as above lower left. 1951. Water-colour 38.1 x 25.4cm. Dr. J. Kirker.

Les Baux, Provence. Signed and dated 1951. Oil on canvas 92.25 x 59.6cm. Norman McGrath. R.H.A., 1953; The Neptune Gallery, 1979, No.8.

Cabin, Achill. Study for oil painting of the same subject. Dated 6/9/51. 1951. Pen, ink and water-colour 15 x 27cm. Niall Meagher. The Neptune Gallery, Dublin, 1979. Reproduced on Russell Hotel menu cover.

Bunnafreeva, Lough Croaghaun. Signed and dated September '51. 1951. Water-colour 53.3 x 35.5cm. Desmond McGreevy. The Irish Exhibition of Living Art, 1952, No.77. (On loan from Michael Scott).

[Study] Bunnafreeva – The Haunted Lough of Croaghaun, Achill Island. 1951. Water-colour 22.8 x 29.2cm. Mrs Maura Coldrick. The Neptune Gallery, Dublin, 1979, No.27. Reproduced as a greeting card, 1951.

The Metal Bridge. Signed and dated lower right. 1951. Water-colour 45.7 x 33cm. Sheila Iremonger. R.H.A., 1965, No.213.

Garden Front, Somerton Lodge. Signed and dated, lower right. October '53. 1953. Ink and wash 13 x 34cm. John Ross. R.H.A., 1975, No.41 [possibly]. The Neptune Gallery, Dublin, 1979, No.20.

Untitled. [Fishing Boats in French Harbour]. Signed and dated 1953. Water-colour and crayon on board 47.6 x 74.9cm. Bruce Arnold. The Neptune Gallery, Dublin, 1979, No.29.

Precipice of Croaghaun. Signed and dated, lower right, see **The Red Precipice.** 1953. Water-colour and sepia 55 x 43cm. Peter O'Farrelly. The Irish Exhibition of Living Art, 1955, No.85.

Bog Wood and Gold. Signed and dated 1953. Water-colour 50.8 x 63cm. Jenny and Donal O'Donovan. R.H.A., 1953, No.173; The Neptune Gallery, Dublin, 1979, No.9.

Untitled. [Artichokes]. Signed and dated 1953. Water-colour and crayon 60.9 x 35.5cm. Kirsten Douglas. The Neptune Gallery, Dublin, 1979.

In Memory of a Garden. Signed and dated 1952. Water-colour on board and wicker with a leaf. 56.5 x 41.5cm. Mrs Sheila Hanna. R.H.A., 1952, No.190.

Untitled. [Bog of Allen]. Signed and dated. Shows Cement Roadstone quarry in the Bog of Allen. 1952. Water-colour 26.6 x 36.8cm. Neptune Gallery, Dublin, 1979, No.28. Reproduced in Cement Roadstone Calendar.

Punchestown Races. Inscribed 'Punchestown, Co. Kildare', unsigned. 1952. Water-colour 48.3 x 32.4cm. Daithi Hanly. R.H.A., 1952, No.187.

Glenmalure. c.1952. Water-colour. R.H.A., 1952, No.174.

Le Lavandou. c.1951. The Irish Exhibition of Living Art, 1951, No.89.

The Devil's Footprints, Curraun. Signed and dated, lower right. 1954. Watercolour and sepia 74 x 58cm. Peter O'Farrelly. Irish Exhibition of Living Art, 1954, No.101.

Road through Curraun. Inscribed as above lower right and dated 13/9/51. Unsigned. 1951. Watercolour 48.2 x 33cm. R. Pye.

Howth Castle. Commissioned for *Ireland of the Welcomes,* the official magazine of Bord Failte, the Irish Tourist Board. Signed lower right but undated. c.1953. Ink. *Ireland of the Welcomes,* Vol.3, No.1, May/June 1954, p.23.

Inistioge. Illustration for 'Kilkenny Classical', by Hubert Butler, *Ireland of the Welcomes.* Inscribed, signed and dated 24/4/53. 1953. Ink. *Ireland of the Welcomes,* Vol.2, No.2, July/August 1953, pp.18-19.

John de Gray's Castle and St. Finian's Tower. Commissioned for *Ireland of the Welcomes.* Signed lower left and dated. 1953. Ink. *Ireland of the Welcomes,* Vol.2, No.3, September/October 1953, p.14.

The Royal Tombs of Ennis. Illustration for 'Heart of Ireland' by Kees Van Hoek, *Ireland of the Welcomes,* 1953. 1953. Ink with crayon. *Ireland of the Welcomes,* Vol.2, No.3, September/October, 1953, pp.16-17.

Headfort House – limestone fireplace in entrance hall. Commissioned for *Ireland of the Welcomes.* Signed and dated. 1953. Crayon, wash and pencil. *Ireland of the Welcomes,* Vol.2, No.5, January/February, 1954, p.26.

Headfort House – Italian Cypress Avenue. Signed lower right and dated. Commissioned for *Ireland of the Welcomes.* 1953. Sepia. *Ireland of the Welcomes,* Vol.2, No.5, January/February, 1953, p.27.

Headfort House – The Terrace and House. Commissioned for *Ireland of the Welcomes,* signed and dated. 1953. Ink. *Ireland of the Welcomes,* Vol.2, No.5, January/ February, 1954, p.29.

Castle Leslie, Glaslough. Commissioned for *Ireland of the Welcomes.* Unsigned, undated. 1954. Ink. *Ireland of the Welcomes,* Vol.2, No.6, March/April, 1954, p.28.

Curraghmore House. Commissioned for *Ireland of the Welcomes.* Signed and dated. 1954. Ink. *Ireland of the Welcomes,* Vol.3, No.2, p.31.

Fota House. Commissioned for *Ireland of the Welcomes.* Signed and dated. 1954. Ink. *Ireland of the Welcomes,* Vol.3, No.3, September/October 1954, p.31.

St. Michan's Church St. Signed and dated lower right. Designed as a Christmas card for Jamesons Distillery. 1954. Sepia.

Jamesons from St. Michan's Churchyard. Inscribed lower right as above. 1954. Sepia and crayon 17.5 x 27.4cm. Jenny and Donal O'Donovan.

Portrait of a House. Watercolour. R.H.A., 1954, No.169.

Untitled. Signed and dated. [Driftwood, vivid red sky]. 1954?34? [1954]. Watercolour 55.3 x 73cm. Charles Henry de Gale Price. Neptune Gallery, Dublin, 1979, No.10.

Phoenix on Curraun. Watercolour. R.H.A., 1954.

Rotunda of the Cypresses, Villa d'Este. A sketch in ink, watercolour and crayon also exists in the possession of Jenny and Donal O'Donovan. 1959. Watercolour 24.2 x 47.5cm. Jenny and Donal O'Donovan. R.H.A., 1959, No.126. Reproduced as a Christmas card.

Listening to the Sea, Achill. Signed and dated. 1959. Watercolour 73 x 44cm. Charles Henry de Gale Price. R.H.A., 1959, No.147.

Untitled. [View of a Quarry]. Signed and dated, lower right. 1958. Watercolour. Cement Roadstone Calendar.

Le Moulinot, Vermenton, Yonne. Postcard sketch, inscribed as above and dated 21/9/59. 1959. Pen and black ink 10.3 x 15.2cm. Jenny and Donal O'Donovan.

The Terrace of Le Provençal Grens with a view of the Iles d'Hyeres. Postcard sketch, inscribed as above. Verso: dated 4/10/59. 1959. Pen and black ink on card 10.3 x 15.2cm. Donal and Jenny O'Donovan.

Front Square, Trinity College, Dublin. 1958. Watercolour on paper. 31.7 x 45.7cm. Norman McGrath.

Front Square, Trinity College, Dublin. 1958. Sepia ink on paper 31.7 x 45.7cm. Sean McSharry.

Studio with Paintings at Somerton Lodge. Signed and dated. 1957. Watercolour 69.8 x 50.8cm. Norman McGrath. The Neptune Gallery, Dublin, 1979, No.30.

Avocado Plant in Studio at Somerton Lodge. 1957. Water-colour on paper 69.8 x 50.8cm. Norman McGrath.

Sea Thistle. Signed and dated, lower left. This is one of three versions of the same subject. 1956. Watercolour 34 x 63cm Mrs. N. Baker. RH.A., 1956, No.147.

From Our Window in Collioure, Pyrenees-Orientale. Inscribed as above and dated Sept '60. 1960. Black ink. Reproduced as a greetings card.

Locarda Cipriani, Torcello. Sketch. dated Sept 16, '62. 1962. Ink and water-colour.

Grape Arbour at Torcello. Inscribed lower right as above and dated lower left 9/9/62. 1962. Sepia ink. Reproduced as a greetings card.

S. Giorgio Maggiore from the Zattere, Venice. Signed and dated, Venice 19/9/62. 1962. Watercolour 38 x 62cm. Price family. R.H.A., 1963, No.168; The Neptune Gallery, Dublin, 1979, No.40.

An Island and a Thistle. c.1962. Watercolour. R.H.A., 1962, No.173.

Monastery of Tourliani, Anomeria. Inscribed as above, lower left. 1963. Watercolour. R.H.A., 1971, No.31.

The Red Precipice. Signed and dated lower left. Similar to **Precipice of Croaghaun** but with radically different colour composed of bright red for the cliffs and green for the sea. 1958. Watercolour 46.3 x 74.2cm. Dr. E.A. Martin. R.H.A., 1958, No.196; The Neptune Gallery, Dublin, 1979, No.11.

The Castalian Spring, Delphi. Inscribed lower left as above and dated lower right 8 x 63cm. 1963. Ink.

In the Plaka, Athens. Inscribed lower right as above and dated 25. ix. 63. 1963. Ink. *The Irish Times,* 9th January, 1964.

Mykonos from the Hotel Leto. Inscribed as above, lower left and dated lower right 2. x. 63. 1963. Ink.

Pool of the Institute Grapponese di Cultura in course of completion and without water. Inscribed lower left as above and dated lower right 16. x. 63. 1963. Ink.

Sea Thistle, Mayo. Signed and dated 1963. Watercolour 54.6 x 81.5cm. Private Collection. R.H.A., 1966, No.159; The Neptune Gallery, Dublin, 1979, No.15.

The R.I.A. Library and Reading Room. Dated 6th August '63. 1963. Ink 30.4 x 22.8cm. Kirsten Douglas. The Neptune Gallery, Dublin, 1979.

Aoife and the Children of Lir. c.1963. Watercolour 64.7 x 48.2cm. Michael O'Flaherty. R.H.A., 1963 No.211; The Neptune Gallery, Dublin, 1979.

Aoife and the Children of Lir. Study for the above painting. 1963. Watercolour 22.8 x 28cm. Jenny and Donal O'Donovan.

Calypso. Signed and dated 1963. Pen, ink, and acrylic on board 39.3 x 49.5cm. Jenny and Donal O'Donovan. R.H.A., 1964, No.108; The Neptune Gallery, Dublin, 1979, No.14.

Mills on Mykonos. Unsigned, undated. c.1964. Watercolour 27.3 x 38.1cm. Mrs. McNicholl. R.H.A., 1965, No.195; The Neptune Gallery, Dublin, 1979, No.32.

Allegro. Signed and dated. 1963. Pen, ink and acrylic on board 50.5 x 60.5cm. Jenny and Donal O'Donovan. R.H.A., 1964, No.1; The Neptune Gallery, Dublin, 1979, No.12.

Untitled. [The Acropolis]. Signed and dated 27. ix. 63. 1963. Pen and ink on board 50.8 x 61cm. Private Collection. R.H.A., 1964, No. 194; The Neptune Gallery, Dublin, 1979, No.13.

White Washing on Mykonos. Signed, lower left. 1966. Watercolour 70 x 43cm. Nuala and Sean Rothery. R.H.A., 1966, No.168; Reproduced in R.H.A. catalogue, 1966.

Theatre at Taormina. Inscribed as above lower left, signed and dated 3/10/67 lower right. 1967. Ink. Reproduced as a Christmas card.

The Garden front, Somerton Lodge. Inscribed as above, signed and dated 27/9/67. 1967. Ink. Reproduced as a Christmas card.

Vaison-la-Romaine. Signed and dated. 1967. Oil on canvas 43 x 57cm. R.H.A., 1967, No.32; The Neptune Gallery, Dublin, 1979, No.17.

Pattern of Avocados. Signed and dated. 1967. Pen, ink and watercolour 45.7 x 58.4cm. Bruce Arnold. R.H.A., 1967, No.198; The Neptune Gallery, Dublin,

1979, No.43. Front cover of the catalogue for the Neptune Gallery exhibition in 1979.

Jaune-Gris-Noir. 1967. Watercolour 20 x 24cm. Sean Mulcahy. R.H.A., 1968, No.112.

The Duomo and the fountain of Montorsoli, Sicily. Inscribed as above, signed and dated 29/9/67. 1967. Ink 27.3 x 30.1cm. Isolde Motley. The Neptune Gallery, Dublin, 1979. Reproduced as a Christmas card.

Crusaders Castle, Parikia, Island of Paros. Inscribed as above, signed and dated 5. iv. 65. 1965. Watercolour. R.H.A., 1969, No.17.

Giardino del Cavaliere. Inscribed as above and dated Florence 14. x. 66. 1966. Sepia.

Atlantic Coast, Achill. Signed and dated. 1965. Watercolour 41.5 x 71.5cm. Jenny and Donal O'Donovan. The Neptune Gallery, Dublin, 1979, No.16.

Church of Ekatontapylion, Parikia, Island of Paros. Undated c. 1969. Watercolour. R.H.A., 1969, No.15.

The Garden Front. Inscribed as above, signed and dated 27/9/69. 1969. Pen and ink 22.5 x 31cm. John Ross. The Neptune Gallery, Dublin, 1979.

Kingsbridge Station. Signed and dated. 1969. Pen and ink.

Cathedral and Church of Sta. Tosca, Torcello. c.1967-8. R.H.A., 1974, No.13.

Sherlockstown Sallins, Co. Kildare. Signed and dated. 1968. Sepia and mono-chrome wash.

Paris Long Ago. Very similar to a photograph of Mary McGrath in Paris, 1954-5. c.1968. Watercolour. R.H.A., 1968, No.144; Reproduced in R.H.A. catalogue, 1968.

Greek Theatre, Epidaurus. c.1965. Watercolour. R.H.A., 1970, No.137.

Capri from Monte Tiberio. Probably study for later oil of the same subject. Inscribed as above, signed and dated 26/10/70. 1970. Ink. Gabrielle O'Herlihy. Reproduced as a greetings card.

Untitled. [View of Piazza San Marco, Venice]. Signed and dated Sept '71. 1971. Pen and ink. Reproduced as a Christmas card.

Anomera – Island of Mykonos. c.1971. Watercolour. R.H.A., 1971, No.27.

Capri from Monte Tiberio. Signed and dated, lower right. 1972. Oil on canvas 55 x 75cm. Jenny and Donal O'Donovan. R.H.A., 1972, No.53; R.H.A. catalogue, 1972.

The 15th Century Cloister of the Dominicans, Dubrovnik. Inscribed as above, signed and dated October 1974. 1974. Pen and ink 30 x 20cm. Jenny and Donal O'Donovan.

Front and Side elevation of Somerton Lodge. Signed and dated Oct. '73. 1973. Pen and ink 23 x 32.5. The Irish Architectural Archive.

Villa Jovis, Capri. Signed and dated. 1973. Oil on canvas 54.6 x 75cm. Jenny and Donal O'Donovan. R.H.A., 1973, No.107; The Neptune Gallery, Dublin, 1979, No.18.

The Castalian Spring, Mount Parnassus. c.1976. Watercolour. R.H.A., 1976, No.131.

Kilbride Lodge. Signed and dated. Designed as a card. 1975. Pen, ink and wash.

Passerelle Debilly, Paris. Signed and dated. 1975. Ink and watercolour on board 50 x 68cm. Jenny and Donal O'Donovan. R.H.A., 1975, No.40.

Untitled. [House of Peter Dunlop]. Several postcard sketches of the house. 1975. Pen, ink and wash. 25.4 x 35.5cm. Peter Dunlop. As postcards.

View of Somerton. c.1975. Wash Drawing. R.H.A., 1975, No.41.

Castletown. Signed and dated, lower left. 1975. R.H.A., 1976, No.28.

Athena. No signed and numbered edition known. Illustration for *The Labyrinth and Other Poems.* 1930. Wood engraving 8.9 x 10.1cm. The Deutscher Gallery, Armadale, Victoria, 1979, No.81; The Neptune Gallery, Dublin, 1979. *The Lady Clare Magazine,* Vol. xxvi, No.3, 1932, p.119. Later used for the brilliant cut glass door panel, in the R.I.B.A.

Inspiration. No signed and numbered edition known. Illustration for poem in *The Labyrinth and Other Poems.* 1930. Wood engraving 9 x 6.6cm. The Deutscher Gallery, Armadale, Victoria, 1979, No.82; The Neptune Gallery, Dublin, 1979. J.W. Mills, *The Labyrinth and Other Poems,* 1930, p.55.

A View of Dublin looking South. View of Dublin with the main buildings and streets indicated. Commissioned but rejected by Bord Failte. c.1953.

A View of Dublin South of the River. Map of the south of Dublin from Merrion Square to the Liberties. The buildings are indicated with scrolls bearing their names. Inscribed as above and 'Drawing by Raymond McGrath'. Unknown Pencil on tracing paper, ink and crayon. 40 x 42cm. 1950s. The Irish Architectural Archive. O.P.W. *Corridor* Supplement 2.

Dublin Railway Stations. Signed Raymond McGrath delt. Shows Amiens Street, Kingsbridge, Harcourt Street and Broadstone Stations. Commissioned as a

Greetings card from Reginald and Eileen Ross Williamson. 1950. Ink.

Russell Hotel Menu Design. Shows a profile crowned with leaves looking at his hand, which holds grapes, leaves and a butterfly. 1950's. Watercolour 20.3 x 22cm. The Irish Architectural Archive. As a menu design.

Russell Hotel Menu Design. Shows fairy or elf gathering nectar. Unsigned and undated. 1950's. Water-colour. The Irish Architectural Archive.

The Royal Hibernian Hotel. Shows Hotel entrance. Unsigned and undated. Also two people seated at a table. White line on black. 1950s. Reproduced as a Christmas card.

Untitled. Designed as a Christmas card from Reginald and Eileen Ross Williamson. Signed. Shows Santry Court, Connolly's [sic] Folly, Co. Kildare, The Ruin, Rathfarnham Castle, The Temple, Drumcondra House, Mapas Obelisk, Killiney, The Wonderful Barn, Leixlip, and the Obelisk, Stillorgan Park. All these names inscribed in scrolls beneath the illustrations. 1946. Ink. Rough watercolour sketches of some of the buildings exist in the Irish Architectural Archive.

El Arco, Palma de Majorca. Signed and dated. 1976. Ink and grey wash. 15.2 x 15.2cm. Beth Bolton. The Neptune Gallery, Dublin, 1979, No.19.

The Pink Nuns. Signed. Watercolour 53.3 x 36.8cm. Jenny and Donal O'Donovan. R.H.A., 1978, No.32; The Neptune Gallery, Dublin, 1979, No.37.

Untitled. [Apprehension; Full length standing man and woman with parrot on swing]. Signed. 1920-9. Pen and ink and brush on card. 18.8 x 16.2. Australian National Gallery, Canberra.

The Granta Lad. Signed and dated. Illustration for poem by Albert Frost. 1929. Ink.

The Great Hall, University of Sydney. Signed and numbered edition of 30. Inscribed in the plate upper right The Great Hall of the/University of Sydney, upper left August/MCMxxiii. 1923. Etching, printed in sepia on wove paper. 19 x 12.5cm.

Design for a Certificate for the Board of Architects of New South Wales, Australia. 1920's. Ink on card 57.2 x 39.5cm. The National Gallery of Ireland.

View of Chapel, Trinity College Dublin. Pencil on tracing paper 41.5 x 59cm. The Irish Architectural Archive.

Advertisement design for the Gresham Hotel. View north from the Gresham Hotel. Sepia and watercolour 17.5 x 41.5cm. The Irish Architectural Archive.

Advertisement design for the Gresham Hotel. 3 views of Dublin, north, south, and a view of the hotel façade. Signed R.McG. Watercolour.

Sketch of Foyer, Old Abbey Theatre and Gallery and Dress Circle. Blue pen and brown crayon on tracing paper. 45 x 57cm. The Irish Architectural Archive. Lennox Robinson and Micheal O'hAodha, *Pictures at the Abbey: The Collection of the Irish National Theatre, Dublin,* 1983, p.47.

St. Werburgh's, Dublin. c.1951. Sketch in the possession of Jenny and Donal O'Donovan. The Irish Exhibition of Living Art, 1951, No.104.

Untitled. [Cellar or bar]. Signed and dated lower right. 1976.

Granada. No signed and numbered edition known. c.1927. Woodengraving 6.4 x 5.2cm. Deutscher Gallery, Armadale, Victoria, 1979, No.60; *Lady Clare Magazine,* Vol.xxii, No.2, Lent Term, 1928, p.49.

The Seven Songs of Meadow Lane. [The Gates of Heaven]. Signed and numbered edition of 50, of which 25 were bound in The Seven Songs. Decoration for the Second Song, *The Gates of Heaven.* 1924. Woodengraving 5.8 x 8.3cm. Deutscher Gallery, Armadale, Victoria, 1979, No.28. *Art in Australia,* December, 1924, p.64.

Christmas Card. Nov. 1926. No signed and numbered edition known. Same block used for 1928 engraving [St. Paul's], except the kangaroo is omitted. 1926. Woodengraving 8.3 x 6.4cm. Deutscher Gallery, Armadale, Victoria, 1979, No.54.

[Janet Frew Waterhouse]. No signed and numbered edition known. The same block as 'I cannot see what flowers are at thy feet' but with the addition of the inscription JANET FREW WATERHOUSE. c.1927. Woodengraving 8.9 x 6.4cm. Deutscher Gallery, Armadale, Victoria, 1979, No.56.

The Castle Derlin built Pendragon. No signed and numbered edition known. 1925. Woodengraving 14.3 x 19.8cm. Deutscher Gallery, Armadale, Victoria, 1979, No.43.

(Gum Trees). No signed and numbered edition known. Water-colour of the same subject exists owned by W. Henningham. c.1925. Wood engraving printed on Japanese vellum. 11.2 x 6.9. Deutscher Gallery, Armadale, Victoria, 1979, No.44.

Bookplate for Raymond McGrath. No signed and numbered edition known. 1925. Wood engraving 11.7 x 7.4cm. Deutscher Gallery, Armadale, Victoria, 1979, No.50. *Art in Australia,* March 1927, p.26; P. Neville Barnett, *Australian Bookplates,* Sydney, 1954, p.154.

The Old Church, Hunters Hill. No signed and numbered edition known. 1921. Etching printed in sepia on wove paper. 15 x 25.4cm. Deutscher Gallery, Armadale, Victoria, 1979, No.1.

Argyle Cut, The Rocks. Signed and numbered edition of 6. 1922. Etching, printed in sepia on wove paper 20.9 x 25.4cm. Deutscher Gallery, Armadale, Victoria, 1979, No.5.

The Irish Embassy, Paris. Signed, lower left. Ink. Office of Public Works Architectural Association of Ireland, The Architecture of the Office of Public Works 1831–1987, AA1, p.111.

Entrance to the Chapel of the Convento de Santa Isabel, Cordoba. 1927. Sepia and watercolour. Irish Architectural Archive. *The Architect's Journal,* January 11, 1928, p.23.

Interior of the Hospital of Santa Cruz, Toledo. 1927. Sepia. Irish Architectural Archive. *The Architect's Journal,* January 11, 1928, p.21.

The Velvet Cloak. Signed and numbered edition of 20. 1922. Etching printed in sepia on wove paper. 11 x 6.1cm. Deutscher Gallery, Armadale, Victoria, 1979, No.12.

Untitled. [View of a quarry near Glencullen]. Signed and dated, lower left. 1943. Water-colour 32 x 44cm. Michael Baker.

Ardmore Point, Wicklow. Signed and dated. 1941. Watercolour. Mill Hill Fathers.

Arklow Harbour. Signed and dated lower left. 1943. Watercolour 31 x 44cm. Gabriel Hogan.

Roman Theatre at Orange. 1950. Watercolour. United Arts Club, Dublin; 1993.

Cliffs and fields near Tintagel. Watercolour. c.1938-1940. Combridge's Fine Arts, Dublin. 1940, No.15.

The Abbey Theatre. 3 pencil, ballpoint and crayon drawings on paper. 54 x 41cm. Ink. Abbey Theatre, May 6, 1953. The Abbey Theatre.

*Compiled by
Catherine Lawless*

347

SOURCES

ARCHIVAL SOURCES

Australian National Gallery (A.N.G.)
British Broadcasting Corporation Written Archive Centre (B.B.C.W.A.C.)
Clare College Cambridge Archives (C.C.C.A.)
Gonville and Caius College Cambridge Archives (G.C.C.C.A.)
Irish Architectural Archive (I.A.A.), to which Jenny McGrath O'Donovan gave a substantial amount of her father's material in 1978.
Imperial War Museum (I.W.M.)
McGrath Papers, Bray, Co. Wicklow
Mitchell Library, State Library of New South Wales (M.L.S.L.N.S.W.)
New York Public Library (N.Y.P.L.)
Pritchard Archive School of Architecture, Newcastle University (P.A.S.A.N.U.)
Royal Hibernian Academy Records (R.H.A. Records)
Royal Institute of British Architects (R.I.B.A.)
Victoria and Albert Museum (V. & A.)

LETTERS FROM ENGLAND

Laura Coates Cohn	16 Feb. 1990
Ken Entwistle	8 July 1991
Nicholas G.L. Hammond	24 Feb. 1990
John Harris	21 Sept. 1979
Leslie Hayward	10 Apr. 1990
Neil A. Hutchinson	6 Mar. 1991
Simon Jervis	(undated 1990)
L.J. McDonald	26 Feb. 1990
Andrew O'Rourke	31 Aug. 1990
David Regan	2 Feb. 1992
Deirdre Sharp	6 Mar. 1990
Dennis Sharp	13 Mar. 1991
Gavin Stamp	18 Feb. 1990
Peter Thornton	2 Mar. 1990
Nicholas Townsend	15 June 1993
Peter Varley	4 May 1978
	(written to Mary McGrath)

LETTERS FROM AMERICA

Betty Ahlm	(undated 1990)
Francis Keaveney	7 Sept. 1992
Paul Mellon	11 Oct. 1990
Lance M. Neckar	8 Apr. 1991

LETTERS FROM AUSTRALIA AND NEW ZEALAND

Tim Beaglehole	28 Aug. 1990
Baiba Berzins	16 Mar. 1987
Patricia Boyd Davies	27 Jan. 1993
Deborah Edwards	18 Feb. 1992
Les Hollings	3 June 1987
Ronald Horan	30 Aug. 1990
R.N. Johnson	16 Mar. 1987
Philippa Kelly	22 May 1989
Clive Lucas	5 Apr. 1990
David Saunders	29 Feb. 1984
	(written to John Warnock)
Julia Joseph Saunders	5 Jan. 1993
Ken Scarlett	(undated 1990)
Howard Tanner	12 Mar. 1990
Bob Warnock	(seriatim 1990–1992)

LETTERS FROM IRELAND

Charles Acton	15 Feb. 1990
Patricia Boylan	8 Mar. 1990
Edgar M. Deale	7 Nov. 1990
Isobel Dockrell	(undated)
Brian Fallon	(undated 1992)
Karen Latimer	21 Mar. 1990
Brian Lynch	(undated 1992)
Patrick McKeon	10 Feb. 1990
Con Manahan	20 Feb. 1990
Norman Moore	15 Feb. 1990
Elizabeth O'Driscoll	(undated 1991)
Tim O'Driscoll	26 Feb. 1990
Mary O'Reilly	(undated 1994)
Andy Purcell	26 Feb. 1990
Una Redmond	9 Apr. 1990
Anne Robson	15 Feb. 1990
Ann Martha Rowan	25 Mar. 1993
Richie Ryan	28 Feb. 1990
Tom Ryan	15 Feb. 1990
Morgan Sheehy	17 Oct. 1990
Sam Stephenson	28 Feb. 1990
Ronald Tallon	18 Apr. 1990
Mervyn Wall	25 Feb. 1990

LETTER FROM FRANCE

Percy Le Clerc	19 Dec. 1990

INTERVIEWS IN ENGLAND

Peter Bicknell	21 Nov. 1989
Neil Bingham	17 Nov. 1989
Alan and Sylvia Blanc	10 Mar. 1990
Catherine Bond	14 Nov. 1989
Sherban Cantacuzino	Mar. 1990
Gordon Cullen	7 Mar. 1990
Paul Davis	6 Mar. 1990
Sylvia Embling	22 Mar. 1990
Maya Hambling	20 Nov. 1989
Alice Hemming	16 Nov. 1989
David Jacques	21 Mar. 1990
Simon Jervis	12 Mar. 1990
Paul Koralek	13 Mar. 1990
Jill Lever	23 June 1993
Joanna Millett	8 Mar. 1990
Michael Moody	15 Nov. 1989
Angela Nevill	13 Nov. 1989
Derrick Oxley	13 June 1993
	(by telephone)
Karin Arup Perry	24 Nov. 1989
(Sir) James Richards	13 Mar. 1990
Seán Rothery	19 June 1989
Jeanne Sheehy	9 Mar. 1990
Phil Targett-Adams	6 Mar. 1990
Nicholas Townsend	11 Mar. 1990
Lis Townsend	11 Mar. 1990

INTERVIEWS IN U.S.A.

Max Abramowitz	23 May 1989
Barbara May Chermayeff	23 Nov. 1990
Serge Chermayeff	23 Nov. 1990
Mary Kiersey Corcoran	16 May 1989
Paddy Corcoran	16 May 1989
Eileen McGrath Frost	21 May 1989
Reggie Malcolmson	16 May 1989
Molly Wade McGrath	6 Jan. 1992
Norman McGrath	23 May 1989
Hazel Guggenheim McKinley	10 Nov. 1990

INTERVIEWS IN AUSTRALIA

Kingsley Aikins	24 Apr. 1990
Pamela Bell	8 May 1990
Margy Burn	14 May 1990
Roger Butler	10 May 1990
Edward Farmer	2 May 1990
Allan Gamble	4 May 1990
Elaine Haxton Foot	25 Apr. 1990
Edith Heaton	3 May 1990
Wendy Pye Henningham	1 May 1990
Alfred Jones	8 May 1990
Colm Kiernan	27 Apr. 1990
Michael Kirkpatrick	26 Apr. 1990
Harold Mathews	15 May 1990
Andrew Metcalf	25 Apr. 1990
John McPhee	10 May 1990
Sean McSharry	25 Apr. 1990
Gwen Mitchell	26 Apr. 1990
Ken Pye	26 Apr. 1990
Ruth Pye	26 Apr. 1990
Andrew Sayers	10 May 1990
Merle Selvage	27 Apr. 1990
Jac Smit	2 May 1990
Elwin Smith	2 May 1990
Ken Smith	4 May 1990
Ivor Smith	2 May 1990
Stella de Vulder	2 May 1990
Bob Warnock	27 Apr. 1990
Peter Webber	4 May 1990

INTERVIEWS IN IRELAND

Charles Acton	21 June 1990
Eoghan Buckley	7 May 1991
Maurice Craig	7 May 1990
Pat Cuffe	22 Feb. 1990
Patrick Delany	2 Oct. 1991
Liam Egan	10 Apr. 1990
Daithí Hanly	5 June 1989
John Healy	10 June 1989
Paul Hogan	18 July 1994
Máirín Hope	21 June 1990
Eddie McParland	July 1990
Jenny O'Donovan	5 May 1989
Cathal O'Neill	5 May 1989
Oscar Richardson	23 Feb. 1990
Seán Rothery	10 June 1989
Herbert Unger	15 June 1989

INTERVIEWS IN FRANCE

Jean Stempowski	15 Apr. 1989
Jacqueline Stepowska	16 Apr. 1989

INDEX

Italics denote a book or periodical.

Quotation marks denote a work of art or writing.

356